I0132065

AFFECTIVE JUSTICE

AFFECTIVE JUSTICE

||||||||||||||||||||||||||||||||||||||||||||||||||

THE INTERNATIONAL CRIMINAL COURT

AND THE PAN-AFRICANIST PUSHBACK

Kamari Maxine Clarke

DUKE UNIVERSITY PRESS *Durham and London* 2019

© 2019 Duke University Press
All rights reserved
Designed by Amy Ruth Buchanan
Typeset in Minion Pro and DIN Neuzeit Grotesk Bold Condensed
by BW&A Books, Inc.

Library of Congress Cataloging-in-Publication Data
Names: Clarke, Kamari Maxine, [date] author.
Title: Affective justice : the International Criminal Court
and the Pan-Africanist pushback / Kamari Maxine Clark. Description:
Durham : Duke University Press, 2019. |
Includes bibliographical references and index.
Identifiers: LCCN 2019013454 (print)
LCCN 2019980367 (ebook)
ISBN 9781478006701 (paperback)
ISBN 9781478005759 (hardcover)
ISBN 9781478007388 (ebook)
Subjects: LCSH: International Criminal Court. | African Union. |
Criminal law—Africa. | International crimes—Africa. | Criminal justice,
Administration of—Africa. | Criminal justice, Administration of—
International cooperation. | International criminal courts—Africa.
Classification: LCC KZ7312.C537 2019 (print)
LCC KZ7312 (ebook) | DDC 345/.01—dc 23
LC record available at https://lccn.loc.gov/2019013454
LC ebook record available at https://lccn.loc.gov/2019980367

Cover art: African Union Summit meeting, January 2013, Addis Ababa,
Ethiopia. Photo by the author.

This book is freely available in an open access edition thanks to TOME
(Toward an Open Monograph Ecosystem)—a collaboration of the
Association of American Universities, the Association of University
Presses, and the Association of Research Libraries—and the generous
support of Arcadia, a charitable fund of Lisbet Rausing and Peter
Baldwin, and the UCLA Library. Learn more at the TOME website,
available at openmonographs.org.

Dedicated to my father, the late

LINTON CLARKE SR.,

whose quest for understanding complexity

and whose appreciation for the fruits of

hard work has inspired every part of

this book—from its initial problematic

to its concluding thoughts.

CONTENTS

||||||||||||||||||||||||||||||||||||||||||||||||||||

Acknowledgments

This book is the culmination of three phases of field research and was possible with the financial research support of a number of visionary foundations and institutions: the Wenner-Gren Foundation for Anthropological Research, the National Science Foundation (NSF) Law and Social Sciences and Behavioral Sciences divisions, and the preliminary fieldwork grants from Yale University. In addition to those institutions, there are many persons to thank for their support. When in 2012 the NSF announced their biannual funding awards, including my grant to study the International Criminal Court (ICC) and sentimentalized emotional responses to its African indictments, it garnered the pushback of a few Republican US senators and Washington, DC, policy makers. They were unable to see how research about Africa and the ICC could be relevant to US strategic concerns and Americans in particular. Hopefully, it will now become clear that understanding the making of justice in international domains is fundamentally about justice at home. A special thank you goes to Drs. Deborah Winslow and Jeffrey Mantz as well as the then NSF director, Dr. Cora Merritt, for their public support of the research for this book its critical place in informed decision making.[1]

Next, I thank my intellectual lifelines, my central interlocutors during the writing of this book: Sara Kendall and Siba Grovogui have invigorated me with conversations and provocations and remain the bedrock of this work. Also fundamental has been the ad hoc international law working group that began during my later years at Yale and since then has provided me with a lifeline for making sense of the complexities of legality in the mix of postcolonial politics both within and outside of Africa. I thank Ifrah Abdillihi, Sarah-Jane

Koulen, Charles Jalloh, Ademola Abass, Benson Chinedu Olugbuo, Siba Grovogui, Mahmood Mamdani, Dire Tladi, Matiangai Sirleaf, Tendayi Achiume, Sara Kendall, Ronald Jennings, and Adam Branch for their inspiration, brilliance, and commitment to critical approaches to the study of international justice. I also thank my colleagues and workshop guests who offered manuscript input at the author's workshop hosted at Carleton University: Bronwyn Lebow, Erin Baines, Gerhard Anders, Doris Buss, Sarah-Jane Koulen, Umut Ozsu, Betina Kuzmarov, Christiane Wilke, Trevor Purvis, Sara Kendall, Philip Kaisary, Josephine Uwineza, Sukeshi Kamra, Rohee Dasgupta, Karen Hebert, Meredith Terretta, and Marie-Eve Carrier-Moisan.

At the African Studies Centre at Leiden University, where I held my academic affiliation during fieldwork in the Netherlands, I thank the staff, Maaike Westra and Marieke van Winden, and faculty colleagues, professors Benjamin Soares and Ton Dietz. Many colleagues and readers provided support and intellectual engagement throughout different aspects of the process and I thank them all: Olaf Zenker, Jonas Bens, Ilana Gershon, Sean Brotherton, Kristin Bright, Connal Parsley, Mark Goodale, Lucia Cantero, Marcia Inhorn, William Kelly, Tom Zwart, Bas De Gaay Fortman, Chris Gevers, Immi Talgren, Peter Geschiere, Sally Merry, Carsten Stahn, Chris Brown, Stacy Douglas, Stuart Murray, Pius Adesami, James Gathii, Daniel McNeil, Abel Knotterus, Eefje DeVolder, Mahmood Mamdani, Carol Martin, Kristin Cheney, Mariana Valverde, Sarah Trimble, Cynthia Perry, Kerry Rittich, Michael McGovern, Daniel Rosenblatt, Jennifer Hyman, Deborah Thomas, Sheryl Metzgner, Horace Campbell, Richard Wilson, Brenda Chaflin, Wahneema Lubiano, Achille Mbembe, Mark Drumbl, Lynn Chin, Faye Harrison, Jacob Olupona, Francis Nyamnjoh, Stuart Murray, Carolyn Martin-Shaw, Victoria Kumala Sakti, Eric Worby, Shireen Ally, Jill Staufer, Akhil Gupta, Hannah Appel, Sherry Ortner, Andrew Apter, Jemima Pierre, Darryl Robinson, Robyn Kelly, Kris Peterson, Samar al Bulushi, Philipp Kastner, and Andrew Ross.

Many colleagues and audiences where I presented my initial findings were instructive in pushing me to sharpen my focus, articulate my stakes, and clarify how the postcolonial condition is central to the ICC's Africa challenge. Thank you to colleagues and interlocutors at the following universities and institutes where I presented early chapters from this book: Duke University, the University of Pennsylvania, Yale University Law School, the University of Toronto, the University of Illinois–Chicago, Cambridge University, Washington and Lee Law School, the University of Florida–Gainesville, Syracuse University, the Harvard Kennedy School, Harvard University Weatherhead Center for International Affairs, the University of California–Berkeley Law, the University of Toronto's Centre for Criminology and Sociolegal Studies and Centre for Diaspora and Transnational Studies, the American Society for International Law, the American Anthropological Association, Law and Society Association, Kent University Law School, The Hague Institute for Global Justice and the Grotius Centre for International Legal Studies at the University of Leiden, the National University of Australia, the Free University of Berlin, the University of San Francisco, Queen's University, Cornell University Society for the Humanities, Haverford College, Cornell Political Theory Workshop, the Anthropology Department at the University of California–Los Angeles, The AfriMatrix Reading Group, the University of Chicago Anthropology Department, the Department of Criminology, Law and Society at the University of California–Irvine, the University of California–Berkeley Department of Anthropology, and the departments of Law and Legal Studies, the Institute for African Studies, and Global and International Studies at Carleton University.

During the second half of the research for this study, the Department of Anthropology at the University of Pennsylvania was invaluable in housing the project and shepherding its growth. The collegial support from the Race and Empire Reading Group gave me the initial opportunity to clarify the relationship of race and affect. Deborah Thomas, John Jackson, Noah Tamarken, and Nichole Carelock were central interlocutors in helping me make sense of the politics of race as it related to legal theory. Shortly afterward, I also spent the remainder of my sabbatical at the University of Toronto, hosted by the Centre for Diaspora and Transnational Studies. I am thankful to Ato Quayson for the engagement and that of my colleagues: Rinaldo Walcott, Antonela Arhin, Alissa Trotz, Mariana Valverde, Ruth Marshall, and Kerry Rittich.

The researchers and interns who worked on this project were central to its consolidation, and I cannot thank them enough. Tina Palivos and Sarah-Jane Koulen were the administrative and intellectual support for this project for many years. Tina was the organizational and administrative bedrock who held things together, and Sarah-Jane led the research agenda in both The Hague and Addis Ababa. I could not ask for a better core team of dedicated graduate students and always sophisticated thinkers with whom to have worked. I am forever indebted to them—now well into their postdissertation lives. Ifrah Abdillihi began as an intern during the research phase of the project in The Hague and continued as a researcher in Kenya and, along with Sarah-Jane, was central to insights that emerged. I am grateful to Ifrah for her intellectual agility and cannot express enough how fortuitous our meeting really was.

Other researchers in The Hague included Edward van Dalen, Annika Kress, and Tommie Leisink, and I thank them for their work. Alongside Ifrah, Brenda Kombo and Muoki Mbunga worked tirelessly with us in Kenya. In phase 2, Thomas Saunders and the wonderful law interns in Addis Ababa helped to make a difference as we worked in the shadow of the African Union political actors. I thank Luladay Berhanu, Ahadu Yeshitela, Tewodros Dawit, Bethel Genene, and Ingrid Roestenburg-Morgan for their African-based data collection. Special thanks to Godfrey Musila, Ania Kwadrans, Andrea Sobko, and Shermineh Salehiesmati for their research on the African Court Research Initiative and to my Carleton-based research assistants: Patricia Wallinger, Meghan Boyer, and Roselyn Wanjiru—thank you. Also thanks to my research interns: Irene Wang, Patricia Wallinger, Michelle Musindo, Afreen Delvi, Leonardo Rivalenti, Kayla Bose, Monica Lung, and Sean Havel.

Fieldwork and participant observation was made interesting with the passion and dedication of some of the key players at the Coalition for the International Criminal Court (CICC). Thanks to Bill Pace for the permission to conduct fieldwork at the CICC, to Steve Lamony from the CICC–New York office, and to the dedicated staff in The Hague: Amielle del Rosario, Sunil Pal, Matthew Cannock, Niall Matthews, and Alix Vuillemin. Other colleagues working with civil society organizations were critical to my understanding of the ICC and human rights in Africa. I cannot mention them all, but notable influences were African Legal Aid, headed by Evelyn A. Ankumah; the Pan African Lawyers Union, led by Donald Deya; Raymond Brown and Wanda Akin from the International Justice Project; Chris Dolan from the Refugee Law Project, Makerere University; Lucy Hovil from the International Refugee Rights Initiative; James Gondi at the African Center for Open Governance; and Alpha Sesay at the Open Society; as well as various NGO workers on the front lines in Kenya: Aimee Ongeso from Kituo Cha Sheria and Nelly Warega and Lydia Muthiani from the Coalition on Violence against Women.

Other African NGOs and particular persons stand out as having propelled the project in decisive ways: Njonjo Mue and Otsieno Namwaya, Kenyan researcher, African Division, Human Rights Watch; Haron Ndubi, lawyer and human rights activist; the executive director of Haki Focus, Saida Ali; the Coalition on Violence against Women–Kenya; Elizabeth Evenson, head of the International Criminal Justice program, Human Rights Watch; Stella Ndirangu, program manager for international cooperation at International Court of Justice (ICJ), Kenya; Abdulkadir Noormohamed, complementarily program officer at Open Society Initiative for East Africa; Njeri Kabeberi, executive director of the Centre for Multiparty Democracy Kenya; Esther Waweru, program officer in legal affairs (civil and political rights), Kenya Human Rights Commission; and Désiré Assogbavi with Oxfam International.

At the ICC, support and engagement have been generous and productive. Thank you first to the ICC prosecutor, Fatou Bensouda, and the deputy prosecutor, James Stewart, as well as to various legal representatives working for survivors: Mariana Pena, Anushka Sehmi, and Wilfred Nderitu. A special thank you to Oriane Maillet, Fadi El Abdallah, Alexander Khodakov, Fiona McKay-Head, Paolina Massidda, Phakiso Mochochoko, Shamila Batohi, Shamiso Mbizvo, Luc Walleyn, Jennifer Schense, Thompson Chengeta, and Maria Mabinty Kamara. And though the ICC does not have an equivalent defense office, we have also benefited from the candor of the various members of the defense legal teams working with ICC defendants: Logan Hambrick (assistant counsel, defense, Ruto/Sang case), as well as those in various ICC field offices, including Göran Sluiter, Karim Khan, and Dov Jacobs.

Members of the African media and outreach units were very helpful. I cannot name them all here, but Solomon Moriba, from the Special Court for Sierra Leone, and a range of others were invaluable, including Andrew Mwenda, Ngunjiri Wambugu, Parselelo Kantai, Okiya Omtatah Okoiti, Maina Kiai, Tom Maliti, and Rosemary Tollo.

We conducted more than two hundred interviews and focus groups over the two years of fieldwork data collection, so it would be impossible and unethical to name them all here. But a number of focus group members stand out. The first group were members of the Mau Mau Veterans organization in Kenya: Evanson Wainaina Waritu, James Kinyua, Joseph Waweru wa Thirwa, Loise Wangui wa Kamau, Lydia Wahu wa Muiruri, Magdalena Wanjiku Kamau, Monica Wambui wa Gitau, Muhinya wa Kinyanjui, Mwangi wa Murimi, Ngaruiya wa Kanyua, Thurugu wa Gitombo, Wanjiku Thigira, and Wanjiku Thuku. I extend thanks to another group of Nubian-Kenyans in Kibera. Thank you to those at the African Union (AU): AU Department of Political Affairs, Dr. Khabele Matlosa, Ibraheem Bukunle Sanusi, Olabisa Dare, Salah Hammad, Jhon Kiubaje, Idriss Kamara, George Mukundei Wachira, and Semiha Abdulmelik; head of legal affairs, Vincent Nmiehelle; Justice Sofia A. B. Akuffo, judge and president of the African Court of Human and Peoples' Rights; Matthew Brubacher, AU Special Taskforce on the Lord's Resistance Army (LRA); Zinurine Abiodu Alghali, senior policy officer training, Peace Support Operations

Division, Department of Peace and Security; Adelardus Kilangi, AU Commission on International Law; and Moawia Ahmed.

Interlocutors at the various governments and embassies were especially critical in helping with basic accommodations, intellectual insights, and professional friendships. I cannot thank them enough: Reta Alemu Nega of Ethiopia; Jongi Joseph Klaas, the first secretary, South African Embassy; Ambassador Dr. Monica Juma, Kenya; and Thomas Whitney, US Mission to the African Union.

While we were in Addis Ababa, the Institute for Security Studies and Addis Ababa University were excellent hosts and provided central support for this project. I thank the staff and researchers at both the Addis Ababa and Pretoria offices for their insights and passion about these issues: Ambassador Olusegun Akinsanya, Anton du Plessis, Philip Kasaija Kapuuli, Solomon Ayeledersso, Ottilia Anna Maunganidze, Berouk Mesfin, Yemi Tadesse, Golda Keng, and Samrawit Tsegaye, as well as Hirut Woldemariam and Elshaday Kifle Woldeyesus from the Human Rights Centre at Addis Ababa University.

Thank you to the anonymous reviewers of this manuscript. Your sharp and incisive insights have helped to strengthen the book in so many ways. Appreciation goes to Oxford University Press and Cambridge University Press for permission to reprint revised versions of chapters 1 and 6, respectively. Thank you to PoLar for permission to reproduce a revised and earlier version of the introduction. Thanks to *Human Rights Quarterly* for permission to reprint a version of chapter 3. Of course, the related publication and editing teams represent the unsung heroes and heroines of this work, and I am thankful for their attention, care, and commitment to making the book a reality. Appreciation also goes to Anitra Grisales for her insights from the very early days of this project, as well as for her ability to pose key questions when I was wading in the forest of trees. A sincere thank you goes to my editor at Duke University Press, Ken Wissoker, for his commitment to this project and its "forest of trees"—even when it was not always clear where the trees where.

Deeply felt appreciation goes to my immediate family: Evon Clarke, Linton Jr. and Kathy Clarke, Sheryl and Brian Metzgner, Kathy Clarke, Terry St. Denis-Clarke, and Simone and Ashton Clarke for their emotional support during the long life of this work. A heartfelt thank you to Linton Clarke, my late father, and Viola Clarke, whose influence shaped what this work became. And to my extended family, Herbert Williams, Cliff Macfarlane, and Marie Mabinti Dennis, thank you for your support throughout. Finally, to those in my everyday life: Thank you to Ronald Crooks, whose life lessons have shaped the path of this work, and to Stephen Appea for your ongoing invigoration and engaged input on what this book has become, from the early days to the present. To Talia Clarke-Crooks and Joseph Clarke-Crooks, you have both grown up with this book looming around us, invigorating family conversations, and navigating jealousies around the time spent carrying out the fieldwork and writing. Your genuine curiosity, childhood innocence, and loving support have given me hope that newly reconfigured worlds are possible—even as the old worlds continue to weigh us down. I could not ask for a better support network, group of interlocutors, and family of supporters. However, I alone take responsibility for the shortcomings of this work.

Preface

Assemblages of Interconnection

On the plane en route to Addis Ababa, Ethiopia, to attend my first African Union (AU) summits, I sat next to an American missionary about to launch a new church project in neighboring Kenya. Though excited about the newness of his contract, he was wary of the difficulties Americans encounter living in African cities. He was concerned that his way of life was different, and that he would have to shift his standards and become at one with his parishioners. Though he never used language that was explicitly shocking and derogatory, it was clear that he saw his role as bringing a much-needed form of humanitarian enlightenment to Africa. This was made palatable through the way he spoke of Africa's cycles of violence and poverty.

And then came the discussion of my work. After the usual niceties, he launched with a pointed interrogative: "Has the International Criminal Court [ICC] convicted Kenyatta and al-Bashir yet?" I paused, first out of shock from his presumption that I—another North American—was like him and in ideological conformity with his worldview. And though the charges against President Kenyatta and Deputy President Ruto have since been dropped by the ICC prosecutor's office, at the time I responded with resignation about not knowing how things would play out. And, also with resignation, I offered a familiar American trope, that "they were innocent until proven guilty." To that, he insisted that if I wanted to talk about innocence, I should focus on the innocent African victims who needed justice. Here the presumption was that the deceased and the survivors were innocent, and the African elite needed to be stopped, that blood was on their hands and wealth in their pockets. For him, convicting the sitting presidents of Kenya and Sudan would secure justice for the survivors of Africa.

I could not resist turning to similarly troubling issues at home: at the time, America's wars in Iraq and Afghanistan that have led to the death of thousands of innocent civilians. But to my interlocutor, America's war on terror was a just war—unlike what he saw as the irrational violence in Kenya and Sudan. He spoke with passion, and his assumptions about justice presumed that those two trials were key to ending impunity in Africa. As this soon-to-be resident of Kenya spoke, I could not help but think about the kind of life that he was preparing himself for and how important the discourse of justice abroad was for him in explaining America's place, his place, in improving the world's future. I also thought about what the latent sense of feel-good humanitarian discourses did that were popular among many of the northern missionaries, NGO workers, and journalists that I have met throughout Africa. While on the plane that day I began to think about the words that my intimate stranger used, the images and feelings associated with the words, and the way they danced in our imaginations and became entangled by other histories and consolidated our different feelings of justice.

According to his notion of justice, understood as the legal protection of those victimized by violence, it was not necessary to extrapolate further—at least not beyond what he had already. He and I knew what he meant, and yet so much was partial and unnecessary to spell out. The rest was expressed through sentimentalized expressions—tone of voice, word emphasis, facial expressions, hand motions, and bodily responses. These nonverbal cues reflected the type of affective bodily responses that accompanied the aspirational dreams of justice writ large, and through their passionate utterances they constituted our alliances. What was not as evident was how the feelings of what justice is were produced through particular educational knowledge domains and perpetrated through various emotional regimes that contribute to how feelings are embodied as legitimate.

A similar set of justice convictions also propelled through emotional discourses was predominant during the course of my fieldwork in Nigeria, Ethiopia, and Kenya between 2013 and 2017 and highlighted the ways that alliances were formed through sentimentally uttered discourses. In those cases, it was not the benevolent missionary but the African civil society activist whose affirmations of justice-as-law were rooted in much more than prosecutorial justice. While carrying out research, my team and I traveled from place to place, soliciting reactions to the ICC's indictments of African leaders while also following ICC cases, collaborating with thought leaders on various online platforms, and serving in a consultancy capacity on various research and policy strategies. What unfolded over the course of this phase of study was my reckoning with the complexities of international criminal law through assemblages that necessarily involved the foregrounding of embodied affects in relation to their regimes and hegemonic knowledge forms. This became evident through the collection of contradictory responses about the perceived culpability of African leaders.

While many felt that various leaders of African states were corrupt and uncommitted to the life of the ordinary person, some still defended them because of their recognition of Europe's history of extraction and underdevelopment of Africa and the way that those histories are part of the contemporary plunder of the region. Others defended their leaders, insisting that the problems were structural—that although independence produced political freedom, it did not free African states of entrenched political, economic, moral, and religious formations that were part of the plunder of Africa's resources. Those who refused to defend African leaders for various failures often turned to international bodies such as NGOs or legal instruments as the only solution to Africa's postcolonial crises. Many no longer believed in the possibility of partisan politics solving Africa's structural inequalities. With the sense that long-standing leaders like Robert Mugabe and Jacob Zuma were pillaging Africa's resources, they instead resorted to the promise of the law—with its aspirational mantra of certainty, promises of objectivity, and predictability. One response that characterized this retreat to law in the midst of ambiguity and dismay is best illustrated through the emotional plea of a colleague from an East African country working for a prominent African NGO. In response to a presentation at a meeting that sought to depict the ICC as a political force characterized through a history of European colonial instrumentalizations, he immediately rose up in the audience and declared without hesitation, "I am a proud African. Yet, I have lived personally under a repressive regime, experienced the abuse of power, and have survived it."

Then he continued, "This debate [about the value of the ICC] has been poisoned by our leaders. We should not replicate this misrepresentation at this forum. We must speak to each other through the letter of the law. We must stop posturing and debate frankly."

Claiming an eyewitness and insider standpoint, my colleague was impassioned and compelling. He spoke with conviction and his voice trembled with frustration and anger. His statement reflected the conviction of someone who reveled in what his country has offered the contemporary world, but bitterness about its human rights failures. He was a member of its ethnic majority and enjoyed the benefits of that class, but he worked tirelessly to ensure that those he saw as less fortunate would have a fighting chance. This was the spirit of his conviction; this was his expectation of contemporary democracy in Africa, and international law was the tool to address such injustice. Yet he remained dismayed and carried it in his words and his body, through his utterances and work commitments. His leaders had not enabled democracy's promise in his lifetime, and his mission was to address that.

With legal justice as the solution for protecting Africans victimized by repressive regimes, it was not necessary for my colleague to extrapolate—at least not beyond what he had articulated already. We all knew what he meant by the role of African repressive regimes abusing their power; that statement alone, and its delivery, articulated through familiar tones of anger and deep disappointment, provided the opening for his claim that Africa needed legal solutions to political problems.

A third prominent public throughout the African continent are those who insist on using structural inequalities connected to the Africa-and-ICC debate and on both using the law and going beyond it. One public intellectual from a West African country spoke passionately about African attempts to extend the criminal jurisdiction of the African Court and create the African Court of Justice and Human and Peoples' Rights in relation to a perceived double standard inherent in international legal spheres. As he declared in a public forum in Addis Ababa, "The desire for Africa to prosecute international crimes goes back to the 1970s. It was not just a matter of African leaders evading justice. Africans were concerned with the fundamental legal basis and the justifications for prosecuting crimes against Africans."[1] He made a sentimentalized plea to remind us that, as he said, "[The] desire to prosecute international crimes predates the ICC and was motivated by the fact that Africa discovered that there were certain crimes that affected Africans (like Apartheid) but the rest of the world was not interested."[2]

This statement, articulated with passion and paradox, formed the basis for the speaker to talk about the inability of Africans to use criminal law to address mass atrocities that were arguably related to colonial plunder of Africa, as well as the paradoxes related to the contemporary deployment of international criminal law to arrest African leaders. It represented a profound set of claims against international injustices argued passionately by African peoples of all class backgrounds and experiences, for it reflected a desire to highlight the complexity of African concerns within the larger histories of plunder and injustice. For those whose life worlds were compromised by colonization and whose temporalities and spatial orientations reflect *things African*, the ICC can look and feel like colonialism itself—what Hannah Appel called the "abdication of sovereignty" alongside the denial of colonial liability for violence on the African continent. From unsettled land dispossession to the absence of criminal liability for corporate violence, the political decisions that shape the ICC involve making sense of how one lives with the sequel of colonialism."[3]

To all three interlocutors—the missionary from the United States, the civil society activist, and the public intellectual and scholar—law had the potential to provide a way out of the poisoned politics of the postcolonial state. Yet for others it has the potential to obscure political inequalities. They all spoke passionately and in animated ways about the importance of international legality for Africa's future. For the first two, the senses of justice were connected to an organizing logic about liberal equality that tells us that everyone is entitled to rights and freedoms, and that the law exists to ensure that we get them. This justice narrative presumes that individual equality can be guaranteed judicially. The third interlocutor was concerned with how structural inequalities can exceed the juridical and how related justice discourses can often conceal those realities. In all cases, legal knowledge and its tools, affects, and particular discursive strategies that were appropriately legible to the context at hand served as key component parts of the connection between the actors.

In keeping with these sentiments argued in Africa and beyond, *Affective Justice* is about the way that such justice discourses are brought into being through the sum of their parts—technocratic knowledge, affects, and emotional regimes. It is concerned with how these assemblages of justice are felt, experienced, and institutionalized, such as the ICC or the newly forming African Court of Justice and Human Rights. For it was these related and complex sentiments that on July 17, 1998, led 120 of the world's leaders to sign the Rome Statute to establish the International Criminal Court. At the heart of this justice discourse was a legacy and set of sentimental commitments against mass atrocity violence that is said to have continued from various twentieth-century trials, including the Nuremberg tribunal of the late 1940s. Part of this discourse was the insistence that various publics, constituting the international community, have a responsibility to protect those victimized by such violence. Also central to it is a vehemently articulated anti-impunity discourse that insists that no one (high-ranking leaders, politicians, presidents, rebels, or ordinary citizens) should be beyond the reach of the law.

Like the other examples I have opened with, these feelings about the importance of justice are enabled through the law and communicated with various narratives that perform a particular type of work. The ICC anti-impunity narrative insists not only that justice means individual perpetrators should be punished, but that a perpetrator's official capacity should not bar him or her from criminal investigation. Understanding justice not solely in relation to the visible application of the law at all costs, but also as negotiated assemblages of feelings about inequality and power, allows us to recognize how other narratives about the ICC in Africa reflect people's ambiguities about Africa in relation to other spheres of global power.

To understand the logic of the competing ICC responses, we must think about the effects of the past on bodies and on people's futures, and how those futures are mediated and institutionally represented as well as regulated and simultaneously itinerant. It requires that we explore how the past collides with the present to produce our bodies and our imaginaries, and it involves wrestling with the interplay between temporality and the role of sentimentalized narratives.[4] These feelings of justice or injustice are complex and insist on including African independence and sovereignty aspirations alongside post-1960s histories of postcolonial despotisms, state failure, and embedded structural inequalities. In this regard, various African responses to the ICC and related postcolonial justice projects emerged within an acute temporal and spatial awareness of Africa's economic and political challenges in the world and the bodily responses to such inequalities. For while many hold various African leaders responsible for despotism and state failure, they also recognize the inequalities that pervade the African postcolonial state—such as the reality that many economic and political decisions about African states are actually made outside of the geographical boundaries of those states.

From agreements made during independence talks, to the role of economic speculation and investments, to structural adjustment, mineral extraction, and market competition with Chinese competitors and beyond, many see the way that modernity has prescribed a particular set of practices that already constrain the ability of the state to provide for its citizens. The stakeholders, informed by the recognition of some of these realities, also use particular affective narratives to make their claims. From their ambivalence about African leaders to their accusations of international institutions as extensions of histories of imperial plunder, the articulated narrative responses reflect a particular way of expressing the complexities of justice through a rethinking of the political. The narratives also produce expressions about who we are, what we stand for, what matters, and why; thus, they are vulnerable to be driven by our bodily affects. As expressive manifestations that involve particular enactments of feelings, these affects are expressed, understood, and ultimately sentimentalized in particular ways—using specific narrative tropes and related strategies for enforcement and alliance.

These emotive narratives about justice are critical to this book, which takes as its point of departure an ongoing debate about whom the ICC is indicting and why—and how individuals in social movements are engaging and institutionalizing or contravening those developments. The book is about responses to judicial inequalities that do not always find expression in legal frameworks alone, as well as the social imaginaries that are shaped by perpetual campaigns for legal justice. Such campaigns are effective because of the techniques used to mobilize sentimentally shaped action.[5] Time and time again, as we spoke with interlocutors on the African continent—politicians, academics, leaders, judges, investigators, diplomats, lawyers, children, survivors of violence, the homeless, and members of NGOs and of civil society, it was clear that international law—with its temporal and spatial particularities—was seen as both a beacon of possibility and the basis for the continued plunder and inequality in Africa. But with justice articulated through the support or rejection of the ICC or the support or rejection of an African court with criminal jurisdiction, it was also clear that the validity of my colleagues' positions at the meeting that day, and many meetings before and after it, were not rendered legitimate because of their experience or facts, but because of the profound affective performance and sentimentalism that accompanied their speech acts and the institutionalized forms that reinforced such narratives.

Affective Justice explores both the subjective and agentive processes and the structuring fields through which individuals respond to social injustice. By examining the role of sentimentalized justice narratives manifested in and through bodily expressions, verbal utterances, biomediated hashtag campaigns, international laws, and claims about justice, we can see how various affectively shaped social regimes determine what is acceptable and authoritative, and what is not. The book is about the strategies of international justice brokers and the sentimentalized imaginaries of many of the African interlocutors with whom I conducted my research.

Studying Affective Assemblages of Justice

How can transnational justice ethnographies explain the complex workings of postcolonial affects by what Bill Mazzarella describes as preserving the traces of past encounters and bringing them into the present as potentials? How can political and legal anthropology be used to study the affective body by exploring the "pragmatics of institutional practice"?[6] How can the study of institutional practice shed light on the workings of affective resonances and their sentimentalized deployments of international legal tools? To answer these questions, I had to begin and end the research for this book in the middle of things—feelings about the joys and horrors of the African past, aspirations for a new future, conversations on planes, disputes at conferences, observations of international court cases, incomplete responses to images of violence, successful indictments after seven to eight years while survivors of violence still await assistance, heart-wrenching testimonies, and feel-good humanitarian gestures—all manifest in and through bodies but also inscribed and partially observable through institutional practices. The nature of these unsettling realities has led me to examine the manifestations of sentimentalized emotions that underlie rule of law assemblages. My goal is not only to study such assemblages ethnographically through their embodied practices, as many have done in the anthropology of affect literature. It is also to fill the gaps in the political and legal anthropology literature as well as the international law and politics literature with a study of entanglements that focuses on how various approaches to justice, communicated through sentimentalized strategies and engaged in institutional practices, are expressed and have effects in daily life.

Research for this book began in the midst of public debates about whether ICC justice was biased and involved the targeting of Africans alone. Questions of ICC bias and selectivity pervaded anti-ICC discourses and ranged from accusations that the court is racist to questions about how Africa's "failed states" contributed to breeding grounds for wars, violence, and even more indictments by the ICC. These questions were sometimes met with public agreement and at other times with laudatory responses from a range of ICC actors, judges, stakeholders, academics, and civil society groups that all included a familiar refrain—that with its birth in the resolve to stop the arbitrariness of violence, and thereby protect victims, the ICC's justice is a blind justice whose sole objective is to end impunity. Yet over the past four years of data collection at and in relation to international criminal trials at the ICC in The Hague, in civil society organizations, at AU summits and meetings in Addis Ababa, at postviolence sites in Kenya and Nigeria, at the African Court in Tanzania, the Extraordinary African Chambers in Senegal, and in the Assembly of State Party UN annual meetings, conference rooms, and workshop halls, it became clear to me that in order to understand the challenges of the ICC as an international justice institution, we must grapple with the paradoxes of contemporary justice. And if, following Talal Asad, we see the public sphere not as an "empty place for carrying out debates" but as a space "constituted by the sensibilities—memories and aspirations, fears and hopes—of speakers and listeners," actors and agents, then nowhere is there a better domain for exploring the making of justice than through affective practices and inquiries into their institutionalization, retractions, and, at times, waning popularity.[7]

In order to understand the ways that sentimentalized expressions of international justice are manifest in various globalizing publics, I assembled a research team to work on this project from 2012 to 2014 and then, with new funding, took on a new cluster of short fieldwork trips and ongoing and engaged consultancy project work from 2014 to 2018. Throughout 2012, my team spent eight months in phase 1 of the project in The Hague, exploring the many contours of ICC justice in its first ten years of existence. In an effort to understand the affective practices involved in the rise of the ICC's rule of law movement, we trained a small group of interns and conducted interviews, archival work, media documentation, and trial observations.

In 2013 we spent six months in Addis Ababa, Ethiopia, at the African Union—the continent's foremost Pan-Africanist organization concerned with fostering integration, collaboration, and a high standard of living for the citizens of Africa—where we interviewed AU staff, conducted participant observation at its events and summits, and set the terms for collaboration on a research project related to the emergence of the African Court. This was an important moment to work within the complexities of the AU, as the organization was also undergoing exceptional transformation. At that time, it was developing a new architecture of peace and security, forming a political structure, and developing new institutions and treaty agreements. A general reconceptualization of Africa's responsibility for addressing growth, violence, and political turmoil was underway throughout the continent. Significant funding possibilities for civil society groups and talk of justice and strategy were underway. We documented the aspirations and strategies for building a renewed Pan-African movement and how those hopes were manifesting in the newly evolving debates about the extension of the criminal jurisdiction of the African Court as a way to take on transnational crimes in Africa, against Africans. Despite the pushback against the ICC, the faith in international legality—this time in Africa—as a way to address political violence remained interesting to us. It highlighted the way that legal hegemonies travel and take shape not only through institutions of power, but also through emotional frameworks of expectation or emotional regulation—a notion that I take up later in the book.

In 2013, we also set up a team of researchers in Kenya and Nigeria to work with survivors of violence, understand the complexities of postviolence contexts, and observe the postviolence rectification strategies underway. In Nairobi and its surrounding areas there were also significant mobilizations that involved judicial and nonjudicial approaches. I then traveled to northern Nigeria in 2014 to understand related fallout from postviolence attacks waged by Boko Haram, whose abductions of over two hundred girls from a boarding school led to a short-lived global protest mobilization to return the girls to their families. In both Nigeria and Kenya, our goal was to make sense of the meaning of justice for everyday people in two of the regions that are, for the ICC, sites of ongoing interest. To the AU, the ICC's interest reeked of the selective targeting of African cases—as many often exclaimed—and this discourse drove our inquiry and puzzlement.

The final phase of this project involved closer research collaborations (2014–2018) with the AU and African Court advocates. If my research team felt like classic anthropological interlopers during the first two phases, by this final phase the consultative practices became central to the form of participant observation that underlined this work. I became part of an advisory team involved in the expansion of the criminal jurisdiction of the African Court tasked with contemplating the new judicial architecture and helping to critically assess and reshape its design. Through the formation of the African Court Research Initiative, we provided technical assistance to the African Court, as the legal office labored to create a better and more responsive African Court protocol for the African continent. We worked with international law experts and as partners with various organizations to ponder the challenges ahead for an African Court with jurisdiction to adjudicate criminal cases. Some of this work was based in cities such as Arusha and The Hague, as well as in various consultancy and advisory settings in Addis Ababa. It involved working with scholars, lawyers, diplomats, advisors, and civil society groups to procure research data, assess negotiation documents, engage with and study the adoption of strategies, and do ongoing advisory work.

By the end of the last phase, we had spent over six years working at the heart of ICC and Africa issues—a rhizomatic process that could not be accomplished by just one person and whose scope reflects the face of new global ethnographies. During the analysis, we coded data and mapped particular emotional responses that shaped the data analysis. By focusing on various sentimental emotions coded as anger, fear, vengeance, pain, sympathy, and victorious joy, we attempted to make sense of the emotional contours of international justice at the ICC, the AU, and in related spaces of international justice assemblages. We analyzed the manifestations of those affects and emotional expressions through our readings of particular speech acts that allowed us to reflect on the way that various emotional expressions were articulated and institutionalized through various discourses and campaigns. In the end, our observations collected during all three phases of this research helped to ground my understanding of the management of violence, the sentimental fortitude that governs it, the contestations over how it should be managed, and what social regimes, historical imbrications, and institutional forms are involved in the shaping of the narratives and feeling rules through which the legitimacy or illegitimacy of international justice is expressed. Ultimately, as *Affective Justice* outlines, recognizing the relevance of affects in shaping how justice is materialized is key to understanding how justice is made legible, institutionalized, disentangled, and also remade anew. This, I hope, will contribute to the much needed development of an anthropology of international justice of the twenty-first century.

Introduction

Formations, Dislocations, and Unravelings

On April 27, 2007, the International Criminal Court (ICC) issued arrest warrants against Janjaweed militia leader Ali Kushayb and Sudan's minister of humanitarian affairs, Ahmed Harun.[1] Then on July 14, 2008, the ICC prosecutor requested an arrest warrant against Sudanese president Omar al-Bashir, which was issued on March 4, 2009.[2] Since it came into force through the Rome Statute in July 2001, the ICC, a court with jurisdiction among 123 member states, has implemented mechanisms for punishment of crimes against humanity, war crimes, and genocide committed after July 1, 2002 (when the Rome Statute went into force), and also hopes to do so universally for the crime of aggression.[3] As one of many institutions engaged in the growth of the rule of law movement, the ICC is constituted through a multilateral treaty order that enables the jurisdictional reach of international legal institutions and their associated liberalist principles. The court's much-vaunted call for an end to impunity is represented in its moral discourse of supporting victims through the pursuit of those most criminally responsible, including heads of state.

Under the Rome Statute for the ICC, state actors under the jurisdiction of the court have agreed to suspend their sovereignty over the adjudication of particular international crimes and have instead ceded that responsibility to the ICC. The popular expectation is that states under the ICC's jurisdiction will be held responsible for protecting the lives of their citizens from mass atrocity violence, thereby committing to ending the impunity of those who are seen as having evaded justice for too long.[4] By attributing to high-ranking leaders (rather than lower-level actors) the responsibility for mass atrocity violence, the ICC has perhaps done more than any other international institution to promote the need to end impunity. But it has also borne the brunt of significant critiques in response to local controversies, all the while calling attention to its selection strategies and legitimacy.[5] One such controversy has emerged because court agents can trigger its jurisdiction through a state self-referral for investigation and possible prosecution under Article 13(a) of the Rome Statute. However, given that upper-level leaders are unlikely to investigate their own actions honestly, jurisdiction can also be triggered through the prosecutor's *proprio motu* (one's own initiative) referral power (Article 13(c)), as well as through a referral by the United Nations Security Council (UNSC) (Article 13(b)). The latter has been controversial because they can also involve referrals of nonstate parties that have not consented to the Rome Statute's jurisdiction. More than half of the states that are permanent members of the UNSC—the United States, China, and Russia—have refused to suspend their sovereignty and submit their states to the jurisdiction of the ICC.[6] This reality has been described by African publics as a cloak of equality in the midst of incommensurably unequal domains.

From its inception in 2002 until the fall of 2018, the ICC has pursued twenty-two cases in nine situations across several African states: Central African Republic, Democratic Republic of the Congo, Ivory Coast, Sudan, Uganda, Kenya, the Republic of Mali, and Libya. It has issued indictments for thirty-six individuals, including twenty-seven warrants of arrest and nine summonses to appear before the court.[7] From the cases of alleged African warlords to the indictments of African leaders—such as President Uhuru Kenyatta and Deputy President William Ruto of Kenya, President Omar al-Bashir of Sudan (not a party to the Rome Statute), and Laurent Gbagbo of Ivory Coast—the predominance of African defendants has led to suspicion about the fairness of prosecutorial justice. Growing numbers of African and other postcolonial stakeholders have begun to see the anti-impunity/rule of law discourse as highly biased and uneven.[8] This was especially the case following the ICC judge's refusal to accept the prosecutor's request for authorization to begin an investigation into whether crimes were committed in Afghanistan by the US military.[9]

In response to perceived structural injustice, some African leaders, such as Rwandan president Paul Kagame, have offered passionate utterances, as when he stated that the ICC appears to have been "put in place only for African countries, only for poor countries. . . . Every year that passes, I am proved right. . . . Rwanda cannot be part of colonialism, slavery and imperialism."[10] This comment, made in the context of President al-Bashir's indictment in 2009, reflects the perspective of many on the continent who have begun to perceive the ICC not as the mechanism for a more hopeful future, but rather as a force that seeks to continue a long and tragic history of exploitation, racism, and external control of African states and economies.

When the ICC prosecutor issued the arrest warrant for President al-Bashir in 2009, it marked the first time that the UNSC had invoked its referral power under Rome Statute Article 13(b) to refer a particular situation to the ICC prosecutor.[11] The referral was predicated on the UNSC's determination that the situation in Sudan constituted a threat to international peace and security under Article 39 of the United Nations Charter, and that the prosecution of the perpetrators of the human rights violations in Darfur would help to restore peace and stability in the region.[12] The government of Sudan objected to the exercise of this jurisdiction, arguing that both the UNSC and ICC violated the country's sovereignty given that Sudan had not ratified the Rome Statute for the ICC and, therefore, had not consented to suspending its sovereignty.[13] In immediate reaction to the arrest warrant against al-Bashir, the Sudanese government expelled more than a dozen humanitarian aid organizations and workers—leaving more than one million people without access to food, water, and health care services—creating controversy and further complicating peace negotiations that were underway.[14] In addition to the Sudanese government, the Arab League, the Organization of the Islamic Conference, and some members of the UNSC (most notably China) also objected to the arrest warrant.[15]

For its part, the African Union (AU) responded by requesting that the UNSC defer the ICC prosecution against al-Bashir, arguing that a legal process would "undermine ongoing regional peace efforts in which Mr. al-Bashir was actively participating."[16] The UNSC responded minimally to the AU request, considering it only briefly and declining to act on it.[17] When the UNSC refused, the AU called on its members not to cooperate with the ICC's order.[18]

That the state agents of the AU, initially strong supporters of the ICC, have recently adopted an oppositional stance is especially telling. The AU is the largest Pan-African organization, with an expanding mandate to achieve greater unity, solidarity, political cooperation, and socioeconomic integration for African peoples. In regard to President al-Bashir's indictment, the AU insisted that the "search for justice should be pursued in a way that does not impede or jeopardize efforts aimed at promoting lasting peace."[19] It also reiterated a concern about a possible "misuse of indictments against African leaders."[20] In the end, the UNSC denied its request, resulting in the AU's 2011 decision not to cooperate with the arrest and surrender of al-Bashir to The Hague. Until April 2019, when an army-led military coup in Sudan led to the end of his thirty-year rule, he has been traveling to various African ICC member states without arrest. After this period, African leaders continued to insist that they would not support ICC-led regime change. If al-Bashir is to be prosecuted, "it would not involve handing him over to outsiders."[21] As of summer 2019, the controversy is ongoing and is part of a broader debate about international justice—what institutions and people have the power to name it, deliver it and why—and is at the center of what I refer to as *affective justice* and that this book takes up.

How do justice institutions like the ICC or the African Court for Justice and Human and Peoples' Rights operate with effectiveness and force when they do not have universal jurisdiction, enforcement power, a police force or military, or the assumed loyalty of a citizenry, as a state does? In this book, I show that they can be explained through a practice theory in which embodied affects, emotional regimes, and technocratic forms of knowledge reflect the interplay among embodied and regimented practice that I call affective justice. This, I argue, is central to the power of such justice institutions and the justice formations they seek to produce.

Affective Justice as a Theorization of Rule of Law Assemblages

Notions of justice have tended to be mapped out against three broad categories of understanding: philosophical, analytic, or practice oriented. The contributions of Jacques Derrida and John Rawls have been especially important to developing a coherent philosophical understanding of justice as a domain by which fairness is established through rights and duties and in relation to achieving justice through the law.[22] As an analytic category, justice has been understood as an expressive domain through which people organize their ideas about what is morally right and fair as well as what is ethical.[23] When understood in terms of practice, justice is seen as being produced and challenged by the materiality of people's actions through which meanings of justice are lived. Anthropologists have long engaged in documenting practice-oriented meaning making and how notions of appropriateness and inappropriateness are produced through sociocultural behavior. Yet philosophical and analytic perspectives have been privileged in discussions of international justice, and the contributions of an anthropological focus on practice have been less prominent. This book begins to address that gap by illuminating how affects as embodied practices shape emotional responses and how those responses can, through the intensity of their force, produce international justice in particular ways. Affective justice seeks to illuminate an important process that has remained obscure in the theorizing of international justice: that is, how various forms of legal, political, and economic instrumentalism have produced the force of law, sociomoral affects, and embodied practices that constitute international publics.

Affective justice is the term that I advance for understanding people's embodied engagements with and production of justice through particular structures of power, history, and contingencies. Central to it are the ways that affects, as embodied responses, constitute publics by dislodging identity from its classification domain and relocating it to a domain of practice and regimentations of feelings. This approach allows us to highlight what people do with emotions and is connected not only to affects and their subjectivations, but also to the biopolitical strategies through which life and its human possibilities are managed. As I show, this happens under regimes of knowledge and power, through which law and technocratic and capitalist processes are deployed. Seeing justice through the workings of these affective embodiments, emotional regimes, and biopolitical processes demonstrates that contemporary international justice mobilizations do not gain their power through singular and formalized law-making processes, in relation to which people supposedly engage with and buy into meanings of justice. Rather, they gain their power through the conjunctures amongst legal ephemeral, and embodied imaginaries. *Affective Justice* shows that this happens through technologies, particular legal feeling expressions and narrative devices that are used to expand, displace, and end injustice, thereby producing the basis on which justice is felt.

Affective justice as a practice reflects embodiments of feelings that are manifest in feeling expressions and embodied practices, including the spoken word, legal actions and innovations, or electronically mediated campaigns. In an attempt to shape justice institutions and conceptions of justice, ICC and AU agents, nongovernmental advocates, and civil society activists vie for control of social norms or challenge those norms to produce new ones. Thus, seen through the remit of the ICC, affective justice reflects the way that people come to understand, challenge, and influence legal orders through the biopolitical instrumentalization of technocratic knowledge as well as through their affective embodiments, interjections, and social actions. The practices involved are infinite and span from treaty drafting, ratification, and adjudication to trial attendance, language negotiations, and joking, to refusals that involve rejections, withdrawals, and noncooperation declarations, as well as the development of countercampaigns. What connects these practices to law's power are the embodied feelings and emotional expressions that drive such acts and circulate them globally. It is these practices that are at the heart of this book and clarify the central role of affective justice in the making of contemporary international criminal law.

Yet international justice, like other forms of justice, is often presumed to be outside the realm of these practices of construction. It is seen by many of its advocates as objective and nonprejudicial, with precedents that are external to sociocultural, political, and precognitive scrutiny. In the realm of cognition, a growing number of contemporary brain scientists have argued that the mind responds to precognitive sensory impressions and processes to produce culturally appropriate emotional responses.[24] Gaining inspiration from this literature, humans translate precognitive affect into hyperlocal cultural terms of understanding that are in turn expressed through emotions and regulated socially and adopted into actionable concepts. *Affective Justice* posits that emotional articulations of bodily processes constitute a critical link connecting the precognitive body to the making and unmaking of sociolegal and political institutions, and that this site of translation can be examined through observations of how affects are legally materialized, discursively and performatively. As the individual feels and expresses, social practices shape what ultimately counts as justice. By introducing a language for clarifying the assemblages of precognitive, sociopolitical, cultural, and moral processes through which justice is produced, *Affective Justice* explores how justice making is enmeshed in bodily affects that give rise to emotional expressions and various racialized iconic figures. It explores some of the ways that bodily affects and their emotional potentialities are entangled in the constitution of international justice and focuses on the way that bodies, psychology, and social practices come together to produce the terms on which justice is materialized, disaggregated, ruptured, and made legible again. The lived material and/or sentient body, the social body, and the body politic—each of these bodies, coproduced and intersecting, is being mobilized through affectively propelled biosocial and social forms. What emerges is an illustration of how affects can shape, through emotional and institutional manifestations, the form that justice takes. It insists that justice is a product of sets of competing practices that are shaped and expressed materially and socially. And constitutive formations of justice are represented within social feeling regimes and emotive performances that provide clues to how social relationships are deployed to enact what justice becomes. As a constellation of competing sensations, these feelings are materialized socially and provide possibilities for theorizing justice through entanglements that include contingency and structural inequality.

At its base, *Affective Justice* argues that international rule of law formations such as the ICC and, as I discuss later, the African Court do not produce legal processes that articulate justice in stable and predictable ways.[25] Rather, such institutions reflect a complicated and precarious array of infinitely deterritorialized interrelationships among a wide variety of actors who possess differential forms of power and privilege, including citizens, technocrats, judges, advertisers, investigators, evidence procurers, airlines, tourists, those victimized by violence, those being investigated by prosecutors, and so forth. International justice cannot be a sacrosanct, stand-alone space for justice making understood through identity categories such as "survivors" or "perpetrators." In these realms, affects that emerge from a violation or perceived offense produce responses that are irreducible to a singular identity or action or delimitation of power. Rather, the ICC—like other domains of justice making—exists within assemblages that are constituted by networks of emergent properties, manifest in what Gilles Deleuze and Félix Guattari refer to as "component parts."[26] The components as part of international justice function through a set of factions that shape international criminal law moral imaginaries: the figures of the *perpetrator*, the *victim/survivor*, and the *international community* that activate the affective possibilities through which justice is articulated and embodied. In these imaginary spaces, invocations such as the "victim to be saved" and the "perpetrator to be stopped" are deployed as proxies through which law's architecture is retooled, constantly resharpened, and remade anew—as needed. Thus, in order to understand the international management of contemporary mass atrocity violence, we must account for how these affective domains actually constitute law's power in ways that congeal but also redirect meanings of justice.

Characteristic of national and international law assemblages is the idea that social entities—their formations and their existence in practice—are component parts of international criminal justice formations while also being entangled in other relations. As one of a broad array of legal sites, international criminal justice functions within an assemblage of actions, emotions, linkages, reactions, connections, utterances, metaphors, and so forth. From the complex worlds of investigators to the rulings of judges, lawyers, and those victimized by violence, as well as those charged with the perpetration of violence, the assemblage is far reaching. It is more than the sum of its component parts. Through the combustion of those parts, international criminal justice is propelled through affects and emotional domains that communicate what justice becomes. This way of orienting justice formations in the context of whole units being seen as "inextricable combinations of interrelated parts" departs from the idea that social relations are structured hierarchically or are reducible to other things.[27] Rather, sets of relations and their practices—like international trials that involve attorneys, spectators, perpetrators of violence, security staff, prison guards, activities of media companies, images, the objects of violence such as land or political parties, botched trials, interpreters and misinterpreted translations, legal statutes, nongovernmental organizations (NGOs), images that shape imaginaries, audiences, students, convicts, interns, news reporters, securitization companies, transportation companies, hotels, airlines, and so on—are component parts within a contingent patchwork of relationships.

Central to this book, therefore, are these meta-formations, working alongside micropractices that constitute the international criminal justice assemblage in the contemporary period. The formations do not exist through a universalizing global domain in which fairness and equality constitute international justice everywhere. Rather, international justice gains power through the various affects that are grounded in the deep-seated histories and inequalities whose dispositions are sometimes already inscribed in people's psychic or emotional worlds. Thus, when attempts to rectify injustice are dislodged from sites of suffering to sites of remediation, they have the ability to become aligned with already meaningful moral commitments, such as feelings of structural inequality that are emotionally expressed through anger and public protest. From the meanings of the Nuremberg trials for international justice advocates to the absence of international institutions intervening into colonialism and apartheid, it is through practices that are imbricated with histories of injustice that international institutions gain their power, that law gains its force.

Examining the role of affects in theorizing "the global" requires, then, that we go beyond the fiction of the global as all-encompassing spaces in which competing forces are counterpoised. Making sense of the globalization of international justice involves inserting into justice making the practices, embodied feelings, and regimes of regulation that are constituted through it. As knowledge and media technologies proliferate and advertising and campaign strategies become more sophisticated, these various entanglements come together through deterritorialized component parts of international justice assemblages. As an intensified manifestation of law making and justice practices, this book shows that international justice involves globalizing processes not because there exists a domain called *the global*, but because its processes are imagined and practiced as *global*, and in the context of such imaginaries they travel, dislodge meanings, and remake them in new spaces and contexts. This is how international justice travels—through embodied domains that inspire legal inventions, protests, and contestation and lead to their rearticulation in new ways. And it is precisely the dynamic basis upon which justice is embodied that discusses the aspirational realities of international criminal law.

Conceptually inspired by Deleuze and Guattari, this patchwork of justice-making practices contains antigenealogical and irreducible components that interact with each other while also maintaining their properties.[28] Applied to international legal spaces, such properties of the composite parts connected to technocratic knowledge involve authorial language, hierarchical relations, and temporal and spatial scales, as well as interactions that, while messy, present themselves as objective and honoring legal certainty. Thus, contemporary rule of law assemblages function through particular and often mundane affective regulatory mechanisms that are spread through a variety of institutions and discursive channels, including campaigns, indexes, slogans, and contemporary technological tools such as Twitter and Facebook.

Ultimately, the prevailing methodological questions of this book concern the field at the scale of transnational ethnography that is rhizomatic in form but highlights the way that global linkages reflect nodular stems of knowledge, practice, and sites of meaning making that spread rapidly through horizontal networks through a range of powerful legal, aesthetic and political mechanisms, such as campaigns that motivate particular calls to action, even as they leave open itinerant possibilities. The key, following Deleuze and Guattari, is to make sense of these formations that defy not only linear lines of causality but also elude the traditional multisited ethnographic methods that have become popularized in contemporary anthropology.[29] By introducing ways of articulating the complexities of international criminal law institutions and actors, *Affective Justice* provides a tool kit for making sense of the rhizomatic realities of culture and power that has shaped both the ICC and the Pan-Africanist pushback.

To make sense of such complexities, sociologists have explored justice through structural fields as a way to understand culture and power relations.[30] Others have examined the way that legal processes work and shape their constituencies.[31] And some, attempting to clarify the workings of global or transnational theories, have examined legal processes in relation to vertical, horizontal, and structural approaches through their effects.[32] Concepts such as scales of justice and actor-network theory have been developed to make sense of the entanglements between law and the global and transnational social spaces within which it operates.[33] I present a way of studying international legal processes and practices by mapping various affects that are manifest in emotional practices that shape and are connected to the component parts of international justice making, especially in relation to the mobilization of the law through appeals to emotion.

As my methods suggest, the actions of judicial institutions, the emotional responses to which these actions give rise, and the sentimental articulations that seek to direct affects into action have no real beginning or end. Their time scapes start neither with the Nuremberg trials as the central marker nor with the 2002 temporal jurisdiction of the ICC. Nor do they start with the acts of violence by which liberal legality identifies culpability. Studying international justice movements necessarily involves looking at the making of component parts, which exist through what Deleuze and Guattari refer to as "ceaselessly established connections between semiotic chains, organizations of power, and circumstances relative to . . . social struggles."[34] The result is an understanding of the social field as an assemblage of different aspects of competing regimes of knowledge and sentimental expressions of this knowledge, which occupies different status designations and meanings depending on the site of inquiry and field of power.

In its focus on social practices fueled with emotional manifestations, *Affective Justice* presents an approach to justice that considers technocratic knowledge production and its biopolitical domains, the role of affects and their emotional expressions, and the representational regimes that manifest through interpretive and institutional practices. While justice is knowable by social and humanistic scholars through its materialized forms, such as anger and joy, the subjective experience of international justice involves a constellation of components that are not simply arbitrary. In other words, affective justice is not an essential form of justice that can be applied universally to different contexts and people. Nor is it a form of expression that binds particular social groups and not others. It is a product of immaterial and material practices that find their expressions in bodily or social meaning making. Materialized through expressions, representations, discourses, and feeling regimes that shape the way that justice is embodied and expressed by people, affective justice is constituted by complex assemblages that communicate through convergent, itinerant, and even divergent component parts. By introducing the concept of *reattribution*, which I use to describe a particular form of refusal that involves redirection, I offer an explanation for how those engaged in African international rule of law circles are rethinking justice by dismantling its meanings in time and place and embodying new formations, even as those new formations may one day become just as hegemonic as the ones they are protesting. These formulations call on us to think differently about the relevance of mechanisms such as treaties and preambles. They open up new possibilities for understanding how legal architectures are historically confronted, challenged, and even dismantled. For example, the imposition of legal experiments in Africa to constitute the colonial state and its contemporary modes of governance and sociality were constitutive of mass displacement and devastation of earlier forms of practices. That displacement involved imperial domination of Africa's ancestral lands, the uprooting of the peoples from those lands, and the restructuring of social organizations, forms of governance, languages, and taxonomies that were foreign and lacked popular legitimacy.[35] This meant that so much of Africa's relationship to legal justice enabled this pillage and was instrumental at best. Though it would be wrong to draw direct or facile linkages, it is clear that the continuity of violence and the plunder of Africa's land and peoples are related to residual colonial inscriptions.[36] Yet, the relationship between colonial injustice and contemporary violence is rhizomatically entangled. This is why we observe a wide variety of African responses to institutions such as the ICC. Some involve NGO- and court-propelled social networks such as those engaged in anti-impunity advocacy. Others involve groups that are rethinking the causes and remedies of structural injustice.

As feelings of political actors are projected onto sites of legal action, those actors jockey for power to establish the core assumptions that underlie beliefs about why something like violence erupts or how it should be mitigated. What we see is that affective justice is a domain of practice, a psychosocial as well as conceptual domain for making sense of the way categories are assembled and people's relationships to them are materialized, and how they are rendered visible through some actions and made invisible through others. This process of justice making operates within contested spaces by which people engage in forms of refusals and recalibrations. In the context of a Pan-Africanist pushback, the book explores the way that refusals are generative of new component parts of the assemblage. Though there has been significant scholarly work attempting to clarify the complexities of assemblage theory and to theorize large social entities and notions of global assemblages in different social universes, little attention has been given to the moral universes that shape justice practices in international rule of law regimes and how they combine with other instrumental and technocratic regimes.[37] And even less attention has been given to the way that these new formations have led to the redesigning and repurposing of emergent assemblages whose force is propelled by constant interrelations between history, personal memory, structures of legal instrumentality, and affective resonances, including refusals, reattributions, and endorsements. This negotiation is embedded in assemblages that are not neatly structured in relation to distinct micro-, macro-, and meso-formations. They are messily embroiled in structuring histories and impromptu manifestations that shape how international justice feels. This book presents case studies that emerge from multisited ethnographic research to show how regimented feelings about perceived injustice shape the opportunities and limits of international justice.

In the first decades of its formation, the ICC has been riddled with politicized disagreement and struggles over its perceived legitimacy and institutional power. In particular, some of the most vocal critics have focused on the ICC's anti-impunity sentiments, reified in the institution through frequent invocation of "victim" and "perpetrator" narratives. The terms for the rise of the sentiment of the duty to prosecute that emerged from the 1980s to 1990s were critical for deepening the emergence of the discourses that framed the contemporary rule of law movement. The same was true for the later African postcolonial advocates who joined forces with them to establish the deepening of the moral authority and power of legal accountability for mass atrocity crimes committed by high-ranking leaders. However, this was followed by subsequent emotional refusals by African states because of the ICC's focus on prosecuting African leaders. African critics subverted this narrative by complicating the pursuit of the African perpetrator with the image of the anti-imperial freedom fighter, thus erecting a substantive challenge to the hegemony of the victim-perpetrator binary and its emphasis on individualized guilt over structural injustice.

In international law, the duty to prosecute serious international crimes was first established in a series of treaties recognizing specific atrocities as requiring intervention. The Convention on the Prevention and Punishment of the Crime of Genocide (Genocide Convention) recognizes genocide as an international crime, imposes individual responsibility, and requires state parties to try to punish perpetrators of genocide.[38] The Geneva Convention requires states to "search for persons alleged to have committed, or to have ordered to be committed, . . . grave breaches [of the Geneva Convention], and . . . bring such persons, regardless of their nationality, before [their] own courts."[39]

Of late, the notion of a duty to prosecute has been recognized with such a high degree of prevalence that the International Committee of the Red Cross (ICRC) asserts that there is an obligation under customary international law for states to investigate and prosecute international crimes.[40] Yet a vibrant Pan-African pushback against demands for legal accountability has also unfolded through the initiative of the AU, which has refused to cooperate with ICC arrest requests and has built leverage through threats and actual withdrawals from the Rome Statute. In turn, a global network of progressives—including radical and mainstream members of the African and African diasporic economic and cultural elite—have launched vehement demands for international institutions to pursue justice through accountability outside the confines of African state influence. By organizing grassroots and networked struggles to end corruption, address decimated legal systems, and make perpetrators accountable for mass atrocity violence, various members of the middle- and upper-class transnational elite have mobilized political support to attempt to rectify the perceived failures of African states. As these actors make evident, politically charged emotions are at the heart of contemporary international justice.[41] To understand these processes, we have to turn to how the emotional expression of feelings solidifies sociality in our globalized, contemporary world.

As illustrated, various stakeholders—international lawyers, judges, prosecutors, victim-survivors, defendants, witnesses, African leaders, NGOs, civil society organizations, and everyday citizens—use sentimentalized emotional appeals to contribute to how justice is imagined and the terms through which it is invoked. These affective expressions are not just peripheral. They perform a particular type of discursive work that takes shape through a range of modalities, such as biomediated campaigns, utterances, figures, and symbols that compel constituencies to act. These modalities are profoundly critical in that they shape not only the vocabularies for guilt and innocence, but also contribute to the regimentation of social imaginaries that determine which expressions are deemed legitimate, appropriate, or unacceptable to particular audiences. By detailing the sentimentalized affects of publics for and against African leaders being adjudicated at the ICC—representatives of the court, various NGOs, ICC intermediaries, the international community, and those victimized by mass atrocity violence—*Affective Justice* shows how emotional or feeling regimes are intimately linked to competing interpretations of justice. I explore how histories and structures of power shape, narrativize, and enforce sentimental affinities and practices, how those practices relate to the construction and reception of justice narratives, and how political and racialized subjectivities are made in that process. I analyze these complex processes and document why such approaches to studying justice are critical for making sense of contemporary international justice and the range of responses to it.

Situating Affective Justice through the Study of Emotional Affect

Sociocultural anthropology has long been interested in the study of emotion, and over the past decade, research on emotions in the field has recognized the various affective factors that shape the lives of individuals and, through emotional embodiments, the structure of society.[42] Despite the insights opened up by anthropologists theorizing the study of emotions, political-legal anthropological approaches have been slow to apply the study of affective embodiments to complex macro-global formations within which emotions circulate.[43] Influential political-legal anthropologists have explored how people make and remake their social worlds in conditions of conflict and instability, and much of this work examines notions of violence and social reconstruction through the focus on the daily texture of meaning making.[44] However, these anthropological studies do not take up the role of affects and emotions in mobilizing postviolence practices. Nor are they concerned with the larger global assemblages within which such sociopolitical practices circulate.

Among legal anthropologists engaged in the study of transitional justice and international court institutions, even those texts that focus directly on emotively driven practices miss the opportunity to move beyond frames that individualize emotions and embed them in legal solutions. Richard Wilson's *Incitement on Trial: Prosecuting International Speech Crimes* demonstrates this point. *Incitement on Trial* is about the type of speech practices, what he calls revenge speech, that can contribute to violent crime and examines how various armed conflicts are driven by racial, ethnic, national, or religious hatred. By demonstrating the need to address the relationship between speech acts and various mass atrocity crimes, the optic of analysis is focused on how particular speech acts contribute to crimes against humanity and genocide. It highlights the role of ordering in the perpetration of mass atrocity violence and argues that incitement should be seen as a form of complicity, in turn leading to criminal liability. In advocating a framework for monitoring political speech, the book rethinks notions of criminal liability as a measure for culpability.

Further work by Wilson also illustrates this focus on individualized criminal culpability.[45] Wilson is concerned with criminal liability, hate speech, and postatrocity violence, and argues that not only have human rights become the central language of justice worldwide, but the survivors of mass atrocity violence want legal accountability for such atrocity violence. By mapping various approaches to the anthropology of international justice that reorient justice in broader terms, he argues that, given that survivors use human rights language to advocate for the legal accountability of political leaders who commit those crimes, analysts need to pay attention to the calls for legal accountability for perpetrators of violence.[46] Advocating the development of a framework for recuperating survivors of violence against various offending political elites, this kind of legal triumphalism depends on the presumption of a "victim/survivor" versus "perpetrator" dyad.

As morally important as it is to support the cause of survivors of violence, the dyadic "survivor" versus "perpetrator" construct advocated in Wilson's approach actually works through affective and emotional practices that should not be disarticulated from what such emotions do in the world. To omit this analysis and emphasize only survivors as the subject of inequality misses the importance of understanding not only what hate speech does to produce such constructs but also how such speech acts operate within larger domains of power and inequality. By focusing on individualization and relegating to the margins an analysis of the construction of perpetrators of violence as being outside macro analysis, Wilson contributes to an anthropology of international justice through the production of a liberal and individuated moral universalism that disarticulates the conditions of its making.

Where a rapidly growing body of critical scholarship has begun to explore the particular ways in which emotion and affects work through regimes of expression and practice to construct particular social logics, most studies remain at the micro level of the individual, as does Wilson's concern with the "survivor" and the "perpetrator."[47] While this optic provides part of the story of violence propelled by hate speech in the contemporary period, it misses the ways in which the grammar of suffering disguises the structural conditions of its making. Focusing on hate speech without locating it within broader domains of emotional power makes it difficult to reckon with the complexities of justice in the contemporary period. This book demonstrates that it is critical to understand that those designated as both survivors and perpetrators of violence exist within larger structures of inequality, and therefore both are part of the exercise and problem of power. Contemporary forms of international legalisms are part of a larger tyranny of violence that does not stop with the individualization of criminal responsibility and trial performance. They exist within colonial inscriptions of plunder and extraction that structure the forms of violence within which they circulate. They are constitutive of the continuation of empire in the contemporary moment, and their expression through affective registers is a manifestation of how affects constitute the emotional body and shape the basis on which contemporary justice alliances are manifesting. Moving beyond the individualization of survivorship and toward an analysis that can detail actual assemblages of power and their embodied manifestations will allow us to analyze features that have been widely neglected in the development of the anthropology of justice literature.

Following Sara Ahmed's work on what emotions do in the world, *Affective Justice* explores what people do with those emotions through the study of a particular international criminal justice assemblage.[48] I bring sociocultural theorizing of justice into the contemporary moment by considering how affects shape sociopolitical consciousness and how they are practiced and rendered visible, and also how they are deployed to reframe constituencies in relation to emotional alignments. This rethinking of the deployment of emotions has critical implications for how we understand justice-making practices through visceral, heartfelt expressions, exclamations, and outbursts that conjoin people according to their emotional practices rather than according to their identities. With this point of departure, this book moves us toward an anthropology of international justice that takes seriously the role of affects by showing how they are embodied and how they manifest in emotional expressions. In an attempt to clarify the framework through which affective justice practices play out, I outline three component parts—legal technocratic practices, embodied affects, and emotional regimes—that shape international criminal rule of law assemblages.

The first component is the domain of legal technocratic practice, which is primarily concerned with the biopolitical management of life and death. Biopolitics is understood as exercising power over bodies, ranging from various techniques of subjugation to the control of people and constituencies.[49] It involves the management of the population as a political problem, and, by extension, it involves the legal basis on which bodies are managed through particular legal technical classification measures. Following Foucault, economic, political, psychological, and classificatory domains are key to the ways that the body and the population have been and continue to discipline citizens.[50] In international legal assemblages, biopolitics is involved in the implementation of legal processes to manage the body and to train its stewards and publics to participate in the formal or informal implementation of legality. Legal technocratic classification is connected to biopolitical practices that combine relationships between biology, politics, and technocratic practice—in this case, legal practices.[51] It is a form of disciplinary power that exists across different scales to classify populations juridically as well as to manage life and render some deaths acceptable. These legal technologies for managing life and death are structured in relation to various scientific-legal rationalities that are at the heart of international justice landscapes. In ICC assemblages, like other justice domains, the management of violence is also a biopolitical problem in which state leaders participate in the codification of laws in order to legally manage life and punish those who offend those laws. In the road leading to the Rome Statute for the ICC, this process involved complex technocratic practices over many years—from the drafting of the treaty, to its negotiations, to its ratification and legal promotion. This biopolitical process has produced the social fields in which regimes of international legal knowledge, like other justice domains, have taken shape and circulated through particular narratives.

If we see this biopolitical process of making international criminal law as the production of a rationalizing regime in which determinants for victims and perpetrators are popularized, then it is also important to see this process as central to shaping the basis upon which international legal morality is being normalized and—by extension—how a biopolitics of feeling about those victimized by violence is established through narrative.[52]

Central to such technocratic practices are the ways in which some justice practices (their ontologies and temporalities) displace other practices. This process of displacement is what I call *legal encapsulation*. Legal encapsulation is an adaptation of Susan Harding's notion of narrative encapsulation, which involves the production of dominant narratives that displace others.[53] It is a discursive technocratic practice that, in the negotiation of justice, turns attention from structural equality to the language of the law and the iconic survivor of mass atrocity violence. This biopolitical production of law works through technocratic institutions, such as courts, and morally driven protections of survivors or "victims," leading to the displacement of the political basis upon which injustice might be addressed and replacing it with the celebratory belief in an international judicial order to save lives. In understanding how legal order operates, it is important to note what it displaces and how those forms of displacement ignite affective responses to other conceptualizations of justice, such as redistributive justice or substantive equality.

Another nexus of such displacement, is the hegemonic production of legal temporality, which is a particular way of structuring culpability and, thus, legal possibility. Legal temporality, or what I call *legal time*, is an organizing mechanism through which the culpability of the body is inscribed temporally and spatially and made relevant within particular biopolitical orders.[54] While ICC actors use a strictly defined temporal period to assess which acts of violence are eligible for prosecution, others seek to place those instances of mass violence within the context of historically inscribed inequalities that have a much longer time line. Many people in Africa regard contemporary violence as a function of colonialism or postcolonial corruption that reflects a kind of collective complicity rather than the trespasses of charismatic leaders that the anti-impunity movement pursues. Accordingly, African critics of the ICC have begun to reattribute culpability from high-ranking leaders to certain groups they deem responsible for underlying factors. Thus, legal time intersects with *judicial space*, such as how the strict post-2002 temporal jurisdiction of the ICC correlates to the centering of The Hague as the neutral site where ICC-brokered justice is performed.

The second component, embodied affects, represents the sensorial sphere within the psychological body through which particular affects are manifest. Rooted in the philosophical ideas of seventeenth-century philosopher Baruch Spinoza and later expanded by French theorists Gilles Deleuze and Félix Guattari, the concept of affect continues to energize psychoanalysts, social scientists, and cultural theorists.[55] From notions of affect as part of the "pre-subjective interface of the body with the sensory world," my approach to affect speaks to the visceral domain in which, following Charles Hirschkind, "memory lodges itself in the body."[56] With the recognition that such affects also involve forces and intensities, I approach embodied affects as experienced through bodily impulses yet propelled by particular sustained social sensibilities. In these domains, powerful and productive sentiments such as anger, pain, and hope are experienced bodily in relation to international justice controversies—especially when people feel that justice is not delivered as promised.

This space of embodied affects is where itinerant and emergent justice potentials are found. It is here that identity is called into question and alternate ways of making sense of human alliances are given life. What we see is that bodily responses are not necessarily tied to specific social identities. Rather, they are a product of complex neurological and physiological processes that make it possible to see affects in far more itinerant ways.[57] The way that justice sensibilities are held and felt allow us to characterize people's alliances based on their interior commitments. Following Brian Massumi, states of intensity that are nonlinear and unpredictable are open to creative potentials and possibilities.[58] This is an approach to understanding potentialities through a notion that affects are presocial and exist before human intentions and subjective beliefs. Affects reflect neurological and bodily brain functions and, in that regard, they speak to complexities of the interior life of the individual.

The third component part, emotional regimes, is connected to the first and second component parts but involves the domain of the social in the manifestation of affects. It has to do with the emotional displays of embodied responses through particular discursive tropes. Following William Reddy, an emotional regime is a "set of normative emotions and the official rituals, practices, and emotions that express and inculcate them," and they are a "necessary underpinning of any stable political regime."[59] I extend this concept to think about how emotional regimes shape emotional climates and underpin popular, contemporary notions of justice and people's emotional engagement with them. Through certain kinds of representational practices, emotional responses circulate within sometimes related or competing networks of meaning production. These meaning domains are indexed by icons, words, utterances, color deployment, and hashtags often circulated through technologically driven campaigns. Through the encoding of bodily meanings and experiences, certain archetypal figures (e.g., "victims," "perpetrators," or "freedom fighters/heroes/heroines") serve to reinforce the discursive appropriateness of images or symbols. For example, the ICC's oft-repeated mantras "Justice now" and "No one should be above the law" as well as the AU's Silencing the Guns campaign function in similar ways to appeal to the production of universalist imaginaries that seek to translate feeling into action.[60] Appeals to sympathy or empathy mobilize the power to activate citizens, crafting the human rights citizen-consumer as an actor who has choices about what to prefer and how to engage.[61] Feelings operate through agencies that are embedded in particular historical inscriptions and are part of itinerant responses that are often collective but never fully predictable; they may or may not align with the emotional climate being produced by justice campaigns.

The public that resides in the emotional landscape produced by the ICC and its allies can be glossed as the international community, to include celebrities, ordinary publics, and Africans on the continent and in the diaspora. Through similar strategies, the public that resides in the landscape produced by the African Court and its allies can be glossed as the new Pan-African movement shaped by African leaders. In the contemporary period, these new publics are being constituted in person, at sites of judicial activity, as well as online, where humanitarian and legalistic concepts circulate and concretize through the emotional imaginary, producing particular feelings about justice that compel actors to participate in various ways. Their messages become effective because they represent contemporary institutionalized norms through which expressions of emotional conviction are consolidated and regulated. Spectacularized through legal rituals and grassroots mobilizations, various campaigns and their afterlives have shaped epistemological frameworks of justice and law as modes of power, social ordering, and knowledge production.[62] These formations have led to the rise of a new class of mobile experts on the rule of law (judges, civil society activists, prosecutors, and defense attorneys, etc.) who are engaged in the exchange of techniques and transnational practices. While this outcome is well understood, little attention is devoted to the aesthetic and affective production of rule of law feeling regimes, which render the calls to action by these experts viable and compelling. Furthermore, what the framing of emotional regimes offers us is an opportunity to consider the dynamic interplay between embodied feeling, sociality, and power. Here we see the conjuncture of emotional responses with perceived senses of injustice that may be materialized through various sensory impressions. This, in turn, may produce forms of refusal or ways of reassigning the effects of displacement. One of the central ways that these forms of reassignment occur as a result of perceived displacement from legal encapsulation is through what I call *reattributive practices*.

In analyzing how these competing discourses jockey for influence over the application of justice in African contexts, the existence of affective regimes and the tropes through which the materiality of emotions are manifest allow me to introduce the concept of reattribution. Reattribution is a process of reassigning guilt through rhetorical strategies that appeal to subjective and supposedly universal emotions but that shift the ontological domain on which competing conceptions lie. In law, attribution refers to the determination of whether a particular act can be attributed to another entity, such as a person, corporation, or government. It emerges from the concept of liability and relates to the determination of responsibility for wrongdoing. But my use of reattribution in this book extends it beyond an oversimplified tie to the legal parsing of wrongdoing. It relates to the affective dimension of justice making through the process of actively refusing, directing, and redirecting meanings of justice through sentimentalized discourses that, at times, shift how culpability is understood.

The distinct discourses described above—frameworks aligned with the ICC or with its critics of public intellectual pragmatists (described in the preface) —represent competing emotional domains that drive the way people comprehend and engage with notions of culpability and justice. These differences are mapped across particular spatial and/or temporal landscapes and shape the emotional fields and embodied responses that arise. Both temporality and spatiality shape the way that everyday relationships are experienced and felt, for they highlight the contours of affects that develop through the layered influences of history, culture, power, and individual agency.[63] Reattribution, then, contributes to the production of affective justice through its role in the entanglement of complex bodily, biopolitical, and socially regimented configurations.

These three interrelated domains—legal technocratic practices, psychosocial embodied affects, and emotional regimes—come together messily through the rule of law movement to constitute affective justice. As the enmeshment of these component parts, an alliance between the instrumentalization of the law and expressive embodiments of its regimes propels us to articulate what justice is and to clarify meanings of justice through their materialization. Together these components form an international criminal justice assemblage that does not gain its power by focusing on justice for survivors alone. They come together through the production and combination of the figures of "perpetrators," "victims/survivors," and the "international community," which produce compelling domains for the mobilization of affective justice. Defending survivors through legal arguments alone is not how international criminal law surpasses state sovereignty and gains its power. It gains its power through the fusion of its component parts with other contingencies that come together and constitute affective justice.

This book presents a theory of international justice in the twenty-first century that departs from the atomized victim/survivor/perpetrator models or state-centric theories of sovereignty. Instead, it clarifies that international criminal justice as a site of contemporary contestations can only be understood as an assemblage of component parts that are activated through complex interrelationships.

This approach to justice allows us to advance a theory of justice as embedded in embodied and emergent forces, foregrounding affects and their operationalization within particular sociohistorical regimes. At the center of the rule of law movement are not only histories of proclamations, treaties, laws, categories like "victims" and "perpetrators," and so forth; there is also the sensorium—feelings, smells, sounds, historical narratives—that informs the work of international justice. They inspire feelings of righting past wrongs, which is at the heart of the international justice project. But how agents arrive there and come to align themselves with those engaged in similar expressions is where affective justice, as a site for the fusion of various component parts, exists.

Assemblages of Justice Making in Practice

Following the AU's declaration of noncooperation with the ICC's call to arrest and surrender President al-Bashir of Sudan, a number of developments unfolded in summer 2012 when the former president of Malawi, who had committed to hosting the next AU biannual summit in Lilongwe, Malawi, died suddenly.[64] The newly appointed president, Joyce Banda, aware of the ICC's call for the arrest and surrender of President al-Bashir, was expected not only to host the summit but to issue the final invitations to all fifty-three AU member states and their presidents, including al-Bashir.[65] As a new president, Banda began her term by entering into partnerships with a range of international donors. But many of her US-based donors threatened to cancel their financial commitments if President al-Bashir was allowed to come to Malawi without arrest. To them, a visit by him would signify Malawi's unwillingness to fulfill its good-governance commitments. With Malawi's economic constraints in mind, President Banda announced to the AU leadership that if President al-Bashir were to attend the nineteenth AU summit in Malawi, her country would have no choice but to fulfill its ICC obligations to arrest and extradite him to The Hague. According to Banda, "Malawi is already going through unprecedented economic problems and it would not be prudent to take a risk by allowing one person to come and attend the summit against much resistance from our cooperating partners and donors."[66] Rather than stopping at disinviting al-Bashir and affirming an obligation to arrest him, President Banda disinvited the leaders and advisors of all fifty-three AU member states. Within the next four days, the summit was relocated to the headquarters of the AU in Addis Ababa, Ethiopia, and new invitations were issued to AU heads of state, including President al-Bashir.

Ethiopia set a precedent that has been replicated at subsequent AU summits. At the most recent summit in June 2015, South Africa declined to turn over al-Bashir to the ICC. Given South Africa's status as a BRICS country and its recent history of human rights promotion and constitutionalism, this development was curious to many onlookers, who had expected the state to embrace its international treaty obligations.[67] In summer 2016, the controversy around ICC expectations of African states peaked at an AU ministerial meeting, when delegates discussed the contradictions of the duty to prosecute and the status of requested ICC amendments. The ministers complained bitterly about what they saw as inequality in the ICC related to its referrals through the five permanent member states of the UNSC, which lacks African representation. Articulating positions in animated and colorful language, they took issue with the overall focus of the ICC on selecting African cases and insisted that this perceived bias has political consequences. To the chagrin of various African human rights civil society organizations working for predominantly Western-funded NGOs, the debates were invigorated by angry civil society demands for checks and balances against unchecked African governmental power; leaders met this criticism by publicly calling out the imperial continuities of international legal injustice. The result inspired the call for a coordinated strategy for African states to advance a collective withdrawal from the Rome Statute that established the ICC. What unfolded were emotionally driven expressions of dissatisfaction, leading three African states to declare their intentions to withdraw from the treaty.

Burundi was the first state to formally announce that it would withdraw from the ICC through a decree from its parliament. President Pierre Nkurunziza's government began proceedings following the April 2016 opening of an ICC preliminary investigation of violence in Burundi. The violence unfolded following a third-term presidential bid by President Nkurunziza. This led to imprisonment, torture, killings, rape and other forms of sexual violence, and disappearances. The UN Independent Investigation on Burundi released a report naming officials who, it claimed, orchestrated the violence against perceived political opponents, and citing evidence of rape, disappearances, mass arrests, torture, and murder.[68] The report estimated that large numbers of those victimized by violence were opposed to the proposed third-term mandate of President Nkurunziza. The government of Burundi dismissed the report as biased and politically motivated, denying its allegations. Later, Burundi announced its withdrawal from the ICC.[69]

South Africa was initially a visible champion of African state enthusiasm for the ICC. Following the Burundi decision, however, it declared its intentions to withdraw from the Rome Statute for the ICC in a public announcement stating that the Rome Statute's treaty obligations were inconsistent with customary international law, which offers diplomatic immunity to sitting heads of state. The declaratory statement sent to the UN secretary-general read, "Under these circumstances South Africa is of the view that to continue to be a State Party to the Rome Statute will compromise its efforts to promote peace and security on the African Continent."[70] The statement incorporated language that suggested an alternative logic for justice on the continent:

South Africa is committed to protection of human rights and the fight against impunity which commitment was forged in the struggle for liberation against the inhumanity of colonialism and apartheid. . . . South Africa, from its own experience has always expressed the view that to keep peace one must first make peace. Thus, South Africa is involved in international peacekeeping missions in Africa and is diplomatically involved in inter-related peace processes on a bilateral basis as well as part of AU mandates. In complex and multi-faceted peace negotiations and sensitive post-conflict situations, peace and justice must be viewed as complementary and not mutually exclusive.[71]

Following the release of this statement, NGOs submitted a complaint to the South African high court rendering the ICC withdrawal declaration unconstitutional. The high court concurred and ordered President Zuma to retract the notice of withdrawal.

The Gambia was the third country to communicate its intention to withdraw from the ICC. Its announcement was made by its minister of information and promoted by former president Yahya Jammeh. Justification for withdrawal centered on what was seen as the ICC's practices of selectively focusing on African human rights abuses. As noted, the minister announced that the ICC was being used for "the persecution of Africans and especially their leaders while ignoring crimes committed by the West," furthermore stating that "there are many Western countries, at least 30, that have committed heinous war crimes against independent sovereign states and their citizens since the creation of the ICC and not a single Western war criminal has been indicted."[72] However, in a country shrouded by two decades of repressive rule and a contested election, newly inaugurated president Adama Barrow pushed back against the AU's withdrawal strategy by canceling the notice of intention to withdraw from the ICC and reaffirming his support for the institution.

Various organs of the ICC, such as the presidency and the Office of the Prosecutor, are consistently responding to these controversies and challenges by shoring up and projecting the core logic of legal accountability as the sole appropriate and objective strategy for ending impunity. For the notion of sovereignty remains at the center of state processes; participation in the Rome Statute treaty system is voluntary, but when states are seen as signing and then ratifying a treaty to establish an international criminal court, what they are doing is taking responsibility for pursuing the crimes under the jurisdiction of the court as well as cooperating to adjudicate the crimes under the

Rome Statute.[73] Article 17 of the statute lays out the basis for the admissibility of a case under the ICC.[74] It clarifies that if member states that have ratified the Rome Statute are "unable and unwilling" to "genuinely" investigate a case under the jurisdiction of the court, the ICC can claim jurisdiction of that case, thereby leading to what many see as the suspension of a state's sovereign right to adjudicate the alleged violence.[75] This architecture provides the framework for the 123 states under the court's remit that have ratified the statute—one-third of them being African states.[76] But in order for this technocratic structure to work, the ICC operates through ideas, convictions, willing membership, and some forms of coercion that travel, take root, and circulate in various ways.

The ICC is not simply its building or its capacity to host criminal trials. It is not just about a single location or a single set of founders or judges. Its work is far reaching and multifarious; its beginning and end go well beyond the Rome Statute. Its legal actions precede the making of the Rome Statute, and it follows violence as well as being constituted by it. This global circulation of the rule of law actors and "actants" (Bruno Latour) is centrally propelled by moral convictions to save victims and stop perpetrators of violence. Its mission operates through moral embodiments in which political commitments against impunity are central to how the component parts of the assemblage function. Yet the morality, emotion, and embodied feelings about injustice are core components of the movement's power. The ICC routinely individualizes collective violence through the projection of the figure of the victim in relation to the perpetrator. For example, the Gambian lead prosecutor for the ICC, Fatou Bensouda, has publicly asserted that the Rome Statute is her bible. "It's not about politics but the law," Bensouda explained at a public forum in Albany, New York, in April 2012, as she was transitioning from deputy prosecutor to lead prosecutor of the court. "I will use the law to uphold justice," she asserted. In emphasizing that the court's mandate for justice centers on serving victims through legal accountability, she later argued, "We should not be guided by the words and propaganda of a few influential individuals whose sole aim is to evade justice but, rather, we should focus on, and listen to the millions of victims who continue to suffer from massive crimes. The return on our investment for what others may today consider to be a huge cost for justice is effective deterrence and saving millions of victims' lives."[77]

Prosecutor Bensouda's performative plea for ICC justice was delivered in the name of the "victim." Deploying what I call a *sentimental legalism*, her narrative construction follows a liberalist legal discourse that works through legal encapsulation. It equates justice with the law and invokes a mission of protecting "victims" against powerful perpetrators who have enjoyed impunity for too long.[78] This discourse of "saving victims" by making high-ranking perpetrators individually responsible through judicial trials in effect links the notion of protection—and by extension prevention—to a very particular application of legal justice. It serves as a sympathizing strategy that neatly collapses the protection of victims with the rejection of impunity for perpetrators, and that reifies the legal tool of holding perpetrators accountable as the sole appropriate mechanism for justice.

This narrative is similar to Judge Song Sang-Hyou's plea for the ICC at the Nuremberg Forum conference on the twentieth anniversary of the Rome Statue. In response to US President Donald Trump's and then John Bolton's 2018 anti-ICC United States protectionist speeches, he insisted that "the ICC is a judicial instrument that operates in a political world. . . . We need to keep the ICC objective. . . . We need to defend the rule of law from the interference of politics."[79] These narratives regale a celebratory story of the rule of law operating through objectivity, predictability, and empowerment to end impunity and, ultimately, to curb political violence. As obvious and appealing as this may seem in the abstract, attempts to map this logic onto particular African contexts through legal actions have generated profound disagreement, dis-ease, and discord.

The manifestations of ICC justice also presume a color-blind racial indifference as a fundamental operating principle that renders senses of race and racism unsayable in the international law landscape. This means that for the ICC, the racial politics of African indictments are decentered from the public discourse. Yet the visual practices of seeing race—however unconscious or conscious—are still part of the affective landscapes in that discursive and representational politics of the "victim," and the "perpetrator" have the impact of precluding certain kinds of claims. For if the "victim" looks like a Holocaust survivor, then "victims" of colonial violence cannot be recognized as they are; if the "perpetrator" looks like a black African man implicated in mass rape or torture, then particular North American or European heads of state may not look like perpetrators from their desks. These forms of representations serve to demand certain actions and priorities as well as wield military and enforcement power in response to these representations. Such paradoxical presences and absences of racial difference highlight both the imaginary fiction of race and the lived experiences of structural violence that can surface in the "hidden zones of the unconscious."[80] This dialectics of race is described by Achille Mbembe as an "operation of the imagination" in which he argues that it is in those zones of the unconscious that race is both a site of "reality and truth . . . of appearances" and a site of rupture and effusion.[81] Its appearances are constituted by the "very act of assigning race, and produced and institutionalized through the normalization of human racial typologies in which blackness has been stigmatized."[82]

These consequences of race are a function of modernity in which transatlantic slavery led to the violation of particular black bodies, and later colonialism solidified the ways that those bodies would become governed, resulting in the subsequent structures that produced and continue to produce the very forms of racial inequalities in the first place. Thus the accusations of ICC racism by African leaders are not simply a fictional and strategic invocation of an imaginary category; they are a resurrection of the fictive construction of racial difference that is still felt to be shaping contemporary life in bodily and visceral ways. In the realm of ICC indictments of black bodies, what is the relevance of the racialized body in relation to how international justice works through figures of "victims" and "perpetrators"? And what does studying certain reattributive affects through passionate utterances—such as anger—tell us about structural inequalities as well as particular responses to them? To understand these processes, we have to turn to how the emotional expressions of feelings link sociality and justice in our globalizing world.

Multiple traumas over generations elicit a broad and deep range of emotional responses that show how international law has been complicit in the making of African injustice. Just as the agents engaged in the emergent rule of law movement seek to reattribute impunity with persistent justice, so too are Pan-African justice advocates engaged in the reattribution of its products. Through emotionally infused public refusals of ICC justice, we see attempts to produce and express sentiments that neutralize criminal responsibility and reroute it to other domains of culpability. For some, this is because African leaders are often critiqued for their hypocrisy by proponents of international justice, whereas leaders of economically powerful states are not. The dialectical relationship between the figure of the African perpetrator indicted by the ICC and the seeming hypocrisy of the West makes such emotionally propelled narratives both insidious and compelling. But some African populations also engage in the reassignment of justice against ICC norms while simultaneously struggling with their emotional anger against African leadership for unleashing tyranny and violence against their populations, which includes their complicity in enabling the economic extraction and plunder of African resources. These various and competing responses are rhizomatic and unstable, and they should not be dismissed or rendered invisible in scholarly inquiry.

Consistent patterns of controversy and conflict within justice narratives force us to reexamine the making of international justice frameworks. We need to understand what these justice projects do, how they do it, and in what way the desires and fantasies of their narratives emerge. When peoples' aspirations produce counternarratives, vocabularies, and legal institutions, including new geographies within which to recalibrate justice practices, we must understand how particular affects make them possible and how they circulate to constitute new alliances that are regulated according to technocratic and social practice regimes.

Emotional Constructions and Deconstructions of Justice in African Contexts: Affective Justice and Affective Reattribution in Practice

When the ICC was launched, advocates aspired to use international law as a beacon of emancipation and a solution to a perceived absence of justice across the African continent. The thirty-two African states that worked through their constituencies to ratify the Rome Statute in 1998 initially embraced the rule of law movement as an extension of their commitment to Africa's development. They did so publicly, with ceremonial acceptance and celebratory claims to membership. The memory of the violence that unfolded in African regions in the 1980s and 1990s invigorated a moral conscience to act. In order to embrace the ICC, African stakeholders also had to face and seek to transcend residual feelings of indignity and anger stemming from the inaction of international publics during the Rwandan genocide, the injustice of South African apartheid, and the multiple impacts of European imperialism across the continent. In order to accomplish this emotional transition, many actors within African countries took moral leadership from luminaries such as Bishop Tutu, whose emphasis on truth and reconciliation in the South African context had privileged the setting aside of public manifestations of anger in response to injustice in order to verbalize past wrongs and forge a pathway toward forgiveness. Forgiveness represented the emotional blooming of truth, which emphasized the institutional, not only personal, dimensions of apartheid's violence. The truth and reconciliation strategy involved highly public and often exaggerated displays of emotion, including particular ways of articulating truth and of performing forgiveness in order to produce a new South Africa predicated on collective justice.

In Rwanda, the shocking images and stories of the mass slaughter of over half a million Tutsis—black African bodies—and the inaction of international actors contributed to the eventual establishment of both the role of traditional justice known as *gachacha* (sitting under the tree) and the institutionaliza- tion of the International Criminal Tribunal for Rwanda to adjudicate those deemed most responsible for violence. Gachacha involved its own cultural and performative articulations of justice, in which people were expected to articulate suffering, admit to their crimes, and perform reconciliation. In both examples, we see that emotional displays of forgiveness and reconcilia- tion are not arbitrary. Nor are they necessarily insincere or always predictable in relation to people's national standing. They exist in a domain of personal feelings and practices that operate within and serve to reify particular institu- tions through which justice is negotiated. As I illustrate in chapter 1, emotion- ally regimented conceptions of the "victim" and the "perpetrator," as located within particular racialized bodies, are part of this reification; they are part of the moral imaginaries in contemporary rule of law landscapes.

A close analysis of the work that they do reveals how international and other justice forms operate through emotional constructs and carefully crafted campaigns. For as I introduced above and elaborate in this book, le- gal encapsulation involves legalistic processes that make legible the subjects of the law, and this is where technocratic international processes connect with micro-individual bodily affects and feeling expressions. In the case of interna- tional justice, it is the "victim" and "perpetrator" as fictive constructs who are encapsulated within contemporary international legal frames.[83] In African judicial spaces, a popular counterfigure—the Pan-African freedom fighter, male and black, and the victim of colonial injustices—is propelling the emo- tional domains through which new justice formations are taking shape. What is interesting is how these modes of seeing, engaging, and feeling are work- ing through a biopolitical apparatus involving the pursuit of economic crimes that are taking shape through responses to perceived injustice.

The Freedom Fighter within Pan-African Emotional Regimes

The key to understanding international justice in the contemporary period is to recognize how legal encapsulation produces displacements and how those displacements are leading to the erection of new institutions (in this book de- scribed as the Pan-Africanist pushback). This jockeying to redefine justice en- ables a dialectics of subjugation and emancipatory possibilities. For example, various stakeholders might insist that African independence is a misnomer because independence marked the beginning of neocolonial governance in which African markets adapted to world-market incentives, and that this process not only fueled economic dependencies but also enabled corruptions of justice central to the crisis of the African neocolonial state.[84] Falling prey to structural-adjustment development policies, African leaders dismantled social institutions and privatized the independence-era welfare state. In response to the challenges of postcolonial economic development a sentimentalized Pan-Africanist discourse is now being employed to reorient the terms of justice, from Western judicial mechanisms to politico-economic sites, to achieve a reorientation of structural justice. This push for new justice arrangements has reconfigured the basis on which international justice for survivors of violence has been articulated.[85] For example, during Kenya's anticolonial independence struggle of the 1950s, Jomo Kenyatta—the father of Uhuru Kenyatta, Kenya's president from 2012 to 2016—was indicted and charged for murder but also imprisoned for his efforts to free Kenya from British colonial rule. Although he was convicted as a perpetrator of criminal violence, his track record as a revolutionary inspired reverence from large numbers of Kenyans who viewed him as primarily a freedom fighter for Kenya's independence.

This reorientation of justice focuses on the way histories of plunder and unequal political economic formations in African countries are encapsulating alternate iconic affects—not just the anticolonial freedom fighter but figures like the displaced villager as well. These are now being packaged and disseminated through countercampaigning strategies and affective performances which insist that legal solutions must be firmly linked to a broader dismantling of neocolonial structures of oppression that Africans encounter at every level, from the rural villager to the cosmopolitan head of state.[86] Thus, through the power of reattribution, an emergent *African geography of justice* is developing as a counterpoint to what is seen as hegemonic structures of Western approaches to international justice.

Reattribution through the Reorienting of the Terms of Justice

Various members of the African Union have pushed back against anti-impunity assertions of justice and have insisted instead on the relevance of histories of injustice. While the memory of the Jewish Holocaust and the Nuremberg trials haunts the historical imagination of various anti-impunity ICC supporters, it is not necessarily seen as central to the historical imaginary among those engaged in Pan-Africanist mobilizations. Instead, some of those angered by mass atrocity violence in African countries look to African colonial and neocolonial tragedies, including long years of apartheid violence in South Africa and the genocide in Rwanda, for a countering set of affects. In his opening statement at the Thirteenth Ordinary Session of the Conference of the Committee of Intelligence in 2016, President Kagame aserted, "Accountability for crimes is a principle that the African Union endorses, without ambiguity. But politicizing justice, and deploying it more or less exclusively against one continent, or pursuing it selectively for whatever reason, is not the answer. . . . It is a form of 'lawfare' where international law is abused to keep Africa in a subordinate position in the global order."[87] This notion of the ICC as lawfare—the use of law to engage in social, political, or military battles—implies the deployment of law and its institutions to defeat African authorities through displacing perceived sources of violence. Similar responses of anger against lawfare have included direct accusations of racist and imperial motivations.[88] For example, at the end of an AU session in 2013, the Ethiopian prime minister and chairman of the AU, Hailemariam Desalegn, argued that the "process [that the] ICC is conducting in Africa has a flaw; the intention was to avoid any kind of impunity, ill governance, and crime. But now the process has degenerated into some kind of 'race hunting.'"[89]

For many, then, the ICC has come to embody evidence that colonialism still exists, now in a new form. And yet critiques of the ICC can, in turn, serve to simplify the character of the critics, papering over their own public contradictions. For despite President Kagame's international reputation as a leader preaching reconciliation, a man who as a child escaped death during the killing of ethnic Tutsis and who is now seen as having led Rwandans to rise above age-old divisions and the horror of genocide, he is also popularly seen as having exploited Rwanda's tragic history to produce a Tutsi-dominated authoritarian regime with a track record of suppressing opposition and covering up its own violence. As a strategy for managing this internal contradiction, he and others have sought to attribute Rwanda's violence to alternate sources, including colonial inequalities that led to the invention of ethnic and racial differences.

One form of reattribution has involved blaming European colonialism and invoking sentimentalized narratives in support of the villager displaced by colonial settlers or the anticolonial freedom fighter. Here, the sentimentalized narrative strategies foreground structural injustice as a corruption of the justice principle, thus resulting in sentimentalized expressions that its constituencies were known to interpret as anger. It is with the presumption that justice must be extracted from structural injustice that some African actors display particular sentiments in arguing for political solutions. For example, echoing other angry performances, President Museveni of Uganda expressed his dismay with the ICC's indictment of Kenya's president-elect, Uhuru Kenyatta, and the international pressure to influence Kenya's elections against him. As Museveni said during Kenyatta's inauguration in 2013:

> I want to salute the Kenyan voters on one other issue: the rejection of the blackmail by the International Criminal Court and those who seek to abuse this institution for their own agenda. . . . I was one of those that supported the ICC because I abhor impunity. However, the usual opinionated and arrogant actors using their careless and shallow analysis have now distorted the purpose of that institution. . . . In Uganda's case between 1966 and 1986 we lost about 800,000 people. How did we handle that sad history? Have you ever heard us asking the ICC or the United Nations to come and help us deal with that sad chapter of our history?[90]

These sentiments, communicated to African constituencies and delivered with tones of anger and irony, reflect the perception that the rule of law movement has little space for considering the longer histories of inequality that fabricated underlying structures of violence on the African continent. They also encapsulate the resonant feeling of resentment that France and England (former colonial hegemons) as well as the United States (a contemporary empire) continue to maintain a patronizing relationship with their former African colonies, a relationship that is expressed, among other ways, through deep ties to military training, the use of force, and threats of regime change through international legality. This has manifested not only in military interventions and NGO funding to propel anti-impunity work, but also in judicial control through international courts. The predominance of African cases before the ICC is causing many African heads of state and lawmakers to feel that the colonial management of Africa has returned in the form of international institutions such as the ICC. Articulations of critique and dissent, even by African warlords, can gain strength and legitimacy because of a perception of underlying hypocrisy.

International law insists on an original presumption that justice should be universally protected and pursued for all, and not just for Africans. But the perception of a double standard in practice has led to the angry assertion by many Pan-Africanists that Western liberal, sentimental legalism—embodied by the anti-impunity movement—only serves to erase politics and fill vacant spaces with icons that inspire empty social actions (such as hashtag activism and "clicktivism") without any material gains for African citizens.

The perceived erasure of politics through legal encapsulation is seen as not only rendering invisible deep histories of past injustices but ignoring the political potential of judicial action to create the conditions for future peace and lived justice. Popular global governance mechanisms such as the ICC are seen increasingly as tools for maintaining Western power. Some who are protesting the encapsulation of justice and its effects in African postcolonial states are working to redefine it by retelling history and reattributing culpability. Yet within this dialectic, many contradictions and complexities persist. For example, critics within and outside Africa and its diasporas recognize that it is contradictory for both Prime Minister Hailemariam Desalegn and President Museveni to speak against the ICC while they have been accused of crushing antiopposition movements, leading to the deaths of thousands of their citizens in Ethiopia and Uganda, respectively.[91]

Such postcolonial state concerns, in which the leadership elite are blamed for African violence, are facing serious challenges. On the one hand, in dealing with the internal practices of the state and its economy, they are embedded in limited forms of sovereignty that are constrained by contemporary globalization. On the other hand, not only does the postcolonial state not control key decisions that impact its economy, but state agents have not been able to address its failed social institutions that leave the indigent underserved and offer corruption and illicit violence as viable alternatives to structural injustice. Various African publics approach these challenges and complexities in ways that demonstrate both their ambivalence toward their leaders and the recognition of deep structural inequality that gives rise to state failure. A new generation of African professionals and progressive activists recognizes that the imposition of colonial structures of rule had a crucial determinative effect on the postcolonial conundrum.[92] They point to the myriad ways that, throughout postcolonial Africa, structural inequalities produced and still produce the conditions in which extreme forms of material violence take shape. Within this broader critique, there is a range of positions regarding where to attribute culpability in relation to the unraveling of formal colonialism, the reckoning with African complicity in mass atrocity violence, and the perpetual emergence of neocolonial structures.

Beyond the focus on who should be held accountable for mass violence, the implementation of the Rome Statute and the subsequent events related to the ICC's Africa indictments have also heightened additional debates and emotionally fueled arguments about the ICC's ability to provide justice to survivors, as they themselves define it, and to resolve political violence in Africa through judicial solutions. Many have come to resist anti-impunity arguments that the ICC's forms of legal justice are the best way to pursue justice, rejecting it as a mode of justice activism, citing other structural inequalities as the basis for African violence.

However, by rethinking Wilson's assumptions about the basis upon which survivors are relevant to the international justice project, the reality is that various justice imaginaries—such as the "perpetrator" and the "freedom fighter"—operate through emotionally infused icons that draw on deep-seated histories and psychosocial feelings that compel social action. The freedom fighter becomes an icon of justice, a redemptive body who preserves the traces of past actions and brings them into the present as potentials.[93] As Brian Massumi writes, "The body doesn't just absorb pulses or discrete stimulations; it infolds contexts."[94] Through the vehicle of the iconic body, constructed through sentimentalized affect, we experience the embeddedness of history in future sociopolitical effects. This imbrication of the past and the present through affect shapes what Bill Mazzarella refers to as the "pragmatics of institutional practice."[95] Affects articulated through institutional practice emerge as emotional appeals used to address larger sociopolitical concerns, such as racial targeting—feelings that the ICC is an extension of a colonial disciplinary apparatus. Some emotional forms invoke deeply known histories and reattribute what many see as illegitimate hegemonies of the past to reframe new justice narratives about contemporary events and actors. Similar to the noteworthy interventions like that of Jacques Vergés's "rupture defence"—an attempt to challenge the court's legitimacy by calling into question the basis upon which particular social truths and histories are narrativized—through disjunctural narratives in the legal defenses of Slobodan Milosevic at the International Criminal Tribunal for the former Yugoslavia or Khieu Samphan at the Cambodian trials, we see how narrative ruptures inhere through the telling of different renditions of histories of violence.[96] Similarly, various people who are suspicious of the legal power of ICC-based justice have invoked European colonialism as a continuity of ICC justice. As anti-ICC sentiments are articulated, particular component parts of affective justice are deployed to shape it. And it is here in the spaces of refusal that new legal-justice formations are being assembled in particular ways.

What we are seeing is the formation of new domains of justice making that are not manifestations of an evolutionary progression of judicial justice cascading toward a new, enlightened form.[97] Rather, in response to the feelings of injustice in an unequal world, those pushing back against the justice-as-anti-impunity discourses are reconceptualizing justice and attempting to differentiate African approaches to international law by embedding them in renewed spaces for reasserting the terms by which justice is reembodied.

Institutionalizing New Spaces of Justice: The African Court, Transitional Justice, and Its Pan-Africanist Affective Regimes

In the pages that follow, I demonstrate how various postcolonial affects, embedded in psychosocial responses to various forms of violence, function within particular Pan-Africanist emotional assemblages that—despite the construction of racial imaginaries—constitute the feeling expressions of various constituencies, not always predictable racially or ethnically constituted groups. The dynamics of race making is also about sense-making imaginaries that are not objective or empty.[98] These are lived experiences that foment emotional alignments with others who feel similarly. Embodiments of emotion confer belonging not to social categories that map neatly onto traditional group identity markers as the anthropological field once knew them—Ashanti, Tutsi, Dinka, Kikuyu, male, or female, for example. Instead, by studying the ways that people communicate their senses of obligation through symbolic, verbal, bodily, and technocratic expressions, a focus on emotional responses that align with regional or global assemblages can show how particular alliances are possible and others rendered unfeasible.[99] One of the ways this is done is through feelings about culpability.

Concerted efforts to expand culpability to actions deemed criminal yet not legible within the Rome Statute's legal architecture mobilize persons according to particular feeling climates or personal commitments. The ICC is also not the only tool for addressing mass atrocity violence, nor does it dominate the management of violence. In the case of the assertion of a new dominion, a set of African spaces that buffer the spread of treaty-driven prosecutorial institutions such as the ICC, other domains are defined by the rallying call, "African solutions for African problems." Through such calls to action, justice is reoriented spatially and temporally within deeply sentimental histories of African subjugation. These forms of reattribution highlight the way that emotional regimes function and create a biopolitics of feeling that shapes the emotional climate within which justice is articulated.

The attempt to establish an African court with criminal jurisdiction to adjudicate cases currently pursued by the ICC is a striking example of how reattribution can generate structural transformation, as well as an illustration of how emotions are deployed through historic symbols to regulate sentiments and constitute community. The African Court is the product of spatial and temporal reconceptualizations of international criminal justice as it functions within African landscapes. It is the outcome of an effort to conjure an African geography of justice through sentimentalized invocations of Africa's place in an increasingly interconnected world. But as we shall see, not only is the idea of international justice being reconceptualized in relation to how solutions to violence ought to be addressed, but, in an attempt to move beyond what is seen as the ICC's politically driven core crimes, stakeholders of the African Court project have introduced additional crimes—economic crimes—that they consider to be symptomatic of the "true root causes of African violence."[100] These include piracy, mercenaries, terrorism, corruption, illicit exploitation of natural resources, money laundering, the unconstitutional change of government, and the trafficking of drugs, persons, and hazardous waste. The focus on prosecuting these crimes reflects an effort to articulate a new understanding of what constitutes justice in an African context. It attempts a shift away from the ICC's framework that centers exclusively on individual criminal accountability toward a more expansive notion of culpability that includes corporate criminal liability. Within the logic of the African Court, corporate leaders could be held accountable for their role in seeding the underlying conditions that generate mass violence. The African Court is a concrete example of how a new Pan-Africanism operating at a regional scale is emerging at the site of justice making in order to make new claims on African governance in opposition to perceived neocolonial justice campaigns.

Pan-Africanism has been defined as a "movement of ideas and emotions," reflecting an "underlying unity of emotions and ideas in the black world."[101] At the roots of the movement are deep feelings of dispossession, oppression, persecution, and rejection that appear congruent with contemporary material conditions on the continent. The impetus for Pan-African mobilization emerges from an emotional response to what Colin Legum refers to as a feeling of "loss [that] came [from] enslavement, persecution, inferiority, discrimination and dependency. It involved a loss of independence, freedom and dignity."[102] Pan-Africanist philosophies originated in the late 1800s, and the first Pan-African Congress was held in London in 1900, spearheaded by a range of black intellectuals and African elite students in the diaspora. Pan-Africanism as a coherent political movement was formally launched in 1958 at the First Conference of Independent African States held in Accra,

Ghana, where Patrice Lumumba was a key speaker. The 1958 version of Pan-Africanism held as its prime objective the solidarity of black people around the world and the assertion of "Africa for Africans," which involved the pursuit of independence and the rejection of colonialism in all its forms. Other features involved the aspiration for a United Nations of Africa—a continent unified through regional federations—as well as the reemergence of an African renaissance to recover and recast African societies and cultural traditions into neo-indigenous forms.

One approach to the African renaissance involved drawing on the best of Africa's cultural forms and combining them with contemporary ideas that were deemed desirable. Other viewpoints in the movement included an impulse to construct and project African nationalism as an alternative to tribal and territorial affiliations; the rejection of communism and the reinvigoration of African economies as engines to replace colonial economic markets; the insistence on African societies rather than colonial metropoles as the necessary beneficiaries of development; an adoption of contemporary democratic principles; a rejection of violence as a viable method of struggle; and the adoption of a notion of positive neutrality, which involved the development of what was referred to as a nonalignment movement of African states with global powers, in particular China, the United States, and the former Soviet Union.[103] Thus, it is critical to understand the multifaceted history of Pan-Africanism in order to make sense of its contemporary revivals (such as "African solutions to African problems"). Yet Pan-Africanism, it is important to note, did not critique the myth of racial homogeneity. It contested its inscriptions of inferiority. The paradox of Pan-Africanist narratives is that they produce both a language for the rearticulation of black pride and also reinstate the myth of African unity. The production of Pan-Africanism, then, entails a fiction of racialized and experiential unity and because of this, the terms that define Africanness exist within domains of historical subjugation that shape the ways that postcolonial anti-imperial sentiments emerge and how their related collectivities come into being.

The historically rooted variations in such emotively articulated sentimentalisms foreground the multiple ways African critics of Western liberalism understand culpability. Some African political actors emphasize the injustices of inequality while others call out the indignities of racism. Many foreground a sense of pride in African control of Africa's own future and lift up the African Court as an example of self-determination over matters of criminality and justice. While these points of view are distinct and particular in relation to each other and to the history of Pan-Africanism, they work in concert as they attempt to rectify the legacy of Africa's structural inequalities and shape the contours of new African judicial spaces.

The Work of Affective Justice in the Making of International Justice

As noted, in contemporary international justice circuits, popularly articulated within anti-impunity social movement circles, the "victim to be saved" and the "perpetrator to be stopped" have come to constitute the moral basis upon which action for justice can occur. When the humanitarian and international justice movement uses aesthetic imagery of bodies to be saved in order to assert strategies of rescue, we see a professional human rights class seeking to crystallize and activate an international citizenry around the idea of ending impunity as the preeminent deterrence for violence and suffering. This narrative moves us beyond the direct experience of suffering and into a disembodied, mediated experience where contemporary justice needs an exemplary judicialized "victim" (also see Sara Kendall and Sarah Nouwen, 2013).

Law garners its authority through emotional affects that produce various forms of encapsulation, and through this process power is made real through various emotive appeals. These expressive practices reflect utterances that allow relevant components of justice assemblages to exercise their related capacities yet retain their component properties. In maintaining their properties, new discursive domains are produced and used to further concretize preexisting forms of segmentation. Those victimized by violence who have particular personal stories, captured in sound bites and captions, represent a hyper-embodiment of suffering that can be acted through a biopolitics of protectionism through which the international community engages. The emotive figures for invoking suffering are increasingly racially embodied as black or brown, or Muslim and male, and the responses to such racialized justice sensoria have come to look and feel a particular way. But this is not because of something endemic to race or ethnicity or gender. Rather, because of the way that the symbolics of race operates within particular assemblages of cultural meaning making, power, and possibility, the fiction of difference is reproduced according to particular modes of seeing, feeling, engaging, and speaking. And, as such, in various international justice assemblages involving African constituencies, the manifestation of justice may look different because of the structuring fields, such as various legacies from colonial institutions or the structure of legal temporalities that shape how justice feels in particular spaces. But, again, key here are the ways that human suffering is decoupled from particular spaces and reproduced through moral obligations that shape justice practices in the contemporary period. By exploring how historically formed social locations, personal commitments, experiences, and affective practices that shape people's relationships to institutions like the ICC and the African Union are, as I have argued, regimented through particular structuring devices, such as figures of "victims," "perpetrators," and "freedom fighters," we can tease out the institutional, historical, and moral orders that popularize various international justice emotional regimes.

As a conceptual framework for clarifying international justice assemblages, affective justice resonates at the level of both the individual (subjective) and the collective (social) consciousness. It is both the performative dimension of sociolegal claims to justice—what Marianne Constable, quoting Stanley Cavell, has termed "passionate utterances"—as well as the embodied responses operating through particular regimes of feeling that shape what Justin Richland calls law as both ideation and materiality.[104] These forms of segmentation are manifest in a range of ways, including constructions of racial difference through which particular bodily inscriptions are made meaningful. For the contemporary period represents, as Achille Mbembe argues, the manifestation of black bodies fluctuating between human and object as the defining feature of the modernity of black life.[105] If this has relevance for how we understand suffering bodies and invocations of justice for those bodies, then the larger questions are: What imaginaries have emerged at this junction in the production of international justice? What does it tell us about the modes of seeing, engaging, feeling, and speaking about both perpetrators and those victimized by violence? How do these modes manifest in the embodied affects that emerge in the field of international criminal justice? And what do those affects and their emotional responses tell us about structural inequalities as well as particular responses to them? To understand these processes, we have to turn to how the emotional expressions of feelings link sociality and justice in our globalizing world.

Affective Justice explores such restructuring processes ethnographically, revealing how they are expressed through sentiments, spread institutionally, and work to enforce the contours of emotional expression in particular ways. In legal studies and studies of humanitarian formations, interrogating affect can be a generative way to make sense of what feeling can tell us about the outcomes of various legal rituals—such as trials, testimonies, or political settlements. In the context of violence and its remedies, studying the deployment of emotional affects can help us to understand which emotions are likely to mobilize support and with what discursive strategies.

By bringing together complex transnational processes with the study of private, interior microprocesses such as individual emotions and the regulation of public sentiments, *Affective Justice* invites us to reconceive international justice through assemblages of psychosocial and political meanings that are shaping new and old publics. Taking the products of the international social imaginary as key modalities for understanding the enmeshment of individual sentimental responses and larger entanglements with history and power, this book explores how the breakdown of particular social rules leaves open a space for contesting the terms on which feeling rules are negotiated and justice expressions are regulated in daily life.[106] These attempts to rectify injustice make explicit the way that feelings of justice are expressed in daily encounters with international legality and, as such, how their reattributive rectification highlights the way that new remedies are put into tension.

What are the effects when international justice regimes invoke the figure of the perpetrator as black, African, male, and/or Muslim, and the figure of the victim as female, black or brown, and with child? There is a pressing need to contemplate the role that affects play in justice projects and what imaginaries sustain these formations. And this is where the challenge of global ethnography emerges: the complexities of transnational alliances require that we remain analytically vigilant in our assessment of the categories and scales within which we map these connections and through which we determine the purpose. Through a chapter-by-chapter examination of the making, manifestation, transfer, and institutionalization of feelings about justice, this book explores the interpretive authority of legal stakeholders and publics as influencers of the contours of various body politics. While new rule-of-law institutions are emerging as manifestations of new justice/governance projects, the responses of stakeholders to these institutions are also providing alternatives for reconceptualizing justice and governance that are linked transnationally yet play out in locally complex ways. The practices involved are infinite and span from treaty drafting, ratification, and judicial application to trial attendance, nomenclature adoption, and joking practices, to refusals that involve rejections, withdrawals, and noncooperation declarations, as well as the development of countercampaigns. What connects these practices are the embodied feelings and emotional expressions that drive such acts. It is these practices that are at the heart of this book and that clarify the central role of affective justice in the making of international criminal law.

Affective Justice is organized into six chapters that explore various aspects and illustrations of the three dynamic components we have articulated: technocratic practices, psychosocial embodied affects, and emotional regimes. Chapter 1 opens our inquiry into affective justice by exploring the technocratic workings of legal encapsulation and its genealogies. It analyzes how a particular narrative of justice as law has influenced the definition and protection of victims, as well as the judicialization of politics in the late twentieth to early twenty-first centuries. As the justice discourse progressed, "the victim" was invoked not only as the subject to be saved by new judicial mechanisms, but also as the basis for protection through moral responsibility. By explaining the rise of anti-impunity narratives and rethinking the unproblematized notions of the "victim" and the "perpetrator," this chapter maps a particular set of formations through which to make sense of the rise of legal encapsulation as a component part of contemporary rule of law assemblages. It explores the conditions under which humanitarian discourses have gained traction using forms of sentimental attachment to produce the establishment of international justice. Through that mapping it details the ways in which particular campaigns have been deployed to substantiate such imaginaries.

Chapter 2 turns from the technical mechanisms of legal order to the intersubjective. It explores the role of passionate utterances and sentimentalized origin stories, on the part of both ICC advocates and critics, to consolidate contemporary alliances for and within institutions. By illuminating the workings of affective regimes and their institutional expressions, the chapter explores a key result of reattribution, that of affective transference, which produces particular forms of sentimental attachments in situations that could be argued to have otherwise unrelated causality. The connection between one distinctive national or military trial and a criminal tribunal, or the attempt to connect colonial indictments to the ICC's charges for Kenya's postelection violence, provide examples of the sentimental language and strategies by which these social imaginaries of justice are alternately internationalized and regionalized for institutional purposes. In this chapter, we see examples of how protest speech and celebratory rhetoric have harnessed particular sentimental histories and icons to consolidate communities and institutionalize feeling expressions. We also see how audiences respond to these rhetorical strategies. This moves us closer to understanding the affective politics of social protest through the strategy of reattribution and its unifying and galvanizing potential.

Chapter 3 explores another key affective formation in the international justice assemblage: the ways in which online justice campaigns are deployed to produce a highly diversified international community with newly mediated victims. The Kony 2012 campaign that anti-impunity activists used to bring the leader of the Lord's Resistance Army in Uganda to justice is illustrative. These kinds of campaigns are increasingly propelled by biotechnology and sentimental discourses designed to mobilize publics through new moral regimes of saving people and preventing suffering. The deployment of the #BringBack OurGirls campaign a few years later also reflects these strategies. In this case, the global #BringBackOurGirls campaign was mobilized by concerned citizens, celebrities, activists, and governments worldwide to try and save hundreds of girls abducted in Chibok, Nigeria, and to pursue the prosecution of Boko Haram as perpetrators of that violence. This campaign is a particularly striking example of how political action can be spectacularly driven by emotional reactions and aspirations. Such justice campaigns drive and shape responses to international legality but are not always the most useful or effective ways of understanding real individuals and their social worlds.[107] These campaigns often reveal more about the Western professional class than they do about African victims; they are emotional lenses through which we see only certain positions, and they reflect the traditions of practice through which particular attachments and commitments are emotionally embodied.

This chapter also examines how the temporal immediacy of "the now" structures the demands and expectations about equality, such as how the imagery of girls denied an education by radical Islamic militants became the object of global empathy. However compelling, this popular temporality of justice with its aesthetics of care, compassion, and narrowing sense of time to the urgent now has not added up to its promise of delivering justice. Some of its subjects are pushing back, resisting the hegemonic narrowness of legal time and urging a historical understanding of the root causes for Boko Haram's terror.

In Chapter 4, I extend the previous discussions to consider the workings of reattribution in response to technocratic legal considerations having to do with legal time as an ordering modality of legal encapsulation. By examining how the figure of the perpetrator is produced through the convergence between space/time, culpability, and sentimentality, we see how international rule of law assemblages shape the domain within which emotional regimes propel particular understandings of justice. With its strict understandings and juridical demarcations, legal encapsulation concretizes a sense of stability about who is a perpetrator and how such a figure should be understood and contained. Yet this legal temporality is immediately challenged by questions about jurisdiction, admissibility, and evidence, as well as competing feelings about the reattribution of culpability. The question of who is responsible for violence against those victimized by violence automatically raises ambiguities about how we measure culpability, particularly in relation to political, social, and historical contexts.[108] This chapter explores these issues through the case of Kenya's Uhuru Kenyatta and William Ruto, whose ICC indictments cohere with and confirm the international image of the African perpetrator. Kenyatta and Ruto deflected and challenged that imagery with their own slick, technologically mediated campaign that used reattributive approaches to reconceptualize culpability through a colonial-postcolonial continuum. Further, many survivors protest the designations of criminal responsibility strictly in relation to individual responsibility, especially when they connect historical inequality with contemporary feelings that justice has been corrupted. This chapter also examines temporality and the reattribution of culpability from the perspective of survivors of the type of violence the ICC attributes to Kenyatta and Ruto.

Chapter 5 follows the discussion of affective politics of social protest and campaigns by exploring how new cartographies of transitional justice are being drafted to reframe the debate around the judicialization of African violence. With reattribution as a core component of affective justice, I begin by showing how AU advocates have built key campaigns, such as their "Silencing the Guns" and "I am African, I am the African Union" fiftieth anniversary branding, in order to reattribute justice in Africa. These campaigns operate to reroute emotional sensibilities through new geographical justice imaginaries shape the material and psychosocial body. These imaginaries, in turn, shape Pan-Africanist emotional regimes and mobilize the imagery of Pan-African histories to produce juridical, democratic, and economic possibilities on the African continent. By linking histories of Pan-Africanist sentiments to the affects that shaped the work of the Malabo Protocol—the treaty that amends the African Court of Justice protocol to establish a new African court with jurisdiction over human rights and general and criminal matters—the chapter shows how its formation involved attempts to gain authority by incorporating the relevance of deep inequalities in Africa's history. This unfolded as the drafters of the protocol also innovated new ways for political actors to navigate the relationship between legal and diplomatic strategies. Ultimately, the chapter rethinks the classic tribunal-centric purview for understanding violence and its causes and instead explores the remaking of African regional institutions as an example of affective justice.

Institutionalized affects are central to how the judicialization of politics is taking shape in the contemporary period, and, in this light, chapter 6 explores what technocratic legal instruments are being envisioned as alternatives when ICC justice approaches are deemed inappropriate or do not work in the contexts in which they are intended. By examining various judicial possibilities and limits, this final chapter highlights various African actors and their attempts to manage the judicialization of justice. These have manifested in an effort to expand the list of actionable crimes to include those that have enabled violence in Africa, as well as modes of responsibility that include corporate criminal liability. This introduction of new modes of liability represents particular attributions of culpability that go well beyond the individualization of criminal responsibility. Rather, they highlight attempts to reattribute the terms for justice through legal and overt forms of political rearticulation. The crimes adjudicated per the African Court's Malabo Protocol and the provision that grants immunity to sitting heads of state—contrary to the Rome Statute's insistence on the irrelevance of official capacity—highlight how important it is to include the history of Europe's plunder in Africa, its legacies of inequality, and the perception that the ICC continues to control the terms of African subordination in how judicialized justice is both resisted and strategically used through the African Court.

These issues lie at the core problematic of the formation of the African Court, especially in relation to the ICC. For, ultimately, the emotions that have produced the responses to legal encapsulation are not unrelated to the goals, objectives, strategies, and deliberations of the project of liberalist lawmaking itself. They are constitutive of it and require that we uncover the structures of social politics that shape how individuals express emotional responses. Ultimately, we see that feelings of justice are not separate from power and its interpretive impetus for legitimizing social action. They are fundamentally expressed through histories of meaning making around inequality, equality, and the regulatory body politics that shape how sympathies are conjured and produced. The aesthetics of expressions, reactions to perceived racism, and claims of inequality highlight the extent to which emotions are a function of power, legality, hierarchy, authority, and legitimacy, as well as sites for exercising and enforcing feelings and feeling structures through their alliance with various institutions.

In the pages that follow, *Affective Justice* aims to show how international justice works through attempts to regiment itinerant emotions and regulate particular social imaginaries. This is how liberal legality gains its power and how alternatives are produced. Through these domains of power, affective justice practices are mobilized through the law as tools of legitimation and its various component parts to create the sense of immediacy, urgency, and international priorities. These affective justice mechanisms are powerful because they shape public feelings and have the power to erase some forms of political violence while placing others at the center of global moral concern. Understanding contemporary violence and its management by international justice projects, such as rule of law assemblages, should involve thinking about the way that international justice institutions are imbricated in complicated histories and networks and, as a result, how unsettling emotions emerge from those imbrications.

Is there unity to this justice formation? The context of mass atrocity violence has no unifying metaphor. The coming into force of the ICC has produced an assemblage of intensities, spatial and temporal, whose affects are rhizomatic and conflictual, turbulent and nonuniform. Ultimately, the component parts of affective justice come together to constitute the nexus of legal technocratic practice, emotional affects, and particular emotional regimes and provide a promising site for understanding the relationships between law, discourse, and feeling and between knowledge and power. The practices that produce justice making are often invisible and may only become evident long after tensions are documented. An investigation of affective justice makes these practices visible in real time.

PART I

||||||||||||||||||||||||||||||||||||||||||||||||

COMPONENT PARTS OF THE
INTERNATIONAL CRIMINAL LAW
ASSEMBLAGE

CHAPTER 1

Genealogies of Anti-Impunity

Encapsulating Victims and Perpetrators

I cannot and will not forget the innocent Kenyans who are no longer alive to tell their story. I will not forget those who did live to tell their stories of survival—and who have waited too long for justice. These survivors are crying out for more justice, not less. I will continue to fight for the justice they deserve.

—FATOU BENSOUDA, prosecutor for the International Criminal Court

The words above, articulated by the prosecutor for the ICC, were part of Fatou Bensouda's closing remarks at a press conference on the opening of the trial of William Ruto and Joshua Arap Sang. With determination to address injustice against those victimized by Kenya's 2007–2008 electoral violence, her words index how the rule of law, in this case the Rome Statute for the ICC, has become a proxy for the defense of those victimized by violence. But do all political actors invest confidence in the law as a primary mechanism for justice? Consider Bärbel Bohley, a prominent East German opposition activist who famously observed, "We wanted justice, and we got the rule of law," in critique of the contemporary conflation of justice with law.[1] Consider William Ruto, the deputy president of Kenya, who during his pretrial hearing for crimes against humanity attempted to broaden the bid for justice by expanding the terms of victimhood. In a conciliatory, reflexive, and assertive tone, he argued that there were two types of "victims" following Kenya's postelection violence, casting himself within one category. According to Ruto, there were "the post-election violence victims, whose lives and property were destroyed and deserve justice and truth; and another set of victims which I belong to, victims of a syndicate of falsehood and a conspiracy of lies choreographed by networks that are obviously against truth and justice."[2] Ultimately, he claimed, he was a victim of structural violence at the hands of the ICC.

Some people received Ruto's remarks sympathetically and affirmed his plight. To others, his claims were laughable and defiled the very idea of suffering. The executive director of the NGO Coalition for the ICC responded to Ruto's invocation of victimhood by insisting, "States should not be distracted by the efforts of certain leaders to portray themselves as victims when the Court guarantees fair trial rights. The Assembly should stay focused on strengthening the Court's work and impact so that the actual victims of ICC crimes receive redress."[3] A year earlier, then–deputy prosecutor Bensouda had responded to a similar sentiment in which members of the African elite claimed the ICC had victimized them:

> What offends me most when I hear criticisms about the so-called African bias is how quick we are to focus on the words and propaganda of a few powerful, influential individuals and to forget about the millions of anonymous people that suffer from these crimes . . . because all the victims are African victims. Indeed, the greatest affront to victims of these brutal and unimaginable crimes . . . women and young girls raped, families brutalised, robbed of everything, entire communities terrorised and shattered . . . is to see those powerful individuals responsible for their sufferings trying to portray themselves as the victims of a pro-western, anti-African court.[4]

The language Bensouda uses reflects a *juridified* notion of justice in which agents of the court equate justice with legal accountability and claim moral responsibility as its motivation.[5] In this case, the narrative construction of justice as law invokes the mission of protecting survivors against powerful "perpetrators" of violence who have engaged in the exemption from punishment for too long.

The ICC's legal mission presumes that in order to protect those victimized by violence, justice must be understood as the objective manifestation of law. Bensouda's remarks also privilege contemporary definitions of suffering. For her, survivors of "brutal and unimaginable crimes" occupy a category of persons whom the law must protect. The sacred space of victimhood must not be open to expansion. But Ruto's remarks, however controversial in context, do open up space for noticing how the notion of the "victim" in Kenya's postelection context has become popularized to refer specifically to those subjected to violent physical attacks on the body. While ideas about structural, political, and economic violence once had a place in progressive politics on the African continent, Ruto's remarks cast in relief the narrowing of definitional spaces within which judicial processes are playing out. This delimitation of who is a "victim" and what constitutes victimhood has been accomplished through the popularization of a victim-protection discourse and is not unrelated to the rise of the construction of the perpetrator, to which I return later in this chapter and in the subsequent chapters.

It is presumed today that to utter the words "victims want justice" is to assume that victims want adjudication. We can see this illustrated at a February 2014 status conference in the ICC case against Uhuru Kenyatta, now president of Kenya. Fergal Gaynor, the victims' case representative, told the following story about the survivors he represents:

> I referred earlier to a woman I met who was gang-raped by Mungiki attackers and then doused in paraffin and set alight. She was lucky to be rescued. Nine months later she gave birth to a little boy. His biological father is a Mungiki rapist. The woman explained all of this to her husband—who, as you will recall, was himself hacked repeatedly by the Mungiki and left for dead that same day. He understood his wife's hellish predicament. And today they are raising together that little boy. Conceived through rape he is being raised in love. What does he [the husband] want—taking into account the horrors that he and his wife were subjected to? His answer is justice. With justice, he told me, "There can be reconciliation." But if there is no justice he won't be able to find it in his heart to forgive.[6]

Gaynor concluded with the following: "For there to be *true* reconciliation there must be truth. For there to be truth, there must be evidence—all the evidence that is necessary to uncover the truth. For there to be evidence, there must be state cooperation and for that, the accused must give the order. . . . Justice ultimately is truth. It is the whole truth in all its measures. It is the rejection of those who try to create obstacles for reaching those truths. . . . They say in Kiswahili, 'Haki huinua taifa.' In English, 'Justice elevates a nation.'"

In this passage Gaynor connects the notion of true reconciliation with justice, which is fundamentally achieved through legal measures. The implication is that one may uncover the truth of violence only through juridical deliberations. This concept of justice, he argues, will produce the conditions for an elevated nation. This reduces justice to legal justice or legal accountability as the precondition for reconciliation. The language of legal encapsulation underlies this veneer of justice as law, erasing the political and economic realities of violence by judicializing them. The impacts of this reduction are especially notable in cases where poverty has contributed significantly to the conditions for and vulnerabilities to violence, such as in Kenya, the Democratic Republic of the Congo, and the Central African Republic—all countries where the ICC has intervened.[7] Gaynor's rhetorical strategies appeal to the listener's sorrow and sense of righteous indignation when faced with innocent civilians whose personal lives have been destroyed by violence.

The form of sentimentality that we see in Gaynor and Bensouda's speeches has its roots in the humanitarian ethos of giving, holding accountable, protecting, and saving. Seemingly benign and benevolent, the judicialization of justice has been used to justify and enable mechanisms that safeguard the property of elites and protect foreign investments. Even as practices of affective justice are aligned with particular assemblages that include emotional regimes and technocratic legal knowledge, the exercise of power includes the state security apparatus, which has also been shaped by biopolitical mechanisms, including external state intervention, military action, economic assistance, and health aid.[8] Neocolonial systems of dependency, in turn, reinforce Western legal approaches, creating a feedback loop of assemblages that guarantee particular forms of control and contestation. Through the coupling of emotional incitement and material intervention, the individualization of criminal responsibility in relation to the defense of a certain kind of "victim" has become central to discourses of justice in the contemporary period. Holding a figurehead such as William Ruto responsible for mass crimes under his watch (and possibly at his behest) is one example of this discourse in action. Legal encapsulation can be brought to bear on explanations of how displacement functions and why it is not easily measured as an outcome of justice but comes into view with attention to emotional affect. Through these displacements others are also refusing hegemonic justice forms of legality and engaging in counterprocesses that, while they involve the application of the same legal doctrines, are reconceptualized and propelled through a spirit of refusal. This happens through narratives that are personally or publicly communicated and that become aligned institutionally with specific emotional communities, such as those that ICC prosecutor Bensouda constituted through anti-impunity organizing. As such, the particular figures that emerge are narrativized in particular emotional registers. In this case, Bensouda's liberalist legal discourse emerges through particular ways of organizing subjects and then erasing the conditions of their making. Yet those engaged in the instrumentalization and dissemination of this discourse do not necessarily recognize how their speech acts depend on affect. Indeed, on the contrary, liberal legality requires a belief in its predictability and objectivity as well as the power to exercise its principles. In theory, feelings are disavowed and disappeared because they signal subjectivity. However, if we recognize that, in practice, emotions respond to particular types of social experiences, then we can see how particular sentimentalized feelings can be mobilized to place emotion in the service of a differentiated objective.

Let us turn to another example to highlight the contested and divergent nature of the victimhood discourse. In this case, Kiamu is a survivor of the effects of postelection violence in Kenya. He claims the category of victimhood in terms that question the ability of the ICC to secure a reparative form of justice:

> One of the biggest weaknesses of Kenyan criminal law is that we do not have a scheme for compensating victims of crime and the idea that these people of the 2007 violence are the only victims of crime. They're not the only victims of crime. I'm also a victim of crime. I lost ten teeth—I nearly died; the state isn't compensating me. The best the state will do if they find the guys who beat me, they might even hang them, but they'll never pay me a coin for the injuries I've suffered. We've had victims in this country since the colonial times, so if you're going to address the system of victims of political violence in Kenya we do it holistically. We begin with the day the British landed here, the evictions that the settlers did—today the biggest landowners are settlers. All of these issues need to be addressed.

Here we see not only a strong conviction about the limits of culpability in domestic and international criminal law, but also a critique concerning the inability of international law to adequately protect or compensate those victimized by violence.[9] Kiamu claims the status of a victim not only by talking about his social category but also by invoking narratives of loss, suffering, and the pain of erasure. In doing so, his narrative establishes and reproduces particular rhetorical structures that invoke the listener's sympathy and have the potential to secure emotional affinities. Kiamu does this while also problematizing the legal encapsulation of "victims."

Today, some of those victimized by violence are popularly understood to be individuals we have a responsibility to protect. And various people engaged in the production of sentiment about victimhood often invoke justice in relation to narrowly tailored legal processes. As this narrative becomes normalized, law is increasingly seen as the proper domain for vetting sociopolitical issues. The figures of both the "victim" and the "perpetrator" are central to the production of an emotional domain of action around which the rule of law, human rights law, and humanitarianism have come into being alongside larger biopolitical processes.[10] Thus, what is important is not so much that those figures have emerged, but that the law can only rescue someone who has already been victimized ex post facto—after the fact. This makes it impossible to presume that legality can end suffering in and of itself. Rather, this chapter shows how law's biopolitical techniques contribute to the technocratic management of violence through its emotive and aspirational force. Seen as such, what international legal invocations of the victim to be saved do, as I have shown elsewhere, is to produce imaginative hauntings of a "victim," like a specter or a ghost.[11] The figure of a victimized body has both a presence and absence that structures international justice projects in particular ways. As such, the idea of an individual "victim" has been, in turn, reduced to someone who suffered physical violence perpetrated against their individual body. Structural forms of victimhood caused by deep and persistent conditions of economic or political disenfranchisement fade from the new justice discourse. This development reflects a new international order in which the desire to manage violence and the need to mobilize extrastate support for the defense of particular survivors have become part of a critical narrative triangulation—victims, justice, law—that is deployed through affective justice.

In an attempt to understand how the biopolitics of justice has gained influence in the definition and protection of survivors as well as the articulation of action against "perpetrators" of violence, this chapter explores the ways in which legal encapsulation has taken shape and has regimented particular emotional expressions of justice. In this regard, the language of justice as law has been deliberately crafted over time. As the language of individualism rose in significance, the focus on the individual criminal responsibility of state commanders became central. And alongside that narrative circulation is also the relevance of historical, colonial, and postcolonial developments in African landscapes in which global domains of structural inequality have become manifest in a range of sentimentalized justice practices.

A significant part of European involvement in Africa over the past few centuries was founded on and structured by the interrelationship of settler colonialism and the emergence of capitalism. When the management of African violence is understood in relation to the workings of white supremacy, patriarchy, and particular legal logics, we see how the twenty-first-century emergence of justice as law sentiments is not unrelated to the structural inequalities within which postcolonial Africa's violence is unfolding. From the postindependence failures of African state experiments in the 1960s through the 1990s, African dependencies on International Monetary Fund (IMF) and World Bank projects contributed to states becoming increasingly economically and politically vulnerable to neocolonial forms of extraction and control. By the early twenty-first century, a highly orchestrated and carefully designed international campaign of human rights law, humanitarian law, and international criminal law emerged with Africa as its focus. Postconflict African states became experimental sites for a new generation of technocratic knowledge—including legal scholars and practitioners (mostly from North America, Europe, and Australia), who amassed armies of interns and graduates eager to deploy the tools of legal education while launching and advancing international careers.[12] These actors alongside freshly minted legal professionals in Africa and other parts of the Global South (all of whom I later describe through the figure of "the international community") participated in the development of international legal practice and scholarship and collaborated with—at times were led by—northern technocrats committed to using law, such as domestic and international prosecutions, to rectify violence.

In *The Justice Cascade: How Human Rights Prosecutions Are Changing World Politics*, Kathryn Sikkink argued that the enactment of international and domestic judicial prosecutions across the globe constitutes a new trend in world politics. It signals a turn toward holding state officials criminally accountable for human rights violations. By examining how prosecutorial justice is establishing a new basis for morality, she charts a trajectory of increasing demand for individual prosecutions and argues that they reflect a radical change toward social insistence on accountability through prosecution. This development reflects what she calls *justice cascades*. From the Nuremberg tribunals and Tokyo trials, to the prosecutions of Pinochet and Milosevic through ad hoc tribunals, to the coming into force of the ICC, Sikkink argues that a new norm that centers individual accountability has spread across the world. She favors an explanation that focuses on the accumulated impact of a growing body of advocates across the world who have embraced this framework for justice. Thus, justice cascades as a metaphor for the emergence of legal encapsulation in the contemporary period reflect the shift in the transformation of the legitimacy of the norm of holding high-ranking leaders accountable for various international human rights crimes. As she argues, "Norms are intersubjective, that is, they are held by groups of people. But norms start as ideas held by a handful of individuals. These individuals try to turn their favored ideas into norms. . . . When these norm entrepreneurs succeed, norms spread rapidly, leading to a norms cascade."[13]

While it is empirically true that we have seen an increase in the number of judicial mechanisms in the contemporary period, there are in fact many ways to account for their rise. To suggest that a widespread and enthusiastic acceptance of new justice norms is the primary factor is to miss the significance of the consolidation of technocratic knowledge, affects, and emotional regimes in shaping the terms by which affective justice has emerged to constitute international rule of law assemblages. For Sikkink, the expansion of demands for accountability and the spread of new norms are being applied equally across the board, but I argue that these realities continue to be asymmetrical because they are infinitely varied and temporally explosive. They are shaped and guarded by persistent structural inequalities between the Global North and Global South. As the ICC indictment statistics show, and as we have already seen some of their critics argue, prosecutorial justice is practiced differentially according to geography, with postcolonial regions—characterized by deep underlying economic difficulties and evacuated institutions—deemed more in need of international judicial intervention.

Furthermore, to presume that the rise and spread of criminal trials is indicative of new forms of justice patterns that are cascading and producing new norms is to misrepresent the actual rise and spread of the rule of law mechanisms that various stakeholders are deploying. What I aim to show is that the judicialization of politics and the manifestation of what Sikkink refers to as justice cascades are not arbitrary or objective. Nor are they reflections of the natural progression of prosecutorial justice in the contemporary period, as Sikkink suggests. Their contemporary manifestation structures the possibilities around which legality functions and is a result of various processes of delimitation. The justice outcomes highlight the limits of legality in politically shaped conditions of turmoil. In an attempt to demonstrate how forms of technocratic power circulate and combine with particular emotional regimes to constitute affective justice, it is important to understand how contestations over notions of justice respond to various forms of displacements by anti-impunity activists that lead to reattributions of justice. As central promoters of legal accountability in the name of survivors, anti-impunity discourses are often divorced from the actual biopolitics of the rule of law movement. However, the separation of political-economic and legal processes from affects and regulatory regimes of power misses the way that histories of plunder and corruption are deeply bound up in histories of inequality and institutional destabilization in the African postcolony. This disconnect also misses the way that articulations of the rule of law have become naturalized and how the particularities of African postcolonial contexts are deeply tied to Western imaginaries that situate African populations or leaders as lacking order, susceptible to violence, or simply evading justice.

Similar gaps are evident in the prominent counterarguments related to political and legal issues raised in the contributions of political scientists Kathryn Sikkink and Beth Simmons in *The Future of Human Rights*, where they argue that there is no evidence that the dominant approach to justice underway in criminal tribunals actually displaces other ways of thinking about justice. However, when we demonstrate how such forms of legal justice represent the encapsulation of justice through the figure of the victim, we see how this displacement functions as an erasure of other justice mobilizations. Thus, quantifying the trial as a measure of justice cannot be easily measured as an outcome; instead, what comes into view is what other justice modalities come into play.

This chapter seeks to explore a key component part of affective justice—the deployment of international law's technocratic power and its embeddedness in particular structures of emotion. It seeks to show how a particular hegemonic rule of law discourse of justice and individual criminal responsibility has, through an assemblage of component parts, narrowed the category of "victim" in particular ways. This narrowing has resulted in a substantive disjuncture in which a new (post-1999) conception of justice is being propelled through particular emotional regimes aligned with the emergence of neoliberal forms of economic and political governance. International rule of law formations combined with the emergence of transitional justice as a concept and gave rise to an NGO-led movement of anti-impunity that centers the court as the site of justice. By reifying the act of holding perpetrators accountable for mass violence, the anti-impunity movement has introduced and defended a logic by which structural inequality is addressed through judicialization. The emotional push-back from various Pan-Africanists is invigorated by questions about what this says about the politics and geographies of violence.

To understand how this has come about, we must pay attention to the ways in which emotional regimes have been deployed in the post–Cold War era. In this moment, the reorganization of sovereignty, democracy, and various neoliberal forms of economic expansionism with the defense of the victim at its base is not accidental. This construction represents a particular alliance between economics, politics, morality, and the law, which reflects the link between affective sentiments and liberal legality. With these developments, the passionate, sentimental mobilization of what I call anti-impunity demands has been key to the establishment of new norms in support of criminal prosecutions as the solution to mass atrocity violence. The affects that augment these justice forms have come to be seen as legally necessary, and, following Karen Engle, they are central to the perceived relevance of criminal prosecutions as appropriate mechanisms for holding "perpetrators" accountable for violence in the twenty-first century.[14]

When we foreground the deeply political and historical nature of violence in Africa and point to the importance of recognizing that Africa's contemporary violence is deeply embedded in its histories of destabilization and plunder—a process that continues even today, in subtle form but nonetheless damaging—we see that the story about prosecutorial justice takes on different forms of relevance. Instead, a particular discourse of ending the impunity of African leaders has emerged as the triumphant call of the twenty-first century without regard to the conditions of inequality and the histories of inhumanity and structural violence that pervaded black life prior to and during colonialism and well after it. This discourse is symptomatic of a deep-rooted problem in the African postcolony; as we shall see, the structural conditions of inequality—what Thabo Mbeki and Mahmood Mamdani have referred to as the political nature of African violence—are rendered secondary.[15] This marginalization has contributed to the legal encapsulation of the victim and the perpetrator—developments that are not seen as solutions by everyone, including some of the "victims" that trials are meant to help. And, as I show, what we see is how the black body or the discourse related to the African woman or child to be saved becomes part of the way that both the imaginary and its related sensorium are playing out in new internationalist biopolitical regimes.

Neoliberalism, the Washington Consensus, and the Rule of Law

The history of the contemporary state form with its new international justice mechanisms, like the history of the African state, is a modern experiment. The origins of contemporary transitional justice can be located in World War I and then traced through the Cold War.[16] This phase saw the emergence of the December 11, 1946, UN General Assembly, which affirmed the principles of international law recognized by the charter of the Nuremberg Tribunal, as well as the December 10, 1948, UN General Assembly, which adopted the Universal Declaration of Human Rights.[17] Many scholars have characterized the post–Cold War period as a phase of accelerated democratization in which new democracies flourished after the collapse of repressive leaders.[18] This period saw the application of the universal exercise of international law through the extradition of Chilean ex-dictator Augusto Pinochet, arrested in London after being indicted by Spanish lawyer Baltasar Garson. Through this narrative, legal scholars like Ruti G. Teitel, among others, have identified a third phase—post-1990s—characterized by heightened political instability and violence and the subsequent increase in international peace strategies that feature pressure to institutionalize criminal prosecutions. The progression of these three phases has resulted in prosecutorial justice as the new norm.

And where the state experiment in the Global North led to the establishment of democratic institutions, the establishment of states in Africa followed not only colonial forms of governance that were fundamentally extraction oriented, but forms of governance with diminishing institutional capacities. Independent African states retained colonial boundaries and began to establish their institutions in keeping with these archetypes for the new postcolonial experiments. But there were challenges that primarily had to do with the production of national and homogenous unity in the midst of heterogeneous sovereignties and competitions over governance.

From Africa to Latin America and from East Asia to South Asia, the former colonies tried various governance experiments following independence. By the 1960s, newly postcolonial African states began to struggle to establish new democratic models that reflected new constitutions. Even as constitutional democracies were being birthed in Africa, Western states were transitioning to the market economy as the basis for state governance. Even as new African independent states attempted to establish social market principles carried over and adapted from imperial governments, former colonizers were embracing neoliberal economic reforms involving deregulation and the reduction of state influence, the elimination of price controls, and the diminishing of trade barriers in favor of market freedom.

Neoliberal reform had profound consequences as African states, with their nascent institutions, were pulled into the international economy and compelled to negotiate terms of extraction and compensation with their former colonial powers. As imperial forms of colonial protectionism were withdrawn, many African states experienced chaos even as economic extraction persisted in new forms. The shift to independence signaled a precarious period for postcolonial states, in which they were "exposed, weakened, and stripped of their monopolies on violence."[19] One result was a vulnerability to attacks from dissident groups from within nation-states and regions. When conflicts in Africa erupted after the end of the Cold War, there was no remaining imperative for Western powers to intervene in defense of Western interests.[20] In the absence of century-old institutions of colonial power, new domains of power emerged through, at times, the exercise of brutal force. Extreme forms of violence manifested in brutal dictatorships, such as former president Hissène Habré's regime in Chad. This had the effect of widening gaps between the state and various constituent communities, and further weakening the governance systems that were in place.

The recent histories of the Democratic Republic of the Congo, Somalia, Liberia, Kenya, Nigeria, Mali, Sierra Leone, and Congo-Brazzaville all fit this trajectory. Each has a history of authoritarian dictatorships, rebel groups, and various international companies and governments deeply embroiled in controlling land and or extracting resources. This dangerous interplay has deep roots. During the scramble for Africa, Western powers dictated mineral and resource extraction. Over time, the colonization process led to the creation, institutionalization, and exacerbation of various ethnic or religious tensions that persist today. Colonization, the conditions of decolonization, and the reassertion of neocolonization form the bedrock of instability and mass violence that has given rise to most of the contemporary cases being taken up by the ICC.[21]

Given this history, it is no surprise that the contemporary period (1980s to the present) has been rife with the eruption of challenges over governance. Electoral disputes in Kenya, Ivory Coast, and Sudan, for example, led to mass violence. Accordingly, the rule of law has emerged as the barometer for the measure of progress in Africa, without regard for the deeper work of rebuilding the social, political, economic, and legal institutions decimated by generations of extraction and exploitation. There is now a persistent impasse between what is legible to rule of law mechanisms, which individualize mass atrocity violence, and the more complex and far-reaching explanations and solutions that acknowledge the tumultuous impact that Western powers have had in Africa.

Over the past twenty years, Africa has suffered ten civil wars directly related to struggles over land redistribution and mineral extraction. These conflicts have caused widespread destruction and untold numbers of killings and rapes, ultimately leading to the militarization of everyday life. This violence is traceable to colonial legacies and the ways in which postindependence states attempted to control their capital cities and rural regions—with minimal success in the latter—through military takeovers and the autocratic suppression of opposition movements and democratic constitutionalism. In what is known as Françafrique, France is seen as being in a neocolonial relationship with its former African colonies. In Anglophone Africa, we see the deployment of British and American military interventions that seek to shape the management of African political stability and economic growth, the most dramatic of which was the use of military operatives to accomplish successive coups throughout Africa in the 1960s, '70s, '80s, and '90s.[22] In Nigeria, for example, the discovery of oil in 1966 (just ten years after independence) led to decades of struggle over control of petroleum wealth. This contributed to the formation of a highly centralized federal body and minimal long-term development of state institutions. Uneven distribution of power between federal and regional/local governments led to the development and maintenance of patronage politics that saw the political sphere as the central site of social advancement. This led to the autocratic tightening of political power and a series of military coups as the primary mechanism through which political competitors could agitate for power.

By the 1980s, a new international liberal economic order arose to advocate for deregulation, privatization, and the enhancement of private-sector development. In 1981 the World Bank published what became known as the "Berg Report" (named after author Elliot Berg) on accelerated growth in sub-Saharan Africa.[23] Among the key recommendations were market-oriented policies and reductions in government expenditures. These recommendations were soon reflected in World Bank and IMF lending practices; loans were granted in exchange for commitments to market-stimulating reforms (structural adjustment policies).

In 1989, English economist John Williamson coined the term *Washington Consensus* to refer to a strongly market-based approach to development. It highlights ten relatively specific economic policy prescriptions considered central to the standard reforms for the economic and political crises in the Global South. This framework was promoted by the IMF, the US Treasury Department, and the World Bank. Its prescriptions dictated policy approaches to macroeconomic stabilization, economic opening with respect to both trade and investment, and the expansion of market forces within the domestic economy. Themes such as "stabilize, privatize, and liberalize" became the mantra of a generation of Western consultants who came of age traveling to meet with political leaders in southern countries to offer economic development advice.[24] These technocrats inspired a wave of reforms in Latin America and sub-Saharan Africa that fundamentally transformed the policy landscape in these regions toward privatization, deregulation, and trade liberalization.[25] The market-driven reforms proved to be ill suited to deal with public health emergencies, poverty, and social inequality that were in fact exacerbated during this period.[26] This resulted in a cycle of underdevelopment in which the poor grew poorer and the only avenues for profit were extractive industries such as oil, mining, or plantation agriculture—industries that are characterized by violent and exploitative labor conditions. Meanwhile, state institutions ranging from the police and military to schools and hospitals were underfunded, with workers generally under- or even unpaid.

Given these conditions, it is not surprising that contests for political control (i.e., access to wealth) have triggered electoral violence in many postcolonial states, and that in some cases intra- and interstate rebel groups have emerged to vie for political influence and the control of extraction industries. In the midst of political strife, international organizations have generally brokered structural changes that ultimately benefit Western states and corporations in negotiating and sustaining agreements that continue to funnel most of Africa's extracted wealth out of the continent.

In short, neoliberal policies failed to result in economic development and actually did the opposite, exacerbating inequality.[27] In evaluating the failures of the dictates to stabilize, privatize, and liberalize, the World Bank turned its focus from African states to institutions. What resulted was the merger of mainstream development theory with the ideology of the rule of law. Those technical experts engaged in development praxis recognized that economic growth also required the institutional transformation of property rights, legal institutions, and the judiciary. They worked through Western-rooted international institutions such as the World Bank to articulate a new rule of law discourse in which good governance meant a new set of policy strategies aimed at securing economic growth not so much through market efficiency crafted by structural adjustment as through the consolidation of democracy, the upholding of human rights, and the reduction of corruption.[28] In fact, the 2004 World Bank rule of law definition, which was part of the unveiling of its twenty-first-century development policies, centered the need for legal predictability and property rights protection as requirements for good governance.[29] The assumption was that if neoliberal policies had failed, it was because of the absence of a secure institutional environment, rather than flaws in the policies themselves.

The law and legal institutions—component parts of international rule of law assemblages—were central to this new discourse, which signaled that transparent legislation, fair laws, predictable enforcement, and accountable governments would be essential to maintain order, promote private-sector growth, fight poverty, and achieve legitimacy.[30] The ultimate strategic goal was to ensure predictable market conditions. The challenge was to measure governance and commitment through the development of predictive indicators. The World Bank developed a Worldwide Governance Indicators ranking system in which it categorized countries in relation to six aspects of good governance: voice and accountability, political stability and absence of violence, government effectiveness, rule of law, regulatory quality, and control of corruption.[31] The World Justice Project's Rule of Law Index is said to measure how the rule of law is experienced in daily life in a cross section of households. Based on data collected from over 100,000 households and 2,400 expert surveys in ninety-nine countries worldwide, it highlights forty-seven indicators that are said to index the following themes: constraints on government powers, absence of corruption, open government, fundamental rights, order and security, regulatory enforcement, and civil and criminal justice.[32] It also produces data for analyzing various challenges, regional strengths, and best and worst practices.

These indicators were used by foreign-aid donor agencies to allocate funding according to various predictions of compliance.[33] As Sally Merry and others have described, "An indicator is a named, rank-ordered representation of past or projected performance by different units that uses numerical data to simplify a more complex social phenomenon, drawing on scientific expertise and methodology. The representation is capable of being used to compare particular units of analysis (such as countries or persons), and to evaluate their performance by reference to one or more standards."[34] Indicators are said to produce systems of knowledge in which various phenomena are ordered, even as particular claims are asserted according to legal, moral, and scientific measures.[35] Indicators have thus become part of the new democracy of the twenty-first century. They purport to measure compliance as well as predict volatility, risk, and economic viability.

The shift to the rule of law, and the associated support for its principles, institutions, and measurable indicators, opened up space for the UNSC to operationalize the notion of international justice through the establishment of various ad hoc tribunals and, subsequently, the ICC. In addition to serving as a measure for various state conditions and a predictor of a range of outcomes (including state stability, fragility, and the probability of violence), the new rule of law indicators mattered greatly in postcolonial Africa because they played a critical role in the renewal of IMF and World Bank loans, as well as in ensuring the ongoing support of international donors.[36] It is not only that historic patterns of structural inequality are illegible to these judicial frameworks, but also that they are used, via the mechanism of indicators, to justify the perpetuation of neocolonial dependency and disparity at the institutional level.

The Limits of Transitional Justice: The Transition from Forgiveness to Legal Accountability

Even as international institutions were reconfiguring economic neoliberalism and associated pro-democracy institutions, they were also articulating new humanitarian principles embedded in various UN resolutions and international treaties. This new discourse reconfigured the reach of law and located the individual at the center of foreign affairs. The figure of the individual was cast in two key roles: the high-level "perpetrator" criminally responsible for mass atrocities, and the "victim" to be saved from the perpetrator's violence. This rule of law discourse centered on the individualization of criminal responsibility became known as *transitional justice*, which can be defined as a form of justice that is associated with political change and, in particular, can serve as a legal response to the violence of repressive regimes. It is a post facto measure used to enable postviolence transitions to peace once conflicts are over. It advocates for justice strategies to redress mass violence, especially when it is state sponsored or connected to armed conflict aimed at overthrowing government regimes.[37] The tools of transitional justice were developed through the spread of truth commissions, the formation of quasi-judicial mechanisms that document past abuses through truth telling, all with the goal of achieving a political transition.[38] The South African Truth and Reconciliation Commission (TRC) was among the first to popularize the potential of transitional justice.

In the aftermath of widespread systematic violence in South Africa, emotional discourses of forgiveness were everywhere in the public sphere, and people were being compelled to display bodily suffering by performing forgiveness. In 1995, following the toppling of South Africa's apartheid regime, the new government established the TRC to document "the truth" about the past violence of the ruling apartheid government and repair the consequences of race-based exclusions that structured South African life. The objective was to lead the nation through a collective transition from the wounding and anger under apartheid to forgiveness and restoration. It was assumed that those who were able to forgive were ultimately better off than those who were not able to do so.[39] Chaired by Archbishop Desmond Tutu, the TRC centered themes of individual guilt, forgiveness, and reconciliation, rather than on institutional change and reparations, deploying a religiously infused logic built not only on a moral basis but also on a deeply emotional one. As noted by the former minister of justice, Dullah Omar, the commission was "a necessary exercise to enable South Africans to come to terms with their past on a morally accepted basis and to advance the cause of reconciliation."[40] Apartheid had oppressed generations of South Africans and led to the escalation of conflict, resulting in violence and human rights abuses. No section of society escaped these abuses. As a response to the far-reaching consequences of apartheid, the TRC forums required moral and emotional performances of a necessary forgiveness in order to usher in social buy-in to a postapartheid landscape.[41]

Albie Sachs, a former African National Congress activist, explained that the TRC's open hearings were central to its effectiveness: "To me, the most important part of the truth commission was not the report, it was the seeing on television of the tears, the laments, the stories, the acknowledgements."[42] This utterance highlights the way that emotional displays related to experiences of violence are central to the conversion of those experiences of violence into new states of reconciliation.

Bishop Tutu took the opportunity to preach that forgiveness should inhabit the spaces opened up by truth telling. As he has uttered passionately, time and time again, the wounds of hatred and anger created by the apartheid system must not overtake society. He said, "There was no place for retaliation in the new society that emerged after independence."[43] Describing the TRC as an "incubation chamber for national healing, reconciliation and forgiveness," he insisted, "When I talk of forgiveness I mean the belief that you can come out the other side a better person. A better person than the one being consumed by anger and hatred. . . . If you can find it in yourself to forgive then you are no longer chained to the perpetrator. You can move on, and you can even help the perpetrator to become a better person too."[44] Many of the stories told at the TRC reflected a progression from truth to forgiveness. Though affectively embodied and reflecting the angst and pain of subordination, they also emerged in the context of sentimental forgiveness strategies that conferred legitimacy on new forms of South African governance. These strategies were also deployed to attempt a postviolence transition in the aftermath of the Rwandan genocide (April to July 1994) and were articulated in keeping with predominant regimes of expression and feeling.

The period following the Rwandan genocide saw the deployment of passionate discourses that centered the practice of saving victims and holding perpetrators accountable at the core of justice. For example, the musician and peace activist Jean Paul Samputu spoke about how God had shown him the way and that he was surprised that people found it hard to forgive Christians (because of the church's moral and political culpability during the genocide). He stressed that, for him, "forgiveness had nothing to do with the perpetrator but rather meant a release from the bondage of hatred."[45] Samputu reminded his constituencies that "it was human-beings who did this—the world should learn from Rwanda. . . . We live in a world where the culture of revenge reigns, forgiveness should be our permanent attitude."[46]

A woman on the same podium added that sometimes being a Christian can complicate forgiveness because of the undue pressure on Christians to forgive others. But in clarifying different forms of forgiveness, she drew a distinction between psychological forgiveness (promoting improved health and well-being) and Christian forgiveness, which she described as being "based on the fact that God has forgiven me." Then, after a short silence she reflected, "That's quite overwhelming for me. If God can forgive me, who am I not to forgive others?"[47]

What became clear was that forgiveness also required the acknowledgment that a "perpetrator" had committed an offense. And while some victimized by the brutalities of the apartheid regime did offer forgiveness, the overall "perpetrators" of such violence did not generally acknowledge their wrongdoing.[48] The forgiveness projects that were generated through transitional justice projects provided a wealth of testimonies in which ordinary citizens shared their experiences in dealing with forgiveness, always structuring them in relation to particular emotional structures of expectation. But the figure of the "perpetrator" remained elusive. The "oppressor role" was glossed as the apartheid system writ large, white racism, histories of inequality, and President de Klerk as a symbol of a racist minority, but with no particular person or people from whom to extract accountability. For example, during a South African TRC hearing, one witness, a teenage daughter of one of those victimized by apartheid's violence, described the incident in which her relatives were murdered: "The police ambushed their car, killed them in the most gruesome manner, set their car alight." When asked whether she would be able to forgive the people who did this to her family, she answered, "We would like to forgive, but we would just like to know who to forgive."[49]

The absence of an individualized "perpetrator" was seen as a weakness of the South African TRC. Critics argued that, as a quasi-judicial mechanism with no adjudicatory power, the TRC placed a burden on the forgiveness of survivors rather than holding the "perpetrators" accountable and offering recourse for what was seen as some of the worst kinds of structural and physical violence.[50] The International Center for Transitional Justice (ICTJ) was established in light of this critique. The development of the ICTJ signaled a key shift in the advancement and transformation of justice strategies in the last decades of the twentieth century. As advocates in a right-to-truth movement, survivors of violence began demanding investigations into human rights violations to unearth information about the fate of survivors as well as identification of "perpetrators" of violence.[51] Citizens demanded that their leaders and government institutions had a responsibility to locate them and facilitate trials to adjudicate wrongdoing. This movement shaped a new consciousness about people's right to rectify atrocity through legal remedies.[52] New legislation was crafted in response to this assertion of rights. In cases of international crimes (crimes against humanity, genocide, and certain crimes of war), formal amnesties as seen in South Africa or Rwanda would no longer be seen as a legitimate political solution to mass violence.

This paradigm shift from forgiveness to legal accountability laid the foundation for the institutionalization of the anti-impunity movement that proposed legal trials and convictions as tools for change. International tribunals that hosted multiple trials of named "perpetrators" became the testing grounds for determining whether the deployment of criminal justice in postwar contexts could be used to advance political transitions. As a vehicle for those victimized by violence to reconcile past harms, it led to the emergence of the emotionally infused category of the "victim" of violence as a problem to be addressed in legal as well as moral terms. However, it was the moral register that had become critically relevant for African states following the Rwandan genocide, the long history of antiapartheid struggle in South Africa, and Liberia and Sierra Leone's civil wars, in relation to which international intervention was late, marginal, and ineffective. In that regard, much of my earlier research on the making of the ICC documented that African state diplomats signed on to the Rome Statute with the expectation that judicial mechanisms should ensure that the "international community" would never again stand by and watch genocidal violence on the African continent.[53]

The notion of the "international community" is itself an important site of discourse that merges humanitarianism with foreign policy making and international criminal law mechanisms that are sustained by a responsibility to protect discourse.

"We Wanted Justice, and We Got the Rule of Law":
The Core Responsibility of the "International Community"

In September 1999 in The Hague, Netherlands, on the centennial of the first international peace conference, Kofi Annan, then secretary-general of the United Nations, delivered a critical speech in which he challenged states to address "two equally compelling interests" at once.[54] Titled "The Effectiveness of the International Rule of Law in Maintaining International Peace and Security," Annan's speech called first for the production of an effective response to human rights abuses. The second interest was concerned with the development of a mechanism through which states could act with universal legitimacy.[55] Galvanized by this challenge and the movement it represented, the Canadian government established the International Commission on Intervention and State Sovereignty to reconcile the relationship between state sovereignty and the responsibility of the international community to act in the face of "mass violations of humanitarian norms."[56] It published a report in December 2001 titled "The Responsibility to Protect," which introduced a critical doctrine for the development of key principles of legality related to the protection of survivors.[57]

Following the 2001 failure of the international community to act to prevent or stop the Rwandan genocide, the African Union reinforced the idea that the international community had a responsibility to protect populations in crisis situations.[58] Article 4 of the AU's constitutive act asserts "the right of the Union to intervene in a Member State pursuant to a decision of the Assembly in respect of grave circumstances, namely war crimes, genocide and crimes against humanity."[59] Some four years later, the UN General Assembly produced a declaration called "Principles and Guidelines on the Right to a Remedy and Reparation for Victims of Gross Violations of International Human Rights Law and Serious Violations of International Humanitarian Law." This declaration articulated a universal set of guidelines for survivors. Also by 2005, the AU had adopted the Ezulwini Consensus, which provided African states with an African regional tool to address mass atrocities.

A foundational pillar of these declarations was the right to protect, the idea that states have a responsibility to protect populations from gross human rights violations including crimes against humanity, war crimes, genocide, and ethnic cleansing. Where states fall short or in fact perpetrate crimes, then the international community has a responsibility to step in to assist or usurp states in fulfilling this primary responsibility to protect a population.

If a state fails to protect its citizens from the four crimes of concern, and if it has failed to maintain peaceful measures, the international community has a responsibility to intervene using the most effective and appropriate means, ranging from coercive measures to economic sanctions, with military intervention as a last resort.[60]

The discourse of a right to protect is not simply a moral architecture constructed in the contemporary period. The notion of an obligation to protect those victimized by violence was driven by a force of law deployed across sovereign borders through international institutions afforded expanded jurisdictional reach. This expansion of activity reflected a fundamental shift from the regulated affairs of the state to the expansion of global governance mechanisms known to operate from the north to the south, particularly in Africa and Latin America. This geospatial dynamic reflects the continuity of economic dependencies and a persistent need to manage political compliance through legal means. The establishment of new ad hoc tribunals, international treaties, decrees, and charters promoted the legal frameworks that made this possible. The notion of the individual to be protected joined with new international humanitarian and judicial mechanisms that provided the vocabulary for popularizing radically new and fundamentally transformative formations.[61] Key to the development of these mechanisms was a deeply retributive justice system focused on punishing the guilty, but with minimal powers to confer reparation and restoration for the survivors.

As the second decade of the twenty-first century progresses, the plight of survivors in postviolence conflict situations remains within the realm of retributive justice approaches, such as criminal tribunals but has been institutionalized in only particular places, such as the Global South, and not other places. International discourses about victims of violence were critical in establishing a profoundly astute justice discourse. The formation of judicial mechanisms to protect "victims" was only part of the story. In shifting from development priorities to judicial measures, not only were the sites for adjudication deeply selective, but the popular definition of justice became narrower and far more restrictive and, with it, who counts as a "victim" deserving of that justice, and the discourses surrounding it, were articulated through the dialectical pinning of an individual "perpetrator" whose impunity was to be stopped at all cost. And yet, the complication is that in the African region, a differentiated form of international justice was developed through the African Union Commission and related bodies. The rise of a new hegemonic anti-impunity justice trend requires that we consider these emergent formations

and the pro-accountability discourses that sought to override African cultur-
alist forms of justice differentiation through an emotively moral individualization of criminal responsibility that insisted on a justice stance that required
criminal trials as the optimal approach to ending impunity.

The Emergence of International Criminal Justice and Its Differentiated Formations

In an age characterized by neoliberal precarity and a post-1968 disenchant-
ment with the potential of radical politics, notions of saving victims and
ending impunity have become predominant throughout the Global North.
Increasingly, campaigns to project these ideas globally are reflected in the discourses and actions of citizens in the Global South and connected diasporas.
From Palestine to Mali, and from the Philippines to Chile, anti-impunity activists are engaged in missions to save those victimized by political violence.[62]

The rise of various national and international concerns about how to manage violence has led to the development of solutions forged within a paradigm
of global security and protectionism. Some of the solutions have prioritized
the essential role of anti-impunity, insisting on the radical dismissal of the immunity of heads of state, a core principle that has long pervaded international
customary law. Known as the exemption from punishment or freedom from
the injurious consequences of an action, the notion of impunity galvanized a
movement intent on eradicating the differential and unequal application of
justice.[63] Activists insisted that no one is above the law. Stamping out the exceptionalism of leaders whose actions contribute to mass atrocities, international criminal law took shape as a viable mode of justice that renders official
authority irrelevant in the eyes of the law. This core value of anti-impunity
that is enshrined in the Rome Statute dates back to the World War I era. In
March 1919, in the war's aftermath, the Commission on the Responsibility of
the Authors of the War and on Enforcement of Penalties recommended the
formation of a high tribunal. Built into its architecture was the rejection of immunity for all—including leaders and governmental heads of state.[64]

With a commitment to ending impunity, this contemporary movement is
driven by the foundational ICC dictum that no one is above the law. This has
contributed to the individualization of criminal responsibility through which
a vociferous anti-impunity movement has taken shape. After World War II,
the Nuremberg and Tokyo international tribunals built their case law around
the Charter of the International Military Tribunal. Under Article 7, the charter stated, "The official position of defendants, whether as Heads of State or
responsible officials in Government Departments, shall not be considered as

freeing them from responsibility or mitigating punishment."[65] A subsequent decision by the tribunal in a Nuremberg case reaffirmed this principle in an October 1946 judgment; it noted that "the principle of International Law, which under certain circumstances protects the representative of a State, cannot be applied to acts which are condemned as criminal by International Law."[66] This was echoed by the International Military Tribunal sitting in Tokyo. In 1950, the UN General Assembly adopted the Principles of International Law Recognized in the Charter of the Nuremberg Tribunal. Principle 3 of this document states, "The fact that a person who committed an act which constitutes a crime under international law acted as Head of State or responsible Government official does not relieve him from responsibility under international law."

A further example of this early judicial development that I highlight as an example of technocratic knowledge is illustrated by the words of Robert Jackson, a leading American lawyer, judge, and writer of the twentieth century who served as a US Supreme Court justice from 1941 until 1954. During 1945–1946 he was the architect of the international trial process and then the chief prosecutor of the surviving Nazi leaders at Nuremberg, Germany. In the absence of precedent for legal individual criminal prosecution in European states, he, among other analysts, invoked emotionally charged moral grounds for pursuing legal accountability for victims of Nazi mass atrocities.[67] As part of his opening statement at the Nuremberg trials, he articulated a goal of achieving justice for survivors by punishing those who bear greatest responsibility for crimes against the peace:

> The privilege of opening the first trial in history for crimes against the peace of the world imposes a grave responsibility. The wrongs which we seek to condemn and punish have been so calculated, so malignant, and so devastating, that civilization cannot tolerate their being ignored, because it cannot survive their being repeated. That four great nations, flushed with victory and stung with injury stay the hand of vengeance and voluntarily submit their captive enemies to the judgment of the law is one of the most significant tributes that Power has ever paid to Reason.[68]

Here the opening is focused on the condemnation and punishment of those whose actions led to mass violence and required that other nations intervene and sacrifice their citizens in the interest of humanity. To further buttress the moral force of his emotional plea, he locates the neutrality of allied nations as victorious but resulting in mass injury. He highlights the significance of legal action as subjecting captive enemies to the judgment of the law, clear-eyed and devoid of retaliatory impulses. The invocation of sacrifice and moral duty is clearly articulated throughout his opening, which utilizes emotionally charged expressions of feeling and conviction. Later in his statement, in reflecting on the collective responsibility of the German people, Jackson indicates, "A second paralyzing force involves a mental conflict involving moral values; before which we Americans stand a bit baffled. We have long been taught, and still believe, that might does not make right. And yet we see that all we hold to be morally right is in jeopardy wherever it does not also possess physical might."[69] The call for a moral impetus to "confront evil" that echoes in his statement resounded throughout the second half of the twentieth century. Its relevance was foregrounded at the commemoration of the seventieth anniversary of the Nuremberg trials on September 29, 2016, during which then US Attorney General Loretta Lynch declared,

> Certainly the onslaught of evidence of man's inhumanity to man can leave one dispirited and discouraged. But we cannot—and we should not—give in to despair, because the legacy of Nuremberg is that when we are called to confront the evil that walks this earth, we turn to the law. When we need to mete out justice to those who have reaped the whirlwind and revel in the chaos resulting therefrom, we turn to the law. And through the law we give voice to those shattered souls who seek redress, and we provide a reckoning to those who trade in fear and trembling. Let us never forget that within these walls, evil was held to account and humanity prevailed.[70]

Feelings of fear and impassioned responses that result in bodily trembling are both affective responses to perceived injustice materialized through sentimentalizations to justify the introduction of legal rituals as remedies. However, there is an irony in the attempt to individualize criminal responsibility as well as render insignificant the official capacity of those who acted in the interest of evil: it can result in the obscuring or erasure of the structural underpinnings of institutional violence. We see this materialized in later tribunals that insisted on official capacity as irrelevant, including the International Criminal Tribunal for Yugoslavia (ICTY) and, later, the International Criminal Tribunal for Rwanda (ICTR).

Article 7(2) of the ICTY statute stated that "the official position of any accused person, whether as Head of State or Government or as a responsible Government official, shall not relieve such person of criminal responsibility nor mitigate punishment."[71] The ICTY asserted that Article 7(2) was declaratory of customary international law. In its Article 6(2), ICTR replicated the sentence, as did the Statute of the Special Court for Sierra Leone.[72]

Innovations that came with the establishment of new and budding international legal institutions presented challenges to the legitimacy of the ICTY. These challenges required that its champions constantly affirm the nature of justice under construction and the moral basis on which it operates. For example, ICTY registrar John Hocking, in discussing the function of the tribunal, clarified the domain of justice as not simply the creation of individuals, but instead as a moral force represented in the shared conscience of humanity:

> Of course, the principal function of the Tribunal is judicial, as indeed it is of the special courts in the region. . . . The Tribunal views the continuation of its work by national jurisdictions as a central element of its legacy and it remains committed to transferring its experiences and knowledge to the domestic justice systems in the former Yugoslavia. . . . In parting, allow me to leave you with the words of Aleksandr Solzhenitsyn: *Justice is conscience, not a personal conscience but the conscience of the whole of humanity. Those who clearly recognise the voice of their own conscience usually recognise also the voice of justice.*[73]

Time and again, the moral force of the work of hybrid courts was articulated as representing the will of the collective whole. This narrativization of society as speaking through the work of international courts was further adumbrated by the tones of voice and the body language of legal actors as they solemnly recounted the horrors of violence. The emotive pleas that surrounded public testimonies are not incidental. They follow particular regimes of expression that are structured by law's logic and the larger political frameworks that propel its interest. The forms of defiance that are often performed in public speeches take their cue from principles of law that have been historically crafted.

As unpacked above, the movement toward anti-impunity is based on the principle of the irrelevance of official capacity with origins in the Nuremberg and Tokyo tribunals and the subsequent work of the International Law Commission that was directed to work on a statute to establish a permanent court.[74] Yet, though the Nuremberg tribunal operated on the principle of irrelevance of national capacity, the draft statute for the ICC did not contain this principle. After the first draft of the Rome Statute was released, a preparatory committee of state representatives formed to discuss it. At a committee meeting in February 1997, the concept of the irrelevance of the official position was approved and consolidated in the draft statute. The suggested article read:

This Statute shall be applied to all persons without any discrimination whatsoever: official capacity, either as Head of State or Government, or as a member of a Government or parliament, or as an elected representative, or as a government official, shall in no case exempt a person from his criminal responsibility under this Statute, nor shall it [per se] constitute a ground for reduction of the sentence.

Any immunities or special procedural rules attached to the official capacity of a person, whether under national or international law, may not be relied upon to prevent the Court from exercising its jurisdiction in relation to that person.[75]

This recommendation was added to Article 24 of the Draft Rome Statute. At its second meeting on June 16, 1998, the Committee of the Whole decided to refer to the Working Group on General Principles of Criminal Law, among which was Article 24—Irrelevance of official capacity, paragraph 2. However, its wording was not altered.[76] The committee then approved the articles as they appeared in the document, and the Rome Statute was approved on July 17, 1998, with the immunity provision dismissed.

Upon signing the Rome Statute, one-third of UN member states had to ratify it in order to establish a permanent court. Over the course of the next few years, neither the preparatory commissions nor the Assembly of States Parties addressed issues of immunity until various African states presented an amendment. At the assembly's twelfth session, the Article 27 passage concerning the irrelevance of the official position of the "perpetrator" was considered.

The first two paragraphs in Article 27 have different functions.[77] Paragraph 1 denies a defense of official capacity. It concerns functional immunity and is derived from texts in the Nuremberg Charter, the Genocide Convention, and the statutes of the ad hoc tribunals. In contrast, Paragraph 2 outlines that no exception exists for "core crimes" under personal immunity. Paragraph 2 of Article 27 concerns immunities that exist by virtue of customary international law, and that protect heads of state and other senior officials by virtue of their particular office or status. Immunity *rationae personae*, or personal immunities, describe those immunities that attach to an office or status. This type of immunity is limited to only a small group of senior state officials, especially heads of state, heads of government, foreign ministers, diplomats, and other officials on special mission in foreign states. It is conferred on those with primary responsibility for the conduct of the international relations of a state, and it is possessed only as long as the official is in office. State officials to whom this type of immunity applies are immune from prosecution for official acts as well as those carried out in their private capacity, whether the act in question was committed while the official was in office or before his or her entry into office. Such immunities stem from the recognition that state affairs are hindered by judicial interference from foreign governments, and the view that immunities are necessary for the maintenance of peaceful cooperation and coexistence among states.

Ultimately, Paragraph 2 amounts to a renunciation, by state parties to the Rome Statute, of the immunity of their own heads of state to which they are entitled by virtue of customary international law. It concerns personal immunity and is without precedent in international criminal law instruments. It outlines that the statute applies "equally to all persons without any distinction based on official capacity. In particular, official capacity as a Head of State or Government, a member of a Government or parliament, an elected representative or a government official shall in no case exempt a person from criminal responsibility under this statue."[78]

With this key development underway, international criminal law as a technical legal strategy for addressing mass atrocity violence took shape. But what is important to note is that these legal developments could not take root without particular emotional assertions about the form of morally driven interventions articulated as being on behalf of "victims/survivors" and "perpetrators" at play. Through the mobilization of members of political and civil society, international and nongovernmental organizations, and social movement activists, the ICC has been advocating for national judicial solutions to mass violence. These developments, with their moral and juridical foci, have moved from a focus on the sovereignty of states and state protections to the protection of individual persons, groups of peoples, and membership in a network of treaty obligations.[79]

This anti-impunity movement emerged against a backdrop in which state actors were seen by their publics as exercising impunity at will. As in the twentieth century, members of the movement responded to widespread human rights abuses—rape and torture, for example—by demanding that institutional mechanisms be deployed to hold leaders legally accountable for criminal actions. This call to end impunity was a call to ensure that no leader would be above the law. And thereby grew the rule of law movement to put in place a legal infrastructure to support legal accountability. However, anti-impunity movement organizers encountered an inherent problem in that despite the institutionalization of the ICC, as described in chapter 6, it lacked institutional enforcement powers. As such, the ICC's anti-impunity principles become effective through the amplification of its affective and emotional practices engaged by NGO advocates, such as the Coalition for the International Criminal Court (CICC).

In communicating the anti-impunity principles at the core of the CICC's mission, NGOs evoked feelings of empathy in response to human suffering through technologically savvy pro-justice campaigns that featured the image of the victimized African body. For example, in 2016, the CICC launched an ongoing campaign in support of the ICC called United by Common Bonds. The website features "ways to get involved," including sharing content on social media, a way to donate to the campaign, videos, and information about the court and the issues it addresses. Sophisticated design and carefully chosen colors seemingly aim to compel visitors to join the fight for justice. With the goal of underlining what they call "the global nature of the Court's mandate and mission," messaging on the site highlights the "continuing desire to see it deliver justice to victims in all parts of the world."[80]

Through the work of civil society and NGOs like Amnesty International, African Legal Aid, the CICC, the Coalition for the African Court, and Human Rights Watch, to name a few, competing notions of justice are being propelled by demands for immediate forms of judicial accountability in order to insist upon forms of liberal legality that are legible to other missions. But, as we will see, to assess the impact of these demands we need to look well beyond their mission statements or Twitter characters. Their power is tied to their work within the complex assemblages of anti-impunity formations, and their effects are felt through the impact of legal encapsulation, through which similarly constituted emotional constituencies are formed. This formation can be measured through the way that groups of people deploy figures of those victimized by violence as the key domains by which anti-impunity sentiments are expressed and by which moral subjects and bodies politic are shaped through history and power. And when combined with a particular examination of legalistic products such as indictments, which are seen by some as representing constricted international justice apparatuses, structuring devices such as space and time come into precise focus.

Various NGOs engaged in articulating their work through anti-impunity sentiments have established regional offices both at home and abroad and are working to universalize this discourse, drawing linkages among victims everywhere and presenting a universal legal remedy. As projected by the images in the backdrop of the CICC homepage, the global justice movement is discursively built upon images of the most vulnerable: black and brown women, elders, and children. This contemporary imagery and the discourses invoked in international law circles can be traced in large part to the influential worldview of Ben Ferencz, the former investigator of Nazi war crimes for the Nuremberg trials who himself fled persecution as a small child and identifies himself as motivated by affiliation with the victim population. Popularly billed as "the only living prosecutor from the war-crime trials that followed the Holocaust," his "victim"-oriented, pro-judicial-accountability stance has contributed to the mobilization of an assemblage of justice NGOs, such as what was then the Lawyers' Committee for Human Rights (now Human Rights Watch) as well as Amnesty International and the CICC.[81] Ferencz's collaborators worked with governments and built citizen support for a 1998 Rome conference for the formation of the International Criminal Court, which led to the signing of the Treaty of Rome. This occasion marked the institutionalization of a movement for which the narrative of anti-impunity—that no one is above the law—and the importance of the duty to prosecute reached far and wide. This narrative was propelled by many who suffered abuses at the hands of violent government regimes and became influential advocates of international criminal justice, including Thomas Buergenthal and Juan Mendez in Argentina, or African civil society workers like Netsanet Belay, the Africa director for research and advocacy at Amnesty International, who previously spent over two years in an Ethiopian prison as a prisoner of conscience. These activists working through the law or with large NGOs or human rights institutes engaged in affective justice strategies that shaped the rise of a duty to prosecute during the 1980s and '90s. This shaped the moral authority and power associated with appeals from those victimized by violence at the hands of their governments.

As discussed in the book's introduction, the radical impacts of the duty to prosecute that became popularized at the Nuremberg trials led to the reclassification of criminal culpability in the post-1990s treaty construction period and the assignment of guilt to individual leaders, especially African leaders. Central to the notion of anti-impunity for those indicted for mass atrocities was a form of reattribution of guilt articulated through an emotionally charged dictum, uttered publicly and privately in both formal and informal contexts, that no one is above the law. Also known as the "irrelevance of one's governmental capacity," this dictum is often articulated with absolutist declarations that everyone—from powerful state leaders to impoverished members of rebel groups—must be held accountable equally to the standards of prosecutorial justice. In the post-Nuremberg era, advocates refined and disseminated passionate convictions that the rule of law cannot be questioned or overturned, and they deployed a related justice narrative that "you're either with us or against us" to condemn any public critique. Ferencz himself engaged in political negotiations and strategic lobbying at the Rome conference for the establishment of the court. In his public speeches and private conversations throughout the development of the NGO anti-impunity movement, he and many others contributed to the iconic continuities that linked the ICC to a post-Nuremberg social imaginary. To accomplish this, Ferencz was known to draw on his moral authority not only by claiming to have seen the results of Nazi violence against victims, but by narrating how he played a central role in holding some of its commanders judicially responsible for crimes. As he recalled in an article for the popular magazine *The Atlantic,*

> I saw crematoria still going, the bodies starved, lying . . . dying, on the ground. I've seen the horrors of war more than can be adequately described. . . . The capacity to destroy life on earth has grown incredibly in the course of my lifetime, which increases the need to set up a mechanism to try to prevent that from happening. . . . There are perpetrators of crimes, and there are victims of crimes. They are ready to fight and die for their ideals; they cannot have a fair judgment. You need a third party—a court— in order to determine the facts.[82]

Ferencz's worldview assumes that the solution to mass violence is a third-party institution, namely an international court that is autonomous and has the power to determine the facts of horrific violence. Here, justice is understood as being exercisable through legal methods and through the call to action to "protect victims wherever they are."[83] A call to action is a particular, regimented strategy. It reconfigures the spatial authority of international justice, in which citizens who are victimized by mass violence are within the reach of the objective redemption that international justice renders possible. This has engendered a popular discourse that supports the reformulation of the contemporary sovereignty principle through a movement that claims moral responsibility beyond borders.

By insisting that international publics have a moral responsibility to protect victims everywhere, the component parts of affective justice are highlighted through advocates' use of this narrative. For example, introducing particular sentiments of saving alongside the moral responsibility to act, anti-impunity advocates established the building blocks to produce a legal solution out of a twentieth-century sociopolitical process. It is this legal solution, sentimentalized through saving and holding accountable, that liberal legality represents. Supplemented by a linear narrative of activism from Nuremberg to Rome, Ferencz communicated a universalist and color-blind mission shaped by the Rome Statute's preamble: that all peoples are united by common bonds that could be shattered at any time by violence, and that millions of children, women, and men have been "victims of unimaginable atrocities that deeply shock the conscience of humanity."[84]

As a key icon of international justice, over the past fifteen years Ferencz (and his family, including his son, Don Ferencz) has been called on to open and close key ICC events and to speak at receptions. He also delivered the Office of the Prosecutor's closing argument for the ICC's first trial, that of Thomas Lubanga, with a statement that included invocations of "ending impunity" through the legal pursuit of individuals responsible for what is often articulated as the worst crimes against humanity. This emotional enactment of justice through the enfolding of those victimized by violence into the core justification for international legal action reflects legal encapsulation in its most hegemonic form. This domain of biopolitical technocratic practice is most vividly seen in the anti-impunity movement and manifest in the use of international law to save the "victim" from "perpetrator" impunity.[85] While legal encapsulation was once a response to the blatant and brute power of worldwide state practices and violence with impunity by their leaders, today the assemblage has shifted its entanglements and produced a highly vocal and institutionalized response to state violence. Within this structuring field, then, affects are felt bodily and are knowable when they converge with particular feeling expressions.

From Technocratic Knowledge to Postcolonial Emotional Regimes

With the combined expressive and instrumental impetus behind Africa's participation in the Rome Statute system, as well as the adoption of a range of other international treaties, African state agents inserted themselves and mobilized to build new institutions. These included the signing of international law treaties and the erecting of international crime and investigation divisions that wedded domestic state action with the expansion of human rights and international criminal law institutions, shifting the focus from states and state protections to the protection of persons and peoples.[86] In doing this, emotional expressions of justice were articulated through anti-impunity activists' reinforcement of regimes of suffering and protection. In other words, though protections for minorities and those from the Global South were differential and uneven, discourses invoking the responsibility to protect citizens from violence and the rights of survivors were seen as a means to support the increasing responsibility of state actors to protect citizens.

Since the early 1990s, African sites of violence have continued to provide the spaces and subjects for new policies to address violence, seek truth and justice, and enable reconciliation in fractured societies. As evidenced by the implementation of international criminal tribunals such as the Special Court for Sierra Leone in Freetown, Sierra Leone, to the ICTR in Arusha, Tanzania, to the Extraordinary African Chambers in Dakar, Senegal, to the Hybrid Court for South Sudan, it is clear that the emergence of the rule of law has not only involved African actors, but has also left deep imprints throughout the continent. However, the justice approaches did not emerge only as a result of the rise of legal accountability mechanisms or the cascading of criminal prosecutions. African Union–driven approaches to anti-impunity in African contexts have also been shaped by disappointments that led to alternate possibilities through which new policy frameworks touted as reflecting African traditions were institutionalized. One such domain of invention driven by particular emotive histories was the development of the Transitional Justice Policy Framework, shaped by a group of elder statespeople who were a part of the African Union's establishment of a group of a small number of high profile African leaders named the Panel of the Wise. This group of recognized leaders approached the management of violence with the assumption that peace and justice are interrelated and that those engaged in justice work should be sensitive about the timing of indictments, especially where peace talks are underway.

By the late 1990s and early 2000s, the euphoria following the end of apartheid in South Africa and the promise to rectify the international community's failure to intervene in the genocidal violence in Rwanda gave many the feeling that the ICC could provide redemption for histories of violence. Many African state negotiators and political actors participated earnestly and enthusiastically, offering technocratic cooperation and public advocacy to help establish and ratify the Rome Statute of the ICC. They were committed to the rule of law's potential as a protective device for the future. For stakeholders in several engaged African countries, the transformative potential of law was less about the symbolism of international justice that Nuremburg represented for so many anti-impunity ICC advocates in the Global North than about the hope that international legal justice might finally offer a possibility for deterring future violence in Africa, a continent that has long suffered violent plunder from external and internal agents. Motivated by this vision, African governmental representatives participated earnestly in the adoption of a movement that equated legal accountability with justice. In turn, the ICC's predominantly European and North American staff worked in concert with African civil society, and under the expectations of primarily Western donors, to cement the ICC as the key modality for constraining the arbitrary abuse of power where states are deemed unwilling and unable to do so. However, the ICC's framework is structurally limited. It does not have universal jurisdiction and can act only in those states that have signed and ratified the Rome Statute. This means that at the time the ICC was unable to pursue perpetrators of violence in places like Iraq, Afghanistan, the United States, and Syria. This had implications for the appearance of ICC justice and made the court vulnerable to accusations of inequality, racism, and selectivity in favor of African countries.

In response, the Panel of the Wise contributed to the formal development of an African Transitional Justice Policy Framework that foregrounded what are seen as shared African values on democratic governance, human rights, peace and security, and rule of law. In this formulation of African values, strengthening the rule of law is just one component of a larger transitional justice modality for addressing impunity and armed violence in Africa. Central to the emergence of an African justice discourse is the production of an affectively claimed African geography that is Pan-African in scope and expression, and that seeks to differentiate international justice through a sense of African shared values. Such values presume that African justice requires an understanding of the contexts and deep histories within which such violence has unfolded. Cultural and political considerations can be factored into justice solutions alongside a range of other priorities, such as various issues concerning national cohesion, socioeconomic rights, African solidarity and cohesion, and transformative development.[87] The case of South Sudan's Commission of Inquiry and the subsequent establishment of the Hybrid Court for South Sudan are examples of this approach and of the role of sequencing in allowing peace talks to play out. The strategy is said to involve the invocation of a Pan-Africanist logic that is differentiated from dominant assemblages of anti-impunity and rule of law.[88]

Contrary to the ICC prosecutor's choice to request an arrest warrant against Sudanese President Omar al-Bashir on March 4, 2009, the Sudanese government, the AU, the Arab League, and the Organisation of Islamic Cooperation objected on the grounds that such an action by the ICC was destabilizing for peace talks, which were to be revived in Doha, Qatar.[89] Several African and

Arab members of the UNSC, supported by permanent members China and Russia, proposed a resolution to renew the United Nations–African Union Mission in Darfur, the joint AU-UN peacekeeping mission formally approved by UNSC Resolution 1769 on July 31, 2007, to bring stability to the war-torn Darfur region of Sudan while peace talks on a final settlement continued.[90] Using Pan-Africanist language to invoke the need for an African approach, the AU called on the UNSC to invoke Article 16 of the Rome Statute to defer the processes initiated against Bashir on the grounds that a prosecution of the president could impede the prospects for peace in the region.[91]

To contain the broad backlash against the ICC in Africa, the AU established the High-Level Panel on Darfur in March 2009, headed by Thabo Mbeki, with a mandate to recommend approaches for reconciling the demands of peace, justice, and reconciliation.[92] The report, released in October 2009, recommended balancing these demands by establishing a hybrid court composed of Sudanese and non-Sudanese judges and legal experts, introducing legislation to remove immunities for state actors suspected of crimes in Darfur, and forming a "Trust, Justice and Reconciliation Commission."[93]

In May 2011, the Doha Document for Peace in Darfur (DDPD) was finalized at the All Darfur Stakeholders Conference.[94] The government of Sudan and the Liberation and Justice Movement then signed a protocol agreement on July 14, 2011, committing themselves to the document, which established the framework for the comprehensive peace process in Darfur. The DDPD was the culmination of two and a half years of negotiations, dialogue, and consultations with the major parties to the Darfur conflict, including all relevant stakeholders and international partners. The UN-AU Mission in Darfur lent technical expertise to the process and continues to support the dissemination of the DDPD as well as to urge nonsignatory movements to sign on.[95] Many argue that the establishment of the DDPD and the threat of prosecution have led to serious delays in the overall implementation of the accord and the lack of a permanent ceasefire.[96]

As one AU negotiator, whom I will call Abdul, shared with me, "The issue is complex and the threat of prosecution and the creation of an international judicial solution is part of the problem. We have tried to insist on an African approach, a staggered approach that is politically savvy, in order to achieve peace first and justice later." By emphasizing the sequencing of peace and justice as an "African approach," Abdul attempted to attribute to Africanness not only an interest in prioritizing peace and the end of violence first but also a commitment to judicial justice at the appropriate time. This sequencing has led to the establishment of the Hybrid Court for South Sudan as an African approach that is attentive to establishing peace, addressing political injustice, and investigating and prosecuting individuals bearing the most responsibility for violations of international law and applicable South Sudanese law committed from December 15, 2013, through the end of the transitional period.

Though the court is not yet functional, it is controversial, and there are many who object to criminal prosecutions as a way to address deep-seated historical and political projects. Yet, in keeping with legal technocratic formations as a component part of the international criminal legal assemblage under examination, under the August 2015 agreement, the AU Commission established it as an extension of the sequencing directives outlined in the report from the UN Panel of Experts on South Sudan (otherwise referred to as a Commission of Inquiry).[97] Part of this AU commission of inquiry approach is an affective articulation of justice for South Sudan that is being described as an African-led and African-owned process. As such, discourses abound that highlight particular imaginaries, such as African geographies of justice, through which various AU actors participate in the reattribution of justice.[98]

In contrast, the emergence of an anti-impunity movement most significantly active in European states has involved ensuring that powerful leaders responsible for mass atrocity violence do not use peace talks or quasi-judicial mechanisms (including the law of immunity) as a shield. Also relevant to the component parts of such technocratic legal tools is the role of the United States in offering diplomatic pressure and millions of dollars in funding.[99]

Assemblages of Justice Feelings: Saving the "Victim," Stopping the "Perpetrator"

The component parts of advancing anti-impunity discourses through the ICC are also relevant to the way that emotionally propelled justice discourses are being fueled. Building on the principle that no one is above the law, the new justice formations have involved particular checks on national power. Luis Moreno-Ocampo, the first ICC prosecutor, has commented on the importance and roles of courts: "People have to understand, before the ICC, the way to control crimes was to negotiate."[100] Now that the ICC exists, he explained, "some people were thinking the ICC could be like a new threat for force negotiations; one that could be taken away. This is not the ICC. The ICC is a judicial system."[101] Moreno-Ocampo has also sought to clarify a misconception concerning the role of the ICC in peace processes. "It's not us affecting the peace process. The criminals are affecting the peace process, because what they like to do is to use the negotiations to protect themselves."[102]

A number of key figures in the creation and development of technocratic legal theories in the International Criminal Law School also moved international law jurisprudence beyond earlier twentieth-century principles of state sovereignty.[103] One such figure was Antonio Cassese, who, as president of the ICTY and one of the architects of the doctrine of the criminal responsibility of the offender, documented what he saw as a fundamental moment of rupture in international law. In *International Criminal Law*, he argued for the expansion of criminal responsibility of an offender. To do this, he expanded the term "culpable negligence" (*culpa gravis*) to include unconscious negligence, to move international criminal law to the objective responsibility of an offender for strict liability. However, this also resulted in making individuals and not states sole legal subjects of criminal law. This, he argued, provided a sufficient legal basis for an interpretation of international criminal law that would not disregard the legal concept of state sovereignty.[104]

Cassese and other figures such as Judge Theodor Meron and Professor Cherif Bassiouni idealized international criminal law as capable of replacing state sovereignty. Cassese had been a critical figure in the creation of the ICTY and author of the Tadić decision that established the basis for individual criminal jurisdiction.[105] And Bassiouni was central in shaping the individualization of criminal responsibility. Known as the father of the ICC, he championed the driving of the ICC process forward. For Bassiouni, the "absence of the individual in international law" was an unfortunate development in the history of law. With precedents such as the Tadić decision, international law recognized individual criminal jurisdiction and shaped the formation of a corpus of international criminal law that combined human rights and humanitarian law with criminal law. With the already established moral force under which the notion of the individual "perpetrator" was rendered a subject of the law, and the shift to individuals as a core concern, the idea of the "victim" to be protected also emerged with a vengeance.

The international victims' rights movement took shape with great moral force. It was based on a parallel humanitarian regime guided by the law of war.[106] Like laws of acceptable justifications to engage in war that incorporated dimensions of democratization and political and social transformation, the law of war emerged alongside the legal protection of the "victim." The pressures of laissez-faire globalization affected the ways in which state sovereignty and state borders were being reconfigured. They also had implications for how domestic laws were reformulated through the incorporation of international treaties, and how national laws were reworked with the introduction of bilateral agreements and new regional conventions and formations.

Institutionalizing Compensatory Possibilities for "Victims" as Performative Acts

At the Nuremberg and Tokyo tribunals, as well as the ad hoc tribunals for the former Yugoslavia and Rwanda, the interests of survivors were to a large extent overlooked; their role was generally restricted to that of witnesses. However, as a result of the shift of the new governance architecture, there has been a growing movement, supported by a range of NGOs as well as some states, to recognize the role of international justice in providing not only retributive justice but also restorative justice by permitting survivors to participate in proceedings and receive reparations for the harms they have suffered.

In 1985, the UN General Assembly first adopted the Declaration of Basic Principles of Justice for Victims of Crime and Abuse of Power (the Victims' Declaration), which revolutionized the ordinary usage of the term *victim*. This declaration has been the cornerstone of legal rights for "victims" under international law. It established victims' rights in the criminal-justice process, including the right to access justice, to be treated with basic respect and dignity, to protection and assistance, and to reparation. The restorative dimension came further into play in 1991, when a compensation system for victims of war was created. In the aftermath of the Gulf War, the UN Security Council set up a commission to deal with the requests for compensation stemming from the occupation of Kuwait.

The Victims' Declaration contributed to laying the foundation for negotiations during ICC Preparatory Committee discussions about how *victim* should be defined. Interestingly, after extensive debates about whether legal entities could be included in the definition of the term, a compromise was reached in the Rules of Procedure and Evidence to establish that it may include organizations or institutions.[107] Despite this, the definition popularized by the ICC and the NGO Coalition for the ICC represents the consolidation of the notions of "victims," justice, and law. During the negotiations on the statute, emphasis was placed on ensuring that the core values of the court—to promote greater peace and security through accountability for crimes, as well as the rights and the dignity of the "victims"—would be respected.[108] This issue was crucial, given the clear recognition by states that the ICC should be not only retributive but also restorative.

In keeping with the rule of law momentum, the Rome Statute provides for the possibility of granting reparations to victims. In the negotiations that led to its formation, two principal institutions were conceptualized: the International Criminal Court and the Trust Fund for Victims (TFV). These two institutions were propelled by a ten-year campaign called "A Universal Court with Global Support." Through its goals of state enlistment through ratification and implementation of the Rome Statute, the signing of cooperation agreements and enhancement, and the recruitment of top ICC staff, the long-term campaign involved ongoing advocacy, networking, strategy building, lobbying, and the use of language that reproduced particular affective commitments to "victims everywhere" as the basis of their work. It was against this backdrop that the TFV was established in September 2002 by the Assembly of States Parties to complement the reparations functions of the court. Its mission was to provide advocacy and mechanisms for mobilizing physical, material, or psychological resources for individuals victimized by violence. Today the TFV is administered by the Registry but is independent from the ICC and is supervised by a board of directors. Articles 75 and 79 of the Rome Statute lay the foundation for this restorative, victim-centered element.[109]

The TFV, supported through court-ordered forfeitures and fines as well as voluntary contributions by states, has a two-pronged mandate. The first aspect is the provision of general assistance to survivors or communities of survivors in ICC situation countries. The second mandate involves the management and implementation of reparations for survivors. In a novel phenomenon in international criminal proceedings, Article 68(3) of the Rome Statute grants that victims of crimes under the jurisdiction of the court may also make their views and concerns heard during a trial. Accordingly, the Office of Public Counsel for Victims was established in 2005. As of July 2010, the office had represented approximately two thousand victims and filed approximately three hundred submissions in various proceedings before the court. The office has also assisted thirty external legal representatives in all situations and cases, and provided close to six hundred legal advisors to them.

The Victims' Rights Working Group was created in 1997 under the auspices of the NGO Coalition for the ICC in order to work with various survivors' representatives to help them participate in the proceedings or to inform them of judicial developments as they relate to their case. The Victims Participation and Reparations Section of the ICC's registry conducts regular assessments and evaluations of its work, and sees itself as committed to a reflective learning process as its staff implements the court's mandate in situation countries. The mission is communicated in a prevailing discourse of defending survivors and ending impunity through the rule of law. The centrality of survivors in the trust fund's work is enabled through the mobilization of ICC judicial proceedings.

Despite initial presumptions that the formation of the TFV signaled a revolutionary turn toward centering the oppressed, various stakeholders on the ground have come to rigorously debate whether international criminal trials should be subordinated to other justice-producing mechanisms available on the African continent, as I touched on in the introduction. Their arguments are broad and reflect concerns about the viability of the ICC and its ability to achieve justice, especially if driven by retributive motivations. While the ICC is essentially a punitive institution, the drafters of the Rome Statute and a significant civil-society lobby attempted to include elements of restorative justice that focus on social repair and reconciliation.[110] Yet various victims of violence, once enthusiastic about ICC adjudication, are also ambivalent about the extent to which the ICC is able to achieve the sort of justice real survivors imagine for themselves and their communities.[111] Two large questions emerge: (1) How are we to define whom the court is working for? (2) Has it been able to deliver on the expectations of justice for survivors?[112]

The inclusion of those victimized by violence as a key component of international trials has become one of the main organizing principles underlying the development of twenty-first-century international criminal justice. The limitations and tensions in practice have also become apparent. Accommodating the participation of survivors of extreme forms of physical, sexual, and psychological violence through the structure of trial proceedings and as beneficiaries of reparations through the TFV were heralded as significant achievements. Yet survivors' applications to participate in trials have at times been so voluminous that those involved in data management and registration systems have struggled to cope with the bureaucratic burden. And though the court's promise has been articulated in the name of survivors, many survivors of violence complain of the lack of proportionality between its institutional force and its ability to produce substantive and tangible reparation for those in ongoing need. While on one hand the discourse of victimhood has produced emotional sympathies, on the other hand the identification of certain violations has set the terms by which sympathetic protective action can take place, often limiting the possibilities to certain prescribed channels and outcomes.

Judge Christine van den Wyngaert of the ICC has described the lengthy and cumbersome process of survivor registration at the ICC as a terrain for contending with the aspirations of survivor inclusion and the difficulties of necessary exclusion.[113] She concluded that the "number of victims is becoming overwhelming. . . . The Court may soon reach the point where this individual case-by-case approach becomes unsustainable. It may well have to consider replacing individual applications with collective applications."[114] Judges have, since the start of ICC trials, been grappling with a way to balance considerations of restorative justice for survivors with expeditious and fair retributive justice. Indeed, a ruling by the judges of Trial Chamber V has led to the overhauling of survivors' participation and representation in the case against Uhuru Kenyatta, and is an example of the need for rethinking the ICC's restorative mandate.[115]

Despite the rhetoric, the nature in practice of retribution-driven judicial proceedings may at times deliver undesirable or even incomprehensible results where survivors are concerned. Due to a recharacterization of charges, or a change in the temporal scope of cases, it is possible that, from one day to the next, survivors may find themselves ineligible even for participation, let alone reparations. Organs of the ICC working with survivors or the legal representatives of survivors must deal with the challenges of communicating changing judicial decisions about who is considered a "victim" or whose changing status has caused new forms of exclusion. Competing demands continue to highlight the challenges as they relate to maintaining the equilibrium between the restorative mandate and the retributive criminal justice mandate of the ICC.

What we see from this tracing, in which the emergence of the anti-impunity movement led to a particular conception of individualized "victim" and "perpetrator," is that the increasing judicialization of postconflict transitions actually delimits the potential for deep and pervasive societal reparation. By analyzing the nature of violence being adjudicated in the first place, and linking it to historical processes that have organized subjects in particular ways, we see that the rise of prosecutorial justice has been part of a larger, complex set of histories tied to deeply felt attachments in the Global North to core ideas about society, law, the economy, the individual, and freedom. These attachments have been deployed strategically in the Global South and have been central to the development of a moral impetus around which the rule of law's anti-impunity movement has gained its force, ultimately shifting the justice terrain to a popularly articulated individualization of criminal responsibility. Ultimately, this move to individuating criminal responsibility in the name of "the victim" is also tied to the circulation of an aesthetic that is built on the moral fortitude of saving predominantly black and female bodies.

These aesthetics undergird international justice through a biopolitics of sentimentality in which it is not just an individual universal subject that is invoked in the international psychic but rather a raced, sexed figure that occupies the moral imagination.

As discussed in the introduction, the ordering of liberal legality is also built on an aesthetics of the "perpetrator" to be held accountable. This perpetrator figure, individualized and gendered as mostly male, provides the international imaginary with a sensory depiction within which notions of justice are nested. How did these black and brown bodies come to be seen as the prototypical "victim" and "perpetrator" in international rule of law circuits? As we shall see in the chapters that follow, the technologies of legal power that unfolded alongside the institutionalization of liberal legality did so through a moral call to individualize responsibility for violence that in most cases has its roots in histories of colonial plunder and structural inequality, economic restructuring, and the consequent absence of institutional alternatives in fledgling African postcolonies. These formations point to a moral aesthetics of the "victim" and the "perpetrator" whose sensory depictions appear illegible to liberal legality but are felt among those who identify with its racialized and nationalized aesthetics.

Making Sense of Liberal Legality and Its Sensory Depictions

In the international adjudication of mass atrocity crimes, liberal legalism substitutes collective responsibility for mass crimes with the individualization of criminal responsibility. We see this most clearly in the cases involving ICC indictments of African leaders—black, male, middle aged, powerful. These indictments of individuals being held criminally responsible are not simply to be read as unraced perpetrators. They present black and brown bodies whose presence involves the transmission of sensory impressions about race but whose imagery is often said to represent that violence. The public responses by defiant African leaders about the ICC as racist—as we saw in the introduction—is a statement about racialized embodiments and the emergent feelings that have followed related to its histories of injustice.

Despite its disavowal of subjective affects, the reality is that justice, expressed through liberal legality, relies on emotional affectivities in order to be established as seemingly legitimate. The central dilemma is the dialectic between the work of emotion and the way that emotional inscriptions play out through racial and gendered politics. Because of the incommensurabilities related to the exercise of international criminal justice, the reality of these justice formations is not adequately explained by Sikkink's "justice cascade," which imagines organic and widespread calls for prosecutorial justice as the drivers of its manifestation. Rather, as I have begun to show, the technocratic production of legal justice alongside emotive discourses and the regimes that propel them have combined to produce the tools through which law regulates possibility, and those possibilities in international justice domains are propelled through affective expressions. Thus, articulations of justice do not spread evenly across geographies of time and space. More often they reaffirm sites of inequality, in turn giving rise to novel contestations that mobilize new forms of emotional and conceptual expression.

What is the relevance of examining affective justice in these spaces of structural inequality? In these spaces we see the manifestation of biopolitical legality. This involves considering how the emergence of the African state was always a project of material extraction, economic opportunism, and political and legal impositions but also a project that reinforced particular aesthetic imaginaries for particular purposes. In chapter 2 I begin to take a closer look at the way that technocratic knowledge puts in place the conditions of possibility in which emotional expressions are regimented and fueled. As I will go on to show, sociocultural norms unfold through specific ways of talking, signaling, expressing reaction, or producing practices that enable new priorities to develop. Feelings about and perceptions of justice manifest moral codes that are expressed through particular emotional performances. Certain rhetorical strategies, such as affective transference, are used both to champion international justice formations, like the ICC, and to critique them. In the process, subjectivities and communities of affects arise and impact the work of affective justice.

CHAPTER 2

Founding Moments?

Shaping Publics through Sentimental Narratives

If affective embodiments and the working of reattribution reflect both subjective technocratic and political processes that shape and are shaped by various structuring fields of expression, then how do justice leaders, international lawyers, judges, bureaucrats, and members of various publics who are performing, observing, witnessing, and refusing legal encapsulation tap into prevailing emotional regimes and deploy sentiments that become institutionalized? And how do those emotional expressions become entrenched within institutions like the ICC, NGOs, and the African Union's regional courts, such as the African Court? How are they transferred within constituent publics—from person to person, leader to constituency—and deployed to make new sociohistorical narratives feasible? And, as Sara Ahmed asks, how do emotions align subjects with each other and against others?[1] This chapter explores the way that feelings of alliance and compassion are generated through political speeches and legal narratives that not only make various anti-impunity ICC and Pan-Africanist justice discourses real, but also constitute social alignments through which emotional regimes play out. I begin here with two brief examples to illustrate this process, and then delve more deeply to analyze the different contours of affect that both structure fields of expression and are conditioned by history and individual emotional responses. Taken together, they are transmitted through the production of feeling regimes, and through affective transference, a process felt bodily, their meanings travel and can become manifest through emotive practices.

In 1952 Jomo Kenyatta, the father of independent Kenya and of Uhuru Kenyatta, was arrested by the British colonial army following a state of emergency declared by the British administrators of colonial Kenya. Kenyatta had been indicted the year before, together with five others known as the Kapenguria Six—Achieng' Oneko, Bildad Kaggia, Fred Kubai, Kung'u Karumba, and Paul Ngei.[2] By April 1953, all six were incarcerated for their membership in and organization of the Mau Mau freedom fighters. Kenyatta denied the accusations but was convicted of what many believe were "trumped-up charges." He served six years as a political prisoner until 1960, when the demands for his release grew and native Kenyans gathered daily in the town square to protest the injustice. This mobilization succeeded, and Kenyatta was released. As the story goes, once released, Kenyatta led his people in petitioning for Kenya's independence from British colonial rule. When the first Kenyan elections were finally held in May 1963, Jomo Kenyatta was elected prime minister of the Kenyan African National Union, and it was in that context that he and his advisors negotiated the terms for Kenyan independence on December 12, 1963.

Approximately fifty years later, Jomo Kenyatta's son, Uhuru Kenyatta, became the president of the Republic of Kenya, and with his deputy presidential partner, William Ruto, established their landmark consolidation of two previously antagonistic political groups aligned along competing ethnic cleavages. This consolidation is related to the 2012 indictment of Uhuru Kenyatta and William Ruto by the ICC, which of course did not prevent them from winning the highest seats in government (a situation I explain in more detail in chapter 4). Their election campaign tapped into various emotional sensibilities related to anticolonial struggle and postcolonial Pan-Africanism in order to mobilize the sympathies of the Kenyan people. They did so by presenting the ICC's indictment of Uhuru Kenyatta as a historical continuity of Jomo Kenyatta's political struggle for independence against imperial rule. Kenyatta's popularly hailed 2013 Heroes' Day speech provides an example of postcolonial emotional regimes that celebrate the freedom fighter discourse deployed to cultivate emotional sympathies for Pan-African anticolonial struggles.

On October 20, 2013, Uhuru Kenyatta presided over his first Heroes' Day (known as Mashujaa Day in Swahili), a national public holiday to collectively honor all those who contributed to the struggle for Kenya's independence.[3] That day, Kenyatta's speech began with a characteristic unifying call to the ethnically divided nation and immediately highlighted the importance of celebrating the past. Upon establishing a sense of a shared political community that long struggled for independence from Europe, he went on to reinforce the aftereffects of colonialism and its impact on social and economic inequality. In an attempt to celebrate their independence journey, he highlighted the material and psychological consequences of the colonial project and its impact on their Kenyan forefathers:

> Fellow Kenyans, we are here to commemorate the sacrifice and heroism of many Kenyans whose vision and conviction won us freedom and sovereignty. Colonialism had stripped all Kenyans of their fundamental rights. They had no land, and were considered inferior in their own home. There was neither dignity nor freedom for Kenyans then. Our forefathers waged a struggle of conviction and principle, supported with no resources except the burning fire of humiliation and the indefeasible yearning for independence and respect.
>
> They were brave and noble. Many took up armed struggle in the forests, as others formed and led movements for the civil agitation for independence. The colonial reaction was repressive and brutal. Heroes were killed and imprisoned, while the rest were stigmatized and hunted down like animals. The cost of the struggle was painful, because the settlers did not consider Africans equal human beings worthy of rights.[4]

Kenyatta's narrative about the humiliation of Africans at the hands of colonial administrators and settlers, and the subsequent freedom struggles that ultimately led to Kenyan independence, set a particular emotional climate that formed the backdrop for his audience. He went on to describe how Africans suffered at the hands of colonialists and emerged victorious in their fight against those forces:

> This day marks the official beginning of the worst phase of colonialism, and the most harrowing period of our struggle for independence. The brutality our independence heroes underwent from twentieth October 1952 until the attainment of self-government ten years later defies imagination. It is the reason that we have reverently emblazoned our national flag with the red of their sacred blood. That is why our constitution states that, we the People honor those who heroically struggled to bring freedom and justice to our land. In history, Mashujaa Day is a day written in blood by the hand of our heroes.[5]

After discussing the "brutality" that their "independence heroes" endured, Kenyatta went on to liken his judicial indictment by the ICC to his father's indictment by the British colonial administration in Kenya, thereby connecting the brutality of the colonial past to contemporary international law. The audience—seasoned and acutely aware of Africa's history of colonial domination—was invited to share sentiments of horror about colonial injustice and make a symbolic connection to the other, current injustice: "Our forefathers rejected colonialism and imperial domination in their time. We must honor their legacy, and stay true to our heritage, by rejecting all forms of domination and manipulation in our time. Let us confront without flinching those external forces seeking to thwart our collective aspirations. They may be powerful and rich, but so were the colonialists. They may disrespect and even hate us; we have defeated their ilk before."[6]

When those who attended the event that day and others who watched it on television described their interpretation of the opening of the speech, time and time again they told us that Kenyatta's references to external (read colonial) domination reflect colonial defiance at work. Their reaction reflects the way that popular feelings about Kenyan postcolonial futures are bound up in a particular form of rejection of colonial degradation. What we see is that these sentiments are made real as a result of particular a priori events that shape what the present and future become.

Through the use of partial invocations, Kenyatta succeeds in getting his audience to connect contemporary justice to selective histories of colonial sham trials. The logic is that the political histories of subordination that created Kenya as a colony were the same histories that led Uhuru Kenyatta to a subordinate place in the realm of international justice and politics. These historical logics highlighted the way that morally coherent causalities can be mobilized to produce moral sentiments that celebrate the fetishized victim-survivor. And through the deployment of certain linguistic tools, political speech acts and the sentiments that they conjure articulate partial concepts while still communicating full ideas. In other words, the existence of the violation is so commonly understood that it is unnecessary to spell out. Rather, the listener is made to call on his or her own sense of inequality in order to fill the gaps.

The forms of sentimental emotions involved in such postcolonial justice discourses represent what Russian philosopher Mikhail Bakhtin calls "dialogic" to refer to the ways that contemporary imaginaries are continually informed by past conceptions.[7] This approach to the social retelling of relevant events in daily life can help us make sense of how emotive expressions about the colonial past, as temporally shaped manifestations of social reality, guide how feelings of injustice are understood and attributed through narrative strategies. In this particular example, emotional regimes shape emotional climates through passionate utterances and narratives about stigmatization. As social constructions, these collective feelings reflect individual perceptions but are actually manifestations of how discourses produce groups and how groups of people embody lived emotions. What we see is that through those experiences, they are positioned for the collective effects of the transference of those feelings to the social body. As a product of sociocollective emotions generated through social interactions, emotional climates reflect social norms that establish how people feel or ought to feel and constitute the affective terrain within which public emotions operate.[8]

The study of emotion presumes that such feelings are grounded in particular socio-moral orders expressed through responses that are deemed ordinary. For example, where stigma makes possible the terms for regulating what is acceptable in relation to what is abhorrent, the imagery and discursive concepts that are invoked produce the terms for shared collective sentiments. President Kenyatta's reference to the ordinary aspirations in Kenyan dreams of freedom from "imperial domination" was juxtaposed with his suggestion that there were "external forces seeking to thwart [their] collective aspirations." The political reality of colonial trials (often seen popularly as sham trials) and their parallel with Uhuru Kenyatta's indictment by the ICC was conjured to produce a key moment of linkage. As he affirmed, "They may be powerful and rich, but so were the colonialists." In this way, Kenyatta attributed the same colonial armature of subjugation to the ICC.[9] This did not involve an explicit reference to the ICC. There was no need to name it. Rather, the point was sharpened with the profound declaration, "We have defeated their ilk before," referring to external judicial bodies such as the ICC in which the colonial is tied to the international (read: European). Invoking the word *ilk* to refer to a type or kind of imperialist, Kenyatta symbolically equated the colonial subordination of black Africans under British imperialism to the known fact that, to date, the ICC has only indicted Africans. His conclusion: Kenya's Mau Mau revolutionaries used constitutionalism to defeat their oppressors, and so will Kenya's contemporary democratic vanguard.

By comparing his own ICC indictment to the arrest and political conviction of his father some fifty years earlier, Uhuru Kenyatta attempted to make personal meaning out of historical and contemporary realities through a cultural template of subordination and an emotional process known in psychoanalysis as transference.[10] Transference represents the common ascription of one person's emotion to another, or to an object. For Freud, it was connected to the process of projecting unresolved issues in one's primary kinship relationships onto others. I use *transference* here to link intersubjective cultural fields to show how it is used in metacontexts such as crowds and large audiences.

Affective transference, as an intersubjective process fueled by emotional regimes, is not only employed by those protesting the presence of the ICC in Africa. We also see it in the rhetorical practices of those engaged in the anti-impunity rule of law movement, such as the members of the ICC's Office of the Prosecutor (OTP). Key to this analysis is the understanding that once those narratives are articulated within their own component parts where they are seen as being socially legitimate, they have the power to mobilize sentiments that are shared by others and create new enmeshed alignments in that process.

In the ICC's early days, the court gained popular traction as a symbol of protection for victims and as a means of ending impunity. The domain of state authority, which had (since the Peace of Westphalia in 1648) long dominated approaches to sovereignty, began to topple. Theories of a state's responsibility to its citizens transformed with the emergence of a new moral order, which took shape with the emergence of the responsibility to protect, or R2P, doctrine, as explained in chapter 1.

Members of the OTP, such as Shamiso Mbizvo, remind us that the court was set up on behalf of the "international community to intervene when the nation-state fails." As she suggested in a keynote speech at a conference on the ICC and Africa in The Hague in May 2014:

> The final text of the Rome Statute of the International Criminal Court is the culmination of almost a hundred years of hard work, unyielding determination, and stubborn hope on the part of people all over the world, from many walks of life, who have all shared the vision of an independent, permanent International Criminal Court. The ICC exists to hear the voices of victims of the most atrocious crimes, when their cries fall on deaf ears. It is a Court that was set up to intervene on behalf of the most vulnerable, when their own governments fail to hold their abusers accountable.[11]

Mbizvo's discussion of the existence of the ICC as a culmination of "almost a hundred years of hard work" in order to establish a mechanism to intervene on behalf of the "most vulnerable" suggests a historical continuity over a longer period of time than the mid-1990s, when international law was instrumentalized morally and politically. Like Kenyatta's symbolic linkages, she described the contemporary ICC's formation metaphorically as a one-hundred-year road to Rome culminating in the formation of the Rome Statute for the ICC. This is a sentimental narrative construction that tells a celebratory story about a long and sustained road to justice that often involves efforts to end the impunity of a perpetrator and to rescue a victim through international legality. But when the ICC is examined dialogically, it becomes clear that even though the formation of the Rome Statute for the ICC was shaped by a range of very limited attempts to hold postwar leaders and commanders responsible for war crimes, there was also an absence or suspension of justice mechanisms in various colonies in the Global South.[12]

This chapter reveals the gaps in the production of particular founding narratives and their imbrication in legal and historical formulations. We see how emotions are deployed through sentimental rejections of the Rome Statute narrative to replace it, through affective transference, with new originary narratives that are used to attribute different meanings of justice. Kenyatta's linguistic strategies highlight the emotional politics of social protest that are aestheticized through postcolonial imaginaries of injustice. Illustrating the effectiveness of the emotional architectures he built through his particular rhetorical practices, informants reported that these narratives were inspired by Africa's colonial history and the subsequent objection that various Pan-Africanists have to Western dominance. The embodiment of such imaginaries generates a response to domination by rearticulating new histories that fold into the present.

Like Kenyatta's dialogism framed in relation to continuous indictments by foreign bodies, Shamiso Mbizvo's articulation of the histories that led to the formation of ICC justice is an example of a related set of emotional regimes underway. In this case it serves another set of politics. In both examples, the retelling of their public histories invented links of significance to present morally provocative sentiments around which to mobilize action. In these cases, the sentimental invocations pointed to many things—the perpetrator of violence to be held accountable, or the colonial perpetrators who were never held accountable, or the degradation and fortitude of those whose struggles for justice have been pivotal. All of the sentimental invocations stigmatized European colonial injustices to preclude particular readings of contemporary violence without attention to the roots of inequality. Ultimately, what we see in these examples is the transmission of sentiments of saving and protecting, as well as expressions of African redemption from injustice, for they are key to the way that references to particular types of violence work in liberal democratic speech making. The goal is to show how public speech making is critical to how affects are institutionalized in international rule of law assemblages and how political publics are produced in that process.

The Road to Rome

Today, the popular contemporary story of the birth of the Rome Statute and its judicial legitimacy is based on a particular history of the ICC that sets the beginning of the road to Rome in the early nineteenth century. That story, as told by various representatives of the ICC, often begins with the 1872 founding of the International Committee of the Red Cross, when a permanent court was proposed to respond to the crimes of the Franco-Prussian War. And if those narrative origins are not emphasized, the attempt of the 1919 Treaty of Versailles to try German war crimes of World War I or the 1948 Convention on the Prevention and Punishment of the Crime of Genocide are seen as key to the founding history of the court.

In this story, World War I is seen as contributing to the launching of the first global effort to use international and domestic criminal jurisdiction to address international crimes. Following the war, the Allied and Associated Powers (i.e., Great Britain, France, Russia, and the United States) convened the Commission on the Responsibility of the Authors of the War and on the Enforcement of Penalties to inquire into culpable conduct by the Central Powers (i.e., Germany, Austria, Hungary, Bulgaria, and the Ottoman Empire). The commission was charged with considering the feasibility of asserting criminal jurisdiction over particular individuals, "however highly placed," accused of committing breaches.[13] Objectors to this approach, led by a predominantly American delegation, claimed that if heads of state and other state actors were held liable for collective actions, state sovereignty would be diminished.[14] They also took issue with the reality that no precedent existed in law for such an approach.[15]

In 1919, the commission presented to the Paris Peace Conference its final report on which crimes should be prosecuted before an international high tribunal composed of representatives of the Allied Powers, or before national tribunals.[16] The United States advanced four fundamental objections to this approach, among them that to prosecute a head of state outside of his national jurisdiction would violate the basic precepts and privileges of sovereignty.[17] From here, the potential liability for German and Ottoman defendants proceeded down separate paths.

The Treaty of Versailles ended the war with Germany in 1919 and required it to accept full responsibility for causing the war, make territorial concessions, and pay reparations.[18] It was Article 227 that proposed the establishment of an international tribunal composed of representatives from the United States, Great Britain, France, Italy, and Japan to try the former German emperor, Kaiser Wilhelm II.[19] By the time the Versailles treaty had entered into force, the kaiser had fled to the Netherlands, which refused to extradite him for trial.[20] Article 227 never came to fruition, and the Allies never enforced any other penal provisions of the treaty.[21] In the end, only a few prosecutions took place in domestic courts in Germany, and those who were prosecuted received disproportionately low sentences or were acquitted.[22]

Following World War I, a number of policy makers and lawyers, often described as constituting the international community, took action to build institutions to settle international disputes. The League of Nations announced a commitment to safeguard the peace of nations without resorting to war and in 1920 recommended the creation of a permanent international criminal court.[23] The proposal was rejected as premature; instead, the Permanent Court of International Justice, the precursor to the International Court of Justice, was established with civil jurisdiction over states.[24] Following that narrative trajectory, the most critical period in the development of modern international criminal law (ICL) occurred in the period following World War II. Two international tribunals were established for adjudicating international crimes that occurred during the war: the International Military Tribunal for the Trial of German Major War Criminals (the Nuremberg Tribunal) and the International Military Tribunal for the Far East (the Tokyo Tribunal).

The Nuremberg Tribunal was established through the London Agreement of August 8, 1945, between the four victorious Allied Powers: France, the Soviet Union, the United Kingdom, and the United States.[25] The tribunal convened from November 20, 1945, to October 1, 1946, during which time it heard the matters of twenty-one Nazi defendants.[26] The Tokyo Tribunal was, by contrast, established by a special proclamation issued by the Supreme Allied Commander of the Far East, US General Douglas MacArthur, with the agreement of the Allied Powers.[27] The Tokyo Tribunal convened from May 3, 1946, to November 12, 1948, and was heavily influenced by the United States, with prosecutions led by a single American chief of counsel chosen by MacArthur (with associate counsel from the Allied Powers).[28] In addition to these two tribunals, hundreds of trials occurred before military and civilian tribunals in various locales in the zones of occupation of the victorious powers.[29]

Many scholars of international law argue that it is difficult to overstate the significance of the post–World War II period to the field of international criminal law. They insist that "these legal proceedings established many core principles of the field."[30] Indeed, the establishment of a mechanism in which high-ranking state officials could be held individually criminally responsible for international crimes created a set of discourses that were profoundly powerful.[31] Many scholars have shown that the Nuremberg and Tokyo tribunals made explicit the commitment to holding various officials responsible for their orders to lower-ranking officers to facilitate or directly perpetrate violence. The argument that is often made is that by rejecting the basis for both state sovereignty and discarding principles of immunity through a movement that insists on the irrelevance of official capacity, this post–World War II movement certainly produced a few examples where those culpable for mass crimes were held criminally accountable.[32] However, as is well documented in the literature, for every instance in which European sovereign heads of state were held responsible for violent mass crimes in Europe and South America, there were a plethora of other situations where this was not the case. While the Nuremberg example provides a mechanism for understanding particular instances of criminal liability of commanders, British or Dutch or Spanish imperial forces, for example, engaged in gross violations with impunity.[33] Significant populations involved in self-determination or independence struggles in the Caribbean, Latin America, and Africa, and indigenous and First Nations peoples, were arrested, indicted, and subjected to violence. Yet, if we presume that "international" refers to a wide range of countries and populations, then the absence of the criminal prosecution of former colonial leaders in places like England or even France during twentieth-century independence struggles calls into question the often-told narratives about the trend toward criminal prosecutions.

The recent history that the OTP and many others within the field of international criminal justice call the road to Rome is one in which the immediate post–World War II period witnessed the United Nations emerging from its predecessor, the League of Nations. This was followed by the emergence of an international human rights regime that led to the drafting of the Universal Declaration of Human Rights, the International Covenant on Civil and Political Rights, and the International Covenant on Economic, Social, and Cultural Rights. The codification of ICL continued with the development of the 1948 Convention on the Prevention and Punishment of the Crime of Genocide and the four Geneva Conventions of 1949.[34] And in 1947, the UN General Assembly requested that the International Law Commission (ILC) study the possibility of establishing an international judicial body for crimes such as genocide, war crimes, and crimes against humanity.[35] As the story is told, in the early 1950s the ILC was invited to assess the interest, thus the potential, for establishing a permanent international judicial institution. Codifying the

Nuremberg and Tokyo principles into a Draft Code of Offenses against the Peace and Security of Mankind would provide the subject matter jurisdiction for the proposed tribunal.[36] But it did this with numerous stops and starts, dealing with pressure to abandon it during the Cold War and over various ideological and political disagreements over the type of crimes that would be under the subject matter jurisdiction of such an institution.

In the early 1990s, a range of parallel developments unfolded. The story told is that at the prompting of Trinidad and Tobago and with an emphasis on transnational crimes like drug trafficking and money laundering, the General Assembly once again prompted the ILC to draft a statute for a permanent international criminal court.[37] This took shape alongside an initiative by Trinidad and Tobago to make a concerted effort to address various transnational crimes such as drug trafficking and money laundering.[38] Also during this period, Resolution 780 was adopted on October 6, 1992, by the UNSC to establish a commission of experts to document violations of international law.[39] In response to the commission's recommendation, as well as to calls from a wide spectrum of international actors, on May 25, 1993, the UNSC unanimously adopted Resolution 827 to create the International Criminal Tribunal for Yugoslavia, an international tribunal to prosecute those responsible for crimes committed in the former Yugoslavia since 1991.[40] The following year, the genocide in Rwanda led to the establishment of the International Criminal Tribunal for Rwanda.[41]

Additional ad hoc tribunals were later established (out of the UNSC) to respond to crimes committed in Sierra Leone, East Timor, Lebanon, and Cambodia. The ILC completed a draft statute in 1994 that formed the basis for consideration by the Ad Hoc Committee on the Establishment of an International Criminal Court and then a Preparatory Committee on the Establishment of an International Criminal Court.[42] And while this popular trajectory was seen by many in the growing rule of law movement as a positive development, the ILC's project and the subsequent General Assembly deliberations led to the consolidation of the UN's ICL assemblages, resulting in the formation of the ICC.

On July 17, 1998, 120 of the world's states came together to complete the negotiation for the adopted text of the Rome Statute for the eventual establishment of the ICC. By 2002, the Rome Statute came into force and was celebrated with a profoundly historical century-old origin story. Yet even some of international criminal law's juridical architects, such as Antonio Cassese and Cherif Bassouni, never accepted—empirically, legally, and normatively—the dominant road to Rome narrative, because they understood that up until 1993 such an institution was not enough to destabilize the modern legal concept of sovereignty. The story that is often left out of the road to Rome trajectory is the narrative that highlights the way that the moral responsibility to protect those victimized by violence led to the viability of the ad hoc tribunals and eventually the ICC. Also relevant is the reality that the early innovators who attended the conference in Rome and participated in the early negotiations that led to the eventual treaty often recognize each other as founding mothers and fathers of the statute, invoking familial relationships through which to establish propriety and recognize its originary prestige. From Nuremberg narratives to Tokyo to Rome to Kampala, these kinship descriptions of first, second, and third generations committed to ending impunity for victims and stopping perpetrators continue to pervade its discourses. Insistence that never again will the world allow impunity to soar without recourse remains at the heart of the anti-impunity movement. These sentiments are what make affective justice a critical domain for the study of the embodied feelings that propel justice making. This is very different from the linear story above and illustrates the process of reattribution at work in this example and throughout the book.

In Nuremberg and Tokyo, the reality of defeat in war led to the setting of the conditions for prosecutorial justice. As Mahmood Mamdani has helped to clarify, the hidden prerequisites for trial, in all these cases, were (1) a war, that was (2) won decisively by one side, and to which one might add (3) the historical institution of "unconditional surrender," which includes the concession of sovereign power.[43] By contrast, in the African situations that the ICC has taken up, very different conditions led to the court's reach. The contemporary protection and invocation of justice for victims were related to the inability of African states to use decolonization to move toward new frontiers that would disrupt spheres of inequality, ethnic patronage, and poverty that prevailed in the post-1960 independence period.

The Road from Rwanda, Not Nuremberg

Violence in the former Yugoslavia and then Rwanda, Liberia, and Sierra Leone led to the formation of new judicial institutions that also contributed to a new set of discourses about the ICC. These further reinforced the emotional contours of international law. From Kenya to South Africa, Namibia to Mozambique, Zimbabwe to Algeria, independence negotiations from the late 1950s to the mid-1990s were brokered without attention to criminal prosecutions of former colonial powers. Even as various African leaders were strategically optimistic about the potential of using international justice in their newly independent states, they also knew that unless the roots of inequality were addressed, violence would remain a mode for managing law's failures.

The postwar momentum to develop permanent ICL institutions resulted in the criminalization of certain forms of conduct, the establishment of particular types of jurisdiction, and the individualization of criminal responsibility in which particular members states and the UN, as stakeholders in criminal justice, became engaged in advocacy to use criminal justice to address mass atrocity violence. However, when various African advocates decried the timing of such forms of institutionalization, they often commiserated that when international criminal justice was needed to intervene in colonial and post-1990s periods, there were no judicial institutions available to them. The absence of international institutions to intervene in wide-scale violence in places like South Africa, for example, was seen by many of those concerned with the structural inequality of justice as reflecting the same architecture that produced the Treaty of Rome. From 1948 to 1990, apartheid in South Africa was an international crime without an international criminal court to prosecute it. However, after the UN General Assembly classified it as a crime against humanity in 1966, the Organisation of African Unity (OAU) attempted to lobby for the establishment of an international penal court in the 1970s to prosecute the crime.[44] Initially, its stakeholders had hoped that they could establish a criminal chamber through the African Charter of Human Rights, but they abandoned this when the UN Security Council affirmed in 1984 that apartheid was a crime. This opened up the possibility of establishing in the late 1980s a UN international penal court in order to prosecute various apartheid crimes on the basis of universal jurisdiction. But the reality was that in order to pursue apartheid as a crime, national states had to enact legislation to prosecute individuals through universal jurisdiction.[45]

When the Rome Statute crimes were negotiated, apartheid offenses were eventually dropped as a core standalone crime. Instead, apartheid was collapsed into crimes against humanity and subject to a post-2002 temporal jurisdiction. This meant that the period of brutal domination of South African or Kenyan natives was beyond the temporal reach of the court. Instead, the international rule of law movement took hold of post–civil rights judicial agendas propelled by various agents of change in the US, Europe, and Australia. And, as the story is often told, the late 1980s and early 1990s led to the establishment of new judicial institutions that dealt with a range of crimes in which criminal responsibility was narrowly tailored to the present and the future goals of ending impunity. The irony is that when African stakeholders needed prosecutorial justice against colonial domination, international law could not be mobilized to provide viable solutions because of the temporal framing. And although African state brokers participated to varying degrees during the Treaty of Rome negotiations, and even as the law was deployed to establish African independence and membership in the newly changing world order, they were well aware that there were limits to its use as a tool for justice against economic plunder in Africa.[46]

State actors that were actively engaged in the ICC's success, such as England, the Netherlands, Spain, and Portugal, came to be seen by various African state actors as engaging in international lawmaking both as an instrument of historical subjugation and as a tool for social change. Kenyan history and memory of native subjugation provides a vivid example of this relationship. It shows that even as African states signed on to the Rome Statute in response to the demands of new democratic forms of constitutionalism, for a range of leaders and their publics in the Global South, post–Cold War democracy has an internal tension. Structural violence was written out of the ICC's social history, which the narratives reflected. As discussed in chapter 1, African states were often persuaded to ratify the Rome Statute for the ICC by institutions like the World Bank, the International Monetary Fund, the European Union, and various NGOs funded by northern governments or philanthropists.[47] Instead, the ICC emerged as a mechanism for protecting other types of "victims"—of African postcolonial violence—while the prosecution of northern perpetrators, such as those states that were at war in Iraq and Afghanistan, were for some in the North seen as unthinkable. This is because the violence in these contexts was either protected by particular state's nonsubmission to the jurisdiction of the Rome Statute, like the United States, or because between 2002 and 2017 the crime of aggression was not yet operationalized and therefore not justiciable. And with the revision to the crime of aggression, states that were parties to the Rome Statute but did not want to submit to the amendment were able to register a reservation. The example is telling.

At the time of entry into force of the Rome Statue in 2002, Article 5(1) included the jurisdiction of the court over four crimes: (1) genocide; (2) crimes against humanity; (3) war crimes; and (4) aggression. However, Article 5(2) stated that the court will activate jurisdiction over the crime of aggression only after a definition of the crime and the conditions for such jurisdiction are established.[48] The Kampala Review Conference in 2010 fulfilled this mandate, and over thirty state parties ratified the provisions for the amendment of the original text to include the agreed-upon definition and conditions for jurisdiction.[49] The sixteenth session of the Assembly of States Parties in December 2017 decided on the activation of the jurisdiction of the court over the crime of aggression, establishing it in Resolution ICC-ASP/16/Res.5 by consensus on December 14, 2017.[50] However, the assembly's resolution explicitly called for it to "enter into force for those States Parties that have accepted the amendments one year after the deposit of their instruments of ratification or acceptance and that in the case of a State referral or *proprio motu* investigation the Court shall not exercise its jurisdiction regarding a crime of aggression when committed by a national or on the territory of a State Party that has not ratified or accepted these amendments."[51] Many describe this ICC resolution as reflecting a compromised position between the majority of the state parties on one side and a small group of northern countries on the other (Britain, France, Canada, Japan, and Norway). According to our documentation of the negotiations, initially these countries had been calling for further clarity on how the amendments in Kampala would be interpreted. As the interpretation of the terms for the crime of aggression became clearer, they advocated for an opt-out alternative in which they could still remain as parties to the Rome Statute but register a reservation for the crime of aggression.[52] The result was the brokering of the crime of aggression with limited jurisdiction in which the crime would only apply to those who ratified the Kampala agreement (thirty-five states at the time of this analysis), thus submitting to the subject matter jurisdiction under the crime of aggression.[53]

Following the December 2017 Assembly of States Parties, the narrative that circulated among significant numbers of African state representatives was that, once again, northern countries had found a way to create exceptions to the universal application of justice. During the 2018 African Union Summit that I attended the following month, on the heels of the ICC's Assembly of States Parties meeting, various narrative explanations and expressions of anger circulated about ICC states parties that had not ratified the Kampala amendment exercising what some have called de facto immunity.[54] In other words, and except in the case of UNSC referrals, the stories that circulated clarified what they saw as the injustice: by not adopting the amendment and allowing for reservations, predominantly European and Asian states were seen as being able to shield themselves from the subject matter jurisdiction of the crime of aggression.[55] The ability to opt in and opt out and apply the law at will prevailed in their angry discussions about the ICC pursuing only African cases—or, as I've heard many times, "the ICC being put in place to shield the West and pursue the rest."[56]

Given these feelings of structural inequality, documenting the persistence of these ironies makes it all the more important to examine how global power becomes manifest in particular international institutional forms and how structures of inequality are not only felt but expressed and circulate through particular narrative modes. We see this through the sentimental foundations of Kenyatta and others' anti-ICC protest speech or the seductions of the OTP's celebration of judicial possibility, and it explains how and why such feeling regimes circulate and are at times taken up uncritically, even as other critiques of the African postcolonial state project are launched. These complex affects that are embodied and manifest through particular emotional regimes matter because they influence the way people understand the rule of law in the contemporary period, and thus how people's perceptions of law's inequality (or promise) drive public engagement.

As I show here, these seductions do not work through preestablished sentimental formulations; rather, it is through affective transference that people deploy affects and consolidate them with narratives of power. Histories of law and its perceived legitimacy or illegitimacy are actively created within regimes of meaning and require work to sustain their seductions as rational.[57] These narrative tropes are often sufficient, then, to provoke actionable results.

Feelings of anger, resentment, and the victory of the survivor are made real in such anti-impunity circles not through their exacting historical equivalences but through an emotional discourse of the "victim to be saved" that works to align like-minded participants. As one interlocutor following Mbizvo's speech commented, "I may not have agreed with her rendition of the history, but she's right. 'Victims' need us to carry the torch for our generation." Or as another insisted, "For me, it didn't matter whether I agreed with her; in some ways I didn't because her rendition of ICC history seemed flawed. But her speech made me feel victorious all over—all over my body. We all wanted to be part of the movement that she described. We wanted to be counted."

Similarly, in reflecting on Kenyatta's speech in Nairobi, one attendee shared the following: "I'm not a supporter of Kenyatta, but when he gave that speech I felt something; there was something inside of me that tingled, that wanted to cry, that felt robbed and depressed. That feeling brought us together because we all shared that unfortunate [colonial] past."

These comments suggest that the intensity of bodily feeling and its connection to particular sentiments perform sentimental work that can constitute groups, through what Émile Durkheim referred to as "collective effervescence," the simultaneous sharing of thoughts and actions that excite individuals and, in so doing, can lead to group unification.[58] These processes are social but are also emotional and affective. The bodily sensations that people describe are connected to their feelings of shared agreement, their sense of victory or anger from historical conditions of dispossession, and are key to making sense of the emotional manifestations in the afterlife of the law. They call on us to ask hard questions that explain why significant numbers of leaders, academics, members of civil society, and policy makers who may have formerly supported the ICC's potential have since advocated withdrawing from its jurisdiction and vice versa; why some (such as various members of civil society groups in African cities) who were suspicious of the ICC have joined the rule of law anti-impunity movement because they lost faith in their leaders. These shifts in emotional attachments are as elusive as they may be real, but they are key to understanding how shared emotional responses help form alliances— even if momentary.

Seeing law through the way that public utterances retell its history of relevance illuminates the connection between affects and political engagement and raises questions about what contemporary international criminal law really is, within what terrain it has operated, and what it can do given the political constraints within which it exists. Thus, a deeper reflection on the speeches delivered by Mbizvo and Kenyatta to their respective audiences can shed light on how people's relationship to the law is tied to the emergence of contemporary socio-moral orders through which social formations are constituted and disaggregated and emotional climates regulated.

Moral orders operate within knowledge regimes that are propelled by the justice imaginaries that I go on to explore in this book. By discursively representing these figures as moral objects of compassion and retribution, some people engaged in what Thomas Laqueur has called "sympathetic passions," which he describes as bridging compassion and action.[59] These sympathetic passions or emotional calls for action shape the sentiments that its advocates deploy. As a way of defining justice through the production of emotional affinities, the imbrication of legal encapsulation on contemporary rule of law formations has led to particular justice imaginaries with affective valences and ordering logics. And yet, tracing assemblages of affects involves tracing affects in nonlinear ways—not from cause to effect but in relation to courses of events and their materialities, socialities, and aesthetics. This involves thinking about how a standing ovation at a public talk or a loud and unified roar in a crowd during a political speech crystallizes and solidify stories or events. What we see is that certain historical lineages articulated through affective transference in public talks become feasible, thinkable, and acceptable because of the way justice is articulated. They set tones for emotional climates and shape existing fields of justice. Through these processes of public symbolic deployments and emotional community formation, we see how affective transference works—not through knowable emotion but through the constitution of emotional camps that are regimented in particular ways.

Legal encapsulation reinforces these discursive practices. As a product of technocratic knowledge applied to various campaigns for promoting justice, it is seen by those whose feeling regimes are constituted through the anti-impunity movement as essential for protecting those victimized by violence and holding perpetrators accountable. The constructed figures—"the victim" and "the perpetrator"—are key component parts of anti-impunity assemblages as they provide the aesthetic icons through which technocratic legal practices can be instrumentalized.

Yet even with these component parts, attempts to counter prevailing justice narratives abound in the contemporary period. They emerge as narratives that contravene other stories and reflect struggles over the knowledge production through which necessary alignments take shape. This process of alignment is how reattribution gains its power. For, as a process of resignification, it is shaped by controversies around meaning making and contestations around the power to enforce those meanings. But as we shall see below, as affects that are operationalized with others, the process of social transference can be known not through actual experiences, but through the way that sociopolitical consciousness can be assessed by how subjects articulate justice feelings as echoing their past experiences. These descriptions set in motion potential futures while also tapping into past experiences of injustice.

Affective Transference and the Remaking of History

Shamisu Mbizvo's audience included a room full of approximately seventy-five scholars of international law, human rights law, and the literature and anthropology of law, as well as a range of historians of Africa and the West who were committed to various ways of studying international law's impact on and relationship to Africa. Immediately following her speech, she received a standing ovation, even from colleagues who remained skeptical about the court's work. Uhuru Kenyatta's speech was delivered to an outdoor assembly of thousands committed to new possibilities for justice through the coalition parties. In both cases, the narratives about international law were framed in relation to different historical formations. For both speakers, the past was interwoven with the present to make the contemporary period meaningful.

Like Kenyatta's narrative, Mbizvo's retelling of the ICC's past reflected morally coherent explanations concerning the making of the Rome Statute. The moral mission that led to the establishment of the contemporary rule of law movement was tied to its judicial inheritance—the protection of victims as the basis of its pursuit of judicial accountability. In both speeches, messages about interrelationships between the past and the present responded to various past events and made the present meaningful. Yet the viability of those attempts to link past and present is more about the speaker's ability to use affective transference to communicate sentiments that are meaningful to others than they are about real modalities of interconnection or the ascription of stigma.

To critique international criminal institutions, Kenyatta identified an ongoing violation to foreground a stigma that demarcates what is or is not acceptable. He then forged a community of survivors by using language that invokes Kenyan citizens as beneficiaries of yesterday's freedom fighters. From the opening, in which the "sacrifice and heroism of many Kenyans . . . won us freedom and sovereignty," to his later invocations of "our forefather" in order to index kinship, we see attempts to constitute a community. Once senses of community were constructed, Kenyatta reconciled the substantively disjunctural historical narratives. He decentered the violence of the colonial project and brought it into relevance with the ICC's African trials. By grounding his intervention in Kenya's history of colonial violence and the popular perception of colonial sham trials, Kenyatta engaged in the transmission of feelings of resentment—from one person to another, from a leader to his constituency.[60] Here transmission is possible through a colloquial knowledge about the colonial past and its related subjugation that is embodied in preexisting responses to loss, sham trials, and experiences of poverty. Suggestions about Africa's place in an unequal past conjure sentiments that produce parallels with the contemporary world order where feelings of anger from past inequality prevail.

Affective transference is possible with the invocation to celebrate the survivors of that inequality. The reference to "their ilk" highlights how Kenyatta is, in turn, stigmatizing colonial institutions whose continuities contribute to feelings of anger at play. Transference was possible and effective because the histories of colonial violence and its related dispositions were decontextualized from their earlier historical logic and recontextualized into contemporary realities.[61] Through the realization of the relevance of the past to the present, members of the public gained an opportunity to constitute alliances with each other. The message was contingent on knowledge about colonialism, the relegation of colonial trials to sham trials, and African subordination, which were critical to the connections that audience members had to make. It was the decontextualization and recontextualization that characterized the magnetism of the emotional regimes being shaped, that oriented the way Kenyatta's message was received. The achievement of transference allowed the sympathetic listener to create mutually linked freedom fighters and revolutionaries out of both Jomo and Uhuru Kenyatta.

Throughout Kenyatta's speech, and in response to his passionate utterances, the audience applauded, and large numbers shouted for more. When he finished, their applause continued, almost uncontrollably. Affective transference happened through the rhetorical frenzies elicited in the speeches. Passing from person to person and group to group, the forms of collective effervescence created what Margaret Wetherell refers to as pulses of energetic relations.[62] By engaging vociferously with the rhetorical link ("their ilk") between Kenyatta's fight against the ICC and the larger anti-imperial struggles over the past century, the audience that was there that day confirmed the effectiveness of the conjuncture of like-minded feeling expressions with performative displays of agreement.

Eight out of ten of the people we polled confirmed that they were Kenyatta-Ruto supporters. They described the moment as one where "the people spoke," or where "Kenyatta and Kenya could be vindicated." This was in keeping with the top-trending hashtag of 2012, #KenyaDecides. Said one woman to our question about the relevance of colonialism to this moment: "It's true that colonial rule happened long ago but it is relevant today. My family would not be poor and without land if it weren't for the British. Kenyatta can reverse that—Kenya Decides!"

Another agreed and insisted, "Kenyatta is not to be blamed. He defended his people. He was like Jesus. And like Jesus, he delivered."

Through the deployment of certain linguistic tools, the political speech act and the sentiments that it conjured reflected people's application of partial concepts while still communicating full ideas about heroism, retribution of colonial wrongs, and hopes of reconciliation. The violations present with the invocation of colonialism and the historical use of colonial law to oppress the Mau Mau fighters were so commonly understood that it was unnecessary for

Kenyatta to spell them out. Rather, the listener was made to call on his or her own sense of inequality in order to fill the gaps.

The use of the unsayable is powerful because as a rhetorical strategy in justice circles in Kenya around ICC issues, it operates within particular feeling regimes that shape alliances. What it enabled out of the experience of affirmations on that Hero's Day was an embodied sense of "Tuko Pamoja"—meaning "we are together." The sense of history shaping the present emerged from senses of displacement and deliverance. Accordingly, past subordination becomes a reflection of itself in the present. This is where the violence of the colonial past is effectively communicated through the embodiment of subjugation. And, as such, notions of justice are made real through the crafting of postcolonial narratives that the law is seen as being unable to deliver. Through spheres of resignification, representations of ICC justice as injustice and new histories are mobilized through public speeches, silences, selective memories, and referential musings.

As another attendee, Irene, told me in response to my question about that unspoken element in the speech: "It was what he didn't say that made us all come together. Anyone who understood the connection was able to decide whose side they were on—the oppressor or the oppressed."

When I asked her how she felt and whether she could still say that the pain of colonial oppression was embodied, she quickly responded by saying in a low and remorseful tone, "As long as people are displaced from their land, suffering knows no time." By this, Irene was suggesting that the infraction still continues to be felt in the present and shapes people in particular ways. This demarcation of a shared feeling is a product of affects through which particular alliances with others are being formed. They are powerful not because their embodiments are knowable or certain. They are powerful because the feeling regimes within which they operate are constitutive passionate alliances that, in turn, shape social manifestations. The shaping of the social is therefore not about the truth of the feeling. Rather, it is about affective justice—that is, the way that the feeling of the moment is produced, embodied, communicated, and/or made to constitute particular relations.

Many of the responses we received from informants led them to construct a hero figure out of Uhuru Kenyatta. Not only did they speak of how Jomo Kenyatta—the father—sacrificed his life for his people, but they also linked it to how the son, Uhuru Kenyatta, mobilized forces to defend his people from displacement and violence. These claims were fueled through emotionally affective articulations—through an enthusiastic appreciation for the contribution of their leader and his social-familial lineage. Yet not all of those polled were traditional Kenyatta supporters. Instead, they were from a range of ethnic groups and political party affiliations. They nonetheless reported to us that they were taken by the transformative frenzy of the moment. Among those who voted for the opposing party, they still reported that they believed that it was important to rethink how we understand culpability. For many, collective culpability was the framework through which to attribute responsibility.

Time and time again, people spoke of the colonial other, the ICC, or other forces that were to blame for the postelection violence. Their language reflected feelings of oppression, disdain, subjugation, injustice, loss of land, and the importance of a deliverer to return their land to them. They acknowledged local corruption, Somali-Kenyan terrorism, and so on. And while many complained bitterly about Kenyan politicians and inherent corruption, others also articulated the problem of violence as being outside of the conditions of their making. One attendee responded to a question about culpability with the following insight: "No, I didn't vote for Kenyatta . . . but I believe that he is a pawn in a larger game. . . . The Kenyan mafia is relevant here. . . . The game is also being controlled by the West; back then it was the British, now it's Europe and America."

In the context of the embodied impact of Kenyatta's speech and the rhetorical frenzy that led to chants from the crowds, we see how feelings mediate one's relationship to the past, the present, and the future. For example, narratives of subjugation and violence became embodied through the retelling of such histories of subjugation. In the retelling, the narratives passed from person to person, and through the creation of pulses of energetic relations, emotional alliances were formed that become socially relevant.[63] And through the embodied experience of participating, of being there, of feeling anguish and being reminded of the histories that continue to propel Kenyan subjugation, people deployed emotional tools to make sense of particular messages and assess the way the message calls them be taken in—to be engaged bodily in experiences of public feeling. These public feelings have the ability to reinforce particular assemblages of socialization in which particular expressions, such as "We've defeated their ilk before," become more acute.

Through the circulation of concepts (and slogans, as will be seen in chapter 4) that align with past narratives, invocations of togetherness—however fictive—highlight the way that morally coherent causalities can be mobilized to produce moral sentiments that do particular forms of momentary work. Protest speech or celebratory rhetoric demonstrates these dialogisms. As a partial practice, protest speech is a powerful modality because it makes emotional transference possible in contexts that might be substantively different otherwise. Kenyatta's disjunctural history provided the emotional fodder to align the public's inventory of social feelings with their social alliances. This connection between particular types of violence and historical facts that are evidently disjunctural can produce new social truths by constituting "the real" dialogically through realignments of the social. This happens not because the audiences are uninformed but because of the power of available historical tropes and icons and their relevance to constituting the meaning of alliance and connection.

What the example of Kenyatta's public speech shows us, therefore, is that substantively disjunct histories can be made real through the iconic construction of Jomo Kenyatta as hero and freedom fighter, and thus, through the articulation of the relevant continuities, Uhuru Kenyatta as inheritor of that iconic meaning. The production of the real, therefore, involves the deployment of histories that are ultimately sustained through subsequent networks of socialization. Those histories, as retold, become powerful because of the feeling regimes within which the iconic signs invoked operate in relation to particular nationalist founding tropes. The success of affective transference is possible precisely because icons, narrative tropes, and affective embodiments have the power to demand of publics an opportunity to become aligned with others in response to particular momentary and historical feelings. And though the feelings may be temporarily unstable, they tell us something about the assemblages and alignments at play and not necessarily actual sustained convictions over time. Once articulated, these discourses can be sustained through particular knowledge convictions, affective practices, and ongoing forms of biomediation that can shape the networks of socialization through which group alliances are produced and embodied and stories about group histories are told.

For her part, Mbizvo's use of social transference allows her to establish ICL, the ICC, and its actors—the OTP—as the heroes and heroines of "victims" and survivors around the world. Utterances such as, "The ICC exists to hear the voices of victims of the most atrocious crimes, when their cries fall on deaf ears," can be used to suggest that the judicialization of political issues can offer tangible solutions. As such, discourses that might normally operate in the unconscious through words such as *victims* or *ending impunity* can be formulated through a specified inventory of popular references that are more socially familiar than they are individually experienced. Themes of long historical connections establish particular affective resonances and connect socially or institutionally to emotive templates. Accordingly, past subordination becomes a mechanism for articulating contemporary inequalities, but the past is always signaled dialogically. That is, it is seen as building on the present, thereby constituting a reflection of itself in the present.

Celebratory rhetoric also requires particular affective alliances to congeal. For this to happen, the roads of emotional causality must be presented as part of a dialogic continuum in which gaps in the social retelling of the past provide a space for indirect connections to be made between socially relevant developments. In Mbizo's description of ICL's one hundred years of development, for example, what we see is the profound imagery of the grand march to establish the permanent court as the ultimate evolutionary form of justice for all. A plethora of key ICL scholars—from Beth Van Schaack and Ronald Slye to Kathryn Sikkink, Cherif Bassioni, and Antonio Cassese, to name only a few—have popularized these narratives about international criminal prosecutions shaping new senses of justice for those victimized by violence.[64] The related events, people, and the power relations that enable emotional sharing contribute to the establishment of the ordinary logic of law's work. This use of sentimentality is emotionally pervasive in the literature. Who wouldn't want to protect those victimized by violence?

Social Transference and the Institutionalization of Embodied Affects

What I have shown in this chapter is that substantively disjunct histories are often made real not through actual historical equivalences but through the symbolic construction of the "victim" fetish—be it a survivor of election violence or a persecuted anticolonial freedom fighter. This type of knowledge production involves the deployment of sentiments of compassion and responsibility around the protection of victims who are connected to the culmination of a one-hundred-year history of judicial strategies that are ultimately sustained through subsequent networks of socialization. It is also shown through the resignification of the narrative of the "victim/survivor" of colonialism through which particular tropes of imperial justice are used to hold imperialists accountable. What we see in the study of the transference of these passionate utterances is how structurally dissimilar phenomena can be decontextualized and recontextualized to produce otherwise contested assemblages.

For the ICC's OTP under Fatou Bensouda, this involves the encounter with new 1990s moral sentiments in which the promise of the ICC's one-hundred-year historical trajectory demonstrates the construction of international law's moral legitimacy as a crucible for social change. The movement's mantra that "no one is above the law" informs the OTP's invocations of their work as being centrally about protecting victims. When understood in relation to affective transference, we see how hope for judicial legitimacy—meaning the instantiation of legal processes as viable and with the potential to achieve legal fairness, certainty, and predictability—can be breathed into new justice experiments.

For various African leaders and their publics, alternate notions of judicial justice involve articulating new vocabulary for analyzing the historical underpinnings of violence and the dialogic presence of the ancestors within. In the end, determining which justice mechanisms are appropriate is central to how new moral orders are being mobilized to inspire sentimental responses to injustice. Notions of justice are made real through the crafting of postcolonial narratives that the law is seen as being unable to deliver. Through spheres of resignification, representations of Hague justice as injustice and new histories are mobilized through public speeches, silences, selective memories, and referential musings. Their truths become manifest in sentimental attachments that accent the cadence of daily life. In the end, such attachments establish the moral logic that shapes the way that various publics achieve the feeling that justice has been served in the contemporary period.

In both cases, such passionate utterances are central to the social alliances that are formed—as in a celebration-day crowd or in the spaces, like The Hague, in which international justice actors engage in the production of affective justice. As we shall see in chapter 3, once the affective domains are narratively constituted through particular histories and sentimentalized in particular ways, a key component of their effectiveness involves the embodiment of their convictions as demonstrated in various justice campaigns. With the increasing relevance of a "victim" through processes of legal encapsulation, this embodiment of justice reflects affective justice and is critical for understanding the actual making of international justice through its place in the life of the law.

CHAPTER 3

Biomediation and the
#BringBackOurGirls Campaign

Making Suffering Visible

In the spring of 2014, #BringBackOurGirls was mobilized and quickly popularized by politicians; concerned citizens; celebrities such as Kim Kardashian, Angelina Jolie, and Whoopi Goldberg; and the first lady of the United States at the time, Michelle Obama. The articulated goal was the return of the more than three hundred Nigerian girls abducted from a school in Chibok, Nigeria, by Islamic militants in the Nigerian state of Borno—one of twelve states that instituted criminal sharia law in 1999. The support of a global network interested in protecting those victimized by the abductions led to a transnational mass mobilization in which governments and citizens committed millions of dollars in a short period of time to launch campaigns that would lead to the demand for and return of innocent girls to their families and to their dreams of postsecondary education.

To briefly recap the events that led up to the #BringBackOurGirls campaign: on April 14, 2014, Boko Haram, a militant Islamic group based in northern Nigeria, went to Chibok to kidnap girls boarding at the local school. The girls were staying there overnight before taking a national entrance exam to gain admission to postsecondary education. Boko Haram first attacked the village, then the local military base. Then its militants disguised themselves in official government uniforms and at 11:45 P.M. they entered the boarding school by announcing to the girls that Boko Haram vigilantes were going to attack the school and that they were there to protect them. They then abducted 330 Christian and Muslim (though predominantly Christian) girls ranging from fifteen to eighteen years of age.[1]

A month prior to the abduction, the schools in the area had closed for fear of terror attacks by Muslim rebels. But the boarding school in Chibok had re-opened so that the girls could take their final exams. Witnesses say the girls were aware of the risks of seeking an education in an environment known to have denied that opportunity to girls, but because they wanted to pursue their education to one day become doctors, lawyers, and teachers, they took their chances to prepare for the national exam.

Boko Haram is an Islamic militant group based in West Africa whose name means "Western education is sinful/forbidden." The group has been suspected of a range of attacks throughout Nigeria (and recently in Cameroon and Chad) since 2009, with the goal of establishing an Islamic state. With approximately six thousand fighters and control of over twenty thousand square kilometers of northeastern Nigeria, the group has emerged as a major force that has pledged allegiance to the Islamic state, also known as ISIS or ISIL. The militant group's leader, Abubakar Shekau, claimed responsibility for the girls' abduction, stat-ing, "Western education should end. Girls, you should go and get married. . . . Western education should fold up. I abducted your girls. I will sell them in the market, by Allah."[2]

Related sources said that the abducted girls were taken into neighbor-ing Chad and Cameroon and sold as brides to Islamist militants for USD $12 each. The militant leader said the girls were being held as sexual slaves. In response to the kidnapping and potential sale of the girls into sexual slav-ery, widespread condemnations circulated rapidly on Twitter. In a red-carpet interview, Angelina Jolie—Hollywood Academy Award winner and famil-iar symbol of ICC justice—confirmed her pro–prosecutorial justice position: "The important thing . . . is to understand that this happens because these men think they can get away with this and they can do this. . . . We have to start arresting people for this, we have to start bringing them to justice and we have to start making it an absolute crime that puts fear in these men so that they think twice about this kind of action."[3] Similarly, John Kerry, the US sec-retary of state at the time, spoke at a press conference in Addis Ababa, where he declared that the United States would support Nigeria's efforts to find the missing girls: "The kidnapping of hundreds of children by Boko Haram is an unconscionable crime, and we will do everything possible to support the Ni-gerian government to return these young women to their homes and to hold the perpetrators to justice."[4]

Yet supporting the Nigerian government in holding perpetrators of vio-lence accountable has been complex. For while Nigeria's then president Good-luck was publicly advocating retributive justice for the kidnappers, he was privately negotiating amnesty for Boko Haram militants.[5] And over the course of October 2016, the first batch of twenty-one girls who were kidnapped were released to the International Committee of the Red Cross through a prisoner exchange and payment of millions of dollars in ransom. To do this, Switzerland's government used funds from the $321 million that it had been holding since Nigeria's former military dictator Sani Abacha's rule.[6] The International Criminal Court began preliminary examinations of the situation of violence in Nigeria.[7] And by early 2018, further negotiations by international agencies to recover more girls were underway, though not yet successful.[8]

In this age of Twitter, the news of girls being kidnapped and held as sexual slaves went viral through the hashtag #BringBackOurGirls. With millions of tweets within a twenty-four-hour period demanding the girls' release, the media coverage of African girls denied an education by militant Muslims led to the collection of electronic signatures and millions of dollars in aid from leaders, celebrities, and average citizens around the world. Activists in over thirty global cities—from New York and Los Angeles to London and Lagos—engaged in rallies demanding that their governments mobilize sufficient military support to arrest the "perpetrators" and return the girls. The messages were expressed succinctly and with great clarity. The sentiments emphasized compassion and focused on rights and entitlements communicated through a sense of collective responsibility to make a difference.

Over the past decade, scholars have explored the significance of the mobilization of affect for suffering subjects and have also explored the way that new forms of electronic and digital media, such as hashtag activism, are providing renewed platforms to defend injustice and domains for what Andrew Ross refers to as "viral expression."[9] This chapter demonstrates how in public activism emotional manifestations of human suffering have become decoupled from lived spaces through new practices of mediation. It shows how online activism can be seen as symptomatic of a more fundamental process of dislocation seen through the deployment of bodily and biotechnological advocacy. By detailing how messages communicated through large block letters and hashtag activism (rather than aesthetic visualizations of suffering children) are constituting affective justice, the chapter focuses on two interrelated themes. First, it examines how, by erasing the bodily representation of African girls and replacing it with justice messaging, the #BringBackOurGirls campaign built an international social movement in ways that exceeded empathy as the emotional basis for calls to protect African girls. Second, in an attempt to shape an anthropology of international justice, it explores what forms of racial and gendered imaginaries are emerging in the contemporary period and what they tell us about the modes of seeing, engaging, feeling, and speaking about justice at this critical junction. I ask how those engaged in contemporary justice activism use biomediated activism through the decoupling of human suffering from their sites of violence and relocate them to the "international community" with the responsibility to protect. As a component part of affective justice's technocratic knowledge form, biomediation involves redrawing the boundary of the individual self to include media and other electronic technologies.[10] This approach to biomediation represents what I have called affective justice, for it is concerned with the biopolitical entanglements with the body—that is, how to understand it, how movements mobilize affects to save it, and how to manage its violations. The suffering body—materially or symbolically, or the body to be returned, to be liberated—as an analytic opens up a space for a robust interrogation of how new forms of mediation, in the form of electronic media technologies, are being used affectively for social justice mobilization. Through the redefinition of the biomediated body, we see how concepts and campaign demands as well as the tools that transport them are not just manifestations of the social body. They are, by extension, stand-ins for the individual body—our subjectivity, our power, the constructed essence of "the international community."

In this chapter we see how affective justice, referenced through the body of those victimized by violence, is messaged and exported through digital media justice campaigns. In this case, advocacy groups, media outlets, celebrities, and publics on Facebook, Twitter, and various web networks harnessed their resolve to bring this issue to international attention, with the focus on pursuing, arresting, and demanding that Boko Haram correct their actions, and with young African girls at the center of the coordinated campaigns against sexual violence by those deemed terrorists. The tweets and hashtags needed only to combine a few words—"bring back *our* girls"—to assert the global cause of the violated female survivors and personalize the urgency of their return. The use of the possessive *our* highlighted the declaration of a shared humanity—that the girls belong to us and that we have a responsibility to protect them against their captors—while the imperative to bring them back suggested forceful, immediate retrieval by any means necessary.

The emotionally propelled narrative focused on the young girls who were victimized by Boko Haram. But the larger structural forms of victimhood caused by conditions of economic or political marginalization were relegated to the shadows; those impacted by the worst forms of structural violence— the indigent, the landless, those without access to water and health care, for example—were obscured and folded into a discourse guided by the legal responsibility to protect survivors of physical violence, wherever they are in the world. As a form of *do-good activism* in which one can simply retweet a message or sponsor a child to support those victimized by violence, this type of advocacy highlights another set of discourses at play in the individualization of criminal responsibility and the belief that injustice can be pursued through legality.[11] It not only reasserted the urgency of ending impunity through its temporality of the now but also reinforced the construction of the "international community" as a significant subject of international law and as a critical contributor to the emotional and cultural sensibilities that shape the regimes that sustain its networks.

Anthropologists Richard Wilson and Richard Brown argue that the use of humanitarian narratives is critical for the mobilization of empathy.[12] They suggest that emotional engagement and guilt promote particular types of action, and survivors' narratives are key.[13] And while it is true that emotions are mobilized through humanitarian campaigns, and narrative is an important part of that, it is also true, as I will go on to argue, that new technologies, such as Twitter, and online campaigns are leading to the reconceptualization of suffering and are redrawing the body's relation to other bodies. In considering the way that the imagery of a violated body is no longer necessary in global campaigns to enlist empathy and constitute support, we can see that today's biomediated social movements can compel action through concepts and buy-ins to those concepts as a way of consolidating new human-technology-justice assemblages. It is the concept of the "victim" to be saved to which publics are becoming newly aligned or from which they are distinguishing themselves. And these nonspaces of biomediated connection are becoming sites for the formulation of ideological alignments and social positioning and not just the manifestation of humanitarian empathy.

The generative capacity of these types of justice campaigns is aligned with the foundations of contemporary capitalist logic, in which hashtag advocacy connects with expectations of consumer choice—the choice to support a cause, to demand a solution, to donate as needed.[14] Not only are the images and the block-art posters used in ways that enhance people's engagement with it, they also represent contemporary democratic values that tie the logic of freedom to the body to be protected. This body is increasingly being seen as a site of global action. In this merger of freedom (produced through technocratic and legal knowledge), the body, and new technologies that invigorate emotional responses, we see the packaging of transnational protest discourses that stigmatize particular justice imaginaries. In this example, the stigmatization is articulated through emotional pleas using terms such as *barbarism*. And though I am not interested in defending violence, what is important to note here is how in the articulation of "the Other" against the innocence of the survivor of violence, the "victim" becomes not just the girls to be saved. The girls victimized by Boko Haram become the international community itself, represented in block art or hashtags displayed and deployed by celebrity citizens. They become each other—an extension of an international justice assemblage—whose component parts cannot be separated from the whole.

The most effective aesthetic representation no longer depicts the subject who has been violated materially; it is not the survivor around which we locate ourselves, but a set of relations. Thus, while these forms of do-good activism do indeed reflect the articulations of empathy that many scholars of humanitarianism, suffering, and social repair explain through the use of social narrative, it is critical that we extend that analysis to the rapidly changing technological modalities that are constituting new publics in postviolence contexts today.[15] We have entered a new era when international justice assemblages have taken on new capacities and responsibilities focused on judicial solutions, especially in the Global South. This chapter, then, is concerned with why the #BringBackOurGirls campaign and its humanitarian logic was so compelling to its audiences, and what it tells us about the biopolitics of justice and the regimes within which they are circulating in the second decade of the twenty-first century.

Saving "Victims": The Sentimentality of Empathy, Compassion, and Attribution

Two years before the Chibok girls were kidnapped and the #BringBackOur Girls hashtag proliferated, the #Kony2012 campaign was everywhere. The group known as Invisible Children produced and popularized a video titled *Kony 2012* that went viral. Within days, over 120 million had viewed it online, and household names like Bill Gates and celebrities such as Rihanna had retweeted it. Inspired by Jason Russell's travels to Uganda, *Kony 2012* describes the country's twenty-five-year-old war, its violence, and the consequences of that violence: the death and displacement of millions of Ugandans. The film connects Uganda's mass violence to Joseph Kony, the leader of the Lord's Resistance Army (LRA), and demands that, in keeping with the ICC's warrant of arrest, he be held accountable judicially for the violence committed by the LRA. Russell's narration describes Kony as heading "the Lord's

Resistance Army, a Christian terrorist group which has reportedly abducted and forced more than 30,000 children to fight with them since their revolt began in 1986."[16] He then discloses that his commitment was inspired by a promise he made to Jacob, a young Ugandan boy whose brother was killed by Kony's men. Russell vowed that he was "going to do everything possible to stop them." The rest of the story is about how American political participation and stopping a single leader will rectify Uganda's plight.

Russell opens the second story line with advice to his young son. "There are good guys and bad guys in Africa," Russell says, and "the way to make Africa better is to stop Africa's bad guys." Russell's simplistic words about the nature of African violence and the role of ordinary Americans are energized with a compelling narrative about the conditions by which justice can be procured through international participation. The message resounded clearly and mobilized a social movement: by donating money through a simple click of a mouse, and buying a kit that would help fund Joseph Kony's arrest, every American could also be part of the solution to help poor Ugandan survivors. In addition to the twenty-nine-minute documentary, Russell launched a campaign called Cover the Night. It was a call to post around global cities various images of the LRA indictee, Joseph Kony. Russell conceptualized the event as a moment in time when millions would engage in posting the image of Joseph Kony throughout their various communities.

The simplicity of the *Kony2012* message seemed compelling and suggested that Africa can be transformed by *our* philanthropy, through our willingness to save Ugandans. The campaign was one of a series of philanthropic, humanitarian, and justice-seeking gestures communicating that capturing a single commander, a "perpetrator" responsible for mass crimes, will solve one of Africa's most endemic problems: violence. The campaign's aesthetics centered the name and image of the individualized perpetrator, Kony, and used symbolism that depoliticized support for his capture.[17] The imagery employed suggested that regardless of our political leanings (represented by the Democratic donkey and Republican elephant), we can come together in agreement that Kony is culpable and achieve peace (symbolized by the white dove holding the laurel).[18] It also seems to be specifically enlisting US activist consumers in its use of the Republican and Democrat symbols. Other invocations of the activism to stop Joseph Kony insist that the international community should "stop at nothing" to apprehend him.[19]

The campaign was successful in motivating people—from high school students to teachers, parents, and celebrities—to circulate that message in the name of the survivor. Through the invocation of global publics invoking the force of the law, the predominant message was that through the arrest of the perpetrator we will end impunity. However, though profoundly resonant with new justice formulations, the campaign's message was not powerful in and of itself. It was effective in its mobilizations because of its alliance with particular cultural sensibilities that are sustained by time horizons that work through the force of law. With these senses of agitation shaped by particular temporalities of justice, the #Kony2012 campaign contributed to the construction of an individualized "perpetrator" (or in this case, a handful of individuals belonging to political rebel groups) whose alleged crimes aligned with the ICC's post-2002 threshold for temporal jurisdiction, a time determinant that I refer to as legal time. Furthermore, through the attribution of guilt to an individual for violence committed by groups of Ugandans over long years of social unrest, this popular campaign highlighted the workings of retributive justice through a particularly sentimentalized discourse that arresting Joseph Kony would put an end to the war. This is key to the way that those who see themselves representing the "international community" engage in social mobilizations to demand juridical solutions.

The biomediated #Kony2012 campaign prefigured #BringBackOurGirls, in which a similar use of social media unfolded around a globally significant cause in Africa. #BringBackOurGirls began as a local Nigerian movement and was propelled into the international arena through the emotive advocacy of unrelated activist constituencies similarly committed to social change but from different social locations. The social media campaign was initiated on April 23, 2014, during the opening ceremony of a UNESCO event honoring the city of Port Harcourt, when Obiageli Ezekwesili urged Nigerians to support the attempts to return the girls.[20] She encouraged everyone not only to tweet but to actively participate in mobilizing efforts to "bring back our girls." In response to Dr. Ezekwesili's call, Ibrahim Abdullahi, a Nigerian attorney from Abuja, created and tweeted the hashtag #BringBackOurGirls. It was quickly retweeted ninety-five times, including by Dr. Ezekwesili, who had 125,000 followers on Twitter at the time.

On April 30, Nigerian protestors called for action by marching on Parliament in Abuja, which led to further mobilizations around Nigeria and other cities around the world. In Nigeria, the forms of mediation and emotional invocations included the embodied images of girls who were missing, dramatic figures of suffering, and images that produced the terms for not only empathy but also sympathy.

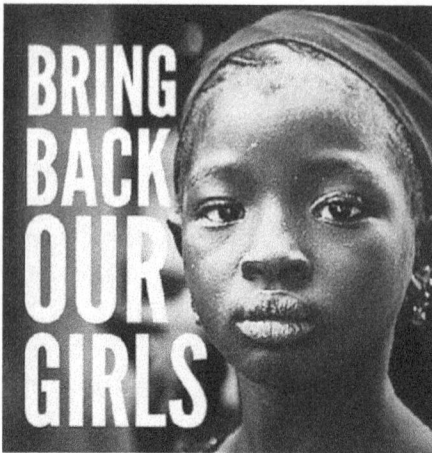

3.1 Nigerian #BringBackOurGirls campaign poster.

This type of imagery represents the classic depictions, by justice and human rights activists in Africa and beyond, of the bodily suffering of those victimized by violence. And yet such images, following Roland Barthes, represent a particular type of horror in which we observe suffering from the standpoint of our own ontological freedom:

> [The] horror comes from the fact that we are looking at it from inside our freedom. . . . Because the creator of the photograph has overconstructed the horror he is proposing . . . we can no longer invent our own reception of this synthetic nourishment. . . . This adds to the reading of the sign a kind of disturbing challenge, sweeping the reader of the image into an astonishment less intellectual than visual, precisely because it fastens him to the surfaces of the spectacle, to his optical resistance, and not immediately to its signification. . . . The literal photograph introduces us to the scandal of horror, not to horror itself.[21]

Such an image, then, is part of the interplay between the image, the conditions that shape our reading of the image, and its alterity—the hyperresemblance of the original.[22] It is the materiality of suffering that both movements indexically reference. In the case of the US-based movement, the advocacy had a different aesthetic.

The story of the girls and the protest movement captured the attention of Ramaa Devi Mosley, an American commercial, music video, and feature and documentary film director based in Los Angeles. She actively promoted the social media campaign to create national awareness in the United States, creating a Facebook page that received more than 43,000 likes by early May

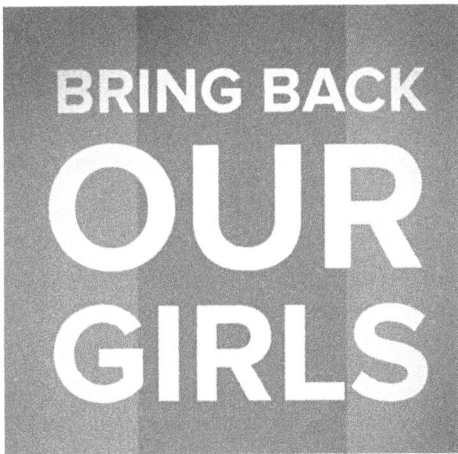

BRING BACK
OUR
GIRLS

3.2 #BringBackOurGirls logo.

and 230,000 likes by July.[23] On May 7, 2014, CNN interviewed her to discuss the abduction of the Nigerian girls. Her campaign caught the attention of many US and international celebrities, who helped to propel the message further.

Designed by Mosley and other US-based digital activists, this campaign was characterized by a different aesthetic of victim suffering that involved a specific form of biomediation. Though they used the same hashtag, #Bring BackOurGirls, as the Nigerian-based campaign, the message and imagery of the international call to social action were both depersonalized and celebritized. Using email, Twitter, and various online formats, they developed four steps for activist mobilization: (1) establishing the brand and posting it on the main website, (2) articulating the mission and goals on the main website, (3) determining the tools for communicating the message (websites, Facebook, Twitter, Instagram), and (4) developing actions/advocacy (rallies, notification of target group, letter writing, petitions, vigils, commercial sales, production of materials, fund-raising). The Twitter and email campaigns were only minimally coordinated. Activists only needed to insert their association's location and their particular details—date and time of march/rally, contact email information—and the networks of alliance could easily grow without prior knowledge of the particularities of the issues. Regardless of their location or affiliation, those interested in advancing this cause were able to access the same official informational templates, use the same block art or petitions, and adopt the same formats.

This imagery uses bold statements in white block letters on a bright red background instead of evocative pictures of the suffering African child. The red calls our attention and signals a visual alarm of danger; the contrasting white letters in all caps, commonly understood to indicating shouting, alert us to the missing girls and their need to be rescued. The red also emphasizes the imperative to return the girls in the name of fairness and signifies passion: the conviction and love that drives the call for action. The use of white, as described by social movement activists, also signifies the innocence of the girls who risked their lives for educational knowledge and personal advancement. These color and design aesthetics articulate a transforming relationship in international justice organizing between the signifier and the signified. They are the aesthetics of a new mobilization strategy being made relevant through the communication of an ideological message that is actively constituting the contemporary "international community." That message is that there is an international commitment to freedom, liberty, and a pro-education democracy in which "no child" is to be "left behind," and we, the "international community," have a responsibility to protect those victimized by exclusions from such universal rights.[24] The visual symbolism of representing the kidnapped girls as an idea—a hashtag message, a red poster with block letters—has taken on new significance in this period: the poster art with its relentless demands, the hashtag and its centering of the person posting it, the petition as a representation of democratic participation. Here, the temporal urgency of a worsening problem, as emphasized in the Twitter messages I discuss below, is reflected in their appeal for action and in the campaign imagery.

The campaign was catapulted to international significance once Michelle Obama joined the cause in May 2014. She tweeted a photo of herself holding a sign with #BringBackOurGirls written on it and through the symbols of her power—African American, woman, wife of the president of the United States of America—her buy-in propelled significant support. This practice of sign holding is a common way for people to publicize their personal feelings about an issue or event on social media. The meme spread, with celebrities from Malala Yousafzai to Ellen DeGeneres posting pictures of themselves holding similarly handwritten signs.

These images should also be seen as an example of a certain type of biomediation in which the sign holder mediates the message of those victimized by mass atrocity violence with her own body, instead of that of the girls. In Michelle Obama's case, in foregrounding her own black (American) body, we can read an attempt to make an emotional appeal by subjecting her body to the cause. Her expression is stern yet concerned; the image is seemingly simple yet powerful. Michelle Obama wears symbolically American red, white, and blue

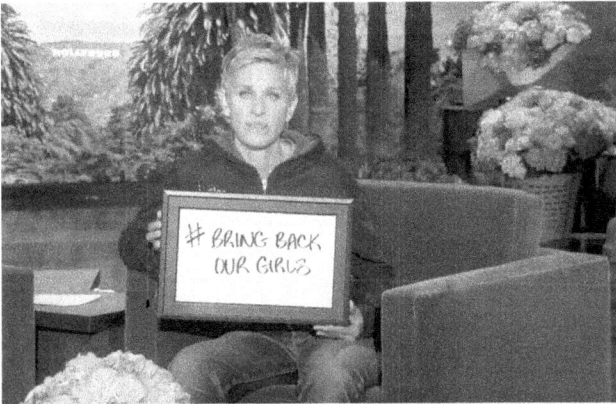

3.3 Michelle Obama, former First Lady of the United States of America.

3.4 Ellen DeGeneres, on the *Ellen DeGeneres Show*.

flowers that bloom hope. Showcasing her straightened hair swooped in big, bountiful, and performatively feminized curls, makeup and manicured nails, a wedding ring, and large silver earrings, the photo, taken in one of the White House sitting rooms, depicts a performance of freedom and liberty, leisure and power. Such a replacement of the suffering girl's body represents a fetishization of the "victim." Here we can see how this type of visual, biomediated advocacy can highlight Western agency over the cause of those victimized. The decentering of those victimized by violence and the recentering of those supporting the cause has led to a radical form of justice encapsulation in which affective justice of the contemporary period is as much about publicizing one's emotional alliances as it is about demanding action. This was clear through their creation of emotive expressions such as "Me too," or "I'm with her." For example, the photo of Michelle Obama displaying the #BringBackOurGirls hashtag was taken on the day that she delivered the president's weekly address, just a few days before Mother's Day 2014 in the United States.[25] Her recorded address began with a sentimental condolence to the families who lost their girls in the Chibok kidnapping: "Like millions of people across the globe, my husband and I are outraged and heartbroken over the kidnapping of more than 200 Nigerian girls from their school dormitory in the middle of the night. This unconscionable act was committed by a terrorist group determined to keep these girls from getting an education—grown men attempting to snuff out the aspirations of young girls."[26]

She continued by reassuring the world of the president's resolve to intervene. "I want you to know that Barack has directed our government to do everything possible to support the Nigerian government's efforts to find these girls and bring them home." As an act of empathy and a complex form of both racial and universal solidarity, she likened the girls to her own, to the daughter of any human. "In these girls, Barack and I see our own daughters. We see their hopes, their dreams, and we can only imagine the anguish their parents are feeling right now. Many of them might have been hesitant to send their daughters off to school fearing that harm might come their way. But they took that risk because they believed in their daughter's promise and wanted to give them every opportunity to succeed." As a call to action, she ended her address by emphasizing themes of resilience, bravery, and hope.

> Right now more than 65 million girls worldwide are not in school. Yet we know that girls who are educated make higher wages, lead healthier lives, and have healthier families. And when more girls attend secondary schools, that boosts their country's entire economy. So education is truly a girl's best chance for a bright future not just for herself but for her family and her nation. . . . These girls embody the best hope for the future of our world and we are committed to standing up for them not just in times of tragedy and crisis but for the long haul.

The humanitarian message—sentimentalized through a Western mother's pain—tells us how critical it is for any child to have a Western education in order to have social mobility in a capitalist democracy contingent on social connections and market competition. This education reflects the liberalist dreams of objectivity, fairness, and a diversity of approaches in ways that emphasize agency, autonomy, and individual power. But this message erases the particularities of the education that is on offer and deemed a girl's birthright. It does not highlight that it is a particular Western (read: universal) education that is assumed, in which other knowledge forms and the inequalities embedded in them are obscured. For example, the idea that the Chibok girls represent the "best hope for the future of our world" is actually incongruent with the Obama girls, for whom the possibility of realizing hopes and dreams of Western education represents a gold standard. Her message also carries unspoken stereotypes of the Nigerian north as backward and irrational while validating tropes of "Muslim girls needing to be saved" or girls having to be "brought back to the West," all made viable through the demand for the return of the kidnapped and uneducated girl as "the victim."

Once Michelle Obama posted the photo on her Twitter account, a range of celebrities rallied around the social media movement—from Angelina Jolie to Mia Farrow, Alicia Keys, Ellen DeGeneres, and so many more—and tweeted messages with similar themes. For example, on the importance of education, Whoopi Goldberg posted, "Fear of education 4 girls in any country condemns the future of that country. WHY HURT YOUR OWN FUTURE #BringBackOur Girls."[27] Ian Somerhalder focused on hope: "Empowering our youth through education is the TRUE key to hope—let's use our voices, innovation&collective power to #BringBackOurGirlsNOW!!!"[28]

Expressions of outrage, tragedy, and demands for immediate action, often in the form of arrests, pervaded these celebrity tweets, as this abbreviated sampling attests:

- Mia Farrow: "A serious search for Nigeria's stolen girls has taken WAY too long"[29]
- Iman: "Let's not forget them! Pls repost #bringbackourgirls"[30]
- Reese Witherspoon: "Sending prayers to Nigerian families who are missing their daughters. It's time to #bringbackourgirls"[31]
- Gina Carano: "Let's bring awareness to the #BringBackOurGirls campaign to get these girls back to their families."[32]
- Rashida Jones: "#BringBackOurGirlsNOW."[33]
- Kim Kardashian: "Heartbreaking! Let's all raise awareness! #BringBack OurGirls"[34]
- Cara Delevingne: "Everyone help and raise awareness #regram #repost or make your own!"[35]

- Kendall Jenner: "This is heartbreaking. please help raise awareness! let's #BringBackOurGirls"[36]
- Kerry Washington: "Amen. '@ABCWorldNews: Michelle Obama joins #BringBackOurGirls movement on Twitter'"[37]
- Naomi Campbell: "#BringBackOurGirls!!! President GoodLuck do something !!!"[38]
- Paula Abdul: "200 girls still missing 2 weeks after being abducted. Keep this in the news #BringBackOurGirls"[39]
- Queen Latifah: "Its time 2 #BringBackOurGirls & put a stop 2 violence!"[40]
- Mary J. Blige: "President Obama addresses kidnapping of Nigerian girls. See what he had to say: #BringBackOurGirls"[41]
- Daisy Fuentes: "This an outrage & a tragedy. The world must demand immediate action."[42]
- Stacey Dash: "Why the hell does it takes 3 weeks and a trendy hashtag to get world's 'leaders' to care about 300 kidnapped girls?! #BringBackOurGirls"[43]
- Chelsea Clinton: "more girls have been kidnapped in Nigeria on top of 200+ schoolgirls already missing. They need our voice."[44]
- Ellen DeGeneres: "It can't happen soon enough #BringBackOurGirls"[45]

In these tweets and demands for international action, we can see how new publics are forming around the concept of "the victim"—"our girls"—as opposed to the black suffering body. These assertions, articulated not only through our social agreement that every child should be free from violence but by the idea of freedom itself, highlighted by a shift from the emphasis on an embodied materiality of victimhood to the importance of justice as law (communicated through ideas tied to justice—democracy, entitlements, rights).

The act of replacing visible African bodily suffering with embodiments of digital social protest movements highlights yet another way that the category of the victim is being encapsulated in the contemporary period. In these new international justice formations, association with the helpless is subverted; the material representation of suffering is no longer necessary to compel sympathy. Increasingly, justice no longer depends on our association with bodily suffering and our acts of pity. Today, the rise of this form of judicialization of justice can be seen through the way that we, the "international community," become proxy "victims" through hyper-embodied representations by celebrities, activists, lawyers, and judges. This formulation requires our agency to demand the immediacy of solutions and to create solidarities through the idea of suffering. Because of the encapsulation of the *victim to be saved*, there is no need to highlight abject suffering and othering. Rather, the resignification of abjection is accommodated by the need to affectively attribute new values and bring our girls into our fold. The idea of "our children" and Michelle Obama's acceptance that the kidnapped girls could be her girls, our girls, represent this shift.

In responding to what online protesters saw as human trafficking of the worst kind—sexual violence against women—select celebrity #BringBackOur Girls tweets about Boko Haram's violence highlighted what they saw as the barbarism of the girls' abduction:

- Jessica Biel: "This is barbaric. Human trafficking needs to end NOW"[46]
- Teresa Palmer: "Take a stand with me! #BringBackOurGirls it's absolutely barbaric and inconceivable that over 200 woman have been kidnapped whilst at SCHOOL in Nigeria. Sadly this apart of a worsening problem."[47]
- Poppy Delevingne: "I can't believe we live in a world where this happens . . . #bringbackourgirls"[48]

Here we see how the idea of the control of females by radical Islamic men is made real through the sentimental plea for freedom from sexual violence. With sexual freedoms at the backdrop of women's rights to life and education, the social grammar of anti-impunity activism went beyond legal accountability. Rather, tropes of barbarism were deployed, and international law's civilizing function took center stage with social media mobilizations against extreme forms of human trafficking and sexual violence. The materiality of the suffering African child or the girl to be saved is overturned, and what we get is the repackaging of humanitarianism through the agency of an activist-consumer making choices about principles they can rally around—justice for women and girls, sexual and educational freedom for women, freedom from sexual violence. These principles are made recognizable through words, block art, a hashtag, and so on (see figure 3.2), rather than earlier aesthetic visualizations of the suffering child, girl, woman, or boy (see figure 3.1) that once required our empathy. Today, by replacing suffering with an aesthetic resignification of victimhood, we see how people see barbarism as the opposite of abject suffering.

Various American celebrities, with their moral influence on social media, began to mobilize support based on empathy for the violated girls, but that quickly transformed into the hyperembodiment of "the victim" popularized through the symbolic resignification of suffering through Western bodies. If we can see that these contemporary justice-for-victims discourses produce illusions (or fetishes) that compel people, then the issue articulated as simply "*our* girls to be saved" should be seen as fictions that blind them and allow them to construct Boko Haram as the *Barbaric Other* and the girls as *Ours*, thereby erasing other relations.[49] What we see, following Hernandez Reguant, is that the aesthetic repackaging of suffering produces it as a condition to be overcome—in which their victimhood is symbolically also our suffering, social suffering. Through clicktivism, using the technological tools of the capitalist order to go online, as agents of change, we can make the decision to support a cause. This modality of humanitarian aid works through the temporality of the now and the imperative to make those demands, not simply in the name of democracy articulated through the international community, but also through the backing of the military-industrial complex. In the case of the latter, the responsibility to protect those victimized by violence has become a legal responsibility of the state and actionable through its citizens. Yet this new form of justice exists within deep inequalities. When designations of barbarism are deployed to comment on practices that are perceived to transgress civility, they reinforce a hierarchy in which particular discourses, such as ending the impunity of Boko Haram violence, emphasize the consequences of violence over the realities of the colonial and postcolonial condition. However, as I will go on to show, it is important to acknowledge how postcolonial inequalities in the Muslim North have shaped contemporary Islamic radicalism today and are thus central to the underlying conditions of violence being obscured by such popular expressions of affective justice.

Histories of Islamic Inequality in Nigeria, an ICC Situation Country

The spread of Islam, predominantly in northern Nigeria, but later in the southwestern region, began a millennium ago. The creation of the Sokoto Caliphate in the holy war of 1804–1808 brought most of the northern region and adjacent parts of Niger and Cameroon under a single Islamic government. However, it did not encompass the Kanem-Bornu Empire, where most of the Boko Haram–related violence has taken place. The extension of Islam within the area of present-day Nigeria dates from the nineteenth century and resulted in the consolidation of the caliphate, and competition over governance of that region continues to be at the heart of Boko Haram's demands.

During the creation of the Sokoto Caliphate, the steady trade of slaves across the Sahara Desert and the Atlantic Ocean (approximately 3.5 million people) accounted for tremendous social strife. Between 1650 and 1860, a steady stream of slaves was held by the Sokoto Caliphate as well as among the Igbo and the Yoruba, which resulted in the creation and sustenance of their ethnic empires. With slave raiding, ethnic and religious distinctions became more pronounced as a form of protection against being sold based on identifiably different associations, such as various types of scarification to distinguish group belonging in particular ways. Conversion to Islam and the spread of Christianity was intricately associated with slavery and efforts to promote political and cultural autonomy through the reinforcement of ethnic and class hierarchies as well as the emergence of various forms of gender dominance. With the encroachment of warring forces from the north and the consolidation of military might from the coast, the British annexed land and eventually colonized the increasingly fragmented region. These distinctions further embedded the seeds of structural violence.

After British conquest in 1903, the consolidation of the northern and southern territories into the Colony and Protectorate of Nigeria led to Nigeria's amalgamation in 1914. As a colony under British rule, the new Nigeria was reconstituted through the goal of resource extraction. Out of 250 to 400 ethnic groups and languages, three dominant ethnic groups—the Hausa in the north, the Yoruba in the west, and the Igbo in the east—emerged through such imperial processes. These three regionally dominant ethnic groups would later become the basis for state organizational logic and public policy. Despite attempts to solidify such heterogeneity into homogeneity, these processes further concretized tensions and divisions that cross-cut concerns about religious values, governance, and resource distribution.[50]

British colonialism contributed to the production of deep structural inequalities that shaped the changing forms of political power in various African polities.[51] Though it lasted only sixty years, colonial rule in Nigeria contributed to rapid change, ranging from the development of extraction economies to the expansion of agricultural products and consumption patterns and the production of particular cultural and moral orders, which grew alongside new educational formats aligned with a modern form of capitalism that distorted economic growth. The creation of new territorial boundaries and the development of roads, laws, and new forms of political order that reinforced British colonial interests led to the emergence of deep regional inequalities within the colony. Those in the south and the east in closer proximity to extractable resources, in particular oil, developed greater intimacies with British rule and benefited from its ideologies of Western capitalist order. After independence in 1960, minimal attention was given to developing state institutions and equalizing them between the north and the south. A highly centralized federal body with little to no accountability formed to replace the colonial administration and further reinforced the development of late twentieth-century structural violence. This pattern was repeated across the continent. Over the years the Nigerian south has benefited from local resources, infrastructure, and general economic development. To this day, the north lacks the type of economic resources, the infrastructure, and the administrative and social institutions enjoyed by the south.[52]

It is these structural inequalities between the Nigerian north and south that have produced the conditions in which the radical Boko Haram freedom fighters emerged. As an Islamic militant group based in West Africa, Boko Haram has led violent attacks against both the state and ordinary people as part of what its members believe to be a divinely guided war for Islam. Since 2009, military attacks by Boko Haram in Borno State and military incursions in neighboring Niger, Chad, and Cameroon have contributed to the uprooting of more than 2.5 million people in the Lake Chad region. Boko Haram's tactics of plunder and pillage have inflicted widespread suffering and reduced large swaths of population to utter poverty. Visible as they are, the atrocities perpetrated by Boko Haram forces against local populations have become the object of widespread condemnation in popular and academic discourses. On the other hand, the systematic ways in which ordinary Nigerians are harmed or otherwise disadvantaged by social and political arrangements that are rooted in the country's long history of disparity between the north and the south are far less visible. Though it works in subtle fashion, structural violence is no less effective in the way it puts individuals and, in some cases, entire populations in harm's way.[53]

The postcolonial Africanist literature has detailed the way that tropes concerning the rejection of Western education have been articulated through discourses of civility versus backwardness by those engaged in the formation of colonial education. This form of colonial education was meant to craft citizens of the state to reproduce colonial governance. To that end, such forms of colonial education reproduced discourses of primitivity and backwardness and fueled the epistemic violence that eventually became characteristic of Islamic militancy in contemporary Nigeria. These narratives made their mark publicly in the early formation of the Nigerian nation-state through early missionary writing and colonial arguments about the native savage.[54] And their effects—the assumption that Islam is backward, antirights, antifeminist—continue to circulate in the contemporary public sphere through electronic technologies, videos, talk shows, nightly news captions, and congressional hearings, where through the invocation of legality they are further concretized in a world deemed secular and without religious bias.

In sum, colonial rule created extreme forms of inequality. Coupled with the creation of a cash economy, a corresponding development infrastructure, the development of religious categories and alliances, and dependence on a national state, the new Nigerian state struggled to meet the demands of statehood, its citizenry, and membership in an international community. As a postcolonial state, Nigeria is, thus, an invention of the modern era whose roots reflect histories of violence, difference, and disparity between the north and the south. The result has been the persistent construction of the people of the northern region as ideologically backward—especially in relation to women and girls. Viewing the kidnapping of the Chibok girls and the related violence inflicted by Boko Haram in the context of the differences between the southern and northern parts of Nigeria, as well as Boko Haram's edict about Western education, reveals the present absence of politics in judicial and social mobilization language. Highlighting these erasures points to the fetish manifested in the figure of the victim. For not only does its demand for instantaneous action preclude the possibility that different forms of politics could be worked out, but it leaves the constituted "international community" with the moral authority to act in particular ways and not in others. Therefore, short-term action—such as signing petitions in order to mobilize government, donating ten dollars, coordinating bake sales and fundraisers—becomes the basis for actions deemed appropriate, as opposed to longer-term structural reorganization, boundary discussions, and shifts in the types of educational values we agree are appropriate for contemporary global citizens.

In the aftermath of violent situations like the abduction of the Chibok girls or the displacement of Ugandans by the LRA, the emergence of the figure of a "victim" to be saved and the "perpetrator" to be held accountable has complicated the way that many in the anti-impunity movement understand the value of lives worth protecting. The discourse then becomes one of rights, freedoms, and rescuing a girl's future. Empathy may be deployed performatively—as a way of inciting us to feel the girls' pain. However, it is the Chibok girls' rights—meaning bodily rights and educational entitlements—demanded by the international community that are presented as the immediate solution.

Yet when our lens for justice is the interruption of an emergency, or the pursuit of arrests or a trial, then justice is possible only through the achievement of those demands, and structural inequality can persist. In other words, if the Chibok girls were all brought back and saved, there would still be no justice per se, as it would not solve the other forms of structural and exceptional violence. Here I am not justifying Boko Haram's violence. I am suggesting that erasing the enabling histories of violence disconnects the plight of the girls from other histories of struggle and instead undermines those politics through the call for the liberal dream of equality and education for all. It is our recognition of a social harm and our sense of that harm as our responsibility to address within particular moral and juridical platforms that compels the idea that we can be and are the agents of immediate change. According to this social justice imaginary, it is irrelevant that Boko Haram's violence is related to the historical struggles between Nigeria's predominantly Muslim north and Christian south.

Through declarations such as "Bring Back Our Girls" that speak to the unity of victimhood, we see the effect of erasing the conditions that produce structural violence. These forms of mediation rely not only on intermediaries who articulate and internalize new signs and symbols, but also on codes and perceptions that shape the meanings that are evoked through brief, emotionally infused Twitter utterances. Through these formats, the declarative demands preclude complex understandings about the nature of inequality and align particular practices with sentimental declarations of abhorrence. Through these speech acts, not only are hierarchies of acceptability established, but the nature of their logic is disassembled from the political conditions and histories that constituted this logic in the first place.

Yet the postcolonial struggles that unfolded in Nigeria following independence did not simply reflect the problem of radical Islamic violence begetting more violence, as one would think in relation to the mobilization against Boko Haram. The discovery and extraction of natural resources like oil, diamonds, and gas has compounded situations of armed conflict across the African continent. Following the discovery of oil and a related brutal civil war, Nigeria was plagued with military coups between the north and the south to control the economic power at the center of the federation. The country experienced ten successive military coups beginning in 1966, just a few years after independence and immediately following the discovery of its oil reserves. The struggle to control Nigeria's government has always been in large part a struggle to control its resources. Minimal attention was given to developing state institutions and equalizing them in the north and the south. Instead, a highly centralized federal body with little to no accountability formed in its place. This pattern has repeated across the continent. So it is not surprising that the race for political control in many African countries has led to extreme forms of violence, military coups, or rebel groups vying for political influence to control various extraction industries.

The ultimate erosion of state capacities to build viable economies for citizens, to command and regulate access to resources in the domestic economy, and to build innovative mechanisms capable of incorporating indigenous cultural traditions to direct future action all represent a more tragic set of realities related the actual violence of inequality.[55] These postcolonial realities call into question modes of liability for violence and question what justice might be if we overlook its fetishes and explore not just the forms of narratives that are deployed but the changing technologies through which new moral formations are taking root. These new strategic modes of mobilization that invigorate emotional strategies in the pursuit of justice are critical for making sense of how the process of encapsulating justice with legality makes structural inequality unintelligible. As a result, the conditions that produce the need for legality—such as structural inequality and spheres of colonialism, imperialism, and racism—are pushed to the margins and erased, while new forms of social alliances are made possible through technologically propelled messaging. This disappearance of a particular type of politics has made Boko Haram leaders' contestations of Western encroachment on northern practices inconceivable.

The #BringBackOurGirls mobilizations have taken shape in response to the symptoms of violence. The use of digital technologies to facilitate changing spheres of protest and engagement clarify how in new advocacy nonspaces, such as hashtag mobilizations, new social commitments are being mobilized. Emotions that connect liberal sensibilities of equal gender rights, sexual freedoms, and the importance of Western education reflect that. I conclude, then, by suggesting that the rise of the construction of an "international community" committed to immediate solutions to social issues has produced a particular constituency motivated by gender justice that is not unrelated to the war on terror—Nigeria's Boko Haram network being a part of the larger deployment of such international war offensives and thus tied to the White House's military interests in the region. Given these alliances, it is important to see such social movement formations not simply as innocent forms of contemporary activism but as reinforcing particular ideological commitments to Western democratic liberal values that are not always shared by all.

Biomediated Alignments and Contemporary Justice

Thus far, this chapter has explored the way that everyday people, celebrities, and activists are working with networks of advocacy groups to mobilize social action around rights discourses. By examining the role of popular practices in mobilizing social action, we see how concepts such as freedom for kidnapped girls or the education of all girls can be invoked as a solution to a much deeper problem. We see that what is articulated as the real work involves enlisting ourselves, as actors, as agents of change. As I have been developing in these early chapters, the "victim to be saved" has become a critical fetish that serves as the basis for contemporary justice. That imagery is not only symbolic and ahistorical but, depending on its alliances with particular publics, can also elicit affective responses in ways that generate social action. It compels our convictions and motivates our compassion. The relationship between our solidarity in defending the vulnerable and our agency to demand the immediacy of resolutions through the pursuit of those deemed criminally culpable is a reflection of the power of contemporary emotional regimes, our technocratic knowledge domains, and the role of technological practices. The consolidation of these component parts constitutes new publics through the articulation of particular moral positions that bind groups of otherwise unrelated people to each other. The portability, immediacy, and rapid circulation of digital technologies have given rise to this proclivity and require that we remain analytically vigilant in our assessment of the alliances that take shape around suffering. We must make sense of when, under which conditions, and who invokes bodies that require our sympathy and when mass mobilizations around biomediated imagery are deployed and how.[56] We also must look at how the suffering body is being displayed and why, how, and when bodies disappear and are sublimated to ideas about our social norms.

The #BringBackOurGirls movement and the actual declaration "Bring Back Our Girls" propelled a discourse surrounding our legal responsibility to act, to defend, or to threaten military action as a key component of international justice. This call for action is a discursive mechanism through which contemporary meanings of justice are being conflated with legality. As a result of these twenty-first-century, technologically driven, affective justice mobilizations, international rule of law and humanitarian circles are calling into question the relevance of empathy to describe the nature of public expressions. Instead, from shifting narratives of suffering and images of bodily dismemberment, new mainstream publics are being enlisted to rally around liberalist values. These developments are shaping global justice advocacy around rights and entitlements and are becoming as much about the emotional expressions of protection of those victimized by violence as they are about the nature of contemporary international assemblages in online nonspaces.[57] Attending to these formations allows us to think about how the idea of suffering can exceed itself and become something else. In this case, the something else expands to become a larger idea around individual entitlements and rights through which new publics are brought into international relevance. And this is critical to how we understand the emergence of international justice in the contemporary period—a site for the deterritorialization of suffering and its relocation in the interest of social change.

By considering these formations in the construction of the international community and the role of the individual engaged in the immediacy of protection as a modality of politics, new online campaigns have become another way to use reattribution to conflate justice and the body with legality. This chapter demonstrates how the legal encapsulation of the victim and perpetrator has successfully created an international community that has internalized the responsibility to protect, but the problem remains that the type of community of action that this generates is rooted in the temporality of the now. The effect of this is a new form of justice in the twenty-first century that negates the relevance of inequality embedded in much deeper histories of violence, and instead focuses on justice demands as urgently actionable and facilitated by new digital technologies as sites for new domains for deterritorialized technocratic knowledge—in this case, biomediation.

CHAPTER 4

From "Perpetrator" to Hero

Renarrating Culpability through Reattribution

Where all are guilty, no one is.
—HANNAH ARENDT, *Responsibility and Judgment*

If the #Kony2012 and #BringBackOurGirls campaigns contributed to the popularization of a particular figure of the African "perpetrator" to be held accountable and the figure of the "victim" to be saved, in neighboring Kenya a campaign with the opposite ideological angst emerged through the figures of Uhuru Kenyatta and William Ruto. Despite being indicted by the ICC and deemed by those in the anti-impunity movement to be perpetrators of Kenya's 2007–2008 electoral violence, these men were resignified and reframed in relation to modes of responsibility that raised the importance of articulating Kenya's violence in the context of the country's history. This treatment of historical context and the role of temporality in attributing culpability are in direct contrast to the approach of international justice campaigns, though equally manipulative. Through the deployment of Kenyatta and Ruto as brave leaders attempting to settle age-old disputes, the two came together as presidential and deputy presidential contenders for the Kenyan federal elections. Their campaign, with its highly produced and compelling message, merged two unlikely collaborators through the rebranding of Kenyan nationalist narratives using sentimental articulations that worked against the growing legal encapsulation trend.

The slick UhuRuto 2013 campaign, introducing the newly merged political party, the Jubilee Coalition, celebrated a new story of national unity by critiquing Europe's ongoing interference in Africa. As symbolic figures of the

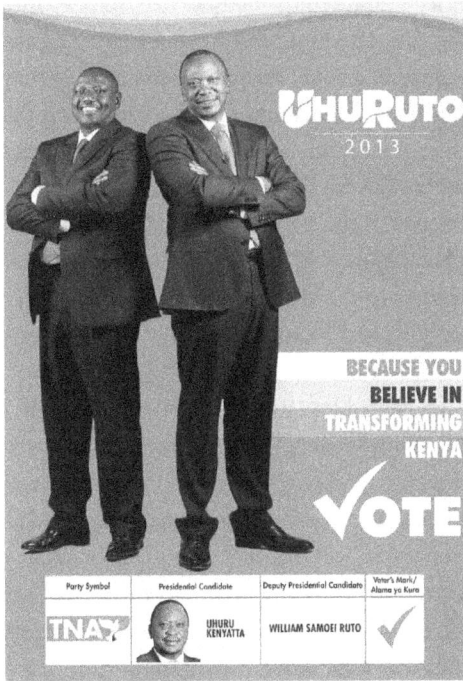

4.1 UhuRuto political
campaign poster.

new postcolonial Africa, Kenyatta and Ruto were made to represent a different story through the Swahili slogan "Tuko Pamoja" (We are together) and with the top-trending hashtag #kenyadecides. Adamant about not letting the West interfere, its message responded to President Obama's warnings—shown nightly on Kenyan news stations—that Kenyans should not elect ICC indictees as the country's leaders. But the refrain prevailed: Kenyans had a right to decide for themselves who their leaders would be.

Through the merger of the names of both leaders, the campaign spearheaded the symbolic unification of historically competing voting blocs to support two leaders now rebranded as figures who would defend against external forces. The resignified image from perpetrator to African freedom fighter was effective (as suggested in chapter 2) because of what Joseph de Rivera refers to as particular historical emotional sensibilities and contemporary emotional climates.[1] As social domains that produce emotional cultural sensibilities, they engage in the socialization of practices and attitudes and create acceptable meanings out of particular political contexts. In this light, #kenyadecides went viral and was the highest trending hashtag of Kenya's 2013 election period.

Tuko Pamoja was deployed as a cultural symbol of unity between two historically competing parties. It was translated into forty-two tribal languages and signaled the diversity of the governing coalition and the coming together of historically fractured political groups. Invocations of Tuko Pamoja on the campaign trail—through speeches, utterances, and salutations—led to the mobilization of grassroots constituencies who prayed and anointed their leaders in defense of what they portrayed as the persecution of Africa's leaders by the ICC. The party's new colors—yellow, red, and black—drew from both Uhuru's National Alliance (TNA) party (red and white) and Ruto's United Republican Party (yellow and black) and was characterized by two hands together with the slogan "Our fate is in our hands."

The Jubilee Coalition's campaign tapped into pro-Kenyan desires for postcolonial justice and succeeded in turning the electoral conversation away from the ICC trials and toward the need for a new agenda for change that addressed the historical roots of inequality in Kenya. This message highlighted the violence of the colonial past and the importance of reckoning with Kenya's contemporary struggles through a sense of the *longue durée* of violence that produces structural inequalities.[2] Thus, in contrast to the ICC's focus on individualized criminal responsibility and strict notions of legal time, this narrative draws on emotional reactions to historical and ongoing inequality and appropriates the discourse of reattribution to reassign blame.[3] But this narrativization could not unfold without the major support of a mediation strategy.

In 2012, Kenyatta hired a British public relations firm (located in the former colonial center) to conduct the relevant strategic market research to understand what they needed to do to win the election. The National Alliance adopted the dove as their symbol and "I Believe" as their slogan. He then hired another UK-based company, BTP Advisers, with a network in European, African, and emerging markets, to develop a campaign that would pull in support and offer a more youthful and dynamic image of the candidates. According to their website, BTP staff see themselves as creating and executing "political and profile-raising campaigns for individuals, candidates, organisations and companies to change hearts, minds and laws and deliver upset and unexpected victories." This company harnessed key sentiments already central to the lives of Kenyans to achieve their main objective.[4] As their website explains, "Our full-time team of consultants, embedded on the ground with the campaign, helped to develop a set of messages that turned Kenyatta's image around. By exposing the weak and flawed nature of the ICC case against him, we made the election a choice about whether Kenyans would decide their own future or have it dictated to them by others. We demonstrated that only Kenyatta understood the concerns of ordinary Kenyans and would defend Kenyan values."[5] Mark Pursey, one of the BTP advisers who led the campaign, outlined that his media strategy involved excessive monitoring of social media and information gathering on their opponent, with the goal of improving Uhuru's image while presenting the ICC process as the machinations of the Western powers.[6]

The campaign message highlighted Uhuru's call to foreign powers to stop interfering with Kenya's internal affairs. This trope, familiar in its form and content, alongside the merger of two traditionally opposed parties, produced a winning package. With input from Kenyatta's defense attorney, the well-known international lawyer Stephen Kay, extensive and detailed commentaries, op-ed pieces, consistent strategic responses to inquiries, and active creation of a positive public-relations message BTP masterminded the Jubilee Coalition campaign to redirect the impact of the ICC's indictments. Central to this was their reorienting of the way that the general public understood issues of criminal culpability—especially the collective nature of culpability—as it relates to who was actually responsible for Kenya's postelection violence. And it worked. Despite the charges of Ruto and Kenyatta's culpability on the international stage, in 2013 a majority of the Kenyan people democratically elected Kenyatta and Ruto to be Kenya's president and deputy president. This democratic election followed the reign of President Mwai Kibaki (2002–2013), who succeeded Daniel Moi's (1978–2002) twenty-four-year dictatorship. The message that the ICC process is deeply political and reproduces older patterns of European colonialism in African affairs, while ignoring Europe's responsibility for its part in Kenya's contemporary violence, continues to resonate and circulate throughout the Kenyan press.

This approach involved contemporary forms of mediation deployed affectively to ignite hearts and minds with the injustices of Europe's violent past and to set new terms for how issues of culpability were understood. But when we deconstruct the hero symbol that the campaign highlights, we see that part of what hastens the transformation of Kenyatta and Ruto from "perpetrator" to "hero" is made possible by clever branding, alliances and complicity with transnational capital, the importance of Kenya-Western trade relations, and the cunning of the untold story of the Kenyan mafia. Indeed, there are few heroes in this story—particularly from the perspective of people who have lived through and survived violence inflicted on them by various African leaders. In talking with ordinary people, even as they complained of the injustices of the African state, we also saw how the reattribution of the individualized "perpetrator" figure by the ICC often led to feelings that international justice has also failed them. Time and time again we witnessed people then dealing with those feelings by shifting the parameters of culpability—a process that I have referred to as reattribution. In this case, reattribution takes the form of reclassifying the basis for culpability through temporality.

As we have seen, the figure of the African "perpetrator" to be held accountable for mass violence committed within a legally limited period of time, or in the context of legal time, has emerged as both a bold symbol of anti-impunity and a key force for social resistance. This chapter builds on a discussion I began in previous chapters about the rhetorical resignification of the figure of the "perpetrator" but looks specifically at counterattributions of culpability in relation to law's temporality. As my research showed, various African leaders use this strategy to deflect blame, protest ICC indictments, and win elections, and African stakeholders, including survivors, also use it to harness such strategies as well. The act of reattribution highlights a genuine ambivalence about international justice prosecutions for mass violence. When the relevance of structural inequalities—and thus the culpability for violence that implicates colonial settlers and authorities or proximate actors—is ignored, the ICC's perpetrator figure functions as a mode of erasure rather than an example of prosecutorial justice cascades, as scholars such as Kathryn Sikkink may suggest.[7] This case, thus, shows how particular sentimental responses to the ICC perpetrator figure and the relevance of legal time have inspired counter-ICC sentiments that are shaping new ways to measure justice in the contemporary period. This happens through the rethinking of culpability.

Culpability is the cornerstone of criminal law and refers to the degree to which one can be held responsible for a particular act or set of results. Rooted in American and European legal traditions, individual culpability treats individuals as autonomous agents who are able to either obey or violate the law, and to bear the consequences of a violation of the law. In the Anglo-Saxon legal tradition known as the liberal justice model, culpability requires the existence of a criminal act (*actus reus*) coupled with the intentional commission of such an act (*mens rea*).[8] As I explained in the introduction, notions of individual culpability introduced to international law in Nuremberg and revived in the 1990s with the International Criminal Tribunal for Yugoslavia, the International Criminal Tribunal for Rwanda (ICTR), and later the ICC, remain a cornerstone of international criminal law today. However, collective violence—as a key feature of international criminal law—has meant that prosecutors in international criminal trials have had to find ways to ascribe liability for collective crimes to high-ranking leaders. They have grappled with ways to establish the linkages between particular actions (or failure to act) of the accused and a given set of acts.

This issue of how to attribute individual guilt for collective crimes has proven difficult in international criminal law circles and among the constituencies and publics expected to internalize such principles. The difficulties have been centered around liberal legalism and the challenges with advocating for direct, individual criminal responsibility—the principle that individuals must be held accountable for their own crimes and not for those of others.[9] In these contexts, legal agents such as the ICC's judges and prosecutor also maintain a threshold of July 1, 2002, for the ICC's temporal jurisdiction over contemporary violence. This narrow temporal sense of admissible time places responsibility for violence in the hands of those who gave the orders, encouraged violence, or did not prevent it. However, others take the long history of colonial and postcolonial injustices into account when assigning guilt for present-day actions. Some of those who experienced or lived through the violence were more likely to hold responsible the proximate actors who inflicted the physical and emotional violence—the police, the head of police, the military, and the foot soldiers—rather than a leader deemed responsible for the actions of his subordinates.

Through this disjuncture we can look for openings to understand how affects and emotional alliances are used to narrativize culpability for the collective violence in 2007–2008. I begin by mapping the circumstances surrounding the violence that erupted following Kenya's 2007 presidential election alongside legal arguments made by the ICC about the leaders' culpability. We then see how the resulting sentimental defiance of those indictments by some Kenyan constituencies takes the form of reattribution, in which culpability for mass violence is redirected through historical and experiential senses of collective culpability. These seemingly different approaches contextualize the temporal and juridical frames through which Kenyatta and Ruto were indicted and the forms of popular refusals that are experienced differently that led to their support and election. Ultimately, these figures are invested emotionally with meanings that map onto either compressed juridical temporalities (the indicted perpetrator) or longer historical narratives (the anticolonial hero), but neither results in feelings of justice being served. For if we see these various anti-ICC sentiments as regulatory responses that buttress feelings against histories of Western domination rather than as ephemeral emotions, then it is what these anti-ICC sentiments do within international rule of law assemblages that is critical for making sense of how the ICC is understood as an extension of European colonialism.[10]

What is relevant is that the history of technocratic imposition of colonial laws in Africa and their related violence exists alongside Africans' bitterness about the role of their African leaders in furthering such problems. For while people's perception of African leaders' abuse of power and the prevalent feelings about corruption and violence with impunity continue to shape the complexities of African landscapes, both the anticolonial and the anti-impunity discourses circulate as social goods that serve to reinforce particular social norms. In so doing, they provide the template for particular behaviors and set new domains for the regulatory ideas around which justice inspires new ideals. Both groups of sentiments are emancipatory in different ways and are shaped by the feeling regimes at play.

Individual Criminal Responsibility and the Case against Kenyatta and Ruto

Adherents to the principle of individual criminal responsibility perform particular sentiments that support the idea that certain types of liability (such as aiding and abetting and conspiracy) can be reconfigured into new modes of responsibility and within strict conceptualizations of temporality. Such reconfigured forms of international legality rely on affective responses to certain narratives, such as the "victim to be saved" or the "perpetrator to be held legally responsible," and are sustained by legal provisions in the Rome Statute. Article 28, in particular, stipulates that a military commander or a person acting as a military commander with effective command and control over their forces shall be individually, criminally liable for the criminal conduct of their subordinates, provided they knew (or should have known) that the forces were committing or were about to commit such crimes.

Article 28 also concerns a commander who fails to take all necessary measures to prevent or suppress the commission of these crimes. The material elements of the crimes must occur within the temporal jurisdiction of the court (from July 1, 2002, onward) and be committed with knowledge and intent. Such a doctrine of hierarchical criminal or command responsibility—established by The Hague Conventions (IV) and (X) of 1907 and first applied during the Leipzig War Crimes Trials after World War I, and then later at Nuremberg— involves the reassignment of the guilt of thousands who committed violent acts to a single chief commander and a few top aides.[11] It highlights a relatively recent development of command responsibility outside of military command structures.

The Nuremberg solution of individualizing criminal responsibility for collective crimes was a moral intervention that was seen to reflect what Gerry Simpson calls the "triumph of liberal legalism and individual responsibility over vengeful politics and collective guilt."[12] This precedent of individual responsibility was heavily influenced by the formation of late twentieth- and early twenty-first-century international criminal law. Yet the challenge is that individualism, as a concept rooted in Western legal traditions, stems from the understanding that a person is only culpable to the extent of their own free will or guilty mind (mens rea). Individual guilt permeates Western legal cultural traditions over concepts such as collective guilt (a people's guilt or historical/structural guilt) or even metaphysical guilt (the notion that a person is guilty simply by existing). It represents what Antonio Cassese has described as the central idea behind individualized liability—a core feature of liberal legality: no one should be held accountable for criminal offenses that were perpetrated by other persons.[13] And though this point was further affirmed with the decision of the International Criminal Tribunal for Yugoslavia Appeals Chamber, which held in the *Tadić* case (written by Judge Cassese) that "the basic assumption must be that in international law, as much as in national systems, the foundation of criminal responsibility is the principle of personal culpability: nobody may be held criminally responsible for acts or transactions in which he has not personally engaged or in some other way participated (*nulla poena sine culpa*)."[14] This conception forms one of the key foundations of international criminal law. Thus, Cassese and a range of other innovators contributed to the popularization of a contrary formulation that was propelled by the notion of attribution. The move to attribution through the individualization of criminal responsibility has actually been seen by many in the Global South as contradicting the foundational principle that no one should be held accountable for the acts of others, because many see the process of attribution as insufficient in addressing issues concerning collective liability for violence. This disagreement not only shows some of the pitfalls of ascribing agency based on military structures to actions among civilians, but also the way in which international criminal law has developed through the authority of (nonbinding) case law between tribunals. We see the precedents applied in the Rwandan genocide trials of civilian command responsibility as well as the Charles Taylor case.[15]

In 2006, an extradition request was issued for the former Liberian president, Charles Taylor, to be extradited from Nigeria to the Special Court for Sierra Leone. This set a precedent for international law norms for a sitting president. Taylor was charged for crimes against humanity and war crimes committed during Sierra Leone's civil war between 1991 and 2002 by another institution that preceded the ICC, the Special Court for Sierra Leone. He was not charged because he was seen as committing those crimes himself; instead, the charges assumed that as a commander he should have prevented such violence (he had command responsibility) or that he was complicit through modes of joint criminal enterprise.[16] These legal developments related to command responsibility are normalized through precedent, but as we will see, they may not map well onto how affected communities understand the causes of violence.

With the individualization of criminal responsibility firmly established as a form of legality for procuring justice for those victimized by violence, the notion of the representative perpetrator indicted by an international tribunal has—since the Nuremberg Tribunal and Adolf Eichmann's trial in Jerusalem—propelled a particular international imaginary of those whose actions (or inaction) contributed to mass crimes that shocked the human conscience. These perpetrators—represented as military leaders, coconspirators, heads of state, and warlords—embodied an individualized presence to be held accountable in various postviolence situations today. At stake in the ICC case against Kenyatta and Ruto were their alleged roles in postelection violence.

On November 26, 2009, the prosecutor for the ICC requested authorization from Pre-trial Chamber II to investigate violence following Kenya's 2007–2008 elections. The Office of the Prosecutor (OTP) argued that it had reasonable grounds to believe that "crimes of murder, rape and other forms of sexual violence, deportation or forcible transfer of population and other inhumane acts" had been committed in Kenya during 2007–2008.[17]

On December 15, 2010, the Pre-trial Chamber granted the relevant permission to indict Ruto, Kenyatta, and others using the conception of superior responsibility. This legal frame involved the doctrine of hierarchical accountability, wherein expectations of supervision pertain to a related liability for the failure to act and were, therefore, further established through the doctrine of command responsibility.

Citing the gravity of the acts of violence and the absence of national proceedings, the prosecutor argued that the cases originating from the investigation of violence during 2007 and 2008 involving the culpability of various high-ranking Kenyan leaders should be admissible before the ICC.[18] The Kenyan government challenged this. Simultaneously, the African Union, in partnership with the Kenyan National Dialogue and Reconciliation team, under the leadership of former UN secretary-general Kofi Annan, recommended that the government establish the Commission of Inquiry into Post-Election Violence.[19] Known as the Waki Commission, it recommended that a special tribunal for Kenya be set up within a given time frame to investigate and prosecute suspected perpetrators of crimes committed during the crisis period.[20] In October 2008, the report indicated that a meeting was held in the state house to coordinate revenge on members of the Luo and Kalenjin ethnic groups; it cited the then-minister, Uhuru Kenyatta, as being criminally responsible for financing and mobilizing electoral support through the Mungiki.[21] Similarly, the Luos and Kalenjins purportedly mobilized their support to attack the Kikuyus (the ethnic group Kenyatta belongs to). The African Union–sponsored Waki Commission recommended that if the Kenyan government failed to set up a tribunal to investigate and adjudicate the cases, then the ICC should take over.

In early 2009, amid increased ethnic party tensions, Kenyan parliamentarians tried to bring forward a bill to establish a special tribunal. In the end, it received limited support and was defeated on two different occasions.[22] Parliamentarians from across the Orange Democratic Movement (ODM, led by Raila Odinga) and the Party of National Unity (PNU, Kenyatta and Kibaki's party) united to defeat it under the slogan "Don't be vague; let's go to The Hague." The public statements made by various ODM and PNU politicians revealed their interest in seeking legal accountability for the other party. The prevailing argument was that no special tribunal in Kenya could be trusted to deal independently and impartially with issues of legal accountability for postelection violence.[23]

On March 8, 2011, the ICC issued summons for the suspects to appear before the court.[24] The prosecutor named six persons (known as the Ocampo 6) suspected of bearing the greatest responsibility for crimes committed during Kenya's 2007 postelection period. The six were divided into two sets of cases representing two historically opposed factions divided along ethnic lines. On one side was Major General Mohammed Hussein Ali, a Somali Kenyan who had been the commissioner of the Kenyan police during the postelection violence; Uhuru Kenyatta (Kikuyu), then the deputy prime minister and minister for finance, as well as the chairman of President Kibaki's PNU; and Henry Kiprono Kosgey (Kalenjin in ethnicity), former minister for industrialization and a member of the National Assembly as well as the chairman of the

ODM.[25] The opposing side included three political agents representing predominant people aligned with the Meru and Kalenjin ethnic group: Francis Kirimi Muthaura, the head of public service, cabinet secretary, and chairman of the National Security Advisory Committee; William Ruto, the minister for higher education, science and technology, and ODM member of the National Assembly for Eldoret North; and Joshua Arap Sang, the head of operations at the Kalenjin-language radio station KASS FM and a radio host at the time of the postelection violence.[26]

Ruto was charged with (1) "Murder constituting a crime against humanity," (2) "Deportation or forcible transfer of population constituting a crime against humanity," and (3) "Persecution as a crime against humanity."[27] For his part, Kenyatta was charged with (1) "Murder constituting a crime against humanity," (2) "Deportation or forcible transfer of population constituting a crime against humanity," (3) "Rape and other forms of sexual violence constituting a crime against humanity," (4) "Other inhumane acts constituting a crime against humanity," and (5) "Persecution as a crime against humanity."[28]

Ruto was alleged to have held a series of meetings in which he distributed money and arms with the goal of commissioning the crimes of murder and displacement of supporters of the PNU (led by Mwai Kibaki, sitting president at the time). Following this, these activities correspondingly fomented the violence following the 2007 election. Ethnic tensions ostensibly worsened when, amid accusations of election rigging, competing parties—the PNU and the ODM—both claimed electoral victory.[29] When Kenya's Electoral Commission announced that Mwai Kibaki was the winner of Kenya's 2007 elections, violence broke out throughout Kenya—particularly in pro-Odinga areas: the slums of Nairobi, the Rift Valley (Eldoret), and Nyanza (Kisumu)—lasting two months.[30] In the end, rioting, excessive use of force (by police and security forces), burning, looting, sexual violence, and murder left 1,200 people dead and displaced thousands.[31]

The prosecutor alleged that Kenyatta organized meetings with various government leaders, the police, and the leadership of the outlawed Mungiki sect, in which he supposedly provided funding, uniforms, and weapons to various pro-PNU youth to carry out their attacks. The Mungiki, whose name means "a united people" in the Kenya Kikuyu language, is known as a mafia-oriented organization and is notorious for its participation in the 2007 postelection violence. Kenyatta is said to have mobilized their support for the purposes of defending Kikuyu interests, leading the ICC to consider him criminally responsible for the violence the Mungiki perpetrated.[32]

In January 2012, the Pre-trial Chamber judges confirmed the charges of crimes against humanity against only four of the six indictees for Kenya's 2007–2008 postelection violence.[33] The chamber did not find that the evidence against Mr. Kosgey met the necessary evidentiary threshold, so the charges against him were not confirmed. In Mr. Ali's case, the judges did not find that the evidence provided substantial grounds to believe that the National Police participated in the attacks in Naivasha and Nakuru, so the charges against him were also dropped, leaving Ruto and Sang versus the prosecutor. By summer 2013, due to various setbacks in the prosecution's evidence, such as the loss of key witnesses for the Muthaura case, the charges against him were dropped, leaving only three indictees overall, with only Kenyatta left in the second case. Though the mode of liability initially confirmed for Kenyatta/Muthaura was indirect coperpetration, after the charges were dropped against Muthaura, the charge against Kenyatta was connected to his being individually responsible for the violence in Naivasha on January 27 and 28 and in Nakuru on January 24 and 27 of 2008. By May 2016, all charges were dropped against all Kenyan indictees because of lack of evidence to convict.

The Limits of Legal Time

When time is juridified, it becomes a matter of concern for law. Operating within the limits of legal time, the ICC cannot see retrospectively beyond its own coming into force in 2002. It is compressed and dehistoricized, bounded by temporal jurisdiction—such as the start date of the ICC's founding statute or the temporal scope of the punishable offense. It also has a substructure in time based on the perceived supremacy of the legislative, constitutional or treaty doctrine. This substructure brings to life the basis on which original intent of legal documents can be determined in time and establishes the basis on which looking backward is permissible. This substructure shapes the basis for the type of legal reasoning through which fundamental values are established.[34] In this case, the Rome Statute for the ICC set out substantive laws and procedural rules through which to address violence. It ascribes guilt based on a particular period within the temporal jurisdiction of the court and highlights questions of responsibility in individualist terms. The ICC examined its temporal jurisdiction over potential cases against Ruto and Kenyatta when it granted the prosecutor permission to commence an investigation of the situation; these considerations are also apparent in the temporal scope of the asserted crimes in relation to the evidence provided to cover the entire time period included in the prosecutor's initial charges.[35] In the end, the ICC's temporal jurisdiction over the Kenyatta and Ruto cases was legally limited by Article 11 of the Rome Statute (*jurisdiction ratione temporis*), which provides that the "Court has jurisdiction only with respect to crimes committed after the entry into force of this Statute."[36]

> The Prosecutor submits that, since the Republic of Kenya ratified the Rome Statute on 15 March 2005 and, pursuant to article 126(1), the Statute entered into force for that State on 1 June 2005, the crimes allegedly committed fall within the Court's temporal jurisdiction. . . . The Chamber concurs with the Prosecutor that the crimes allegedly committed after 1 June 2005, as they appear from the available information, fall within the jurisdiction *ratione temporis* of the Court.[37]

Each of the charges asserted by the prosecutor against Ruto and Kenyatta covered the period from on or about December 31, 2007, to January 31, 2008. However, the ICC narrowed the scope of those charges, finding that the prosecutor had provided sufficient evidence to support the charges only for specific dates. Specifically, in the case of Kenyatta, the ICC held, "Regardless of the broader temporal parameters of the charges, the events of relevance in the present case are exclusively those for which the Prosecutor alleges the individual criminal responsibility of the Suspects, i.e. those that form part of the attack by the Mungiki on the ODM supporters between 24 and 28 January 2008."[38] Eventually, in the case against Ruto, the demarcated period was January 1–4, 2008, and involved violence allegedly committed in the greater Eldoret area.[39] For Kenyatta, the charges were based on his supposed command of murders committed in Naivasha on January 27 and 28, 2008, and in Nakuru on January 24 and 27.[40]

Two aspects of the ICC's decision to narrow the time are worth noting. The ICC decision was based not on a lack of temporal jurisdiction but on the prosecutor's failure to present sufficient evidence to cover the entire time period included in the initial charges. Second, the articles of the Rome Statute that require the ICC to confirm the asserted charges do not expressly require that the ICC parse the time period in days, months, or any other temporal measure, or to otherwise confirm that the time period is sufficiently confined.[41]

The temporal scope of the charges against Ruto and Kenyatta is especially narrow when compared to the scale of the violence that triggered the prosecutor's investigation. As described in the prosecutor's November 26, 2009, Request for Authorization of an Investigation Pursuant to Article 15:

The scale of the post-election violence resulted in a reported 1,133 to 1,220 killings of civilians, more than nine hundred documented acts of rape and other forms of sexual violence, with many more unreported, the internal displacement of 350,000 persons, and 3,561 reported acts causing serious injury. In addition, the social and economic structures of the local communities were largely affected by the widespread looting and wanton destruction of residential and commercial areas. Crimes have been committed in six out of eight Kenyan regions, and particularly in the country's most populated areas, including the capital city of Nairobi, the Rift Valley, and the Nyanza and Western provinces.[42]

In many cases, the multiple crimes had been organized and planned within the context of a widespread and systematic attack against selected segments of the Kenyan civilian population. Groups, and persons belonging to these groups, were stigmatized and deliberately targeted on the basis of distinctive ethnic features and/or presumed political affiliations. Typically, the perpetrators attacked, killed, and displaced members of minority ethnicities in those areas.

One of the most challenging examples of how courts wrestle with problems of strict temporality can be seen through attempts to address continuing and composite crimes, as they force courts to address conduct over a long time rather than in more singular crimes such as murder. A continuing or composite crime is one that necessarily occurs over an extended period, such as apartheid. Unlike murder, apartheid does not occur in a single instant.[43] It involves legal policies, state action, social control, and prolonged practices of exclusion and separation. Continuing and composite crimes also include specific, discrete acts that, by definition, must occur over a longer time frame. For example, the Rome Statute outlaws murder as a crime against humanity. By definition, to be a crime against humanity, the act of murder must occur as part of a widespread or systematic attack against a civilian population.[44] In contrast, when addressing regular crimes such as murder that occur in a discrete temporal instant, courts rarely if ever address the importance of temporal limits. However, with continuing and composite crimes, courts must regularly address the temporal scope of the conduct being prosecuted.[45]

The *Rainbow Warrior* case, one of the most famous examples in international case law concerning continuing violations, set a precedent in shaping how continuing violations are understood. The case is important for the history of international tribunals recognizing continuous crimes. In this case, two French agents were convicted by a New Zealand high court of assisting in the sinking of the *Rainbow Warrior,* a Greenpeace ship docked off the coast of New Zealand (which was going to protest French nuclear testing in the Pacific Ocean). France refrained from detaining the two agents and returned them to Hao, a French Pacific island, in violation of its agreement with New Zealand. In determining France's culpability for refusing to detain the agents, an international arbitration tribunal did not measure France's liability from the moment the agents were removed. Rather, the misconduct was deemed continuous and ongoing, and it included each day the agents remained outside of New Zealand's control.[46]

Continuing and composite crimes force courts to address conduct that continues over longer time periods than simpler crimes such as murder. They create legal dilemmas, not just for questions of jurisdiction but also around questions of evidence and admissibility. In *Prosecutor v. Musema*, the ICTR allowed the prosecutor to present pre-1994 evidence in order to establish the mens rea needed for genocide. Thus, the ICTR jurisprudence allowed pre-1994 evidence of intent but "not of conduct."[47] In this case as well as subsequent ICTR cases, we see an example where the court allowed the introduction of evidence from outside the jurisdictional temporal window.[48] But this contrasts with *Prosecutor v. Jean-Bosco Barayagwiza*, in which the court interpreted its jurisdiction restrictively, holding that no facts predating or postdating 1994 could be used to support a count in the indictment.[49] This case resulted in the conviction of a former Rwandan journalist for incitement to commit genocide as a crime against humanity.[50] It led to the court's attempt to focus on conduct—direct and public incitement—leading to a conviction rather than considering pre-1994 conditions of colonial and postcolonial subordination that fostered the development of extremist Hutu ideologies.[51]

In the last two cases we see inconsistencies in how the ICTR dealt with measures for intent, but what is interesting is that conduct remained within the remit of the court's narrowly prescribed jurisdictional window. The historical and current cases identified here address the limits of legal time and represent compelling examples of how courts wrestled with problems of strict temporality. In the ICC cases relating to postelection violence in contemporary Kenya, a close reading of the ICC's charges reveals the tension between specific instances of criminality (violence) on the one hand, and histories of inequalities and injustices that have occurred over extended periods on the other hand. With this dynamic at play, what we see is how anti-impunity affects are used to shape notions of culpability through the application of legal time and how other senses of responsibility are expressed through the reattribution of such measures of culpability.[52]

The Longue Durée of Structural Violence: Recontextualizing Culpability

In February 2013, Uhuru Kenyatta announced the launching of the Jubilee Coalition with a speech that established the landmark creation of TNA—the political party that was taken over by Uhuru Kenyatta and rebranded to create an alliance of various democratic forces. With a discourse of togetherness, Kenyatta began by highlighting the challenges and opportunities the Kenyan nation was facing. The former had to do with the cycles of violence that caused death and destruction to Kenyans following the ebbs and flows of each election cycle—the most serious being the 2007–2008 violence in which over 1,300 Kenyans died and more than 300,000 were displaced. Central to this violence is the question of land. Shifting the core problems to pre-2002 structural violence, Kenyatta's narrative began with the displacement inherent in the British colonial disenfranchisement of Kenyan natives. As Kenyatta explained:

> You all know that when the colonial government established itself in Kenya it created three categories of land ownership. First was the land taken by the colonial government for its own use, which was called Crown Land, second was the land given to settlers as private land, and lastly what remained was assigned to Africans as Native Reserves. Back in 1954 under the Swynnerton Plan some Native Reserves saw a process of adjudication, consolidation, and registration that gave titles to Africans. At independence our Government inherited Crown Land and renamed it Government land, today this accounts for 13 percent of the country's total land mass. Native Reserves became trust land vested in local county councils.
>
> Even after independence the settlers kept their land under private title, or sold it to Africans on a "willing buyer, willing seller" basis. And today private land is something bought and sold like any other commodity. . . . Private land accounts for 20 percent of our country. Land in those Reserves that were not adjudicated and given back to Africans is now called Community Land under the new Constitution and is to be managed by the National Land Commission. This category of land presently accounts for about two-thirds, 67 percent of the total land in Kenya.[53]

The speech was full of campaign promises that outlined a range of opportunities tied to the land question and ensuring that the nation would recover from violence. "Our nation must heal. Our people must come together, with the realization that—as difficult as it may seem—we need each other. The solution should be obvious to all; we must learn to live with one another, trust one another, to respect one another as Kenyans, love one another."[54]

Later he clarified how this might happen by proposing to provide economic opportunities so that people could procure land viable for agriculture: "As a government, we will provide wider economic opportunities so that people, especially in rural areas, do not feel that the only way they can make a living is tilling ever-smaller parcels of land using a jembe and a panga. We aim to reverse the process of fragmentation and instead institute a process of reconsolidation that will create viable land holdings. While our policies will be deliberate, the process of reconsolidation will be voluntary and driven by the availability of better opportunities across the country."[55]

From the discussion of government land to private land to community land, he articulated a plan for how his government might help citizens own the land on which they live: "The new Constitution recognizes that there is a problem but it does not provide a solution. My Government will be committed to finally giving the Land Answer. . . . My Government will be committed to giving people the title to their own land. . . . Kenyans deserve to have that process completed. . . . We will do this not just in rural areas but also in urban areas where informal settlements abound."[56]

The history to which Kenyatta referred takes us to July 1, 1895, when the region that is now known as Kenya was declared a British-East African Protectorate.[57] British colonialism in Kenya produced a situation of uneven land distribution and a related problem of elite patronage. The colonial government forcefully evicted Africans from their ancestral lands and relocated them onto what became known as the Native Reserves. The confiscated lands were referred to as the White Highlands and represented some of the most fertile regions of Kenya. The British colonial administration imposed laws that also forced Kenyans to labor on European farms with poor social services. They imposed taxation laws, instituted racial segregation, restricted movement through the *kipande* identification system, and curtailed basic freedoms.

Despite their displacement, land and ritual oathing continued to be important for the unification of various Kenyan social groups.[58] Land was not merely a means of economic production but was seen as a divinely inherited blessing that connected them to their ancestors. In response to dispossession, the Mau Mau struggled to reclaim their land and promote equality in the region. The struggle began as early as the late 1940s, though it was most intense between 1952 and 1957, as the Mau Mau intensified their mobilization to establish the conditions for Kenyan independence. With a majority of members from the Kikuyu, Embu, and Meru communities, other Kenyans from various groups—such as the Akamba, Maasai, Abaluhya, Abagusii, and Luo, as well as various Kenyan Indian trade unionists—also participated in what became a movement.[59] With Jomo Kenyatta as a symbolic member, significant social pressure for self-determination led to Kenyan independence in 1963, with Kenyatta as the first president.[60]

Independence came with great expectations around the rectification of past colonial injustices. Kenyatta's government was expected to address land inequalities through a new land redistribution policy. Hundreds of thousands of Africans—mainly Kikuyu—were living either as squatters on European farms in the Rift Valley or in relatively unproductive Native Reserves away from their ancestral lands. Many hoped that Kenyatta's government would resettle them in their ancestral lands. However, instead it instituted a land reconsolidation policy that vexed many of the poor squatters, peasants, and workers. Kenyatta eventually developed a series of strategies for the continual investment of European interests in Kenya while also brokering a deal for the transfer of land to native Kenyans. In order to implement this plan, he borrowed money from the British government to buy back land from European settlers. Instead of overhauling the agrarian inequalities that were established during the colonial period and redistributing land among the majority of Africans who were either landless or land poor, Kenyatta's government introduced the infamous land policy known as "willing buyer, willing seller," which required Africans to buy back their land.

Many saw this postindependence policy as unjust because the majority of Africans were poor squatters, workers, and peasant farmers with very little capital at that time. The popular assumption was that only those who worked closely with the British and earned an income were able to accumulate the necessary resources to buy land or secure bank loans. Thus the early forms of stratification were seen as producing unfair advantages for those who were on the colonial government's payroll during the Mau Mau struggle.

The policy also caused feelings of injustice in many who felt that the terms for buying back land that was initially procured illegally were unfair. According to many of the Mau Mau veterans that we spoke with in Kenya in 2013, this inequality reflected how they understood justice as being about recovering land that had been stolen from them, not holding an individual perpetrator accountable. "Ultimately we have not received any form of justice because the main purpose of our struggle was land and freedom and we have not gotten land. And we are going to demand this land and even if we die our children will continue to demand for this land until justice is done and we have been given what is rightfully ours which is each and every freedom fighter to get the piece of land he fought for in this country."

According to many, issues of culpability must go back to much earlier periods:

> We fought against the British colonizers in order to get our land, and at independence the colonizers all left Kenya and went back to their own country. But now the huge plots of land they owned were taken over by black European, black colonizers and now our struggle today is against these black Europeans, these black colonizers who continue to horde huge plots of land in this country and we will continue to fight and struggle until we get back this land from these black Europeans who own a majority of land in this country.

"Black Europeans" or "colonizers" refers to the home guards—those black Kenyans seen as working closely with the colonial powers, who then took over the bureaucratic governance of the country once the colonizers left.[61] Others in the group we interviewed agreed. One woman, attributing blame specifically to the home guards, added, "They stole our land, they stole our cattle, they stole our chickens, they stole everything that we had and that's why since then we have lived in abject poverty. And it is these home guards, these black Europeans who were working on behalf of the colonial government, of course being overseen by their white supervisors, it is they who have put us in all this mess for the decades we have lived in this country from that period of time from this Mau Mau struggle."

Over time, the emergence of landless squatters unraveled and took on an ethnic dimension, especially during the twenty-four-year reign of Daniel arap Moi. Both Kikuyu squatters and those who acquired land legally in the Rift Valley were seen as foreigners who needed to be forcefully evicted. The reality that various members of the Kikuyu elites—who eventually became known as the Mount Kenya Mafias—had acquired immense wealth and power in Kenya's postcolonial period only made matters worse for those deemed to be foreigners in the Rift Valley. To contextualize the violence that erupted following the December 30, 2007, elections, one must consider the events leading to the elections, which seemingly reveal a nation fractured along ethnic-tribal lines, especially the way that a discourse of evicting the foreigners became a rallying cry for Rift Valley politicians at election time.

Thus, understanding the interethnic consolidation of Ruto's United Republican Party with Kenyatta's TNA, which came together to produce the Jubilee Party and its victory, is central to grasping how accused "perpetrators" of Kenya's 2007 postelection violence, according to the ICC, could facilitate the consolidation of historically opposed ethnic groups, whose candidates then won Kenya's 2013 presidential elections. On one hand, the histories of land dispossession during and following British colonialism produced the conditions through which Kenyatta and Ruto's Jubilee Coalition could be perceived as settling a more than fifty-year-old history of injustice. On the other hand, since Kenya gained independence, political and economic power in government has circulated among the Kikuyu and Kalenjin elite to the exclusion of other ethnic groups, such as the Kamba, Maasai, and Borana, and religious groups, such as Muslims. The recognition of these two realities suggests that the violence actually attests to the way that histories of dispossession became sedimented along various patronage lines. Thus, the attacks against the Kikuyus represented the mobilization of particular ethnic patronage networks to try to change the Kikuyu and/or Luo and Kalenjin monopolization of power in postcolonial Kenya. It is the realization of the deep-seated complexities of culpability playing out through a sense of communal responsibility to protect that has contributed to the recognition of the centrality of proximity and patronage.

The sensibility of collective responsibility—instantiated through oathing, but later sedimented through patronage—thus informs the production of a popular national imaginary in which Ruto and Kenyatta are not widely seen as "perpetrators" awaiting ICC indictment but as national heroes to be protected and celebrated. My informants' answers to the question of who should be held accountable for the violence instead highlights the extent to which collective responsibility is relevant. According to Ngogi, a local Kenyan activist,

> The financing of that violence involved the entire Kikuyu diaspora as well as [the] domestic population. People from southeast London to Texas were holding meetings and sending cash to support the cause. They were planning meetings all over this city. There w[as] supposed to be at one point a huge incident in Umoja and Eastlands where especially Luos were going to be flushed out of the houses that they allegedly occupied. Kikuyu shop-

keepers in Umoja raised a lot of cash and it just so happened that the peace deal came before they were able to carry out the plan.

Here we see not only the complexity of Kenyatta and Ruto possibly financing violence as part of its coperpetration, but a duality where the act of financing the arming of others was seen as a response to the call to protect the collective whole—the Kikuyu against Raila's supporters, the Luo, and others.

Accordingly, what the OTP saw as Kenyatta's legal culpability was actually seen by various members of the Kikuyu elders as a necessary act of communal responsibility in which he—as well as others in Kenya and throughout the diaspora—were perceived as taking critical steps to protect his community from ethnic-inspired violence and to ensure Kikuyu prominence and dominance in Kenyan politics.

Further, Uhuru Kenyatta's rapid rise to power may indicate the importance of the notion of collective responsibility, meaning that Kenyatta was obligated to contribute to the financing of the violence in order to protect his community against other ethnic forces set on displacing them from their land. With this rationale, the sentiment that Kenyatta is a "freedom fighter" and not a "perpetrator" supports a celebratory popular image of him as protecting the collective and not culpable for violence.

Furthermore, admitting to Kenyatta's participation and the role of others in actually financing the violence would be seen as a legal admission of collective guilt during the designated postelection period. Instead, Kikuyus vaguely described Kenyatta's actions as collectively appropriate. Statements such as, "Uhuru stepped in because Mwai Kibaki was asleep." Or "Kibaki was too weak, Mwai Kibaki was useless," and "Uhuru is our hero because he took responsibility when it really mattered."[62] These claims—with their legal implications— speak to the affective sentiments of solidarity and alliance through which contemporary Kenyans are asserting a new narrative about political violence in their country.

According to interview participants, because of reprisal violence on the part of Luos against any ethnic group they felt had supported the Kibaki victory, the Kikuyus, in coordination with their elders, were seen as having mobilized forces to protect themselves in various places; hence the mobilization of the Mungiki forces. Actions taken in the Ruto camp, and by extension the Kalenjins (and Kenyatta through his Kikuyu networks), in terms of mobilization—that is, financing and executing violent acts—were ultimately seen by participants as supporting two principle players: Kibaki and Odinga. The compromise related to this standoff eventually resulted in the creation of a new position, deputy president, as part of the power-sharing agreement in which historically opposed parties came together.[63] Thus, many people saw Kibaki and Odinga as the ones who were most invested in the postelection violence; therefore, though they were not seen as engaging in proximate violence, when respondents were pressed to parse responsibility according to principles of international law, many argued that Kibaki and Odinga should be seen as bearing the greatest responsibility, not Kenyatta and Ruto. When the ICC narrative is overlaid onto Kenyan national politics, we see how what appears in one framework as individual criminal accountability can be reframed as communal responsibility based on a different conceptualization of culpability. Looking after the interests of a people in a complex set of attacks and reprisals cannot be resolved simply through a decontextualized attribution of criminality. It reveals an important paradox—an ambivalence in the data concerning who is held accountable (Kibaki and Odinga rather than Uhuru and Ruto), or whether looking beyond legal accountability may be an attractive way of settling the political foundations of the conflict, which are manifestations of deep-seated responses to structural injustice. This paradox leads to mutual erasures. The first is a legal time erasure that renders insignificant the longue durée of structural violence that continues to be experienced and articulated through daily practice. The second is an experiential-historical time erasure that displaces the encapsulation generated by legal time and instead produces in relation to it the terms through which historical conceptualizations of collective responsibility are experienced and lived. I take up the latter below.

Proximity and the Redirecting of Culpability

Our ethnographic research in Kenya showed that the very survivors of violence that international judicial institutions seek to protect protest the designations of criminal responsibility strictly in relation to individual responsibility, especially when there is an understanding that longer histories of imperial land disenfranchisement created (and were not products of) such forms of contemporary violence. According to a report by the International Center for Transitional Justice, though victims understood that in ICC judicial contexts greater responsibility is borne by those who gave orders that led to violent outbreaks, more than half of those who responded to the question "Who should be prosecuted?" identified direct perpetrators or "foot soldiers" of violence as being directly responsible.[64] Though supportive of the ICC concept in principle, many of those in Kenya classified as "victims" also felt that local and national mechanisms were preferable to pursuing a lengthy ICC process in order to achieve compensation for violence and property loss.[65]

In a 2013 survey that we conducted with survivors of 2007–2008 postelection violence in Nairobi's low-income Kibera neighborhood, an overwhelming majority of residents insisted that criminal responsibility needs to be understood clearly through notions of collective guilt, the role of the police in postelection violence, and the way that the British colonial settlement of the Rift Valley led to the demise of both the Kikuyu and Kalenjin ethnic traditional networks. Thus, individualized criminal responsibility and an expanded perception of time were important. Despite this perception on the ground, international criminal law prioritizes command and superior responsibility rather than holding proximate perpetrators accountable; the expectation is that direct perpetrators will be dealt with under domestic criminal law. Accordingly, for some, the law falls short. This is not only because perpetrators of proximate violence are not being prosecuted in the national context but also because international courts cannot situate crimes historically.

Many of my respondents insisted that focusing temporally on the narrow 2007–2008 postelection violence period as way to measure culpability fails to attend to deep-rooted historical and political issues. Recall that Kiamu, a young Kenyan human rights advocate quoted in chapter 1, maintains, "We've had victims in this country since the colonial times, so if you're going to address the system of victims of political violence in Kenya we do it holistically. We begin with the day the British landed here, the evictions that the settlers did—today the biggest land owners are settlers. . . . My reference point is in the eighteenth century. . . . The ICC has no capacity to address that, so I'll not waste time on it.

Here we see not only a strong conviction about the limits of individual culpability as a framework in international criminal law but also a critique concerning the inability of legal time to adequately encompass historical forms of violence. Despite these other conceptualizations of guilt, it is unlikely that the ICC will permit itself to consider activities that occurred prior to its temporal jurisdiction, thereby violating basic principles of legality.[66] Set against this vexed juridical backdrop, who should be held responsible for contemporary crimes of violence?

Despite the articulation of culpability by the ICC and deep-seated sentiments that supported historical hostilities against warring ethnic groups and parties, public discourses surrounding ICC activity shifted the terms of engagement about justice, increasingly narrating its measure through the longue durée. John, a well-known Kenyan journalist, insisted that in 2007–2008 neither Kenyatta nor Ruto were heads of state, so it is not clear why they would be seen as bearing more responsibility than others.

> Neither of them were running for president. I don't think there was [responsibility] if you look at the violence and protest in ODM strongholds. I think you would see "No Raila, No Peace," not "No Ruto, No Peace," and especially in Kalenjin strongholds. So how on earth do you then begin to design these cases against the two of them? I think that it is possible to finger Uhuru Kenyatta for postelection violence in Naivasha and Nakuru; I think that it is possible. It is much more difficult to [connect him] to the North Rift.

By referring to the slogan, "No Raila, No Peace," John was explaining that those who supported Raila were fighting for his presidency and not for Ruto's (who was in the ODM leadership). After the election results and the announcement that Kibaki had won again, it became clear that Raila, through his ODM supporters, mostly from the Luo ethnic group in the ODM strongholds (like Kibera), refused to accept a situation in which Raila was not going to be in power. Much of this was connected to the problem of the concentration of power among a few families and ethnic groups. From the time Jomo Kenyatta took office from the colonial Home Guards in 1963 to the last election, power was seen as remaining within a very tightly sealed vacuum in which the Kikuyu and the Kalenjin constituted a small community that governed all others and shielded their political and economic elite from accountability to the people and to the law.

The violence of 2007–2008 was, in many ways, seen as a response to the unwillingness of others to concede to the monopolization of power by particular members of the elite once again, which carried over from the transfer of independence. Yet many blamed the media for contributing to the production of the concept that a perpetrator could be responsible for postelection violence by depicting the situation as ultimately being about the ethnic Kalenjin mobilizing against the Kikuyu. As Bornu, a Kenyan political analyst, explained:

> Some say the Kalenjin rose up as a community, though it's not true at all! If you just go back to reports of the violence, the violence was up and down the railway line. There was looting and violence in Mombasa, there were Kikuyu and Kisii evictions in Maasai Land; there was no violence in Central Highlands but Nairobi and going all the way to the border! So the

idea that the Kalenjin were some . . . atavistic, blood thirsty Others just served to demonize them. . . . The ignorance about the Kalenjin was mind-blowing. I mean the Kalenjin were organized so effectively. . . . But when you talk to people in Nakuru or Kikuyus who had family or whatever in Nakuru, there was a point at which the Kalenjin were invading and there was just utter fear. [Because of their fear, people didn't] know what kind of monster [was] coming to attack [them]. But the reality was that the violence was across the board and along party lines and also along a very anti-Kikuyu level. Then you'd have to provoke the question of why is everybody standing up, rising up against the Kikuyu? What is going on? But the Kalenjin were very insistent that that violence was spontaneous, and were very insistent that any form of planning or organization happened after the announcement of the election results, not before.

Bornu's statement highlights that there was not only a sense that the violence was perpetrated across the board by many actors—police, local people, outside forces, militia, gangs—but also that it was inspired by deep-seated histories of disenfranchisement and the monopolization of power throughout Kenya. The ICC's focus on command responsibility not only overlooks the guilt of those who actually engaged in criminal conduct, but in the Kenyan cases it also overlooked the temporality of collective responsibility for age-old political problems. In Kiamu, John, and Bornu's statements, we can begin to see that at the heart of the sentiments being articulated are reattributions of culpability in which guilt for crimes of mass violence is understood in relation to sentimental passions about ethnicity, land, and historical injustices. Culpability is reinscribed onto other bodies, other motives, other actors; the individualization of those acts is delegitimized in favor of addressing such violence through the political settlement of long-standing inequality.

When we asked Marcus, a villager from Kibera, whether he thought Kenyatta was most responsible, he, like many, responded by insisting that many Kenyans believed that Prosecutor Moreno Ocampo was interested in prosecuting those on the Waki Commission's list because the OTP was outsourcing a significant number of its investigations to NGOs and others whom many discredited as being incompetent and far from thorough. As Marcus elaborated:

So, how do these guys end up at the ICC? If not through a process of a kind of political roulette, how does he end up there? That is completely arbitrary; you have twenty people or twenty-plus people fingered for the violence by Waki. . . . I think a lot of people will be asking questions about why isn't so-and-so and why isn't so-and-so on the list, but I don't know by what logic somebody like John Michuki could have escaped. He was internal security minister, the one who directly banned any type of street demonstrations. He was very much involved at the National Security, NSAC, and on top of that Michuiki had said on multiple occasions he was directly ordering the police to shoot to kill Mungiki. But if you are not going to touch Mungiki, I don't know how then you are going to deal with reprisal violence in the north. The other person who should be at the ICC, I mean one would think, would be Maina Njenga [the head of the Mungiki] himself.

By referring to the perception that the OTP accepted the names outlined in the Waki Commission report, Marcus was suggesting that the logic was political and, in some cases, arbitrary. He continued, "If you are talking about the criteria for these kinds of charges to warrant a case at the ICC, I think one of the things that Luis Moreno-Ocampo has been at pains to show is that there was a structured violence, that there was an organization with a hierarchy and so on. It is called Mungiki and his head is Miana Njenga. In many ways one can then begin to understand that there is something legitimate about the angle of Uhuru Kenyatta and William Ruto."

Yet despite this concession about the plausibility of guilt, a range of actors, such as the police chief, members of the police force, and Mungiki gangs were also seen as contributors to violence but were actually dropped from the list. And, as my informant explained, the police were part of this process, too.

The existence of the police also raises questions about why the ICC's prosecution did not pursue the head of the Kenyan police force. Here the presumption was that the violence should not be attributed to one or two commanders. The planning for the violence was said to precede the elections and was mobilized as part of the defense of the Kikuyu. The reality is that there is not only a sense that the violence was perpetrated across the board by many actors—police, local people, outside forces, militia, gangs—but also that the violence was inspired by deep-seated histories of disenfranchisement in which various persons saw themselves as carrying out their obligations to protect their community. But despite the recognition of the responsibility to protect, the point, ultimately, is that they, not Kenyatta and Ruto, were the ones engaged in inflicting proximate violence. Here Marcus maps out the forms of proximate violence relevant to the Mungiki phenomenon:

There are a number of men that were targeted because of their ethnic leanings, and the link between those ethnic groups to certain political leanings. And because of that they were attacked in certain sex-selective ways. You know having their penises amputated, or having them sodomized, and because then when you think about them from the political reasons why it happened, then they qualify as gender crimes. . . . Sexual and gender-based crimes postelection have been downplayed. They're taken as serious crimes related to the election violence. The police have been implicated and other security agents that some victims have described in detail, that it is for sure the people that raped them were security agents that had been deployed to that area or to those places during the period of the chaos.

So, for instance, in Kibera a number of victims have described the attire that the men that raped them were in, and for some of them they describe it in detail; they talk about the way the tear gas canisters were dangling and making noises. Those are some of the noises they remember. So we were concerned that our own security agents have been implicated and that the government has not done anything.

As we see, the realities of intimate violence—rape, castration, sodomy—remain part of the ways that those victimized by violence are also conceptualizing guilt. Those responsible for violence against their bodies are those who actually committed the crimes: the man who raped, the boy next door who killed his neighbor, and the foot soldiers of the security forces who maimed. Yet the problem for many is that because of the ICC indictment, it is the Kenyan government, through the figures of Kenyatta and Ruto, that is being held responsible for those alleged perpetrations of violence, instead of the police and security forces.

In response to our question about whether Kenyatta and Ruto should assume responsibility for the 2007–2008 postelection violence, the journalist Ngugi asks,

> Responsibility for what? Some of the worst violence happened in Western Kenya and, yes, it is often mentioned that Kisumu [is] burning, but it's actually not considered a media epicenter of the violence. And in both cases [they] let the state security forces off the hook. In Kakamega, Bungoma, in Kitale, the vast majority of people that were killed were killed by police bullets usually found in [their] back; they were running away. If you omit that, then all the violence becomes is a long-held ethnic dispute. You know all the rhetoric that influenced—is it called Agenda 4 items?—it is absolute bullshit.[67]

Here Ngugi is referring to part of the national dialogue and reconciliation efforts that took place after the 2007–2008 violence. Four agendas were proposed to address the way forward for Kenya. The fourth and final agenda was to address "long-term issues and solutions" and included points such as land reform, national unity, and so on that have to do with further long-term peace-building concerns. The Agenda 4 items were the last ones agreed to in the Annan-brokered peace agreement. But Ngugi's point is that the issue is a lot more complex than simply ethnicity and land. It is also about the perceptions of narrative erasures and false narratives that are seen as being part of the maintenance of state power. He goes on to suggest that the violence was not simply routine ethnic violence, as it was often framed. He insists that the security forces—those in proximate relation to daily citizens—were actively involved, and people from the Western region were being targeted. "I spent a lot of time, January and part of February, in the North Rift, in places like Kiptere, just around Eldoret town in the outskirts of Eldoret. I was scooping spent cartridges, G3 cartridges. I mean the cops had gone completely amuck . . . because even the security forces . . . were divided along party and ethnic lines."[68]

He emphasizes how ethnically segmented the divisions became:

If you went to the police station in Eldoret town—I remember the first time I went there on a Sunday and a policeman comes striding out. I am coming into the compound and she is coming out, and she is loudly announcing, "This is an ODM zone, so understand where you're coming." I needed security to go into a place called Munyaka, which was a Kikuyu settlement, and she told me, "Eh, listen, my friend, this not the place, and now you have to make special arrangements. You are not going to find people here that are going to go in there." The cops, General Service Unit, Administrative Police, and so on who were shooting up the place in Kiptere and so on were imported, and it was very specific because they were Kenyan police and—again according to locals, again another narrative that's never discussed—Ugandans. But if you went to Moi referral hospitals and you found anyone who was working at Moi referral hospital in January–February 2008, [they say] there was an invasion by Administrative Police–looking types of the hospital at one point, and they said these people could not speak Kiswahili. That is one of the stories you will also hear in Kisumu.[69]

In this passage, Ngugi counters what he saw as false narratives—or massive omissions of facts—in which the proximate role of the police, the security forces, and the use of foreign forces like the Ugandans was underplayed. He insisted, rather, that the state security machine played a major role in the violence and was in fact the largest perpetrator. He argued that when you remove these major players from the story, the violence begins to look like a long-standing ethnic dispute. It involved a range of actors engaged in intimate killing whose affiliations were conveniently segmented along ethnicity and party alliances; but some of the worst forms of violence involved police and security forces from nearby states who were imported to perpetrate violence. The implications debunk Kenyatta and Ruto's criminal responsibility for the perpetration of violence by suggesting that Kibaki had requested assistance from Museveni, who responded by sending security forces from Uganda to parts of the Rift Valley and western Kenya. The report that the "police-looking types" did not speak Kiswahili was taken as further evidence that they were not Kenyan and had been imported. He also seems to suggest that even Kenyan security forces were stationed in different areas, or at least imported into certain hot spots like Eldoret, based on ethnicity and political affiliation. Given the way the security forces were "divided along party and ethnic lines," the Kibaki government was calculating in its deployment of the forces. Thus, Ngugi suggests that there was more at play than different ethnic communities fighting each other.

The key point is that the violence was based on much more than ethnic patronage. It was about the fight to take over government—at all costs—or for the Kibaki government to maintain governmental power and the embodied affects that fueled those struggles. The most pronounced redirections of culpability—from Ruto and Kenyatta to the police, security services, or neighbors accused of stealing—were for the most intimate forms of violence: sexual violence ranging from rape to castration and sodomy. This is one way of assigning guilt to perpetrators of violence through interpretations of proximity, not command responsibility. Another, as we have seen, is through expanded notions of time that reflect the attribution of sentiments about the colonial past and the way the ICC has come to occupy these historical structures of power and exploitation in the eyes of those involved.

Whose Perpetrator, Whose History? Emotional Regimes and the Politics of Attribution

While chapter 3 emphasizes a notion of justice directly tied to advocacy that insists on the immediacy of social action (the temporality of the now), this chapter highlights particular notions of time that not only order the way that legal justice is rendered (legal time), but also make viable the possibilities for understanding culpability in longer temporal periods. These sense-making processes are dialogic, as we saw with the acts of affective transference in chapter 2, and enable people to consider a range of measures for determining culpability. Senses of justice can also be shaped by particular articulations of guilt and innocence that are understood through expectations of patronage, ethnicity, and land inequality. But more importantly, they are propelled through emotional climates, though shared differently and at times constructed and even engaged duplicitously, that produce collective experiences in relation to hegemonic signs. These signs may be historical or contemporary; they may motivate those irate responses that appear to represent anger, or joy, or sadness—all experienced differently perhaps—but what is key is that they are part of an emotional climate that shapes a given experience. It is this experience that contributes to affective community formation and cross-cuts race, gender, nationality, and so on, even as it exists in tension with it. Thus, dissatisfaction about inequality constitutes the way that particular emotional climates are experienced. These feelings punctuate the way that claims and counterclaims are made.

Through reattribution, those engaged in various pro-Pan-African formations deploy particular judgments and narratives in order to undermine the post-2002 linear determinants of legality by which particular foot soldiers, not political leaders, are deemed culpable for violence. Those attributions also have their own institutional and social histories through which regimes form and then are deployed to propel particular narratives for particular purposes. Through claims of guilt or heroism, people attribute culpability. And through this process the figure of the individual "perpetrator" can transform into the figure of the freedom fighter—as seen with Uhuru Kenyatta. For what we see is that these iconic symbols are articulated through particular cultural and emotional lenses that shape judgments, capacities, and moral expressions. As embodied thought, sentiments that shape the meaning of these symbols animate cognition in ways that make interpretation meaningful according to various sociocultural rules. Here various constituencies see the postcolonial condition in contemporary Kenya as fundamentally related to the West and its colonial past. In their attribution of guilt through the longue durée of colonial violence, these Kenyan responses to the ICC's legal designations reflect how definitions of violence and culpability are sentimentally and socially charged and rely on particular conceptions of time as they relate to justice. And through nationalist sentiments and ethnic sensibilities, notions of responsibility are communicated through speech acts, ritual practices, voting behavior, popular campaign icons, and so forth. Ultimately, this is important because perceptions of legal time and histories of colonial and postcolonial degradation can shape ethical horizons for Western legality even as they shape the terrain by which others protest those determinations.

According to one former African head of state who had been in office during the negotiations of Liberian president Charles Taylor's extradition request and who witnessed the subsequent ICC indictments of African leaders, "If I had known then what I know now about extradition and these European courts, I would never have allowed my country to sign on to the ICC [Rome Statute]. Signing on has enabled these extraditions. It's almost like allowing them to take us to the ship, once again." When I asked this leader to explain more about the slave ship metaphor and the idea of external forces controlling African bodies, he likened it to other types of extractions, like "the unfair pilfering of resources, age-old treaties that can't be changed. . . . [They] look like colonialism once again."

The leader's invocation of unknowing consent was echoed in other responses I gleaned from leaders engaged in extradition discussions. On one level, the figure of the African body being extradited to Europe conjures significant responses from those in the West aware of the politics of racialization and its impact on the global order. The imagery of the slave ship speaks to the history of the removal of the black body from Africa and evokes African and European collaborations in historical removals and control of black bodies, as happened during the transatlantic slave trade, as well as the imperial control of Africans through European colonialism. From international legal actors condoning slavery and then later prohibiting it long after its destruction of African societies, to the subsequent colonization of African social, political, and economic life, to the contemporary control of global economic and political institutions, feelings of structural injustice are continually frustrated by new forms of extraction, such as resource extraction, economic extraction, and the general history of external control of Africa's interior. They are part of the dehumanization of African bodies. In addition to the history of the stratification of human value and the sentimental responses to it, the dynamics at play are tied to the existence of an ambiguous set of political exclusions that are in tension with aspirational possibilities of equality through international legality. For the claims of geographic and political selectivity—the idea that some forms of violence are legally actionable by international criminal law instruments and some are not—incite a prevalent emotional response that is also tied to how we understand the place of history and time in shaping questions of culpability.

Though not new to legal anthropology, the notion of legal time is scarcely interrogated in Western jurisprudential circles, particularly with regard to differences in international law (which limits how notions of legal time are conceptualized) and criminal law (which focuses on strict understandings and demarcations in time, rather than reflecting on historical developments or broader root causes). Continuing crimes (such as colonialism or apartheid) lend themselves to less stable assertions about who is a "perpetrator" and create multivalent legal dilemmas. Such questions of jurisdiction, admissibility, and evidence further complicate the parameters by which reattribution responds to encapsulations of justice. Thus it is important to clarify ethnographically what the realm of the social can tell us about contemporary social processes around which notions of time are understood and responses to it registered.

Attributing guilt through strict understandings and demarcations of time is critical to anti-impunity formations in international criminal law. Rather than reflecting on historical developments or broader root causes, ICC jurisprudence has adopted a relatively strict view of temporality with the recognition that nonretroactivity or the principle of *nullum crimen sine lege*—no crime except what is proscribed by law—is one of the central tenets of law. The criminalization of acts occurring over long periods of time is seen as potentially threatening this principle because it is hard to define what precisely is being punished and when exactly the conduct becomes criminal. But this is where the problem lies, for the legal presumptions of temporally relevant responsibility and the growing grassroots conception of who, over what period of time, is actually criminally responsible for acts of violence highlight a hierarchical or vertical disjuncture. This is due to the limitations of attributing the conduct of one person to another—distinguishing between foot soldiers and "those most responsible"—and the problem of legal time as it relates to strict applications of the temporality of violence.

I am not suggesting that those who are responsible for mass violence should not be held accountable for their role in wrongdoing. What I am highlighting here, however, is that competing attributions of culpability reveal substantive differences between social and legal justice in shaping varying understandings of guilt as affective formulations of culpability. They highlight the afterlife of the disappointment with the failure to balance power historically in postcolonial Kenya, set alongside the articulated failure of the law to rectify histories of human dispossession from their ancestral land. We also see how fraught with meaning the assignment of culpability is—especially in contexts in which postcolonial states have failed to adequately address the needs of those victimized by violence.

In the Kenyan political landscape, the individualization of criminal responsibility does not account for the deep histories that produced the conditions under which police violence, ethnic rivalries, and land dispossession were made possible.[70] Rather, there is a realization that the inscriptions of power in colonial Kenya were central to the play of power in postindependence Kenya. And since independence, power has never been balanced or distributed beyond those ethnic groups—the Kikuyu and Kalenjin—who inherited control of statecraft. In postcolonial Africa, the afterlife of imperialism, colonialism, and the violence of dispossession persist deeply in the psychic life of social justice. Alongside historically constituted ethnic divisions there is also an awareness of the ways that imperial injustices remain part of the postcolonial reality—a continuity of structures of economic, legal, and political power. And while the image of the African perpetrator as warlord and killer has been constructed through the law to produce a narrative of the merciless mercenary, the African head of state as perpetrator has been subject to another moral imaginary that represents a new shift in the consolidation of panethnic alliances.

The Kenyan cases pursued by the ICC demonstrate this point and capture the affectivities already in place that the PR firm BTP Advisers used so effectively in their campaign. What they show us is that the attribution of culpability of an African leader to a particular historical moment can actually be explained through affective sentiments of solidarity; not only do Africans want to end violence, impunity, and the abuses of the postcolonial elite, but they also want to reassert a new narrative about the political nature of contemporary violence in Kenya. The Jubilee Coalition victory of 2013 demonstrates how social justice can exceed the legal-political and how an individual's internal feelings manifest in group sentiments about justice and culpability. On one hand, the Uhuru-Ruto Kenyan campaign team was able to implement a publicity strategy that nationalized ethnicity, leading to a merger and consolidation of the Jubilee Coalition and its deployment of a strategic narrative of victimhood. On the other hand, it led to the emergence of a different moral imaginary in which the emotional regime of nationalism galvanized new social domains for supporting the Uhuru-Ruto party. This process highlights the importance of understanding how notions of culpability, circumscribed through temporal frameworks, shape the basis upon which justice is understood and, therefore, on which other alliances are formed.

Justice Corrupted?

Articulating culpability through terms like "superior responsibility" limits the representational life of those deemed most responsible for violence. As I have been arguing, international criminal legal concepts of culpability rely not only on rational reasoning for clarifying the line of command; they depend on a particular production of the guilty "perpetrator" without whom violence would not be possible. But these assertions of culpability and their temporal reconfigurations are not enough to make sense of the deep roots of violence. There is an affective dimension to justice—an emotional connection to it in relation to various time horizons that remain part of the postcolonial condition and which is sustained by the socialization of particular practices and attitudes. These realities highlight the complexities of different understandings of justice—redistribution (dealing with land and structural injustice) versus anti-impunity—articulated through criminal accountability. Their competing claims raise questions related to how justice can be about individual culpability as well as larger forms of structural injustice. Through highlighting processes of reattribution, we can see that some determinations of historical inequality are understood as corruptions of justice, while other feelings of injustice produce new legal innovations to end impunity. Where mainstream constructions of liberal democratic social orders presume the existence of fairness and freedom as the norm, expressions of disappointment point to the problem that without redistributive politics as the basis for justice, a legal order that fails to address inequality can be seen as a corruption of justice.

Similarly, discursive strategies that deploy Pan-African signs of justice through the mythic domain of the freedom fighter, for example, also have the ability to erase acts of violence that evade accountability. In postcolonial African contexts, like that which we witnessed during Kenya's 2007–2008 violence, acts of physical violence were deployed by the very peacekeepers and police and enabled by the very leaders that are expected to protect the people. When those controversies unfold, they often manifest various forms of protest speech that openly contest certain discourses about justice and displace old emotional norms. Those sentimentalized speech acts operate alongside power relationships.

Rather than recognizing the role of the structuring order and its dual fiction as an objective tool, designations of "justice corrupted" depend on the classification of corruption as atypical, as an abberation. But to claim that the failure of justice is an anomaly is to continue to fetishize justice as a veil that hides other relations. Legal time is an example of the fetish of justice; the temporality of the law hides the basis upon which social inequality can be understood. It narrowly circumscribes the possibilities for what justice is and can be and highlights how particular forms of temporality can contribute to the exclusion of other temporal worlds, even as it presumes to be liberatory and justice producing. In other words, the very legal framework that designates culpability temporally can be a tool for exclusion, and justice is legible only within that which is legal. Those formulations that fall outside of liberalist temporal constructions of culpability are rendered unintelligible, thus untenable. The resulting exclusions contribute to the production of fissures in the social order.

Liberal legalist frameworks emerge through particular ways of organizing subjects and then erasing the processes by which such formations take shape. It is accompanied by a belief in the objectivity of the frameworks that serve the law, but these frameworks produce objectivity out of subjectivity. Often, those engaged in this process do not necessarily recognize the constructed temporalities that shape judicial order; they disavow them, instead, because they signal subjectivity. However, if we recognize that the pursuit of justice is fundamentally about domains of inequality, then we can see how feelings about it are mobilized differently yet produce similar results. As we have seen, these developments are differentiated through reattribution, which in some cases leads to refusals of legally circumscribed justice encapsulations, as well as feelings that justice, as the domain for distributive possibilities, has been corrupted. The invocation of corruption may emerge conveniently as a discourse for evading culpability. Or it may be shaped by other time horizons that people identify as the source of the infractions that led to mass violence. Legal time and the longue durée of structural inequality provide the frameworks through which people assess the social order and how justice operates within it.

Ultimately, notions of the culpability of the "perpetrator" or the righteousness of the Pan-African "hero" are made real through the fiction that justice corrupted is an anomaly. On either side of the perceptions of such notions of justice, people engage in reframing law's temporality in order to shift the modalities through which culpability is understood. These processes are at the center of the emotional work of international justice, and it is in the fissures of perceived injustice that legal temporalities are actually made visible. It is these struggles over meaning making and the power to shape and define justice that I go on to explore in chapter 5 through the examination of Pan-African institutions as further examples of reattributions of justice.

PART II

||||||||||||||||||||||||||||||||||||||||||||||||||||

AFFECTS, EMOTIONAL REGIMES,

AND THE REATTRIBUTION OF

INTERNATIONAL LAW

CHAPTER 5

The Making of an African Criminal Court
as an Affective Practice

The year 2013 marked the Golden Jubilee of the founding of the African Union. At the celebratory event in Addis Ababa, Ethiopia, African leaders adopted the "50th Anniversary Solemn Declaration" in which they acknowledged past challenges and successes while rededicating themselves to Africa's progress in technological and economic development.[1] Part of the rededication involved a ritual process in which they articulated eight ideals or pillars of progress for the future. The event was deeply symbolic and emotionally charged.

Sentimental reflections on Africa's unique place as both the cradle of humanity and the locus of dehumanization by slavery, deportation, dispossession, apartheid, and colonialism punctuated the profundity of the moment as the leaders read out the "50th Anniversary Solemn Declaration" in unison:

> **We,** Heads of State and Government of the African Union assembled to celebrate the Golden Jubilee of the OAU/AU established in the city of Addis Ababa, Ethiopia on 25 May 1963 . . . *Reaffirming* our commitment to the ideals of Pan-Africanism and Africa's aspiration for greater unity, and paying tribute to the Founders of the Organisation of African Unity (OAU) as well as the African peoples on the continent and in the Diaspora for their glorious and successful struggles against all forms of oppression, colonialism and apartheid;
>
> *Mindful* that the OAU/AU have been relentlessly championing for the complete decolonization of the African continent and that one of the fundamental objectives is unconditional respect for the sovereignty and territorial integrity of each of its Member States;

Stressing our commitment to build a united and integrated Africa;

Guided by the vision of our Union and affirming our determination to "build an integrated, prosperous and peaceful Africa, driven and managed by its own citizens and representing a dynamic force in the international arena";

Determined to take full responsibility for the realization of this vision

. . .

ACKNOWLEDGE THAT: *The Organisation of African Unity (OAU)* overcame internal and external challenges, persevered in the quest for continental unity and solidarity; contributed actively to the liberation of Africa from colonialism and apartheid; provided a political and diplomatic platform to generations of leaders on continental and international matters; and elaborated frameworks for Africa's development and integration agenda through programmes such as NEPAD and APRM. . . .[2]

In addition to acknowledging the goal of an integrated and clear vision for their union and a quest for peace, they articulated their declaration of priorities: African identity and renaissance; the struggle against colonialism and the right to self-determination of people still under colonial rule; the integration agenda; the agenda for social and economic development; democratic governance; determining Africa's destiny and place in the world; and peace and security. The agenda of peace and security was more punctuated than the others, declaring:

On peace and security—Our determination to achieve the goal of a conflict-free Africa, to make peace a reality for all our people and to rid the continent of wars, civil conflicts, human rights violations, humanitarian disasters and violent conflicts, and to prevent genocide. We pledge not to bequeath the burden of conflicts to the next generation of Africans and undertake to end all wars in Africa by 2020.[3]

They then itemized the steps that they would take to ensure peace and security, from addressing root causes of violence to eradicating emerging sources of conflict to emphasizing conflict prevention. And like all head-of-state events, every part of it was ritualized. But what stood out was the profoundly performative passion that emerged while they read in unison. Bodies moving, words emphasized, but symbolically declarative.

Shortly after this event, and in the spirit of the "50th Anniversary Solemn Declaration," the African Union Commission (AUC) convened a subsequent event—this time a high-level retreat in Durban, South Africa, on April 29,

2014—in which they discussed one of the core issues that emerged as a priority in the establishment of the AU's vision of integration, prosperity, and peace. The gathering was called Silencing Guns in Africa: Building a Roadmap to a Conflict-Free Continent. According to an AU press release on the gathering, Chairperson Nkosazana Dlamini Zuma called on experts to engage in frank and open discussions to develop concrete and innovative solutions to violence. As she stated, "Unless we silence the guns and bury the machetes, the AU vision of building an integrated, prosperous and conflict-free Africa will remain an abstract goal."[4] Attendees dedicated the meeting to reflection on best practices in the realm of good governance and conflict and crisis resolution. They also highlighted emerging trends of concern ranging from Africa's changing demographics to environmental threats and their potential to either incite violence or catalyze solutions. This gathering and its outcomes should be understood as a continuation of decades of transnational contestation over the architecture of peace and justice in Africa.

With the AU's fiftieth-anniversary celebration and the related campaign, the AU leadership has mobilized emotional regimes and Pan-African histories to produce juridical, democratic, and economic opportunities on the African continent. They also presented a new platform for African growth, Agenda 2063, a fifty-year strategic plan for Africa's socioeconomic acceleration, transformation, and progress, following the AU's vision to "build an integrated, prosperous and peaceful Africa, an Africa driven and managed by its own citizens and representing a dynamic force in the international arena."[5] To put this fifty-year continental process in place, the AUC is working with the New Partnership for Africa's Development Planning and Coordinating Agency and is being supported by the African Development Bank and the United Nations Economic Commission for Africa. This long-term project is presented as "a program of social, economic and political rejuvenation that links the past, present and the future in order to create a new generation of Pan Africanists that will harness the lessons learnt and use them as building blocks to consolidate the hope and promises of the founding parents for a true renaissance of Africa."[6]

Though still in development, in Agenda 2063 we can see a deliberate use of the concept of Pan-Africanism, but tied to the more market-oriented language of productivity, growth, entrepreneurship, and transformation. In many ways, Agenda 2063 is part of the African renaissance propelled by Pan-Africanist principles, which calls for changes in attitudes and mind-sets to inculcate particular African values, or what I have been calling emotional regimes driven by various Africanist feeling rules: discipline, honesty, integrity, transparency, hard work, and love for Africa and its people. It provides the opportunity for Africa to break away from the syndrome of "always coming up with new ideas but [having] no significant achievements."[7] And since the popular trope of the corrupt African leaders is inundated with criticism about selfishness, elitism, and turning a blind eye to Africa's poor, the fiftieth-anniversary campaign and its various side events were structured as a counternarrative to such failure-laden imaginaries. Instead, they made clear how Pan-African affects are actually being institutionalized as a counterresponse to the ICC indictments, most significantly the campaigns by its anti-impunity movement activists in Africa and elsewhere. They did this by highlighting themes of belonging to a continent long managed by external forces that is now focusing on recovery, regional integration, democracy, and good governance, and Africa's entitlement to the fruits of its labor.

The following does not attempt to measure their success. Rather, in this chapter I am interested in the way that affective justice techniques are strategically deployed by Pan-Africanists who are working toward Africa's renewed future. In this case, what we see is the way that Pan-Africanism is not used to reference African unity but instead, through embodied feelings of racial subordination, assigned historically to the black body. In this regard, it is important to recognize how critical these racialized imaginaries are in the navigation of international justice. For the ghosts of subordination—the afterlife of subjection—live in the imaginary and draw on history, materiality, and the manifestation of those interiorities to produce templates for African meaning making. What we see is that the racial imaginary is not simply about skin color—black skin versus whiteness, for example. This racial imaginary is about the construction of difference. It is about the way that distinctions based on construction of the black body, the West, and even conceptions concerning culpability or Africa's development converge to produce organizing tropes around which various racial imaginaries are made visible and real. In this regard, Pan-Africanist justice attributions are playing out through the invocation of various slogans, the particularities of their application, and the agreed-upon meanings that shape the way we understand contemporary developments. This process of psychic self-making is part of the geosocial landscape in which internal feelings about Africa and its people merge with various exteriorities in the coproduction of African geographies of justice. But affects, as more than internal feelings brought into being by externalities, reflect structures of emotion imbricated along a zone that intersects with the past, the present, and aspirations for the future.[8]

Though these justice goals are not exclusively Pan-African, nor exclusively racial, when taken together they form the component parts of the AU's new Pan-African assemblage that seeks to overcome histories of exploitation and inequality and reassert Africa's place in the world. As we shall see, sentiments of recovery, overcoming exploitation and hardship, and taking control of Africa's future and its membership in global communities are all part of what is being articulated as the Pan-African renaissance. This demonstrates a return to the foundational principles of self-determination that were necessary to extricate African countries from colonial domination, now with sentiments that propel its agency in creating new solutions for its people. It is a move to a more development-focused agenda involved in the shaping of regional integration priorities through principles of Pan-Africanism and African renaissance. These principles are now being deployed in spatially contingent geographies and are creating possibilities for rethinking what justice is from other sites of meaning making. These new AU spheres are reenvisioning justice in the twenty-first century, embedded in a transitional justice framework that considers foundational structural inequalities while also addressing political and juridical solutions endemic to Africa's histories of violence: structural, psychological, material, economic.

In relation to this strategy, on paper, Agenda 2063's Pan-Africanist framework seems impressive to its onlookers, and much has been accomplished in the first ten years since its inception—at least in relation to norm setting. However, many of the principles that undergird the institutionalization of Africa's new frontiers remain aspirational—as I will demonstrate through the Hissène Habré case—the first international justice case managed by the AU to adjudicate international crimes committed by a former head of state on the African continent. This development of African justice, managed within a regionally contextualized transitional justice framework, is as much about desire, hope, and aspirations as it is about the fears that inaction will lead to the eventual demise of Africa's future. Yet African justice aspirations sit uncomfortably next to the paradox of African development—the realization that the very global capital being sought to build and integrate African economies is also leading to its demise through the displacement of small-scale traders and farmers.[9] With this paradox in the shadow, this chapter is not an evaluation of the AU's strategic goals or the feasibility of Africa's growth and peace plans. It is an analysis of the emotional work that goes into producing and inciting strategic action. In particular, it focuses on African governance concerns over injustice and inequality in the global order and the use of Pan-Africanist emotional regimes to address them. These affects reside alongside a particular set of ontologies that are embedded in the shadows of the colonial past, as previous chapters have been illustrating, and African aspirations to determine its own future.

What is compelling about the use of Pan-Africanist affects as a way to respond to the West are the inherent contradictions that it juggles. On one hand, these Pan-African affects are shaped by messages that are touted as localized and African; yet, on the other hand, it has been well established in the literature that not only are African traditions inventions of complex social encounters with customs and politics elsewhere, they are constituted by the very domains of power that they disavow, such as the European legal systems and its related educational structures.[10] It is this paradox that makes the emotional work of Pan-Africanism an interesting site for the study of feelings and what they do to compel social action. And it is this puzzle that makes the tensions at the heart of Pan-Africanist responses to the ICC even more challenging because, as we saw with Kenyatta and Ruto's campaign branding, emotionally driven institutional sensibilities about justice in Africa are being rerouted through reformulated imaginaries. These imaginaries shape Pan-Africanist emotional domains and histories to produce juridical, democratic, and economic possibilities in Africa.

As strategic formations, the feeling domains that are produced in response to the ICC's anti-impunity approach are not unrelated to the peace and justice strategies in Africa being articulated as an African approach to international law. They are similarly deployed by a cadre of international lawyers, activists, judges, scholars, policy makers, governments, and survivors of violence who are engaged in building strategies to end violence on the African continent and to control the terms through which it is managed. Since its transformation from the OAU, the African Union, a continental intergovernmental body, has demonstrated a renewed energy and growing capacity to resolve conflicts around the continent using particular peace and justice sequencing strategies. Today, the interplay between peace and justice remains one of the most difficult debates concerning international justice in Africa. Some would argue that if peace and a functioning government cannot be achieved, the effort to create a fully functioning state and judiciary will also fail.[11] The range of peace and justice debates in the literature extends from more fundamentalist approaches to justice, ranging from a deep belief that retributive justice prevents impunity to a more conciliatory and gradualist presumption that political settlements for politically based problems are more appropriate.[12] For example, some have argued that courts, as tools available to political actors (the AU) to intervene in conflict situations, can play but a limited role in contributing to the reestablishment of peace, stability, and reconciliation by prosecuting a small number of perpetrators, while others have insisted that because more basic institutions are likely to emerge in contexts in which the guidance available from institutions in a consolidated democracy is missing, in transitional postwar contexts where the political stakes are higher than in a consolidated democracy, keeping the conflict between peace and justice afloat is important.[13] And yet others insist on the reality that there is no binary choice between peace on one hand and justice on the other.[14] For while the range of approaches is often characterized conceptually as either peace or justice, the two are not mutually exclusive. Peace strategies that end violence can be seen as justice producing, and judicial strategies that punish violence can be seen as advocating peace. That is, the peace-justice tension is more appropriately described as a paradox that is built on two sets of contradictory approaches.[15] These ideological differences and conceptual slippages have contributed to the controversies at hand. The problem is the antinomy of two competing principles. One presumes that in order to establish a legitimate and functioning civil society, one must pursue prosecutions for the crimes of the past. The other assumes that in order to secure stability and a functioning government, it is sometimes necessary (and morally acceptable) to forego the judicial pursuit of past crimes.[16]

Thus, the making of an African court with international criminal jurisdiction offers us a lens through which to explore new cartographies of African justice as a symbolically Pan-African question concerned with the particularities of justice on the African continent. It is also a domain of political-emotional regulation. Here, as in previous chapters, we see how particular feeling regimes are deployed to shape new political projects. In particular, I turn to the Malabo Protocol for the African Court, which extended the jurisdiction of the African Court of Justice and Human Rights (ACJHR) to cover individual criminal liability for serious crimes committed in violation of the international law and matters concerning general jurisdiction. I demonstrate how the drafters of the Malabo Protocol for the ACJHR sought to gain authority over the sequencing of peace and justice interventions by discursively recalling the deep inequalities in Africa's histories and infrastructures, while innovating new ways for political actors to navigate judicial contexts.

What is compelling about a case study of the Malabo Protocol and the practices involved in its making is that it features various new institutional

ICC Justice ▷ Individual Criminal Responsibility

Refusals = Returning to Root Causes of Violence

| Trafficking: Humans Drugs Hazardous Waste Arms | Local Cultural & Political Context | Corporate Interests: White Collar Crimes | Corruption | Contemporary Western Political Influence/Pressure |

Historical Conditions of Extraction/Debilitation, Structural Inequalities & Colonial Past

5.1 Root causes versus individual criminal responsibility.

formations through the technical construction of legal authority, but it also features what Connal Parsley has called the "afterlife of the imaginary."[17] The afterlife of the Pan-African imaginary helps us to articulate the way that the new Pan-African renaissance is shaping the authors and the spectators of African social formations. While the making of an African court with criminal jurisdiction is being shaped by a wider institutional campaign around Pan-African histories and struggles, it is also a response to the lack of judicial activity in African jurisdictions for crimes of slavery, imperialism, colonialism, apartheid, and subsequent forms of economic plunder set against the contemporary anti-impunity campaigns that target individual Africans for criminal responsibility for crimes that operate within the afterlife of those spheres of structural inequality.

As I have demonstrated thus far, the anti-impunity campaigns have been driven by the emergence of particular publics whose authority is affirmed through the existence of a victim to be saved and by internationally driven judicial authorities holding the perpetrators of that violence accountable.[18]

As a response to such formations, figure 5.1 highlights the way that the attribution movement symbolized by African geographies of justice reflects the afterlife of the Pan-Africanist imaginary in which conceptualizations of justice require understanding how the colonial past set in place the conditions of underdevelopment that led to the need for its constituents to find new ways to adjudicate the aftereffects of colonialism. What emerges is a particular arrangement of sociopolitical life in which the theater of AU action is not only shaped by the production and institutionalization of new ideas about justice, but temporally driven by an urgency and responsibility to act in a way that is commensurate with anti-imperial, antiexploitative struggle. As we will see, the introduction of economic crimes and criminal corporate responsibility reflects how contemporary forms of Pan-Africanist reattribution is haunted by histories of extraction and violence that are brought into the biopolitics of international justice in Africa.

The Afterlife of Pan-African Sentimentality in the New African Union

The Twenty-Second Summit of the African Union held in Addis Ababa in January 2014, where the AU presented its fiftieth anniversary platform, extended the themes of Pan-Africanism and the African renaissance with themes of African solidarity using the refrain "I am African, I am the African Union." With posters, T-shirts, and images of Pan-Africanist leaders alongside ordinary Africans, the celebratory campaign took on a life of its own in AU discourse. The campaign launch had taken place back in March 2013 at the Sheraton Hotel in Addis Ababa, where various AU commissioners, representatives from diplomatic missions, African ambassadors, and civil society organizations began work to popularize the AU. The goal was to broaden public awareness of what the AU is and does and to encourage citizens of African countries to get engaged. From the Department of Political Affairs to the chair of the Coalition Governance Team, AU representatives described the campaign as a platform for citizen participation in AU affairs and for interaction between member states, the AU, and African citizens. Central to the message was the importance of advancing from the ratification of various AU instruments to their actual implementation so that citizens could reap the practical benefits that could emerge from the aspirations that inspire treaty making in the first place.

The "I am African" campaign was meant to evoke particular emotional responses by connecting Africa's histories of oppression and colonial rule with future aspirations of resilience reflected in a new narrative of African leaders taking control by creating a prosperous Africa. Its green imagery is described by its designers as having been characteristically about African freedom. The AU's governance commitment of African solutions to African problems located its message in the embodiment of its people—commissioners, leaders, helpers, ordinary people—whose images were displayed alongside the "I am African, I am the African Union" declarations.

These declarations were posted in the summit halls, in the town square, on the literature and paraphernalia, and on T-shirts that were distributed and worn by young people throughout Addis Ababa, the capital of Ethiopia. The

Pan-Africanist sentiments of the campaign articulated a reconceived Africa whose mobilizing narrative flowed from Africa's anticolonial struggles, to its political freedom, to its contemporary road to economic and political integration. Its message of perseverance and survival meant to work not simply through its declarations but through the emotive sentiments it conjured in turning injustice to justice. The campaign focused on visual elements of African participation to establish the identity of the AU.

The opening speech at the January 2013 AU summit by its chairwoman, Dr. Nkosazana Dlamini Zuma, best marks what the "I am African, I am the African Union" campaign would articulate as its vision for the future:[19]

> Africa is increasingly seen as the continent of the future, as a place of enormous possibilities, thanks to a young and growing population, our natural resources, but also because of the improving business climate and opportunities, and the strides made in the consolidation of democracy and governance. . . . We do however still have challenges that need to be overcome urgently and collectively. Our continent still has to contend with huge infrastructure backlogs, backlogs in education, health and other basic services, including responding to rapid urbanization, youth development and the need for food security. At the same time, it is a matter of concern that negotiations on global trade issues and climate change have almost collapsed, with very serious consequences for Africa. It is therefore important that Africa remains resolute and determined to overcome these challenges. Central to this, is the institutional [as well as] other capacities to implement our plans at national, regional and continental levels.[20]

Following this opening, Dlamini Zuma, dressed in African garb, proceeded to map the various components of critical importance to the continent, such as building human capacity, promoting economic development, building a people-centered AU, and strengthening strategic partnerships. In this statement the past was invoked to reflect on ideological and political movements as uplift discourses to shift the narratives from African suffering to contemporary regional integration strategies. The assumption was that Africa needed to return to the Pan-Africanism of fifty years ago and use those founding principles to invigorate its future. In articulating this history, she paid homage to the great leaders who made tremendous sacrifices and led their nations to independence, ranging from late "Mwalimu" Julius Nyerere and former president Kenneth Kaunda of Zambia, to Nelson Mandela, Sam Nujoma, Samora Machel, Agostinho Neto, and Amílcar Cabral. And as much as these names mark a particular moment in African independence struggles, they are necessary precursors for setting the moral conditions by which contemporary Africa can join the West in development partnerships.

However, as an ideology, Pan-Africanism was mobilized over the late nineteenth and throughout the twentieth century to encourage the solidarity of Africans in Africa and its diaspora, insisting that the fate of African peoples is intertwined with a common history and shared destiny. Though originated in the African diaspora with an aim to forge a sense of oneness and political belonging between its various communities. Pan-Africanism was dedicated to establishing independence for African nations and cultivating unity among black people throughout the world. There was a sense that "uncritical absorption of Western ideas would destroy the distinctive personality of Africans."[21] It is no surprise that the father of Pan-Africanism, Edward W. Blyden—an educator, politician, and diplomat—insisted on particular approaches to Pan-Africanism, as noted in his 1881 presidential address during the opening of the Liberian College:

> The African must advance by methods of his own. He must possess a power distinct from that of the European. It has been proved that he knows how to take advantage of European culture and that he can be benefited by it. Their proof was perhaps necessary, but it is not sufficient. We must show that we are able to go alone, to carve out our own way. . . . We must not be satisfied that, in this nation, European influence shapes our polity, makes our laws, rules in our tribunals and impregnates our social atmosphere.[22]

It was this sense of indignation that provided the organizational impetus around which Pan-Africanism took shape and that ultimately led to the formation of the OAU.

The OAU—a regional Pan-African organization set up to meet the goals of African decolonization—was established in 1963 with these basic principles to ground its work. Its charter reflected many of the key tenets of Pan-Africanism. For instance, the preamble makes mention of "the inalienable right of all people to control their own destiny" and "the fact that freedom, equality, justice and dignity are essential objectives for the achievement of the legitimate aspirations of the African peoples." In addition, the preamble states that the charter is a response to "the aspirations of our peoples for brotherhood and solidarity, in a larger unity transcending ethnic and national differences."[23] The OAU saw itself as providing the moral authority for the promotion of self-determination. Thus, as a discourse to harness natural and human capital on the continent and enhance the progress of all African peoples, the Pan-Africanism of the 1950s and 1960s took a new turn. From its predominance outside of Africa and in relation to various diasporic communities, it came to be popularized by two of Africa's towering independence leaders: President Kwame Nkrumah of Ghana and President Julius Nyerere of Tanzania, who famously emphasized on a number of key occasions, such as the founding of the OAU in Addis Ababa in May 1963, that "Africa must unite or perish."[24] At that time, thirty-one African heads of state signed the charter of the OAU, formed to create the conditions for African independence by building human and resource capacity for the general enhancement of African people. And although the Pan-Africanism of Nkrumah and Nyerere represented a moment of defying the political, economic, and psychological violence of European colonialism in Africa, truth be told, the new Pan-Africanism today represents the same impetus for regional integration but in the face of new challenges for a continent plagued with unresolved land distribution issues and widespread structural inequalities.

After the Cold War, the security paradigm shifted from a focus on national security (of the state) to issues such as food and water security, land, and environmental concerns—in other words, a concern with internal root causes of conflict. This shift has had a particular impact in Africa, and has led African leaders to expand the mandate of the AU far beyond that of the OAU to activities in the realms of peace and security, human rights, democratization, good governance, and humanitarian assistance.[25] While the OAU was set up in May 1963 to allow independent African states to end the vestiges of colonialism and apartheid, to intensify development, and to safeguard sovereignty following UN principles of international cooperation, the OAU Charter specifically provided for a policy of noninterference in the internal affairs of states.[26] September 9, 1999, marked the end of the mandate of the OAU and the beginning of the new mandate of the AU. It was formally established on May 26, 2001, in Addis Ababa and launched on July 9, 2002, in South Africa.

The AU's Constitutive Act was used to transform the original OAU and establish nine organs within the union that would work to ensure the development of the AU as an engaged body able to ensure the protection of life. The organs include the Assembly; Executive Council; Pan-African Parliament; Court of Justice; Commission; Permanent Representatives Committee; specialized technical committees; Economic, Social and Cultural Council; and financial institutions.[27] Article 6 of the Constitutive Act identifies the Assembly as being composed of heads of states and government and their representatives, as the apex decision-making body of the union. The Assembly is seen as the de facto executive of the union and its functions and powers are often identified as making and monitoring the implementation of the common policies of the union. Other functions also involve receiving, considering, and making decisions on reports, considering recommendations from the other organs of the union, and ensuring the compliance of member states and appointing key officeholders to organs of the union. Through relevant organs and institutions, it is also seen as being responsible for overseeing the management of conflicts and emergency situations and the restoration of peace and security.[28]

A key organizing principle is unity and a common approach to policy areas such as defense; peace and security; economic integration; the free movement of people, goods, and capital; food security; development; and poverty reduction. The new AU marked a shift in promoting both African continental integration and global economic and political membership, and conflict resolution is at the heart of current AU policy concerns.[29] This new form of Africanness articulated through African claims to the new world order may be otherwise read by some as un-African, but the new 190-million-dollar building that the Chinese government gifted to the AU, the dependable and ongoing availability of electricity facilitated by the Italians and French, the organizational structure mapped out in the rotunda with all fifty-three states represented and eligible to vote (like a typical UN General Assembly), are all representative of what Jim Ferguson has insisted are not attempts to be what Africa is not, but claims to power and membership in the global community.[30]

This reconceptualization of the AU represents the complexity of Africa as being as much about the Other as it is about itself; it represents the desire, hope, fear, anger, and joy of modernity that sits neatly next to specters of anticolonial struggles. These affectivities reside alongside a particular set of ontologies, or ways of conceiving of existence; for while the shadows of the colonial past still structure Africa's place in the world, so does the aspiration of significance, of potential, of power. The signs of struggle and survival make hope possible, and power is being claimed in the affective geography of justice, for it offers the promise of a new future. But the signs of struggle being deployed by these new Pan-African campaigns draw on a symbolic, historic framework that is very unlike the roots of the AU's formation. Thus, we must take seriously the ghostly realities of structural violence and how they produce complex political subjects and the actions they take.

The fervor of Pan-Africanism and African geographies of justice in the contemporary period is also shaped by the emotional responses to the failures of international justice to intervene in Africa long before the ICC was a reality. The idea of an African human rights convention and an African court of human rights modeled on the European and Inter-American Court was first proposed in 1961 at the Lagos Conference on Primacy of Law.[31] This proposal resurfaced in 1969 at the UN Seminar on the Creation of Regional Commissions on Human Rights, with specific reference to Africa, held in Cairo. The UN's recommendation to the OAU went unimplemented.[32] Several other initiatives and seminars were held over a period of ten years to discuss and advocate for the establishment of an African commission on human rights or an African court.[33] The call for the OAU to adopt a human rights instrument was reiterated on every occasion.[34] A symposium convened by the UN in Monrovia, Liberia, in 1979 adopted a strong position on the need to create such a body, which reportedly influenced the decision by the OAU Assembly. A series of political events (particularly human rights violations in several African states, such as Uganda and the Central African Republic, that attracted global attention), as well as a concerted campaign to create an African commission, led to the OAU's decision at its February 1979 summit to request that the secretary-general convene a meeting of experts to draft an African charter on human rights.[35] It was here that they proposed the establishment of relevant bodies for the protection of human rights in Africa.[36]

By the late 1990s, the histories of various international legal mechanisms that cross-cut state boundaries soon seemed to offer possibilities to many on the African continent seeking redemption through international law. Before becoming the AU, the OAU sought to prosecute the crime of apartheid in South Africa in the 1970s. From 1948 to 1990, apartheid was an international crime without an international criminal court to prosecute it. However, when the UN General Assembly classified it as a crime against humanity in 1966 and then the UN Security Council affirmed it in 1984, the OAU attempted to mobilize around the establishment of an international penal court to prosecute the crime.[37] Initially, its stakeholders had hoped that they could establish a criminal chamber through the African Charter of Human Rights, but they abandoned the effort when the possibility of establishing a UN international penal court arose in the 1980s in order to prosecute various apartheid crimes on the basis of universal jurisdiction. However, with the consolidation of the UN court with the International Law Commission's project to establish a permanent independent criminal court, the apartheid offenses were eventually dropped from the subject matter jurisdiction of the international court project, and instead apartheid was collapsed into crimes against humanity and established within a post-2002 time limit. The result was that in order to pursue apartheid as a crime, state actors eventually had to enact legislation to prosecute individuals through universal jurisdiction.[38] Ultimately, it was a political settlement that ended apartheid, not prosecutorial justice.

This political solution had the effect of absolving apartheid's perpetrators from decades of violence but also provided the terms for sociopolitical rebuilding through legality. The violent histories that were part of South Africa's nonjudicial settlements were not unlike the histories of Europe's first and second world wars—exclusion, racism, and brute violence. But the legal solutions were different. In South Africa, as in the rest of Africa, the only forms of violence that became legally actionable by international institutions were those that began after various international criminal courts gained jurisdiction. For example, the fallout with international judicial forms was evident with the International Court of Justice's South West Africa (now Namibia) case when many on the African continent lost faith in that institution. Following Germany's loss of territories after World War I, South Africa undertook the administration of South West Africa under Article 22 of the Covenant of the League of Nations. This gave South Africa full power to administer the territory under the League rules. However, when the UN took over the League of Nations in 1946, it worked to grant transitional independence status to Europe's colonies. South Africa refused to surrender its trusteeship mandate of South West Africa. In 1966, Ethiopia and Liberia brought a complaint against South Africa's presence in the region, and the UN revoked South Africa's mandate; but South Africa continued to rule the region. Its attempts to administer racially segregated policies led to the development of black opposition to South African rule and the formation of a Namibian pro-independence movement known as the South West African People's Organisation.

By 1971, the International Court of Justice issued a legal advisory opinion demanding that South Africa withdraw its interests from Namibia. It still refused and delayed Namibian independence until 1988, when the Brazzaville Protocol was signed and led to the formation of a Joint Monitoring Commission with the Soviet Union and the United States as observers. Given the entrenchment of a racially hierarchicalized region with flagrant uses of state violence with impunity, the potential for deploying international law effectively waned. Here, again, the ICC's post-2002 jurisdiction prevented such histories of violence from being legally actionable. Instead, European universal jurisdiction requests lingered, with various activists concerned with violence being perpetrated by various African postindependence leaders.

Keeping these tensions in mind as part of the emotional frameworks of expectation that shape AU responses to the ICC, alongside the AU's refusal to cooperate with growing ICC-Africa indictments, I now seek to clarify the newly unfolding AU structure in relation to the way that emotional, cultural, Pan-Africanist sensibilities are being deployed to propel new AU agendas. By the end of 2013, the AU popularization movement had reached its height, yet it was also mired in contestation. For while Equatorial Guinea's Press and Information Office reported that the campaign was meant to emphasize the autonomy of Africans and their ability to take charge of their destiny, the irony was that many NGOs complained that the "I am African" campaign was part of a moment of AU retooling in which citizen participation was actually restricted, not expanded. These African civil society advocates complained bitterly about restricted access to the AU; because such civil society groups were often seen as being funded by external donors from the West, their legitimacy as advocates of African interests was constantly under attack.[39]

I go on to examine two processes that occurred at roughly the same time and influenced each other: first, the development of African governance and transitional justice policies, and second, the effort to expand the criminal jurisdiction of the African Court through the Malabo Protocol—and through it to clarify the larger transitional justice framework through which to operationalize commitments to peace and justice sequencing. In light of the history of failure around international justice in Africa, I look at what type of future is being imagined when the reorientation of African geographies of justice invokes particular Pan-Africanist philosophical principles alongside forms of counterencapsulation. These reattributions bring together legal and political subjects through encounters in which treaties and peace and justice deals are created and negotiated in order to help them imagine new spaces of justice.

Pan-Africanist Justice Regimes

In its Strategic Plan of 2009–2012, the AUC committed to help facilitate the "establishment of appropriate architecture for promotion of good governance" as part of its continuing work "to achieve good governance, democracy, human rights and [a] rights-based approach to development including social, economic, cultural and environmental rights."[40] To achieve its core objective, the Assembly and the Executive Council have been engaged through coordinated action with one of its branches, the African Governance Architecture (AGA). Alongside the Assembly, the Executive Council houses African leaders and key decision making.[41] Both organs—the Assembly and the Executive Council—are served by the commission and constitute the AU's executive bureaucracy. The AGA is the AU's institutional framework established to coordinate action undertaken by AU organs, institutions, and the Regional Economic Communities (RECS) to support member states in strengthening democracy, governance, and human rights.[42] The rationale for the AGA was that while there are several governance instruments, frameworks, and institutions at the regional, subregional, and national levels, there is little to no effective synergy, coordination, and harmonization among them. These institutions work mostly in silos and do not benefit adequately from each other, even at the level of sharing information and coordinating their activities for effective performance.[43] As such, it is anticipated that the AGA will provide the process and mechanism for enhancing policy dialogue, convergence, coherence, and harmonization among AU organs, institutions, and member states as a way of speeding up the integration process on the continent.[44]

George Mukundi, at the time the head of the AGA Secretariat, noted, "The AGA complements the African Peace and Security Architecture (APSA), which addresses the AU's peace-and-security agenda. The AGA and APSA were designed to bring together principles of democratic governance, peace, and security as interrelated and mutually reinforcing."[45] The ultimate aim of the AGA is to facilitate "the convergence of governance policies, programmes, [and] processes," such as reinforcing the capacity of AU organs and enhancing coordination among them to support members states to strengthen democracy and governance; undertaking action to enhance popular participation in governance and democratic processes across the continent; researching and disseminating information relating to governance, democracy, and human rights across the continent; and implementing shared African values as well as decisions and recommendations of various AU organs and institutions.

Differently articulated, the AGA processes can be seen as providing preventive diplomacy, peacemaking, peacekeeping, peace building, sanctions, transitional justice mechanisms, protection of human rights (commissions of inquiry and fact-finding missions), and humanitarian intervention. The AGA is an evolving mechanism composed of three principal pillars: a vision and agenda; organs and institutions; and mechanisms or processes of interaction among AU organs and institutions with a formal mandate in governance, democracy, and human rights.[46] The African Court on Human and Peoples' Rights is one of the institutions critical to the second pillar, which will give operational expression to the vision for African governance.[47] Similarly, the ACJHR can be viewed as a key institution charged with promoting democracy, governance, and human rights in Africa at a regional and continental level. These components are expected to lead to fully functioning political action.[48]

In May 2009, the AU-commissioned Panel of the Wise presented a report titled "Peace, Justice, and Reconciliation in Africa: Opportunities and Challenges in the Fight against Impunity." The panel is a diplomatic instrument for dealing with violence in Africa, consisting of five members chosen from western, eastern, northern, southern, and central regions of Africa—two former presidents of African countries, a president of a national constitutional court, a former secretary of the OAU, and a head of an independent electoral commission. The detailed report recommended the formation of a Transitional Justice Policy Framework for Africa, which included a range of strategies for dealing with mass violence in Africa. The goal was for AU member states to work toward the establishment of measures that would ensure the protection of those victimized by violence throughout the African continent. As stated in the report, "Justice, peace, good governance, and reconciliation . . . thrive where sturdy and stable democratic values and impulses prevail, and where there is a culture of constitutionalism to constrain arbitrariness and abuse of power."[49] The report stressed that the approach taken in Africa should involve the articulation of common values around the protection of human rights and the development of an institutional architecture with transitional justice at its core. Transitional justice consists of both judicial and nonjudicial measures address the afterlife of human rights violence.

As noted in chapter 1, central to the Panel of the Wise's recommended strategies is the balancing of various forms of judicial accountability with transitional justice goals, as well as sequencing diplomatic, nonjudicial approaches with judicial ones. Recommended strategies included (1) transitional justice and various forms of judicial accountability; (2) balancing of transitional justice goals; and (3) sequencing of these strategies with the presumption that the AU and various political and legal actors should play leadership roles in the articulation of an African transitional justice framework. What is critical here is that sequencing as a core strategy speaks to the place of temporality in how justice is conceived by its stakeholders. It works contrary to the principles of the anti-impunity movement's temporality of the now and its singular concern with judicial accountability. From the violence of traditional empires to colonial imperial rule to contemporary postcolonial struggles, the recommendations of the Panel of the Wise highlighted the history of violence in Africa and its resolve to use politically relevant solutions to address it, even as transnational institutions seek to carve out new domains of territorial, legal, and social reordering.

African-Led Transitional Justice: Peace and Justice Sequencing

Best seen through a set of radically shifting frameworks through which to re-think our approaches to justice, the AU Transitional Justice Policy Framework presumes the importance of an interrelated justice architecture that includes economic justice, political justice (entailed in constitutional and other legal reforms), and justice for crimes committed from the perspective of criminal and reparative justice.[50] Today, the AU Transitional Justice Framework under development is seen as a viable approach to applying sequencing strategies, with several options for determining which AU organs can take action to pro-tect human rights. Its actors see the framework not only as a mechanism for establishing the norms and modalities for state responsibility to its citizens, but also for assisting state actors in recognizing and implementing their ob-ligations. These obligations are not simply to protect those victimized by vi-olence using judicial accountability mechanisms after the fact; they exist to address societies traumatized by various inequalities, such as what we saw in chapters 1 and 2 in Kenya, or chapter 3 in Nigeria with Boko Haram.

New international judicial mechanisms, such as the African Court on Hu-man and Peoples' Rights, have also been designed to implement practices that can help to manage violence strategically. Such forms of action might, at times, exceed judicial accountability but involve other modes of action that are seen as involving preventive diplomacy, peacemaking, peacekeeping, peace building, sanctions, transitional justice mechanisms, protection of hu-man rights (commissions of inquiry and fact-finding missions), and humani-tarian intervention. These strategies include a range of biopolitical approaches that include redistributive politics, the building of respect for institutions and rules that constrain leaders and make them accountable to their constituen-cies, and relevant steps deployed for domesticating, monitoring, implement-ing, and pursuing judicial mechanisms.

Since its transformation from the OAU, the AU (and its components de-scribed above) has demonstrated a growing capacity to resolve conflicts around the continent using particular peace and justice sequencing strategies. In 2002 the AU implemented its first peacekeeping mission in Burundi with the African Mission in Burundi.[51] Since then, it has tried to establish itself as the intracontinental governing body that will attempt to de-escalate conflicts, monitor ceasefires, or negotiate power-sharing agreements following the cessation of hostilities. After the deployment in Burundi, the AU fielded a number of missions, including African Union Mission in Sudan, AU Mission for Support to the Elections in the Comoros, AU Mission in Somalia, AU Electoral and Security Assistance Mission to the Comoros, AU Military Observer Mission in the Comoros, United Nations African Union Mission in Darfur, the African-led International Support Mission in Mali, and the African-led International Support Mission to the Central African Republic, which transformed into the UN Multidimensional Integrated Stabilization Mission to the Central African Republic.[52]

From the violence of traditional empires, to colonial imperial rule, to contemporary postcolonial struggles, the recommendations of the Panel of the Wise highlighted a resolve to continue using politically relevant solutions to address violence in Africa even as transnational institutions seek to carve out new domains of territorial, legal, and social reordering. Since the report's release, there have been a series of consultations to create a comprehensive strategy to go beyond the establishment of norms and address problems of inequality in Africa. The African Union has innovated a strategy of peace and justice sequencing that accommodates a limited function for the ICC while asserting the primacy of African states and institutions in the larger project of creating justice and peace. This approach allows for significant nationally driven, postviolence closure toward the establishment of peace. Courts, as tools available to political actors such as the AU, can be used to intervene in conflict situations by prosecuting a small number of perpetrators, but they play only a limited role in contributing to the reestablishment of peace, stability, and reconciliation. Key here is the implementation of various strategies that do not involve immediately pursuing judicial action before the end of hostilities. One might consider the strategy of using a commission of inquiry as one of a range of sequenced strategies for brokering peace.

The response to violence committed in the ongoing conflict in South Sudan is one example that highlights how the AU's attempts differ from the ICC's approach to the case, as I discussed in chapter 1. Instead, for the first time in its history, in 2013, the AU formed a Commission of Inquiry on South Sudan that was charged with investigating, documenting, reporting, and recommending solutions for peace through diplomacy and negotiations.[53] Some five years later, in 2018, the AU, with the financial support of the US government, began to set up the Hybrid Court of South Sudan. This court is provided for under chapter V(3) of the agreement reached by the South Sudanese parties as an

African-led and African-owned legal mechanism to investigate and prosecute individuals bearing responsibility for violations of international law and applicable South Sudanese law committed between December 15, 2013, and the end of the transitional period.[54] It is to be expected that the Assembly and the Peace and Security Council (PSC) will establish such commissions of inquiry in the future before triggering the jurisdiction of the African Criminal Court.

In a previous situation called an unconstitutional change of government in Guinea, the PSC had endorsed an earlier call by the Economic Community of West African States (ECOWAS) for the establishment of an international commission of inquiry to probe the killing of civilians on October 28, 2009.[55] Following ECOWAS's request, the UN subsequently established such a commission, which rendered its report on January 13, 2010, in which it concluded that there were reasonable grounds to believe that crimes against humanity had been committed.[56] Guinea has since been under preliminary examination by the OTP at the ICC.[57]

Humanitarian intervention is seen as another option on the continuum ranging from diplomacy to military intervention in response to human rights violations. The conflict in Libya provides a different example. On March 17, 2011, the UN authorized military intervention in Libya to protect the country's civilians as a result of violence between Libyan government forces and domestic opponents that had erupted the previous month. Two days after the authorization, NATO initiated the intervention, including establishing a no-fly zone and launching aerial attacks on government forces. In October 2011, after seven months, Libyan rebel forces conquered the country and killed the former authoritarian ruler, Muammar al-Qaddafi. Western media and politicians praised the intervention as a humanitarian success for averting a bloodbath in Libya's second largest city, Benghazi, and replacing Qaddafi's dictatorial regime with a transitional council pledged to democracy.[58]

Some would say that NATO succeeded in Libya. They say it almost certainly saved tens of thousands of lives. It conducted an air campaign of unparalleled precision, which, though not perfect, was seen by some as greatly minimizing collateral damage. It enabled the Libyan opposition to overthrow one of the world's longest-ruling dictators. And it accomplished all of this without a single allied casualty and at a cost—$1.1 billion for the United States and several billion dollars overall—that was a fraction of that spent on previous interventions in the Balkans, Afghanistan, and Iraq.[59] Indeed, many experts now cite Libya as a model for implementing the humanitarian principle of responsibility to protect.[60] However, such arguments are also seen by some African leaders as not providing a full and accurate account of events. There are convincing arguments that the violence was actually initiated by protesters and that Qaddafi's government responded to the rebels militarily but never intentionally targeted civilians or resorted to indiscriminate force, as Western media claimed.[61] Scholars like Alan Kuperman argue that the conventional wisdom is wrong in asserting that NATO's main goal in Libya was to protect civilians.[62] Rather, evidence shows that NATO's primary aim was to overthrow Qaddafi's regime, even at the expense of increasing the harm to Libyans.[63] The biggest misconception about NATO's intervention, according to Kuperman, is that it saved lives and benefited Libya and its neighbors. In reality, when NATO intervened in mid-March 2011, Qaddafi already had regained control of most of Libya, while the rebels were retreating rapidly toward Egypt. Thus, the conflict was about to end, barely six weeks after it started, at a toll of about a thousand dead, including soldiers, rebels, and civilians caught in the crossfire. By intervening, NATO enabled the rebels to resume their attack, which prolonged the war for another seven months and caused at least seven thousand more deaths.[64]

In considering these complex political dynamics in relation to disagreements over how African violence is to be managed, it should not be a surprise that affects and emotional manifestations have been operative in shaping how people position themselves and in what regimes of expression they engage. In reflecting on constituencies who were against NATO intervention in Libya, they argue that in the midst of the civil war, in June 2011, the ICC prosecutor brought an indictment against Muammar Qaddafi and two top deputies and that this action reflected the usual Western imperialist interventions.[65] In supporting such claims, Robert Mnookin argued that the indictment of Qaddafi in the middle of a civil war was a mistake because it precluded diplomatic options that might have ended the bloodshed earlier, and it hampered the West's ability to offer Qaddafi exile in order to end the conflict.[66] In contrast, human rights organizations applauded the prosecutor's actions for underscoring, in their opinion, that dictators could now be held legally accountable under the Rome Statute, and the indictments bolstered the rebels' morale.

People's emotionally charged pushback against the NATO intervention insisted that the indictments may have cut off certain routes to a negotiated solution and an earlier end to the conflict. As early as March 3, 2011, two weeks into the violence, Qaddafi embraced Venezuela's offer of mediation, and on April 11, Qaddafi accepted the AU proposal for an immediate ceasefire to be followed by a national dialogue. The rebels refused to consider a ceasefire until Qaddafi left power.[67] In this regard, scholars like Kuperman maintain that it is impossible to know if Qaddafi would have honored a ceasefire or the promise to negotiate a political transition; however, if NATO had sought primarily to protect civilians, it would have conditioned its aid to the rebels on their sincerely exploring the regime's offers. There is no evidence that NATO ever sought to use its leverage in this manner.[68]

There is evidence to suggest, however, that NATO's approach to the situation in Libya further strained the relationship between the AU and institutions perceived as Western, such as NATO and the ICC. Yet, although the NATO operation in Libya was legalized by the UNSC resolutions, the organization's previous involvement in other conflicts in Africa, such as Darfur and Somalia, had been predicated on requests made by the AU.[69] Since the Darfur crisis in 2005, the principle of AU request has become the norm in AU-NATO cooperation on Africa's peace and security issues, and for the first time, NATO's intervention in Libya was not based on an AU request.[70] The different approaches adopted by the AU and NATO with regard to the Libyan crisis created a clash of positions. This was the first time that NATO had engaged in actual combat in Africa, and yet it excluded African decision making because the AU preferred mediation to military intervention and took a strong position on the need to use diplomacy to resolve the conflict.[71]

Of course, the Constitutive Act of the AU provides for "the right of the Union to intervene in a Member State . . . in respect of grave circumstances, namely war crimes, genocide and crimes against humanity, if it is determined necessary by the Assembly of Heads of State and Government."[72] The AU PSC is to be guided by, among other principles, humanitarian intervention in the circumstances mentioned above.[73] However, there is lack of precision on the scope of the principle of humanitarian intervention, and African state agents have wanted to claim responsibility for the management of violence on their own terms.

These sociopolitical dynamics highlight more instances in which contemporary interventions are seen as resembling colonial and imperialist action and are not unrelated to the form that embodied responses to ICC indictments take. For example, the chair of the AUC, Jean Ping, argued, "Some international players seem to be denying Africa any significant role in the search for a solution to the Libya conflict" and vowed that "Africa is not going to be reduced to the status of an observer of its own calamities."[74] Even if the AU and NATO could not have reached consensus, some argue that a middle-ground approach relying on limited use of force and intensive diplomacy may have fostered a closer collaboration between the AU and NATO.[75]

As the above example illustrates, emotionally propelled forms of reattribution emerged from a sense that reliance on criminal prosecution as the main or sole response to conflict is at best inadequate. Such conflict-laden responses led African states to take action against prosecutorial indictments in the midst of AU peace talks. In 2013, the AU proposed an amendment to Article 54 of the Rome Statute, which refers to the duties and powers of the prosecutor as it relates to investigations, so that certain OTP decisions could be subjected to a decision-making process.[76] This led to disagreements between ICC and AU agents, particularly in relation to the situation in Sudan.[77] These contexts on the African continent clearly point to how various AU stakeholders felt a need to pursue action beyond the prosecution of crimes to address economic justice and political justice, and to approach individual perpetrators with an eye toward reparative as well as criminal justice, when sequenced appropriately.[78]

The official report from the AU High-Level Panel on Darfur has stated that "an outcome which would promote national justice and reconciliation proceedings is . . . required. . . . Criminal justice will play an important role, but not an exclusive one, and must be underpinned by procedures that allow for meaningful participation of victims, as well as reparations and other acts of conciliation. Within the criminal justice system, the investigations, prosecutions, defence and judiciary must work in tandem, or in smooth sequence. Weaknesses in any one element of the criminal justice process would undermine the prospects of a successful outcome."[79]

This report goes on to propose a hybrid court that fuses domestic and international criminal justice procedures and that works in collaboration with complementary domestic alternative justice mechanisms that may function in tandem with various prosecutions—including the ICC when necessary. This approach acknowledges that different institutions and processes have their own distinct roles to play, but need to coordinate and cooperate to achieve the best overall results for peace and justice. Various transitional justice measures underway that have involved truth and reconciliation commissions or institutional reform, including bottom-up traditional or "ethno-justice" approaches, have provided scaffolding for the way that AU and other transitional justice actors are pursuing strategies in the face of anti-impunity constraints.[80] The strategy includes a compilation of transitional justice goals that are embedded in a sequenced temporality relevant to the political foundations of African violence. These strategies speak to the realization that addressing the deep roots of violence in Africa requires more than just judicial accountability. It emphasizes the need for institutional restructuring as key to the foundations of in-equality in Africa.

Now, the passage of the Malabo Protocol in 2014—and the effort to ex-tend the criminal jurisdiction of the African Court and bring it into force—has raised a new set of issues related to how to address the interplay between various peace and justice dilemmas in postviolence contexts. This involves conceptualizing the African Court as one aspect of a wider institutional framework for enhancing human rights, accountability, democracy, and ac-cess to justice on the continent as whole. One way to conceptualize this is through the recognition that AU actors are deploying Pan-African discourses strategically to put in place a differentiated approach to justice that involves the creation of an institutional framework designed to strengthen coordina-tion and collaboration among existing institutions at regional, subregional, and national levels.[81] This differentiated approach involves the shaping of sev-eral transitional justice principles relevant to the African context.[82] These in-clude the urgency to pursue peace through inclusive negotiations, rather than through force or military struggles; the suspension of hostilities and protec-tion of civilians to provide enabling conditions for participation in dialogue and the search for meaningful peace and justice; and, importantly from the perspective of the African Court, a broader understanding of justice to en-compass processes of achieving healing, equality, reconciliation, obtaining compensation and restitution, and establishing the rule of law.[83]

By defining transitional justice to include a range of processes and mech-anisms associated with mitigating conflict, ensuring accountability, and pro-moting justice, the framework proposes a definition that goes beyond current understandings of transitional justice. This broadening includes the consoli-dation of peace, reconciliation, and justice in Africa. The list is voluminous, ranging from activities involving the preventing of impunity, helping end re-pressive rule and conflicts, nurturing sustainable peace with development, social justice, human and peoples' rights, democratic rule, and good gov-ernance. Other activities involve drawing lessons from various experiences across Africa in articulating a set of common concepts and principles to con-stitute a reference point for developing and strengthening peace agreements and transitional justice institutions and initiatives in Africa, as well as devel-oping AU benchmarks for assessing compliance with the need to combat im-punity. With these priorities in mind, it is possible to situate mechanisms such as the African Court and the AGA within the framework of African solutions to African problems, and to see these structures not simply as an example of the spread and expansion of prosecutorial justice norms but as integral to a continent-wide transitional justice approach and process aimed at dealing with past conflicts and securing sustainable forms of justice going forward.

Mobilizing Institutional Values: The Malabo Protocol for the African Court

The Pan-Africanist "Silencing the Guns" and the "I am African, I am the African Union" campaigns were both launched during and after the African Union's fiftieth anniversary, at the same time as the African Court's Malabo Protocol was being debated and negotiated. The strategies around the celebration of the fiftieth anniversary of the OAU/AU point to the way that the message of an African renaissance is mobilizing present action. This celebration provided its stakeholders with the opportunity to reflect on Africa's history and its struggles against decolonization in order to create the terms for a new political, social, economic, and legal platform in a changing world. As noted in the "Report on the Preparations for the Commemoration of the 50th Anniversary of the OAU/AU":

> The OAU has served its time with distinction and tribute is hereby paid to the founders and the vision they pursued with unity. Its greatest success was in relation to decolonization. . . . The most important achievement of the OAU is definitely the liberation of several of its Member States from the yoke of colonialism. At its foundation, only 32 countries were independent and many others were still under foreign domination. Through its Liberation Committee operating from Dar es Salaam since its creation, the OAU has rendered decisive support to Liberation Movements from countries that were still dominated by foreign powers and helped in the attainment of their independence.[84]

The shadows of past Pan-Africanist movements were embodied in the AU's slogans and invoked principles. Remnants of past anticolonial Pan-Africanist movements are uneasily present, always disappearing and reappearing in AU declarations and slogans. While the Pan-Africanism of the past was centrally concerned with resistance against the European enemy, today, the fight against this articulated yoke of imperial power is less evident. In its struggle to consolidate Africa's diverse past, the new AU Pan-Africanism being mobilized in the twenty-first century is desperately committed to economic and political power in African terms, but represents the afterlife of struggle against an obvious colonial oppression.

As noted in the words and speeches of African leaders pushing back against ICC indictments, today the enemy is seen in the very international system in which African states are embedded. Thus, the campaigns that are launched to highlight membership in Africa's past and a shared reorientation of its future demonstrate how African political decision makers engage discursive strategies that account for this presence and absence of power. And where there is a force constructed as non-African and external, such as the ICC court indictments, the politics of Pan-Africanism are mobilized to turn inward to facilitate the management of some of the most extreme forms of Africa's violence on its own terms—within African geographies. The AU's proposal to extend the criminal jurisdiction of the African Court represents an example of this.

As I have been arguing throughout this book, the rise in prosecutorial justice is unfolding within international rule of law assemblages fueled by embodied affects and, therefore, the affective work that produces or unravels these justice projects matters. The journey to establishing the Malabo Protocol for the African Court of Justice and Human and Peoples' Rights is part of a long, complex journey that has taken and continues to take many years; and each of the three sections of the court—general jurisdiction, human rights, and international criminal law—has a separate history that predates the process of vesting the court with both general and international criminal law jurisdiction.[85] As I recounted in the previous section, with the transition from the OAU to the AU in 2000, several organs were created by the AU Constitutive Act, among them the African Court of Human and Peoples' Rights (ACHPR) and the African Court of Justice, both precursors to the African Court of Justice and Human and Peoples' Rights.

The African Court of Justice (ACJ) was envisioned in the constitutive act to be the principal judicial organ of the AU. It was seen as a body with jurisdiction over general international law disputes. The protocol establishing the ACJ was adopted in 2003, and eighteen African states subsequently ratified the protocol, with the effect of bringing the protocol into force.[86] However, its formation was superseded by a decision to merge the ACJ with the African Court on Human and Peoples' Rights.

The African Court on Human and Peoples' Rights was established in 2004 and became operational in 2008. At the time of this writing, the court sits in Arusha, Tanzania, and has jurisdiction over the African Charter on Human and Peoples' Rights and other human rights instruments that were ratified by the relevant states.[87] Since 2008, twenty-three applications for hearings have been brought before the ACHPR with only two judgments being delivered, which continued to raise questions about its effectiveness.[88] This led to the push to establish an African Court of Justice and Human and Peoples' Rights which was motivated, in part, by the desire to establish a judicial mechanism in Africa with not only the ability to function with authority with binding effect, but with international criminal jurisdiction. The eventual proposal to merge the African Court of Justice with the human rights court was propelled by the need to strengthen the African human rights system by enhancing its capacity to engender positive responses from states through binding decisions, given that the decisions of the ACHPR are mere recommendations. This was driven by the eruption of the contentious debate in 2008 on universal jurisdiction following the indictment of Rwandese officials by courts in France and Spain, coupled with the controversy over the ICC's indictment of President al-Bashir in 2009. These developments complicated the path to ratification of the African Court of Justice, and the application of technocratic lawmaking was redirected to the expansion of its jurisdiction.

By this time, the African Court on Human Rights that had been inaugurated in 2006 was engaged in setting up its structures and negotiating a working relationship with the African Commission. During the meeting of experts, ministers of justice, and attorneys general held at the AU headquarters in Addis Ababa in April 2008, the merger protocol known as the Protocol on the African Court of Justice and Human Rights was considered and approved—also taking into account the need for cost-cutting measures. Then the AU Assembly adopted the Protocol of the Merged Court at its Sixth Ordinary Session in Sharm El Sheikh, Egypt, in July 2008 and urged member states to proceed with speedy ratification.[89]

Within months of the adoption of the protocol establishing the merged court, and certainly before the merged court could come into force, the Assembly of Heads of State and Government, during its Twelfth Ordinary Session, held February 1–3, 2009, in Addis Ababa, requested the AUC (Secretariat), in consultation with the African Commission on Human and Peoples' Rights, and the African Court on Human and Peoples' Rights, to examine the implications of the court being empowered to adjudicate international crimes. Thus, at the close of its Thirteenth Ordinary Session in Sirte, Libya, in July 2009, various African leaders urged the AU Assembly to speed up the process and to aim for "early implementation" of its February decision.[90]

However, in late 2009, the Office of the AU Legal Counsel commissioned the Pan African Lawyers Union (PALU) to prepare a draft protocol on the African Court of Justice, Human Rights, and Criminal Justice. The draft was subject to a series of reviews and discussions over the next five years, culminating in the July 2014 adoption of what is often called the "Malabo Protocol for the African Court" (because it was adopted in Malabo, Equatorial Guinea). As a move following the AU's renewed commitment to Pan-Africanism and a more African-centered dispensation of judicial decisions, the protocol amends the merger protocol to add a third jurisdictional chamber—the international criminal law chamber—and also proposes other substantive changes, including renaming the court the African Court of Justice and Human and Peoples' Rights.[91]

As I noted above, these developments unfolded alongside the AU's assessment of the deeply political nature of violence in Africa and the need to hone a range of tools not only to address them but to gain legal authority to manage them. And the development of an African court that includes criminal jurisdiction is one prong of the strategy, for it attempts to shift the understanding of the nature of violence by broadening the crimes of concern to Africa to include economic crimes and the modes of liability for perpetrators of such violence to include corporations.

In 2009, the PALU submitted the first draft to allow the African Court to adjudicate international crimes committed in Africa or against Africans. Well aware of the play of international politics, and in response to Africa's realities, the PALU, under the leadership of Donald Deya, drafted the protocol for the criminal jurisdiction of the African Court, including fifteen crimes in the first draft because they were seen as key drivers of violence that reflect the core challenges of African social realities.[92] The protocol also considered forms of conduct and modes of liability as well as corporate criminal responsibility for international crimes, introduced following the perceived failure of the ICC to address it in the Rome Statute for the ICC.

As the story is often told in the ICC context, France was credited for proposing that the definition of responsibility for the crimes under its jurisdiction should also include responsibility over "juridical persons," defined as the "corporation whose concrete, real or dominant objective is seeking private profit or benefit."[93] Accordingly, there were significant disagreements in Rome over this proposal and inadequate time during the negotiations to secure its inclusion. That the drafters of the Malabo Protocol for the African Court returned to matters of criminal corporate responsibility highlights their interest in making the connection between the commission of economic crimes and the responsibility of corporate actors who are seen as also contributing to or enabling some of the most violent crimes of our times. In reflecting on this issue, one of the key drafters shared with me the following reflections:

Frankly, this was simply about developing a legal strategy. We wanted to figure out how to return to some of the basic principles agreed to already in treaties and agreements previously signed by African states. This involved figuring out how to capture all of the relevant crimes. We asked ourselves, what are the various modalities on the continent? And the answer we kept on coming up with was that there should be many enforcement mechanisms operative. . . . We needed to make those buggers [take] responsibility for their part in Africa's violence.

When I asked him whether this was a revolutionary intervention, he answered,

It's not about sixteenth-to-eighteenth-century colonialism, no. But I guess you can say that this is [a] Pan-Africanist vision that is tied to who we are. I see it as creating possibilities in modern Africa. . . . We did have the sense of how we are going to contribute to creating an Africa that can build itself and take care of itself. I know about the international system and it has a role. But if you look strictly at the constitutional issues in Africa and the need to rebuild state and juridical capacities, the mission connected to this work is all the more important. We saw ourselves as enabling Africa and Africans with a strong legal instrument relevant to the continent.

Later, in reflecting on how it might be done in terms relevant to African realities, he added, "We needed an African governance architecture for the treaty just like we need other international provisions, or various annual democracy assessments that could be used to make this instrument relevant to our needs. We were committed to that—making sure that the vision matched the African architecture underway. . . . This is important because of how much the continent has suffered and how much we have misunderstood its suffering."

Here we see the drafter's vision of the African Court's Malabo Protocol for the new court as being both a response to African inequalities and an expression of the ambitions to make a difference on the African continent in ways that international law has been ineffective. The structure and logic of the crimes replicate the logic of those seen in the Rome Statute for the icc, but what is important is that the geographical location is in Africa and not Europe and that the aspirations reflect the inclusion of crimes that are seen as enabling violence as well as the culpability of corporate actors in contributing to Africa's violence. As such, the palu draft of the Malabo Protocol and the resultant design of an African Court should be understood in relation to the affective terrain that was also unfolding at that time and that eventually led to the institutionalization of particular emotional sensibilities about the ICC as a neo-colonial institution that was targeting Africans and not necessarily addressing the core foundations of violence. As noted in earlier chapters, the controversy revolved around the ICC prosecutor's indictment of President al-Bashir of Sudan on two charges of war crimes and three charges of crimes against humanity in May 2008.[94] The first arrest warrant was issued on March 4, 2009, while the second, relating to the crime of genocide, was issued on July 12, 2010. It was connected to AU actors' emotional responses to the refusal of the ICC to succumb to AU pressure not to proceed in issuing arrest warrants that have the potential to result in regime change. In its February 2009 decision, the AU had argued for an "accommodation" to allow the continental body more time to find a negotiated solution to the armed conflict in Darfur, cautioning that these efforts could be undermined by the indictment of President al-Bashir.[95] In this regard, the AU Assembly at its summit in Sirte, July 1–3, 2009, "expressed its deep concern at the indictment issued by the Pre-Trial Chamber of the ICC" against al-Bashir.[96] In its view, the indictment had prejudiced its efforts to find peace in Darfur. It noted, with grave concern, "the unfortunate consequences that the indictment has had on the delicate peace processes underway in The Sudan and the fact that it continues to undermine the ongoing efforts aimed at facilitating the early resolution of the conflict in Darfur."[97]

It is also clear from the Sirte decision that the AU's concerns over the al-Bashir indictment directly influenced its decision to call on relevant AU organs to speed up work on its request made in February 2009 to investigate the prospects of vesting the ACJHR with a criminal mandate. This is when experts were asked to construct a draft proposal to merge the African Court on Human and Peoples' Rights with the African Court of Justice (in Arusha, Tanzania), thereby expanding the jurisdiction of the African Court to include criminal matters. But, as the trial of Hissène Habré illustrates, anti-impunity frameworks are taking shaping in African geographies of justice as well; emotional regimes that make prosecutorial justice viable are operating alongside a range of other complexities related to the management of violence in Africa.

A Broader Bid for African Justice

Human rights organizations have popularly dubbed Hissène Habré Africa's Pinochet because of the widespread human rights abuses that he committed from 1982 to 1990. When the European Parliament demanded that Senegal, where Habré had been in exile for seventeen years, extradite him to

5.2 The Palais de Justice de Dakar, location of the trial of former president Hissène Habré.

Belgium for trial, Senegal refused.[98] The realization that former heads of state and high-ranking leaders could be tried by a domestic court in Europe ignited feelings of anger throughout predominantly African diplomatic circles. By 2006, the AU's institutional affects led to a united call on Senegal to prosecute Habré. There was a profound insistence that it was not just the "victims" of violence in need of justice but additionally, Africa's reputation that was in need of Habré's extradition and adjudication. In response to the expressed European interests, the AU began to take action to address Habré's order of extradition by establishing a court at the Palais de Justice de Dakar to adjudicate the case against him. This example of an African international trial led by the African Union highlights the working of institutional affects in the shaping of political actions. But it also illustrates the limits of an approach that focuses on individual culpability, even when carried out on African soil.

The Directorate of Documentation and Security (DDS), which was directly attached to the Office of the President, was a principal organ of repression and terror in Chad, and this institutional monster was a product of a widespread mechanism of dictatorial governance that Western states also created.[99] The court found that Habré used the DDS, which distinguished itself through its cruel deployments of all kinds of torture, to manage state security after he seized power.[100] With the reality of oil and prospects of a pipeline at the heart of Chad's development, Habré's dominance in the region was enabled through Western attempts to stave off Libyan interests in Chad's oil.[101] Testimony during the trial revealed that the DDS was propped up by a range of countries—Zaire, Iraq, France, and Egypt, with the United States in the lead. The United States is known to have contributed to the training, support, and growth of the DDS. With additional support from the other states, they all provided cooperation and training for the DDS up until Habré's departure in 1990.[102] The DDS was trained to arrest, terrorize, and squash all those who either threatened Habré's military regime or refused to participate in the National Union for Independence and Revolution—the state party created in 1984 to promote Habré's rule. Through the direction of the president and the party, the DDS spread fear in the Chadian people by arresting, interrogating, and torturing large numbers of the population.

These techniques of governance reflected the vulnerabilities of the postcolonial African state. But, as my interlocutors made clear, it also reflected something far more insidious about the problem with the individualization of criminal responsibility and celebration of the indictment of a single former leader. What they expressed is that while the Habré trial makes a statement about Africa's willingness to fight brutality by making one man criminally responsible, it says very little about how to address impunity through its widespread institutional forms. This example shows us about the feeling regimes that are operative is that the anti-impunity sentiments within the international criminal law assemblage operates within domains that are seen as negating the relevance of history and politics in shaping how we attribute culpability.

However, another arena of action that both responds to these erasures and reflects these African geographies of justice is the expansion of the criminal jurisdiction of the African Court to include a range of political and economic crimes that are seen as enablers of violence. Of course, the Malabo Protocol includes familiar provisions. The subject matter jurisdiction includes all of the Rome Statute crimes; the logic and organization of the court is to be complementary to national courts; it is imagined as coexisting with other international courts; and rather than having mandates and jurisdictions similar to African national courts, it will take effect if states are unable and unwilling to act. The drafters saw the maintenance of the corpus of the current structure of international legal norms as a way to ease any problems with intelligibility that may emerge. But what is explicit and distinctly different is that the Malabo Protocol for the ACJHR is seen as a mechanism for facilitating the end of violence in Africa using a Pan-African vision and an expansion of the crimes and modes of liability specifically relevant to the region.

Working alongside multiple legal and political actors and in concert with those engaged in transitional justice, the PALU drafters indicated that they saw this as an opportunity for African states to contribute to the making of a legally binding instrument. Others said that they felt that it was necessary to produce strong African judiciaries that allow Africans to try their own cases. All saw their mission as groundbreaking, as articulated by Donald Deya, the lead drafter, who asserted that they see the project as "creating possibilities in modern Africa." This idea, which Deya expressed forcefully with conviction and fist waving, was followed by the statement that this is what they felt would contribute to "creating an Africa that can build itself and take care of itself." These affective expressions reinforce the mantra of "African solutions for African problems" that shaped the terrain within which the African Court's own version of attribution is occurring. During the many meetings that I attended and the interviews that I conducted, these claims were punctuated by the affirmation that the AU and African Court project are responding to the need to "rebuild state and juridical capacities" and the conclusion that the PALU saw themselves as "enabling Africa and Africans with a strong legal instrument relevant to the continent."

This articulation clearly highlights legality as one of many options for dealing with the unique predicaments in Africa. When asked whether he felt it was an opportunity for leaders to evade impunity, Deya responded emphatically:

> Various heads of state may have been motivated by other incentives and I cannot speak for them. But what I know is that this will take years to be operationalized. So if al-Bashir wants to use it to avoid the ICC, he'll have to use another route. If the Gbagbos want to use it to save their situation, they'll have to look for another route. If Habré is hoping it will be used for his case, he'll have to continue looking. . . . Just the fact that this was adopted in principle signals something and will force African leaders, international corporations, and others to change the way they do business in Africa.

The court was not designed as an escape route for current indictees by the ICC. It was seen as a space of alternatives for the application of solutions to

Africa's complex histories of structural violence—including imperial plunder and subsequent inequalities that demand innovative solutions. This is innovative in the same way that the African Charter on Human and Peoples' Rights, in 1981, was seen as a space for the incorporation of concepts such as "the right to development, peoples' rights, [and] the duties of individuals," which were introduced to distinguish issues relevant to African peoples from other European legal principles. My interlocutors constantly reiterated that there was very little that was radical or revolutionary about the request to include crimes relevant to Africa's violence. They pointed out that the subject matter crimes were already codified in the treaties and protocols of the AU and of the REC, and were similarly central to basic crimes in international law. As one told me, if there was anything radical, it was the recuperative move to include African-specific crimes that were omitted from the Rome Statute for the ICC because they were seen as too controversial to form the basis for widespread agreement among states.[103]

After a range of meetings, delays, and amendments, in May 2014 a draft was submitted before a ministerial session of a meeting of the Specialized Technical Committee on Justice and Legal Affairs in Addis Ababa.[104] The draft protocol had remained unchanged for two years until that 2014 meeting, when it was revisited and adopted at the Twenty-Third Ordinary Session summit in Malabo, Equatorial Guinea, in July 2014. There, the Heads of State and Government Assembly of the AU adopted a Protocol on Amendments to the Protocol on the Statute of the African Court of Justice and Human Rights (the Malabo Protocol), which suggested the addition of a third section to the proposed African Court, which would have jurisdiction over fourteen international crimes.[105]

The Malabo Protocol thus created the African Court of Justice and Human and Peoples' Rights, which has three sections: general affairs, human rights, and international criminal law.[106] The approved protocol extended the jurisdiction of the ACJHR to cover individual criminal liability for serious crimes committed in violation of international law. It also expanded the terrain of punishable crimes to include new transnational offenses. This was done by including crimes whose subject matter jurisdiction exceeded that of the Rome Statute—genocide, crimes against humanity, war crimes, and the crime of aggression—to address other more pointed political-economic crimes, such as piracy, mercenarism, terrorism, corruption, illicit exploitation of natural resources, money laundering, and the trafficking of drugs and hazardous waste. The inclusion of these crimes has implications for going beyond the

ICC framework, often seen as insufficient for addressing criminal responsibility for Africa's violence. It represents the rectification of concessions made during the negotiations of the Rome Statute for the ICC to eliminate those crimes that were seen as too controversial to include, yet for many were key to addressing Africa's violence.[107]

In this sense, the PALU's draft protocol to expand the criminal jurisdiction of the African Court should be seen as an affective Pan-African project, borne of colonial subjugation and contemporary inequalities tied to Africa's place in the world, but structured to redefine the nature of violence in Africa as embedded in multiple forces of plunder and economic inequalities and multiple actors ranging from individual perpetrators to leaders of multinational corporations and terrorist and gang networks. And though it seems that there is something substantively different about the African Court, the reality is that it is envisioned as operating within a legal realm that is quite similar to other courts elsewhere. Even so, the African Court's Malabo Protocol should be understood in relation to what Deya has called an "African ecosystem," and what I articulate as within particular sociocultural and political ecologies of justice in the context of a range of other mechanisms through which African solutions to African problems are implemented. This approach—which spans judicial and nonjudicial options, alongside sequencing considerations for when such strategies are applied—is an affective form of attribution that highlights the relevance of geographical place in legal decision making.

Various AU peace and security representatives reported to us in a press conference in 2013 that they had a growing disillusionment with the efficacy of the global security architecture and the ICC. They described these disappointments as contributing factors in shaping their efforts to develop a new peace and security framework driven by the need to find appropriate and speedy responses to African security challenges. As Deya clarified for me during one of our many discussions—this time in a room with a number of colleagues who were engaged in the drafting process:

> We see courts, especially those within the continent, as part of an ecosystem of African institutions with which African citizens and their governments are pursuing various goals of mutual interest, including faster economic, social, and political development, and greater unity and integration that is based on a set of shared values. These shared values include a constant and consistent fight against impunity in all its manifestations; development of democracy, good governance, and a just rule of law; and

promotion and protection of human and people's rights. These courts and tribunals ought to be looked at in the context of a number of mechanisms ranging from the African Governance Architecture, the African Human Rights Strategy, the African Peace and Security Architecture, and the Protocol on Relations between the African Union, and the Regional Economic Communities.[108]

Yet, currently, the African Commission on Human and People's Rights is the only functioning tribunal. The criminal chamber is not yet active because not enough ratifications have been made to establish either the African Court of Justice or the merged court.[109] The protocol will come into force thirty days after its ratification by fifteen member states. However, this process takes time, and as of April 2019 only twelve states have signed the Malabo Protocol, and none have ratified it.[110] If it enters into force, the new protocol is expected to work as part of the overall African human rights system and protective sphere, developed over the last two decades, in which the current human rights organs exist. This system is expected to operate alongside the AGA and the APSA. The current and future court has been conceptualized as operating within a system that includes several other institutions, which collectively ensure the protection and promotion of human rights and an end to impunity in Africa.[111]

The passage of the Malabo Protocol—and the ensuing effort to extend the criminal jurisdiction of the African Court and bring it into force—has raised a new set of issues of how to address the interplay between various dilemmas of peace and justice in postviolence contexts. Despite the move to expand the criminal jurisdiction of the African Court, the reality is that in drafting the protocol, AU actors were more focused on the substantive crimes themselves and on ensuring that the prosecutor was not given too much political power than on centering deliberations concerning how legal provisions might guarantee fairness. The actual process by which this unfolded precluded open, public deliberations. Instead, the Malabo Protocol was expedited following the indictments of President al-Bashir and Kenyatta and Ruto before him. This is, of course, unlike the process by which the ad hoc tribunal that adjudicated the Habré trial unfolded. In many ways, the success of the Habré trial being adjudicated in Africa and, as Kristiana Powell has argued, the UN's failures in the face of some of Africa's most profound security challenges—the Rwandan genocide, the genocide in Darfur, the crimes in Sierra Leone, and child soldiering in the Democratic Republic of the Congo—have reinforced a desire for greater autonomy and an internal approach to peace and security on the continent.[112] Similarly, Bruce Jones has written, "It is not entirely un-coincidental that the two places where we have seen the most development of regional options—Europe and Africa—have been the site of the UN's greatest failures in the 1990s."[113]

As the controversy surrounding the indictment of African leaders demonstrated, it appears that the push to create an African criminal jurisdiction is explained by this perceived failure on the part of the ICC as much as it is a search for a mechanism by which African states would exert more control over Africa's future—however that might look. In this regard, PALU was contracted to adopt a broad and long-term approach regarding the development of international courts and tribunals in Africa, whether these courts function at a bilateral, regional, continental, or global level. Stakeholders in the AU see the advent of the African Court with criminal jurisdiction as critical to Africa's future. Yet what is important to note is that the deliberations that led to the production of the Malabo Protocol for the ACJHR arose from innovations that prioritized diplomacy and other political action before prosecutorial action. It is useful to consider these constructed institutional and political components as ecologies of the broader bid for African justice. The idea of a new African Court with criminal jurisdiction represents the AU's attempts to craft new modalities of justice according to contemporary needs for Africa's future. In this case, the new Pan-Africanist struggle is a central component of the affective life of an African Court with criminal jurisdiction, envisioned as a way to remake justice within Africa through particular Pan-Africanist histories of struggle.

African Court as a Sentimentally Pan-African Project

The existence of a treaty to erect an African Court with criminal jurisdiction represents a counterjudicial narrative that encompasses political concerns at the heart of African inequalities. The affective work related to extending the criminal jurisdiction of the African Court highlights the way that African political decision makers engage strategies that account for both the presence and seeming absence of power. As shown, the presence is in its sovereign possibility—the assertion that power is also about its exercise, its ability to mobilize in one's image. It is the potential to mobilize power and affectively attribute it in particular ways. Its absence is in the feelings of inequality and racial oppression that remain illegible before the law. The reality of former

Rwandan president Paul Kagame's anger that the ICC "has been put in place only for African countries, only for poor countries," and that "Rwanda cannot be part of colonialism, slavery and imperialism," quoted in the introduction, points to the problem of inequality and its ability to define new futures. As an uplift strategy, the contemporary approaches to AU justice are deeply tied to the afterlife of colonialism around which new transitional justice mechanisms—relevant to African geographies—are being shaped in ways that reflect conceptualizations of justice writ large. The conundrum of contemporary AU Pan-Africanism is that alongside deep-seated conceptions of the Pan-African liberatory past is actually a deep desire to participate in contemporary neoliberal power, in global power. The resistance to extradition and the anti-ICC mobilizations are expressions of this and are connected to what many psychologists have been known to dismiss as externalities, or what political scientists have dismissed as internalities, but when the affectivities that shape those are combined, they are actually central to new Pan-African sentiments as they are imagined on the African continent.[114] These affective geographies create ambivalences that cannot be simply understood genealogically and mapped out with precision. The recognition of the violence of marginalization operates like ghosts in the present, even as there is a dueling struggle to become part of that which it marginalizes.

For a time in the post-1980s period, Pan-Africanism was seen as either passé or too politicized to be relevant, but as an emotively propelled discourse with significant political power it is being revived today with great moral fortitude. It has come to be revived through the specter of deep-seated African unity, referencing old and new ways, and as a way to make claims to global membership and global capitalism. With free-market capitalism and the entrenchment of international economic interests throughout African economies, political contests are seen as explicitly internal. The AU—as a supranational institution committed to ensuring the maintenance of African democracy, peace, and security—is now claiming to be just as committed to economic development. Yet the shadow of colonialism is useful for understanding affective justice practices as ontological and as informed by the past alongside the present. The call for an African renaissance is a call to reckon with the spirit around which Pan-Africanism became a survival strategy for African states. And today, the struggle being indexed is one in which African worldviews, and Africa, are seen as being eclipsed by external agendas, including those that are often deployed through international human rights principles. This is leading to a gap between imposed structures and actual lived realities transformed through their own structures of logic, and in terms of their own situated struggles and points of tension. In the case of African leaders making decisions about which crimes, when, why, who, and under what conditions the ICC has the power to indict, Pan-Africanist frameworks of expectations are shaping the basis on which African states engage with ICC anti-impunity justice formations.

The Africa being invoked by lawyers, leaders, civil society, and everyday people is an Africa with long-standing and deep patronage commitments to discourses of anticolonial struggle, suffering, and senses of self-determination. What we are seeing today through AU change makers' actions, such as the development of transitional justice and sequencing, is actually the playing out of a reattributive politics working toward the management of Africa's violence on their own terms—albeit not always effectively, given the enmeshment of violence within other component parts of the international justice assemblage. When various AU stakeholders invoke Pan-Africanism as a new Africanist strategy, they are also pointing to domains of affective spatialized control in which neoliberal participation in new globalizing orders is being framed in Pan-African terms. It is through such articulations of African justice that we see how the African Court, as a symbol of African geographies (or ecologies) of justice, constitutes new feeling rules in which the prestige of the past is couched in Pan-Africanist historical domains through which inequality, racial subordination, and structural violence are being rectified. In this way, justice operates through emotional frameworks of expectation and is institutionalized through an assemblage of agents who function with particular forms of authority, desire, dispositions, and imaginaries. Through these assemblages, political actors function, on one hand, as what Hannah Appel calls individuals with unitary will, but it is through their practices through and in relation to the management of violence in African contexts that particular conceptions of justice are affectively articulated.[115] Chapter 6 explores these articulations through various emotionally laden reattributions by the AU: the refusal to arrest and surrender African heads of state, and the refusal to comply with particular renditions of international law that are seen as not being in keeping with Pan-African aspirations.

CHAPTER 6

Reattributions: The Refusal to Arrest and
Surrender African Heads of State

In October 2016, Burundi became the first country to commence the process
of withdrawal from the Rome Statute of the ICC. This move was vindicating
for those who felt that a rectification of the all-African focus of ICC cases was
needed. But it also led to an international outcry by anti-impunity advocates.
When the ICC's Office of the Prosecutor began to speak of launching a preliminary examination into the violence that occurred in Burundi the previous
year, Burundian leaders accused the ICC of acting as an "instrument" to destabilize "poor [African] countries." Leaders also insisted that the ICC's preliminary examination could contribute to "potentially negative forces and their
cronies" committing acts of violence. "Consequently," they noted later, "the
government considers that maintaining Burundi as a party to the Rome Statute of the International Criminal Court cannot be justified."[1]

Following claims that the ICC's actions support a Western regime-change
strategy, President Nkurunziza signed the withdrawal legislation on Tuesday,
October 11, with overwhelming support from Burundi's lawmakers. Later that
week his office submitted a letter of notification to the UN secretary-general,
and according to the rules of Rome Statute withdrawal, they had to wait one
year before the separation from ICC jurisdiction was formalized. Burundi has
now withdrawn from the ICC, while in South Africa there has been an in-
terim decision to stop the withdrawal process at the time of this writing.[2] Pan-
Africanists committed to rethinking justice in terms of structural inequality
and those who are engaged in reattributions of justice within and outside of
African countries are celebrating this move as a welcome restorative action
that responds to inequality in the international system.[3]

The context for the ICC's investigation included the deaths of four hundred people, followed by 168 more, in the capital in mid-April 2015, as well as the subsequent displacement of 310,000 Burundians following politically related violence when the president of the country attempted to amend the constitution and petition for a third term. Given the claims that it was the government's security forces that perpetrated these acts of violence, anti-impunity groups have supported the ICC's investigations and have insisted that the only way that such acts will stop is by holding accountable those who bear the greatest responsibility for those crimes. The chairman of Burundi's national coalition for the ICC voiced similar concerns and invoked "victims" when he said, "This vote is a terrible setback to a country that is facing a serious violent and political crisis. It comes at the very moment that thousands of Burundians thirst for fair, effective and independent criminal justice—as demonstrated by the families of victims that broke their silence and seized the ICC when their cries for justice were ignored by the national justice system."[4]

This was not a singular development. The next week, the South African parliament also submitted relevant paperwork to the UN, notifying them of their decision to withdraw from the Rome Treaty, followed by an announcement of Gambia's intentions to withdraw.[5] The Gambian minister charged, "Despite being called International Criminal Court, [it] is in fact an International Caucasian Court for the persecution and humiliation of people of colour, especially Africans."[6]

Similarly, a particular high-ranking South African government official complained to the media that "every person tried by the ICC has been African," while many other African leaders have echoed Kenyatta in claiming the ICC is "biased against Africans."[7] Interestingly, South African officials were very early supporters and trailblazers of judicial accountability for mass-atrocity crimes, which led to the conceptualization and building of the ICC. They were also the first to produce and implement legislation in Africa that allowed South Africa to incorporate the Rome Treaty into its constitution. However, South Africa's clash with the court and the subsequent pushback began when President al-Bashir of Sudan visited the country for a summit, and the South African government refused to arrest him. It insisted that all heads of state were entitled to immunity under customary international law (CIL).

A number of South African government officials reiterated the point that it does not want to carry out ICC arrest warrants because they are basically "calls for regime change." In response, anti-impunity activists declared South Africa's exercise of treaty withdrawal unconstitutional and enlisted passionate responses to protest this action. Invoking the figure of Nelson Mandela, activists like William Pace, the head convener for the coalition for the ICC, declared, "With its history of injustice, South Africa under Nelson Mandela was a driving force behind the establishment of the ICC. Any withdrawal from the Rome Statute would reverse years of human rights progress. Opposition to the ICC has grown as it has implemented its role, mandated by 124 countries, to bring those most responsible for grave crimes—including high government officials—to justice."[8] Pace then went on, "Victims across Africa have called for justice time and again, either through national judicial systems or, when they fail, through the ICC. The Zuma government is demonstrating a terrible disregard for victims and the powerless in South Africa, throughout Africa and the world."[9] By invoking the figure of Nelson Mandela and the significance of the ICC for survivors, Pace aligned anti-impunity agendas with the heroic figure of Nelson Mandela while insisting that South Africa's participation in the ICC was critical to the moral significance and priorities of the country.

Justice Richard Goldstone concurred:

I am concerned and disappointed at this regrettable action by the South African Government. The withdrawal is quite inconsistent with the provisions of the Rome Statute of the International Criminal Court Act, No. 27 of 2002 and hence unconstitutional and unlawful. . . . I am confident that a South African court will so rule. It is an act that is demeaning of our Parliament and of the people of South Africa. From a moral standpoint, it detracts from the inspiring legacy of the administration of President Nelson Mandela that so strongly supported the ICC and all of the mechanisms of international justice.[10]

Gambia was the third African country to announce its intention to withdraw from the Rome Statute. Its president, Yahya Jammeh, blamed the deaths of over five hundred Gambians (over a five-year period) on the "very dangerous, racist and inhuman behavior of deliberately causing boats carrying black Africans to sink."[11] He called for an ICC investigation of the "manmade sinking" or intentional capsizing of boats carrying African migrants across the Mediterranean Sea to Europe. In an attempt to deflect the attribution of violence from Africans to agents of European nations, he suggested, "If it is not done deliberately, [then] how is it possible that each time a vessel is capsizing, there is the Italian navy to rescue only a few people."[12]

Later, President Jammeh announced, "We have a right to call the ICC to investigate not only cases of Gambians but the case of thousands of African young people who have died on the European coast under unusual circumstances."[13] But these expressions were then followed by retractions from the new Gambian president and the South African parliament. In the fall of 2016, Jammeh was ousted from his twenty-two-year rule of the country, and in early 2017, he was replaced by former opposition leader President Adama Barrow, who subsequently overturned many of Jammeh's policies, including the action to withdraw from the Rome Statute for the ICC.[14] In South Africa, the constitutional court revoked President Zuma's withdrawal notice, finding it "unconstitutional and invalid," and noting that the high court should not have pursued the action without parliamentary approval.[15]

Arguing on behalf of South Africa, South African scholar and former legal advisor Dire Tladi insisted that the ICC position on immunity ignores the International Court of Justice (ICJ) decision in *Arrest Warrant*, which holds that state officials may be prosecuted before international courts under certain circumstances.[16] According to Tladi, a more fundamental problem exists with the AU's postulation that the immunity of state officials, whether personal or functional, under CIL means, in essence, immunity from the jurisdiction of courts of foreign states.[17] This immunity, he argues, is an extension of state immunity from the jurisdiction of other states based on the principle of sovereign equality of states.[18] Since international tribunals such as the ICC and the African Court are not foreign states, the rationale for immunity of states and their officials (i.e., the sovereign equality of states) does not apply.[19]

As a multilateral treaty, the Rome Statute, by definition, is understood as binding only those states that ratify it.[20] Accordingly, the Rome Statute is seen by various AU advocates as not being able to "impose obligations on third States without their consent." Officials of nonmember states thus normally retain all of their immunities even in proceedings before the ICC.[21] In the al-Bashir case, however, the ICC has held that where the Security Council refers a situation in a nonmember state to the court, the entire Rome Statute— including its immunity provision—applies to the nonmember state and that its officials therefore have no immunity before the ICC.[22] Because of this ruling, the debate over whether the immunity provisions of the Rome Statute can be applied to nonmember states in cases before the ICC highlights a raging debate, because various AU officials insist that even if that interpretation is correct, many states, as well as the AU, have argued that Article 27 only lifts immunities before the ICC itself, and does not affect the immunities that such officials enjoy in domestic courts.[23] Under this interpretation, CIL immunities of state officials before domestic courts—recognized in the Rome Statute itself—remain in place, preventing states from arresting al-Bashir, even if that arrest is on behalf of an international tribunal.[24] In response, Sudan began aggressively mobilizing AU member states to weaken support for the ICC in Africa. The AU called upon the UNSC to invoke Article 16 of the Rome Statute to defer the ICC proceedings against Bashir on the grounds that prosecuting the president could impede prospects for peace in the region.[25] But because of the Article 16 trigger that gives the council the power to make a referral, the UNSC sustained its position and failed to act on the AU's request to defer ICC proceedings.[26] As explained in the introduction, the AU directed all of its member states to withhold cooperation from the ICC in the arrest and surrender of al-Bashir.[27]

In contrast to the forms of reattribution taking place in the al-Bashir case, the rulings by ICC judges over immunities have reflected policy positions that Article 27 lifts immunities not only before the ICC, but also in any domestic proceedings on behalf of the court, because otherwise Article 27 would be rendered ineffective.[28] For that reason, Article 98 is seen by African states as not being implicated.[29] Moreover, even if Article 98 applied, Sudan is required to waive any immunity it has under the terms of the Security Council's referral, which requires the government of Sudan to cooperate with the court.[30] According to various ICC spokespersons, there is thus no impediment to the arrest of a sitting head of state such as al-Bashir in a national court, and all state parties are expected to cooperate with the ICC's arrest and surrender requests.[31] In refusing this position, a number of state representatives from mostly African countries, namely, Malawi, Chad, Kenya, Nigeria, Djibouti, the Democratic Republic of the Congo (DRC), Uganda, and South Africa, as well as Jordan, decided not to execute the ICC's arrest and surrender order of Mr. al-Bashir while he was in their territory. Chad did so three times, and Uganda twice. These countries then submitted to the ICC their reasons for their nonexecution of the arrest warrant, and in all six cases the ICC found that the countries failed to comply with the cooperation request issued by the court with respect to the arrest and surrender of al-Bashir, violating their obligation under the Rome Statute. With the exception of South Africa, the court referred all the other countries to the UNSC and the Assembly of States Parties (ASP) for noncompliance with the court's request.

At the thirteenth AU summit, African states agreed to seek an advisory opinion from the ICJ on the question of head of state immunity and the relationship between Articles 98 and 27, thereby seeking a decision on state entitlement to sovereign decision making. In spring 2018, the ICC invited interested parties as well as the AU to make a submission on immunity. And, in July 2018, the African Group in the General Assembly, led by the chair, Ambassador Lazarus Ombai Amayo of Kenya, requested an advisory opinion of the ICJ on the "consequences of legal obligations of States under different sources of international law with respect to immunities of Heads of State and Government and other senior officials. These issues are still underway."[32] In keeping with ongoing disagreements over state entitlements to sovereignty and responsibility for international treaties, disagreements over executive actions reflect the most recent developments in the controversies that this book has been tracing. The response to the ICC's indictment of sitting Sudanese president Omar al-Bashir and continuing efforts to secure an advisory opinion from the ICJ are examples of attributions of justice that follow a particular domain of logic that has a particular history and operates within complex affective justice assemblages.

The issues leading up to the withdrawal from the Rome Treaty go back to the 2010 summit of African heads of state when Malawian president Bingu wa Mutharika raised concerns about threats to state sovereignty in the context of the al-Bashir case. As he said, "To subject a sovereign head of state to a warrant of arrest is undermining African solidarity and African peace and security that we fought for so many years. . . . There is a general concern in Africa that the issuance of a warrant of arrest for . . . al-Bashir, a duly elected president, is a violation of the principles of sovereignty guaranteed under the United Nations and under the African Union Charter. Maybe there are other ways of addressing this problem."[33]

Then there are the indictments of Uhuru Kenyatta and William Ruto of Kenya, detailed in chapter 4, making Kenyatta the first serving head of state to appear before the ICC. Add to the list the June 2011 issuing of arrest warrants for Muammar al-Qaddafi, then president of Libya, his son Saif al-Islam Qaddafi, and his brother-in-law Abdullah al-Sanussi for the commission of crimes against humanity.[34] At its July 2011 summit, the AU Assembly held that the arrest warrants seriously complicated efforts aimed at negotiating a political solution to the crisis in Libya, deciding "that Member States shall not cooperate in the execution of the arrest warrant" against Qaddafi.[35] At subsequent summits, assembly decisions have continued to call for solidarity among AU member states in their opposition to the proceedings launched against al-Bashir, and to call on the UNSC to defer the ICC's prosecutions of al-Bashir, Kenyatta, and Ruto under Article 16 of the Rome Statute.[36]

This all led to what would be the first formal call at the October 2013 summit in Addis Ababa, by some AU member states, for all signatory African states to collectively withdraw their membership from the Rome Statute.[37] The assembly also formally decided, through a declaration of nonextradition, that "no charges shall be commenced or continued before any International Court or Tribunal against any serving AU Head of State or Government or anybody acting or entitled to act in such capacity during their term of office."[38] This was the first declaration by the AU to institutionalize opposition to ICC indictments of African leaders, and it would eventually be codified in the controversial Article 46A *bis* of the Malabo Protocol.[39] But first, the initial declaration was followed by the introduction of reforms to the Rome Statute, especially relating to Article 16 (proposed by South Africa) and Article 27 (by Kenya), one year later at the November 2014 ASP meeting. Kenya also proposed a number of other amendments—one to the preamble highlighting the recognition of regional bodies by the ICC and another to Article 63 on trial in the presence of the accused. But the most controversial was the proposal to amend Article 27, as a key aspect of the deteriorating relationship between the AU and the ICC concerns the applicability of the immunity provision under that article.

Many AU agents approach Article 27 of the ICC statute as a treaty whose rules should be applicable only to state parties. They argue that for nonstate parties, the rules of CIL relating to immunities should remain intact.[40] This position presents Article 27 of the ICC statute as an exception to the rules of CIL—a position that informed AU state decisions not to cooperate with the extradition of al-Bashir, the leader of a country, Sudan, that is not a party to the Rome Statute. This was illustrated by an Ethiopian diplomatic official who explained his irate feelings about the court's hypocrisy: "Sudan is not a party to the Rome Statute. As a sitting president, Bashir enjoys immunity from prosecution on the basis of customary international law. There is no objective reason why as a nonparty to the treaty a judicial body should be able to still exercise jurisdiction and demand the extradition of another black man."[41]

Both the place of politics and the relevance of blackness and inequality emerge time and time again, and they shape the feelings of indignation and the perception that African leaders are being unfairly targeted. Here, emotional climates are enforced through legal interpretation and the recognition of precedents operating within a field of unequal political practices. Among those practitioners engaged in international legal decision making, technocratic practices in international law, based on two primary sources.[42] The first is treaties, and the second is Customary International Law (CIL). Treaties represent international law agreements that reflect "expressly accepted obligations" and mostly bind states that are parties to that treaty. In cases where treaty principles may legally bind states that are not party to particular treaties, it is usually under conditions where the key principles of the treaty are transformed into customary international law. By insisting on the legitimacy of law based on two measures—widespread and uniform practice, and engagement in that practice based on legal obligation—many of its anti-impunity practitioners deem CIL legally acceptable if a given set of norms gain uniform and widespread acceptance. Where various legal principles play key roles in establishing the basis for the legal legitimacy that states adopt, feeling regimes also shape the positions that state actors take.

As I have argued throughout this book, and what most scholarly work on Africa and the ICC dismisses, is the importance of understanding these formations in relation to perceptions of justice—including the deep-seated structures of feeling that emerge within complex assemblages and shape justice alignments. For not only do forms of affective justice take shape within various forms of international legality and through the emotional regimes that shape what is acceptable, but also, particular regimentations are reproduced within the international criminal law assemblage that include component parts within African domains. The examples in this final chapter, like the previous, highlight how alternative formulations of individual responses to structuring histories find their expressions in both legal and sociopolitical forms of action. The formation of these expressions, however, should not be assessed in relation to the production of fixed and temporally consistent identities. Rather, forms of affective justice, manifest in practices, such as treaty withdrawals, are acts that, while legally allowable, are shaped by emotional responses that people, as agents, also choose to embody, within particular conditions of the possible, as they take up particular causes. When these causes take the form of legal and extralegal questions, the result can be alienating for various camps searching for particular rules of order through which to orchestrate justice. This is because legal practices are not simply technical articulations of objective certainty; they are affective and are fueled by histories and assumptions about what one values and presumes, what they mean, and the best steps through which to achieve the goals of justice. Such an approach to technocratic law making highlights how legal practices involve life worlds in affective registers that actually constitute law.

One legal manifestation in the ongoing debate over whether African leaders and heads of states should enjoy immunity has been the emergence of African states that were party to the Rome Statute lobbying for the amendment of Article 27 so that it expressly provides immunity to heads of state.[43] Given the profound sentiments of protest around not surrendering heads of state, African states have hoped that their contrary practice will develop into a regional custom. For law has both an instrumental and expressive function. When we go beyond the instrumental uses of treaty formation, implementation, and decision making, we can recognize that while contestations of treaty provisions have the potential to unravel the sacred bundle that is seen as emanating from Nuremberg and manifest in the form of the Rome Statute, claims of noncooperation and withdrawals not only contest the foundational principles on which the treaty was envisioned but also do something more profound. They provide the terrain on which social actors can articulate their concerns in relation to it. This domain is expressive and unfolds through what I refer to as reattribution—an affectively propelled site of refusal and redirection that is embodied and constitutes alliances through vivid emotional registers. The reattribution of legal frameworks and production of social, political, and legal alternatives provide the basis on which emotional expressions take place and new spaces of possibility are opened up. In this regard, many insist that international law is as dynamic as daily life and that African states have a right to engage in its formation. As chapter 5 recounts, from 2010 onward, AU mobilizations led to the expansion of the criminal jurisdiction of the African Court in order to shift the terms for the management of African violence, often articulated with the refrain, "African solutions for African problems." And, in keeping with this sensibility, one of the most controversial attempts to manage African violence has involved the formation and inclusion of international criminal jurisdiction for an African court, not simply because it stands as a parallel court to the ICC but also because of Article 46A *bis*.

This provision for individual criminal responsibility in the Malabo Protocol advocates the maintenance of personal and functional immunities for heads of state. While it is true that personal immunity for heads of state and high-ranking officials in government does not apply before international criminal tribunals, it continues to apply before domestic courts, unless a waiver from the state concerned is obtained.[44] Advocates in the AU insist that personal immunity applies where domestic prosecutions are concerned. The AU has defended the need for the immunity provision from a doctrinal perspective on the grounds that immunities provided by international law apply not only to proceedings in foreign domestic courts but also to international tribunals, and states cannot circumvent such obligations by establishing an international tribunal.[45] They point to a central concern that there is a conflict between Articles 27 and 98 of the Rome Statute in which African states have competing obligations. While Article 27 removes immunity, Article 98 establishes that the court cannot request that a state act inconsistently with its international obligations with respect to state or diplomatic immunity and must obtain cooperation for the waiver of the immunity. These officials insist that with respect to official immunities for President al-Bashir, CIL allows African states to opt to adhere to AU decisions as well as to decide not to comply with the arrest and surrender of the president of Sudan. This issue was far from resolved for the ICC's July 6 Pre-trial Chamber II decision that states that have ratified the Rome Statute, such as South Africa, and find President al-Bashir on their territory are required to arrest and surrender him to the ICC.[46] However, the International Law Commission has concluded that there are no exceptions to immunity *rationae materiae* for heads of state, heads of government, and ministers of foreign affairs.[47]

The discourses surrounding the immunity provision have arisen out of a concern for the integrity and capacity of an African leader to govern and, as such, an insistence that heads of state should be protected from prosecution while working to maintain peace and stability within their countries. This argument is seen as especially acute in the African region. For despite the delegitimation of political solutions by members of the anti-impunity movement, various AU advocates see the Malabo Protocol as a mechanism that allows for peace and justice sequencing, by which personal immunity is relevant only while a leader remains in power. Supporters insist that in allowing immunity to expire after a leader is out of office, African regional legal modalities can then provide uniquely impactful ways to manage violence on the African continent through the sequencing of peace and justice. Both sets of positions on the irrelevance of national capacity have been vigorously debated among the opponents of this anti-impunity movement—most significantly by those from African states.

It is also worth paying attention to the call by African states for a differentiated regional interpretation of the nonsurrender of incumbent heads of states to international tribunals and courts. They have mobilized to argue that the state practice of immunity for heads of state, foreign ministers, and other high-ranking officials is in keeping with principles in CIL that provide for personal and functional immunities for government officials, and there is no international custom that sets out a contrary rule of surrendering incumbent heads of states. The practice of not surrendering heads of state may also reflect the development of a regional consensus on the rule of nonextradition, which, in keeping with the ICJ advisory opinion request, has become critical at the time of this writing.

The question of immunity, therefore, deals with issues concerning African states as legitimate domains for ensuring the protection of citizens. But it is also an attempt to retain some of the terms of an older order (immunity for heads of state) deemed inappropriate for a global order set on establishing new terms. The implication of Articles 27 and 98 as they apply to nonmembers of the ICC has been the subject of disagreement not only among scholars but among different chambers of the ICC. In a decision that was highly criticized by AU leaders and other prominent commentators, the ICC's Pre-trial Chamber I ruling on whether Malawi and Chad were noncompliant when they failed to arrest al-Bashir, found that "the principle in international law is that immunity of either former or sitting Heads of State cannot be invoked to oppose a prosecution by an international court. This is equally applicable to former or sitting Heads of States not Parties to the Statute whenever the Court may exercise jurisdiction."[48]

The ICC brought its next noncooperation case against the DRC, heard before Pre-trial Chamber II. Here the ICC took a different interpretive approach. The chamber recognized there might be instances where the personal immunity of a head of state of a nonstate party may justifiably be raised before the court and that "the solution provided for in the Statute to resolve such conflicts is found in Article 98(1) of the Statute."[49] It argued that in the case of al-Bashir, because the Security Council resolution imposed on Sudan the duty to cooperate, his immunity was waived, per the requirement of Article 98(1).[50]

In the next matter, against South Africa, Pre-trial Chamber II argued that the obligation of state parties to arrest and surrender individuals for whom an arrest warrant is issued by the ICC emanates from Article 27(2) of the statute and the referral of the situation by the Security Council.[51] The chamber argued that Article 27(2) does not only exclude the application of immunity in proceedings before the court, as South Africa and the AU contended. Rather, it referred to the arrest of such individuals.[52] The court found that where the Security Council refers a situation to the court, Article 27(2) would be equally applicable to nonstate parties. The court rejected the need for Sudan or the Security Council to waive al-Bashir's immunity, as provided under Article 98(1), since it was already removed by Article 27(2).[53]

What this debate demonstrates is how the ICC is articulating institutional assumptions about the power of the UN and—by extension—the ICC. Yet African state actors are pushing back by asserting claims for their sovereignty and making new regional declarations about the practice of immunity for heads of state and high-ranking leaders, in an attempt to set new terms for new justice formations that include economic sovereignty and claims to global membership. These various public positions reflect particular emotional sensibilities that are sustained by legality and its socialization practices.

In chapter 5, we saw how particular Pan-Africanist feeling regimes were deployed to shape the institutionalization of an African transitional justice agenda that included its own court to adjudicate crimes. This final chapter extends that conversation to explore how, with the ICC's refusal to amend various articles in relation to areas seen as contributing to structural inequalities, African leaders are reattributing the scope of international justice practices by shaping a new set of regional norms to better address the long history of violence in the region and provide new opportunities for justice. The proposed amendments to the ICC treaty were seen as setting the groundwork for African state parties to refrain from withdrawing from the ICC, but the failure to adopt those amendments has led to threats and now letters of intent—the first official step—to formally withdraw from the court or to refer the matter to the ICJ. Though Sierra Leone, Ivory Coast, Zambia, Nigeria, Malawi, Senegal, and Botswana were among the African states that countered the withdrawal notifications by pledging their continued support of the ICC, as we will see, acts of withdrawal, referrals to higher bodies, public statements, declarations, and refusals to comply with extraditions are expressions of particular political positions that have an impact on emotionally shaped alignments. Such alignments not only join particular state leaders that have articulated their rejection or disapproval of the ICC, but also constitute anti-impunity alliances through pledges of ICC support. What I am arguing here is that while the emotional states of leaders or negotiators is unknowable, we need to pay attention to the alignments involved in the political jockeying and strategies around withdrawals of support. This can help us understand how complex and controversial actions shape constituents whose emotional worlds are aligned with a position that is produced and socialized through particular emotional regimes. They are constituted not simply through ethnic, national, linguistic, and gender identities, but through embodied feelings about inequality and injustice that shape how international law is perceived and how justice is experienced affectively.

Debating Justice: The ICC's 2013 Assembly of State Parties

In response to the AU's request, the ICC's Assembly of States Parties (a stake-holders' meeting convened annually by the president of the ICC and all states that have ratified the Rome Statute) convened a special November 2013 session titled Indictment of Sitting Heads of State and Government and Its Consequences on Peace and Stability and Reconciliation. At this meeting, state representatives, academics, and members of various civil society groups came together to debate the immunity question. Both the declaration of nonextradition and the proposal by African states to seek clarification on and amendments to Article 27, regarding the irrelevance of official capacity, came to a head at that Twelfth Session of the Assembly of States Parties to the Rome Statute.[54]

The ASP special session was moderated by the permanent representative of Jordan to the UN, Prince Ra'ad Zeid Al-Hussein, and panel speakers included AU legal counsel Djenaba Diarra, professors M. Cherif Bassiouni and Charles Jalloh, and the Kenyan attorney general, Professor Githu Muigai. Multiple sides of the debate were argued. Governments and members of civil society offered input, eventually resulting in the articulation of a range of positions. The then-acting legal counsel of the AU, Djenaba Diarra, welcomed the ASP's decision to hold the debate and to accommodate the AU request. She started with conviction, reminding those in the thousand-seat auditorium that "Africa was left alone to deal with the consequences of Rwanda."[55] This, she said, was why African states took such a prominent role in the establishment of the ICC and form the largest group in the membership.

In saying this, she made a profoundly self-assured statement that the AU has a commitment to peace, stability, justice, and good governance. She explained that the AU had moved from the principle of noninterference in a neighboring state to the principle of nonindifference—in other words, agreeing that a member state has the right to intervene in another member's state internal affairs (to respond to specific crimes, unconstitutional change of government, etc.). It was in that light that the AU had called for the universal ratification of the Rome Statute, she reminded everyone.

Diarra's central message was that the AU was concerned with some of the working methods of the ICC, namely the selective approaches to justice in the way it targets some locations of crimes, like Africa, and not others. Preliminary examinations were opened in Afghanistan, Korea, and other countries years ago, yet there has been no move to trial in those situations, while moves to trial in Africa have been swift. She ended by assuring the ASP that these concerns were genuine and that in the interest of peace, stability, and recon-ciliation, Africa needed to trust the international community. As she noted, "Africa is worried; we need to be listened to, need to be trusted, in the interest of peace, stability, and reconciliation."[56]

As Diarra ended her remarks, she then sat down with stern defiance and various constituencies in the audience whispered quietly. I sat in the audi-ence next to a group of African statesmen who spoke among themselves in support of her call that Africa needed to be listened to. As I listened to them and watched them nod affirmatively and reflected on how empowered they seemed as they smiled. The emotions that they performed aligned with Di-arra and her official AU position, which she articulated clearly and communi-cated with vehement passion. And yet, as I looked over to the section where I had sat earlier that day, I saw various members of civil society sigh and roll their eyes in what seemed to be disbelief. Their responses seemed skeptical of the AU's motives. When I interviewed some later that day, they confirmed my rendering of their response to Diarra's comments; with body language and frowns, they charged that "the AU was full of shit."[57] This response articu-lated the domain of agreement or nuance that—with further conversations—clarified how emotional responses constitute international justice formations.

These two sets of actors—AU officials and various members of interna-tional civil society groups—represent two social alignments that are part of larger assemblages that have been at the heart of this book. Though complex and messy, these emotional responses align feelings about developments in international justice circuits whereby activists, state agents, donors, academ-ics, and others articulate their relations to each other through emotional ex-pressions of agreement, disagreement, or even neutrality. What is fascinating, however, is how such alignments are regulated through emotional regimes produced through people's participation in particular emotional communi-ties. The next presentation supported this.

Kenya's attorney general, Githu Muigai, conveyed Kenya's belief that the ICC is a court of last resort that should complement domestic and regional ef-forts, but its practice of indicting heads of state is actually doing the opposite:

> We intended it to bring to trial those most responsible. The court was to promote justice and promote peace. We intended that the court in general, and the prosecutor in particular, should act in a professional fair manner—we did not expect that they would handle themselves at standards lower than those we expect to see at our level. This is not a license to behave irresponsibly—politically, socially, legally. Over the past five years, we have

cooperated fully with the court. This is a unique situation. The indictment of sitting heads of state is unprecedented and must be approached as such. Allowing for the indictment of sitting heads of state is a threat to the constitutional order and stability in a state—we are not talking of immunities to shield an individual, but immunity to allow a state to continue being a state.

Kenya is the lynchpin in the security of eastern Africa. It is not a country with which the international community should play Russian roulette. We stand with the international community in the fight against terror, against piracy, against drug trafficking, against human trafficking. Yet the sc [Security Council] declined to take seriously our request. Immunity for heads of state is well established and understood in other jurisdictions. We have created a problem within international jurisprudence by allowing double standards to take root.[58]

Muigai pointed to reports on violence unleashed in Gaza and in Sri Lanka, as well as the use of drones by the United States, asking if these situations did not constitute international criminal offenses. His rhetorical strategy garnered the support of those African statesmen and women who felt discriminated against by what they saw as the icc's selectivity of cases that focus on Africa and not on other states, especially powerful ones. In a passionate utterance that emphasized discriminatory practices, he clarified that "they were not being pursued with the urgency they deserve."[59]

Through this claim, Muigai reflected on Kenya's role as one of the most important actors in maintaining peace and stability in Africa, and pointed to the prevalence of terrorism and piracy in the region. With a deeply animated and authoritative rhetorical style, he clarified that the icc trials had a negative impact on Kenya's ability to address the consequences of the 2007–2008 postelection violence (as noted in chapter 4). He argued that immunities for sitting heads of state exist in many domestic jurisdictions, and that this should also apply at the international level.[60] At the end of the day, the icc had the potential to negatively impact reconciliation and stability. As he clarified, "Reconciliation and healing are fundamental; the people must go back home and find a way of living together. When lawyers and judges and diplomats have gone home, the victims are the ones who must live with the consequences."

Muigai's invocation of the icc's selectivity and the realization that the icc had failed to produce reconciliation and stability, thereby failing those impacted by violence, reflected an attempt to disavow the ICC's work. He did this through the rhetorical production of relations of inequality resulting from the ICC's selectivity practices. This clarification works through a pro-African strategic position that demands the application of fairness by ICC advocates. Those in the audience who were aligned with such concerns shared grumblings and support with Muigai.

Attuned to the frustrations of the Kenyan official, the next speaker, Cherif Bassiouni, a key scholar and architect of the Rome Statute, responded that the discussion about amending Article 27 is not about political issues but about rules. He stated emphatically,

> Immunities for heads of state were removed within the Rome Statute framework; this was a conscious choice. There is nothing much to argue about that. You can argue as to the wisdom of that position, but it is a choice made by the drafters. And if, in hindsight, we consider this to have been an unwise decision then we would have to adjust the statute.
>
> Article 27 of the Rome Statute does not reflect customary international law where head-of-state immunity is well established and generally accepted, so what prevails? With respect to ICC states parties, what the treaty says. But to nonstates parties, customary international law prevails. This means that the applicable standards for states parties are higher. How does this influence the policy consideration? Does this persuade states not to become states parties? The immunities afforded to heads of state under customary international law simply relate to the timing of prosecutions/indictments—legal proceedings can commence after an official has left office. . . . In Rome, the drafting committee submitted a package that could not be unraveled. There are a lot of imperfections. We needed to conclude in a five-week period. But, we can now reexamine, [and] reflect on corrections. This is the nature of the beast; the statute is complex. These things need to be revisited . . . in an institution that we all hope will be a long-lasting institution.[61]

Similarly, the next speaker, Charles Jalloh, professor of international law at Florida International University, reinforced the pragmatic position by reminding everyone that Article 27 reflects the manifestation of a "key conviction [that] has taken root in international criminal justice that insists that the law shall apply equally to all persons—the office of the person shall not lead to any form of immunity." Through that entry point he reinforced the point that

Paragraph 1 of Article 27 of the Rome Statute provides that "official capacity of an individual will not be a factor for the purpose of establishing criminal responsibility. Nor will it be considered as a mitigating factor in sentencing. It denies a defense of 'official capacity' to several categories of officials: Head of State or government, members of government or parliament, elected representatives, and government officials."[62]

Like Bassouni, Jalloh was not alone in his insistence on the norms, context, and spirit of the wording of Article 27. The ICJ also held that "an incumbent or former Minister for Foreign Affairs may be subject to criminal proceedings before certain international criminal courts, where they have jurisdiction."[63] As such, many AU practitioners see state practice as confirming that the rules on personal immunities ensure that high-ranking officials and governments accused of international crimes should be prosecuted before international criminal tribunals.[64] This development has established the erosion of functional immunities and has contributed to the circulation of the discourse of ending impunity for the "most serious crimes of concern to the international community." Such immunities are seen as being derived from diplomatic agreements and customary state practice, as well as treaties.[65]

Both of the law professors, one central to the Rome Statute's drafting and the other an important African diasporic international criminal law scholar, spoke on the legal logic and importance of norms. Their alignments agreed with the goals of the irrelevance of official position and the goals and history that immunity represents. Standing behind a tradition of institutionalism to protect against generations of impunity and decades of violence without recourse, the academic call aligned emotional rationalities toward institutional change.

In a prerecorded message, Ambassador Rolf Fife, Norway's minister of foreign affairs, started his comments by reflecting on the early days of the drafting of the Rome Statute. In the last days at Rome, with the final package on the table, there was a sense of universality; they were united in a general commonality of purpose, yet there was respect for diversity. Any new proposals at that point would have unraveled the package. The exercise had a truly cross-regional thrust. Close working relationships, and even friendships, had formed in what Fife called a Band of Brothers. "We had become a melting pot of legal cultures with input from all corners of the world." He also described the willingness to listen and discuss the pros and cons of ideas as characteristic of the moment. He asserted that the ICC legal system was built around the idea of effectiveness, with a goal of removing cultures of impunity for mass atrocities; restricting immunities for heads of state was part of that. He also noted that there was an understanding that the court would not exist in a vacuum and a discussion about how to integrate the court with the status quo—in other words, what the role of the UNSC in peace and security should be. Another core principle is that one is innocent until proven guilty. He reflected on whether the position of an individual also warrants respect and a recognition of the dignity of the post held. This is not to say, he clarified, that this must equal outright immunity, but should result in practical measures to recognize and take into account the dignity of the highest office in a particular state. Ultimately, justice and a functioning judicial institution are key for trust and predictability in a given society. With the spirit of that founding moment in mind, his closing message was that he hoped they would work toward such basic values.

Ambassador Fife's message aligned with the last two messages, where particular social norms and their recognition and incorporation in the spirit of the law were central. Overall, history, politics, and a deep commitment to the spirit of ending violence were all part of what would shape international criminal law. But this conviction had its limits with some members of the plenary and among some in the convention hall. Their emotional expressions and reactions coupled disappointment in the failure of the assumption that no one was beyond the law with a realization that this core principle did not reflect how international law was working in practice. This is so, they argued, because the very values of objectivity that were understood to accompany that commitment failed to guarantee fairness and the universal application of its principles.

The chairperson then opened the floor to commentators. In articulating disappointment and suggestions of race-based selectivity, the representative from Namibia repeated the dominant refrain: "Justice should not be based on selective application. Justice should apply to all continents, to all perpetrators, to all races and to all sexes. Any selective application ceases to be justice and is likely to undermine the objective of the international community in preserving international humanitarian law." He, like Kenya's attorney general, spoke of the similarity of current manifestations of international justice and the all-too-familiar history of colonial domination over African livelihoods.

Through these various remarks, we see attempts both to question what some saw as double standards and to rethink ICC legality through the prism of politics and histories. These comments reflect attempts to clarify international justice through alternate sensibilities. In that case, various AU spokespersons suggested that the future of accountability in Africa must include both legal

and political solutions. These arguments were made not just through the invocation of legal and political logic, absent affective armature; indeed, the affective appeal to histories of inequality or the need to protect survivors are
central to the contours of international justice that continue to play out. Furthermore, as I discussed in chapter 3, while the anti-impunity movement fe-
tishizes the victim as life to be protected, discussions about the immunity of
sitting heads of state also evoke questions of biopolitics and bare life, especially in the context of state sovereignty.[66]

But there is certainly no consensus among African stakeholders, as shown
by the opinion that "the AU was full of shit." On the day in question, those af-
filiated with African civil society organizations chose to challenge the public
assertions by African and non-African state officials by invoking the critical
importance of the law in solving African problems. Several representatives of
Kenyan organizations and governmental agencies delivered powerful public
submissions. Njonjo Mue spoke on behalf of Kenyans for Peace with Truth
and Justice, a coalition of Kenyan civil society organizations, and argued that
immunity effectively means impunity, reminding everyone of the importance
of international law for the weak—the victims of violence. George Morara, of
the Kenyan Human Rights Commission, argued that survivors of the postelection violence in Kenya still support the ICC process, and cautioned that
providing immunity to heads of state would contravene the very reason the
court was created—to prosecute those who bear the greatest responsibility for
the world's gravest crimes. He also warned that providing sitting heads of state
with immunity would create an incentive for them to hold onto power, threatening to entrench dictatorship and impunity.

George Kegoro of the International Commission of Jurists–Kenya warned
against amendments to the Rome Statute and expressed concern that they
could compromise the ICC and render it no longer worth having. Yet immediately following Kegoro's appeal for the integrity of Article 27, Keriako Tobiko,
Kenya's director of public prosecutions, responded dismissingly and with
knowing authority. He reiterated Githu Muigai's assertion that Kenya has, to
date, cooperated with the ICC and will continue to do so. He stressed that the
rhetoric that Kenya has disregarded international law and that it has failed to
cooperate and take seriously its international obligations misrepresents the
truth, disputing the claims of civil society representatives. Rather, he offered
a plethora of examples of ongoing cooperation as well as evidence of Kenyan domestic efforts to put in place measures to prosecute those responsible
for the postelection violence. Part of his message involved pointing to 1,200

domestic cases that have been taken to the Kenyan courts. But he ended by clarifying that complementarity should be a two-way street. Kenya has been cooperating with the ICC, but the Office of the Prosecutor has refused to cooperate with or furnish evidence to Kenyan authorities investigating postelection violence. Tobiko's defense of domestic adjudication was communicated through an emotional response to misrepresentations and inequalities in the international system.

Many individual states submitted comments that afternoon, drawing attention to the relationship between peace and justice, clarifying that the quest for justice cannot be allowed to jeopardize peace and security. There was a general consensus that something must be done to address the AU's concerns; however, many states also said that the integrity of the Rome Statute cannot be compromised, that the independence of the ICC as a judicial institution is paramount, and that Article 27 of the Rome Statute is an untouchable cornerstone of the ICC system. Some state agents reiterated that there is a need to find practical solutions to the problems facing the ICC, while others suggested that these solutions already exist within the law, particularly the Rome Statute and the rules of procedure and evidence. What this debate highlighted was the extent to which varying architects of the AU position were seen as contravening founding Rome Statute principles. But because Africans have become the sole subjects of the ICC, contravention is precisely what the AU intended. International lawmaking, public speeches, protest declarations, and public campaigns, as this book has detailed, provide the context within which shadows of the past manifest to articulate visions and aspirations for the future. They reflect the ordering principles of the past and the grammar of the present, and they clarify the terms on which particular forms of knowledge are seen. Invocations of past solidarity movements help to make legible various social imaginaries, as chapter 5 argued. The Africa that is imagined is indelibly shaped by a history fraught with struggle against an outside colonizer or unjust ideology. It is an Africa that is in crisis—the impunity of leadership, the failure to sustain institutions that can serve the poor. And through affects embodied and emotionalized through political responses, speeches, and social action, we see that the contemporary present cannot be separated from it. It follows that emotional responses to those political developments constitute alliances. They shape constituencies through the feeling rules that emerge in passionate utterances.

After this meeting, stakeholders aligned with Pan-Africanist positions emphasizing structural inequality continued to protest, while those who asserted the need for standards for anti-impunity insisted on the indefensibility of immunity. Such dueling narratives not only set the stage for regulating particular principles about the reach of the rule of law, but also were propelled through invocations of sympathy for survivors or protest against structural injustice. Critical events like these have led to requests for UNSC deferrals of cases under Article 16 and—because of their lack of progress—proposals for particular amendments to the Rome Statute.

Amendments as an Affective Practice

Many arguments have been made regarding the systemic imbalance in international decision-making processes. Their inherent politics result in the unreliable application of the rule of law. P. S. Rao, a distinguished international lawyer from India, argues, "The decisions of the Security Council by design are manifestly political decisions. Accordingly, there is no guarantee that the decisions of the Security Council will reflect either the requirements of law or justice of the world at large. They are essentially reflective of the self-interests of its permanent members, as perceived by their governments, which may or may not coincide with the interests of the parties concerned. Decisions of the Security Council are often questioned for their selectivity and double standards."[67]

Indeed, questions about which states are under the ICC's jurisdiction and the processes of selectivity, as well as the role of the UNSC and its referral and deferral mechanism under Article 16 of the Rome Statute, have raised issues about the fairness of the international system. Under the United Nations Charter, the Security Council's primary responsibility is to uphold international security and peace.[68] Composed of fifteen members, ten rotating and five permanent (the United Kingdom, China, France, the Russian Federation, and the United States), the Security Council is responsible for determining the existence of threats to peace and taking the appropriate action, be it diplomatic or military, to control the conflict.[69] In addition, under Article 24 of the UN Charter, the Security Council is responsible for representing all members of the United Nations to "ensure prompt and effective action," while adhering to the purposes and principles of the UN and its charter.[70] Because of their key role in the establishment of the United Nations, the five permanent states on the UNSC can both vote and veto decisions.[71] They have been granted special overseeing, decision-making status on peace and security in global affairs. Because no African countries currently sit on the UNSC, African state representatives see themselves as lacking fair and equal representation in one of the most powerful international bodies.

On the other hand, the UN General Assembly has long been identified as the main "deliberative, policymaking and representative organ of the UN." A total of 193 members make up the General Assembly, each of whom is allowed one vote on "designated important issues—such as recommendations on peace and security, the election of Security Council and Economic and Social Council members, and budgetary questions."[72] It is essentially the assemblage of member states that "discusses and deliberates on policies, situations, and other international matters," and all decisions related to important issues, such as peace and security, admission of new members, and budgetary matters require a two-thirds majority.[73] Decisions on other questions are decided by a general majority.[74]

Considering the systematic disadvantage that African nations face in UNSC decisions, being legally bound by a UNSC decision to a statute (in this case, the Rome Statute) that a country has not even ratified is not seen as acceptable.[75] As outlined, the case of President al-Bashir in Sudan has been cited as illustrating this seeming inequality, resulting in calls for the UNSC to also defer, under Article 16 of the Rome Statute, the ICC's prosecutions against not just al-Bashir but Kenyatta and Ruto as well. When that was unsuccessful, South Africa, in a meeting on November 3–6, 2009, in Addis Ababa, decided to propose an amendment to the Rome Statute with respect to Article 16 to address situations where the UNSC was unable to decide on a deferral request. This is the original wording of Article 16:

> No investigation or prosecution may be commenced or proceeded with under this Statute for a period of twelve months after the Security Council, in a resolution adopted under the Chapter VII of the Charter of the United Nations, has requested the Court to that effect; that request may be renewed by the Council under the same conditions.

South African officials proposed adding the following two revisions:

2. A State with jurisdiction over a situation before the Court may request the UN Security Council to defer the matter before the Court as provided for in (1) above.
3. Where the UN Security Council fails to decide on the request by the state concerned within six (6) months of receipt of the request, the requesting Party may request the UN General Assembly to assume the Security Council's responsibility under paragraph 1 consistent with Resolution 377 (v) of the UN General Assembly.

Key to this proposed amendment is a larger set of issues related to the desire to address the power disparities of the UNSC through the call for reform. The power vested in the Security Council is controversial, as it allows countries to refer cases to the prosecutor concerning countries that have not submitted to the jurisdiction of the Rome Statute themselves. And coupled with the UNSC's referral for President Omar al-Bashir, a sitting head of state, in 2005 under Resolution 1593, South Africa, joined by a predominant number of African states that had ratified the treaty, felt it important to move to an amendment that asked the ASP to take action if the UNSC did not respond to a deferral request within six months of being notified of it. The request not only asks the ICC to reconfigure how the referral system works but also calls for the UN system to address a structural inequality problem. The unwillingness, thus failure, to address these claims has led to the creation of an African Working Group on ICC Amendments to discuss further reforms, which I attended over successive ASP meetings and informal gatherings.

During the various meetings of the Working Group on Amendments in 2014, Kenyan representatives introduced a proposal to amend Article 27 of the Rome Statute. The original article states:

1. This Statute shall apply equally to all persons without any distinction based on official capacity. In particular, official capacity as a Head of State or Government, a Member of a Government or parliament, an elected representative or a government official shall in no case exempt a person from criminal responsibility under this Statute, nor shall it, in and of itself, constitute a ground for reduction of Sentence.

2. Immunities or special procedural rules which may attach to the official capacity of a person, whether under national or international law, shall not bar the Court from exercising its jurisdiction over such a person.

The first two paragraphs in Article 27 fulfill different functions.[76] Paragraph 1 denies a defense of official capacity. It concerns functional immunity and is derived from texts in the Nuremberg Charter, the Genocide Convention, and the statutes of the ad hoc tribunals. In contrast, Paragraph 2 outlines that no exception exists for "core crimes" under personal immunity. Paragraph 1 of Article 27 provides that official capacity of an individual will not be a factor in establishing criminal responsibility, nor will it be considered a mitigating factor in sentencing.[77] It denies a defense of official capacity to several categories of officials: head of state, member of government or parliament, elected representatives, and government officials. Article 27(1) concerns immunities rationae materiae, or functional immunities that attach to official acts. According to Gaeta, Article 27(1) "excludes the availability both of the international law doctrine of functional immunity for official acts and of national legislation sheltering State officials with immunity for official acts in the case of crimes within the jurisdiction of the ICC."[78]

Functional immunities extend from the doctrine of state immunity, *par in parem non habet imperium* or "equal has no power over an equal," under which no state can exercise jurisdiction over another. Functional immunities serve two purposes: (1) to prevent interference with state affairs through lawsuits, and (2) to protect state agents from individual liability for official state acts both at home and abroad.[79] Since this type of immunity attaches to the official act, serving state officials and former officials may rely on it with regard to official acts they performed while in office.[80] Such immunity does not, however, exist with regard to international crimes (e.g., genocide, war crimes, and crimes against humanity) on the grounds that such acts cannot be considered performance of official acts.

The ICJ held in its 1951 advisory opinion regarding the Genocide Convention that the principles underlying the convention, including the principle of irrelevance of official capacity, were a matter of state practice and CIL.[81] This view has subsequently been upheld in various domestic and international courts. In 1962, the Supreme Court of Israel held in *Eichmann v. Attorney-General of Israel* that Article 7 of the Nuremberg Charter and all of the Nuremberg principles "have formed part of customary international law since time immemorial."[82] In 1998, the English House of Lords ruled on whether Augusto Pinochet could be extradited to Spain for acts of torture perpetrated while he was the head of state of Chile.[83] By a three-to-two majority, the House of Lords held that functional immunity cannot coexist with international crimes.[84] Wirth notes that this amounts to state practice in the UK, and also in Spain, Belgium, and France, which all requested Pinochet's extradition.[85]

Paragraph 2 of Article 27 concerns immunities in CIL, and that protect heads of state and other senior officials by virtue of their particular office or status. Article 27(2) concerns immunities *rationae personae*, or personal immunities that attach to an office or status. This type of immunity is limited to only a small group of senior state officials, especially heads of state, heads of government, foreign ministers, diplomats, and other officials on special mission in foreign states.[86] These immunities are conferred on those with primary responsibility for the conduct of the international relations of a state, and they are possessed only as long as the official is in office.[87] During that time, state officials are immune from prosecution for both official acts and those carried out in their private capacity, whether the act in question was committed while the official was in office or before his or her entry into office.[88] Such immunities stem from the recognition that state affairs are hindered by judicial interference from foreign governments, and the view that immunities are necessary for the maintenance of peaceful cooperation and coexistence among states.[89] Ultimately, Paragraph 2 amounts to a renunciation, by state parties to the Rome Statute, of the immunity of their own head of state to which they are entitled by virtue of CIL but have agreed to waive. It concerns personal immunity and is without precedent in international criminal law instruments. It outlines that the statute applies "equally to all persons without any distinction based on official capacity. In particular, official capacity as a Head of State of Government, a member of a Government of parliament, an elected representative or a government official shall in no case exempt a person from criminal responsibility under this statute."[90]

Kenya's proposed amendment suggested adding a third paragraph as follows: "Notwithstanding paragraph 1 and 2 above, serving Heads of State, their deputies and anybody acting or is entitled to act as such may be exempt from prosecution during their current term of office. Such an exemption may be renewed by the Court under the same conditions."[91] They later proposed to the ICC committee on amendments: "Notwithstanding paragraph 1 and 2 above, serving Heads of State, their deputies and anybody acting or [who] is entitled to act as such may be exempt from prosecution during their current term of office. Such an exemption may be renewed by the Court under the same conditions."[92]

With regard to the proposed amendment, the Working Group Report, led by a Kenyan representative, stated, "The objective of [our] proposal was not to grant immunity to Heads of State, their deputies and persons acting or entitled to act as such, but only to 'pause' prosecutions during their term of office. It was therefore to be understood as a 'comma' rather than a 'full stop.'" Several delegations expressed their appreciation for this clarification but had additional questions and comments with regard to the text of the proposal, notably concerning the meaning of the expressions "current term of office" and "anybody acting or [who] is entitled to act as [a head of state or their deputy]." Moreover, some delegations requested further clarification regarding the term "may" as it was not clear to them who would be entitled to make the decision and on the basis of what criteria. Several delegations recalled that Article 27 was the cornerstone of the Rome Statute and that they were not willing to modify it. There was agreement that discussions need to continue after the thirteenth session of the assembly.[93]

Accordingly, AU stakeholders insisted that in real-world situations, the temporary granting of immunity to sitting heads of state is not antithetical to human rights, as many have argued.[94] The reality is that since no statute of limitations exists for war crimes and crimes against humanity, the eventual prosecution of those guilty of particular violations covered under the jurisdiction of the African Court is a reasonable prospect. They viewed the judicial process as part of a larger political process that needed to also involve peace negotiations and legal accountability sequencing as a strategy, as we saw in chapter 5, that could potentially protect more Africans from repression and violence than international prosecution could ever hope to achieve. As a result, a number of public declarations have shaped particular claims of the significance of African heads of state in some of the most volatile countries in the world, and that to delay investigations against them while they are in office would contribute to the necessary protection of people in the relevant region at risk. But articulating immunity as a pro-justice act involves employing particular sentiments of legitimate state entitlements, protectionism, and obligations of responsibility that are particular to the postcolonial state and its people.

Declarations that highlight these sentiments not only produce legally significant determinations, but, by signaling the aspirational direction of Pan-Africanist institutional practices, they establish certain emotional climates through which particular collective feelings are loosely established. Their protests reflect the recognition of a systemic imbalance in the international system that continues to drive international lawmaking in the contemporary period. As we will see, the assumption was that if the amendment strategy failed, an African Court that respects immunity for heads of state would be implemented, and discussions of treaty withdrawal from the ICC would follow. However, structural compatibility issues related to the ICC and the African Court remain at the time of this writing. For even though the ICC and the International Criminal Section of the African Court of Justice and Human Rights (ACJHR) will exercise overlapping subject-matter jurisdiction, the Malabo Protocol, which created the African Court, does not recognize the Rome Statue.[95] Due to the political climate prevailing during the making of the Malabo Protocol, substantive matters of cooperation with the ICC were not considered. Instead, the African Court only considers cooperation and relationships of complementarity between the African Court and African national courts on the one hand, and regional bodies, known as Regional Economic Communities, on the other hand.[96] Similarly, at the time of its drafting and well after its coming into force, the ICC did not recognize regional judicial bodies such as the African Court. It only gives primacy to national states, and sees itself in complementary relationships with those states. Thus, the frameworks of the statutes that created both courts do not allow for flexible cooperation. Because survivors of violence deserve commitments to a global system that is effective and productive, the stakes are higher than ever before. The lack of a framework for cooperation between the two courts raises significant challenges for those involved. The Rome Statute's obligations require state parties to "ensure that there are procedures available under their national law for all of the forms of cooperation."[97] Accordingly, all state parties are required to carry out arrest warrants issued by the ICC should the suspect be in their territory, for example. Yet, as I have shown, the ICC has faced challenges with state parties refusing to execute these obligations. It is no surprise, then, that this has led to protests against the consequences of ICC strategies in the form of amendments, noncooperation, and even withdrawal.

The expansion of the criminal jurisdiction of the African Court that led to the crafting of 46A *bis* is a further manifestation of the emotional regimes I have been examining throughout this book. As we will see, the claims of inequality and perceptions of selectivity that have prompted the proposed and controversial amendments to Article 27 of the Rome Statute, as well as the ICC withdrawal actions, are central to the relatively late introduction of an immunity provision to the Malabo Protocol, and the justice sentiments that accompany them. This reveals how affects contribute to social alignments that influence perceptions of justice, and how those perceptions shape the way that justice is achieved.

Innovating Immunity and Reshaping an African Regional Custom as a Form of Refusal

Article 46A *bis* of the Malabo Protocol is key to addressing the failure to accept the proposed amendments to the articles on extradition and irrelevance of official capacity in the Rome Statute, as described above, because it explicitly ensures immunity for heads of state. As it notes, "The Court shall uphold the immunities provided for under international law. In particular, no criminal proceedings shall be initiated or continued against a Head of State or Government during his/her term of office." Thus, the ratification of the Malabo Protocol by fifteen states to bring it into force and the subsequent operationalization of the court would, as chapter 5 began detailing, open an alternative avenue for dispensing justice. The strategy involves identifying regional champions—such as Uganda, Kenya, and Ghana—seen as supportive of the African Court to drive the ratification enlistment of African states.[98] This is not simply a legal process.

This process involves securing strategic commitments and a belief in AU policy positions through rhetorical performances, ideological commitments, and strategic moves that align policy positions with legal actions as reattributive acts. For example, at a range of meetings held at different times over the two-year period when I observed various treaty-making negotiations, I documented various African stakeholders calling on "fellow Pan-Africanists who love freedom to take justice in their own hands." Some passionately urged states to recognize that colonialism is long over. As one said, "We need to act against European courts that continue to target Africans and their leaders." This linking of the possibility of justice to regional consolidation and treaty making engages a regional domain of African justice that also involves the invocation of vindicating sentiments through which justice is reattributed as spatialized and expressed as a form of Pan-African freedom.

The existence of such dynamics requires that we not dismiss such practices because of implied disappointments in the workings of the postcolonial African state. Rather, it demands further analysis of the way that refusals and redesignations are taking place in the contemporary period and of the crisis of the postcolonial state. In the case of the AU-supported immunity provision, protests around not surrendering African heads of state highlight the role of various political aspirations that are fundamentally tied to structures of inequality and propelled by particular feeling rules that align the brotherhood of the African statesman with histories of European imperial subjugation. For some of the architects of the AU-supported immunity provision, the Malabo Protocol's Article 46A *bis* is not just about the will for impunity. It is an expression of the goal to establish a contrary regional custom around international treaty norms that have rendered immunity for heads of state irrelevant in some cases (for Africans) yet relevant in others (for Western and various Asian powers). Unlike the current trends in international treaty jurisprudence to make immunity obsolete, for some African stakeholders, like those discussed earlier in this chapter, CIL has long provided personal immunities for heads of state, and African leaders responding to structural injustice insist that there is no reason why the current developments with the African Court Protocol should not be decided according to existing state practice in CIL. This was the South Africa's position when they refused to arrest President al-Bashir of Sudan.

As representatives of South Africa argued in one of the closed meetings that I attended, "We will not promote regime change by arresting and extraditing another sitting head of state." The reality, they insist, is that CIL provides immunity for heads of state and high-ranking senior state officials, and separate provisions have also been upheld that address treaties for the immunity of diplomatic agents, consular officials, representatives of states to international organizations, and state officials abroad on special missions. Similarly, the AU position is that regional customs are norms that develop from practices of states in particular regions of the world. In addition to the role of customary law in the application of personal immunity as a form of international state cooperation, there is a key threshold that for a regional custom to be established it must be continuously and uniformly executed.

The lead authority, the *Asylum Case* decided by the ICJ in 1950, highlights the issue, and many of those engaged in getting ICC or ICJ judges to consider the relevance of this claim point to that landmark case. With impassioned logic, various AU negotiators insisted that in the case between Peru and Colombia, the ICJ accepted that regional customs existed in international law, even if it rejected their relevance in that particular instance. The court stipulated that it relied on an alleged regional or local custom peculiar to Latin American states. Following the court's argument, they concluded that the state that alleges the existence of a custom must prove clearly that such a custom exists and that other states in that region, against which the contested custom is asserted, accept that custom.[99] They also insisted that under Article 98 of the Rome Statute, "The Court may not proceed with a request for surrender or assistance which would require the requested State to act inconsistently with its obligations under international law with respect to the State or diplomatic immunity of a person or property of a third State, unless the Court can first obtain the cooperation of that third State for the waiver of the immunity." Accordingly, states have a sovereign right to determine how to determine how to balance their state responsibility to treaty obligations while also considering their sovereign rights and protections.[100] As noted in the opening of the chapter, the AU Office of Legal Counsel saw their position regarding the amendment of Article 27 as justified and couched it in a legal form—that of their recognition of Africa's development of a regional norm on immunity. Through resolute expressions and impassioned declarations offstage, a number of people supportive of the AU's position insisted to many of us that the AU's legal argument rests on the need for different regional customs, thus practices. They are seeking to develop a regional custom that carves out a limited exception from prosecution of a leader while holding office. This is a critical manifestation of African geographies of justice. It is a refusal to accept the emergence of a particular international legal norm and instead to articulate a regionally differentiated practice. It is what I have called reattribution.

Interestingly, this attempt to reshape the basis for African state practice runs counter to early positions held by many African states and Pan-Africanist national liberation movements of the 1940s–1970s, which refused to use international law for strategic purposes. Rather, African leaders of newly decolonized states in the early postcolonial period argued—often with great success—that general rules of CIL (as opposed to regional rules) were only relevant to Europe, or were Euro-American constructs typically generated behind their backs and foisted upon them without consideration of whether non-European actors had actually given their consent (expressly or tacitly). This argument was exceptionally powerful and far-reaching in international investment law, international human rights law, and (before long) international environmental law. But what is interesting here is that in the contemporary period, African stakeholders are claiming the tools of CIL to facilitate the establishment of new regional customs. Through the communication of these legal positions, which are often articulated with feelings of anger, the notion of differentiated African practices is being harnessed to institutionalize new contours of lawmaking using Pan-Africanist refusals.

However, although AU heads of state participated in the universal declaration of noncooperation with the extradition of President al-Bashir, behind closed doors there is actually no regional consensus on the rule of nonextradition and immunity. If the private debate is an indication of this, we could say that African regional alignments share the affective commitments to equality of states, but they are not aligned with how that should play out. The ethnographic interviews that we conducted in Nigeria, Kenya, and Ethiopia demonstrated this point. From Francophone to Anglophone to multilingual and multiethnic Africans, from the desert to the oil-rich regions, and from the predominantly Christian to the predominantly Muslim or animist, unified decision making has not been easy to achieve. African differences are vast, as are their varied positions on the nonsurrender of heads of state. Furthermore, not all African stakeholders agree with the expansion of the jurisdiction of the African Court and the incorporation of Article 46A *bis*. Nor do they all agree with the call for AU noncooperation with the ICC.

One of the key disputes over the AU's immunity provision concerns whether the one that deals with personal immunity is in violation of CIL—one of two types of immunity in CIL.[101] This immunity attaches to the office or status of a very limited group of senior state officials and is conferred only as long as the official remains in office. The second type, functional immunity, attaches to official acts carried out on behalf of the state. It extends to a broader group of officials and covers them while in office and after they leave office. However, during heated debates between different stakeholders—members of African civil society, various international NGOs, academics, and state representatives—many have raised questions about whether this form of functional immunity covers those acts performed in an official capacity.

The legal questions have been innovative and contested, as have been public responses, through heated debates, that if African state leaders acted responsibly and protected their citizens, there would be no need for claims to immunity. In keeping with this trend in favor of the irrelevance of national capacity, over the past twenty years we have witnessed situations in which national courts have chosen not to apply functional immunity to officials accused of an international crime. Examples include cases against Qaddafi, former Chilean dictator Augusto Pinochet, and Charles Taylor.[102]

In May 2004, the Appeals Chamber of the Special Court of Sierra Leone rejected Charles Taylor's preliminary motion in which he claimed immunity. In doing so, the court emphasized its "truly international" legal status, despite the absence of chapter 7 powers, and found that it was an "international criminal court." It then went on to hold that because of its nature as an international criminal court, not a national court, the paragraph in its statute that denies immunity to officials is "not in conflict with any peremptory norm of general international law and its provisions must be given effect by this Court." The judges concluded that the "official position of the Applicant as an incumbent Head of State at the time when the criminal proceedings were initiated against him is not a bar to his prosecution by this Court."[103] The importance of the distinction between national and international courts for the immunity issue was derived from the ICJ's *Arrest Warrant* case (although the Special Court for Sierra Leone came to an opposite finding). By pronouncing authoritatively on the *Arrest Warrant* case, the ICJ determined whether Congo's minister of foreign affairs enjoyed immunity following Belgium's issuance of an international arrest warrant for crimes committed in Congo.[104] The ICJ ultimately rejected Belgium's argument that there was an exception to immunity for incumbent officials in cases of alleged international crimes. In terms of legal rhetoric, the ICJ could not deduce such a rule from state practice (case law and national legislation), nor could it derive a position from the relevant rules contained in the legal instruments creating international tribunals; according to the court, the latter rules only applied to the specific international tribunals and could not lead to the conclusion that similar rules applied in prosecutions in national courts.

Various AU legal advisors have argued that it is important to see that immunity, though discussed through law, has its greatest relevance in its ability to speak to African realities. Some suggest that because tribal sentiment can lead to electoral violence, not giving heads of state immunity could have a critical impact on how and when one proceeds with judicial action in cases of mass atrocity violence where peace settlements are underway. As one southern African leader told me during my fieldwork, "Weak African states challenged by civil war or political strife need a framework throughout Africa to address how to deal with violence and leaders." And as another high-ranking AU interlocutor explained to a colleague and me during a research meeting:

> We need to be innovative about the immunities issue. The debate is complex, but we need to be much more creative about violence in Africa. What this means is that we need to be active agents in the making of international law. The ICC emphasis has been on African leaders. Customary international law focuses on state practices in order to articulate norms. These opinions are binding. The way we deal with personal jurisdiction needs to be more creative. We need to think about reshaping international law in ways that look at the issues amongst African leaders. . . .
>
> The innovation is that as a region, African states can play a critical role in generating new customs. African states can play a central role in the development of international norms and the creation of complex lawmaking relevant for African changing circumstances. . . . If we consider Africa's role in reshaping international law in ways that look at issues amongst leaders in relation to their ability to generate new customs that are relevant to Africa's uniquely different circumstances, then our approach to the Malabo Protocol, such as provisions like 46A *bis*, for example, requires that we think about personal immunity not in relation to [the] venue/national and international courts division but in relation to nature of the crime.

Why should venue be what is important in African regional contexts? Is it the venue that matters or is it the actual crime—the nature of international harm?

The insistence that the actual crime, not the venue, should be the basis for determining immunity is a point that international law scholar Sarah Nouwen has argued: international law should be the same, regardless of the kind of tribunal in which it is applied.[105] While functional immunity is clearly incompatible with the concept of individual responsibility for international crimes, and therefore of no avail to former officials charged with crimes against humanity and war crimes, it has been harder to prove the emergence of such a rule in CIL with respect to procedural immunity of serving officials. This is because personal immunity is founded on a different principle: granting immunity to certain officials because of the office they hold.[106] She concluded that despite this disregard for the type of crime, there have been several developments that the Special Court could have used as a foundation for finding such a rule, which could have denied former president Charles Taylor procedural immunity while at the same time advancing the emergence of the customary rule—immunity based on the type and severity of crimes.[107] The AU's former legal counsel has adopted this intellectual reasoning as a possible direction for the its future lawmaking and speaks to the emotional commitments to legal innovation that are central to new possibilities in international relations.

As one of my AU interlocutors said, "Africa is tired of the dichotomy between national and international crimes," mimicking that emotional exhaustion in his delivery. With the Malabo Protocol, Africans are saying that they are committed to the subject matter instead of the venue. The argument is that if immunity does not apply in national courts for some offenses, then it should not apply at all in international courts for those particular offenses. Instead, the AU legal counsel's argument, like Sarah Nouwen's, considers the nature of the crime a better route to pursue. This reattribution of legality through other modalities such as peace-justice sequencing and personal immunity for heads of state and high-ranking leaders highlights new possibilities for managing violence through the desire to apply the historical contexts that are relevant to Africa's realities. The AU's work to build alternate models for managing African violence on its terms has been relevant to the AU legal office's logic maintaining that peaceful international relations require a more temporary approach to peace through the institutionalization of personal immunity while a head of state is in office. These measures are seen by AU adherents as reflecting "African solutions to African problems" and they speak to the socialization of particular cultural sensibilities and practices that are transforming the way that states address violence on the African landscape. In other words, the response to the immunity debate is not just about legal doctrine and actionable domains of law. The AU's engagement can be seen in relation to a particular reading of Africa's role in setting new international norms and, in so doing, attending to the forms of political inequality that are seen as deeply pervasive, thereby leading to regimes of inequality.

However, as I indicated above, not all AU actors agree with this perspective, and the incorporation of Article 46A *bis* has received extensive criticism from civil society groups and activists in Africa and around the globe, who similarly argue that such a provision would be a setback in the fight against impunity for international human rights abuses.[108] Some argue that the draft protocol is simply advancing the ideals of the ICC to ensure justice for international crimes peculiar to Africa.[109] Others insist that the draft protocol for the African Court includes a laundry list of crimes and is a project that is not feasible and cannot be effectively implemented.[110] Some scholars of international law, such as du Plessis, have insisted that the AU responses are simply examples of African fraternity; in other words, they represent Africa's elite protecting their own in the midst of mass violence and lack of accountability.[111] And yet others argue that these concerns are purely strategic and serve to derail particular ICC indictments of African leaders.[112]

In May 2014, more than thirty civil society and international NGOs appealed to a meeting of African ministers of justice and attorneys general not to include Article 46A *bis* in its draft of the Malabo Protocol. Organizations including Human Rights Watch, the International Bar Association, the International Federation for Human Rights, Amnesty International, the South African Litigation Centre, the New York City Bar Association, and many others have released statements sharply criticizing the provision as retrogressive and inconsistent with ensuring that perpetrators are held to account.[113] Additional criticism has stemmed from the argument that the protocol contradicts Article 4(h) of the AU's Constitutive Act, which asserts "the right of the Union to intervene in a member state pursuant to a decision of the Assembly in respect of grave circumstances, namely: war crimes, genocide and crimes against humanity."[114]

Those engaged in such criticism argue that if Article 4(h) is strictly applied, the AU should be able to intervene despite declarations of immunity. Some have pointed to additional contradictions with specific articles, including Article 4(o), which obliges member states to respect the sanctity of human life and condemn and reject impunity. For example, they have suggested that the inconsistencies will make it difficult for the AU to be seen as procuring justice in its regional court—as shown through the victim/perpetrator construction in earlier chapters.[115] Some have argued that where immunity attaches to an officeholder, it can create an incentive for that person to remain in office to avoid prosecution. For Idayat Hassan, "Based on the antecedents and attitudes of some African leaders, we can expect immunity for heads of state and their officials to create an atmosphere of impunity for perpetrators of human right violations, thereby encouraging perpetrators to hold onto power for a long time to enjoy the immunity."[116]

This disagreement with immunity for African heads of state may indeed encourage state leaders to stay in office. However, it is important that we see the Malabo Protocol's heads of state immunity as what Ademola Abass calls a "protest treaty."[117] In other words, 46A *bis* is not an objective legal doctrine but an emotionally relevant statement about inequality in global affairs. In this regard, Chidi Odinkalu distinguished immunity in relation to de jure and de facto immunity, in which states that have not submitted to the legal constraints of the Rome Treaty have de facto immunity—that is, immunity in fact. And those that have erected the Malabo Protocol have de jure immunity—that is, immunity in law.[118] Relatedly, and as this book has worked to show, law, formalized through treaties, is a form of expression that has force in particular contexts. But legal norms are not the only way to understand how particular practices are deemed legitimate. In reality, law is negotiated and disputed using legal reasoning in ways that structure what its products become. When we recognize how international law works in the absence of a statecraft and/or police force to compel action, it is important to understand the underlying emotional regimes that shape the nature of affective justice. Expressions of justice through conceptual or narrative reattributions or political protests are critical communicative forms by which law gains its power. To miss this is to misrecognize the place of affects in the life of the law.

As chapter 5 illustrated in relation to the making of the African Court, the debate over immunity and African heads of state is not simply a disagreement with the principle that no one should be beyond the law. It is fundamentally related to the problem of power and history and the emotional regimes that structure the acceptability of particular responses. In the case of the ICC arrest warrants for African leaders, this is seen as happening alongside the violence of economic plunder and structural inequalities that operate in Africa without judicial hindrance. The existence of these perceptions of inequality make it all the more important to explore the making of new international regional mechanisms, not only in relation to their doctrinal formations but also in relation to the sociocultural sensibilities that shape and sustain them.

Treaty Withdrawal as Affective Alignments of Protest

To understand the events that have led to treaty withdrawal as an emotionally affective practice requires that we detail the way that the above recent historical developments led to the contemporary forms of political protest that unfolded following the January 2016 summit.[119] At that time, the lack of progress with the amendments to the Rome Statute led various key African state actors to speak on behalf of states like Kenya, Burundi, Namibia, and South Africa requesting a withdrawal strategy. The AU tasked the Open-Ended Committee of African Ministers on the ICC, formed in 2015 by representatives from various regions of Africa, with the urgent development of a comprehensive strategy, including a collective withdrawal from the ICC. The committee was charged with communicating their strategy to AU member states that are also parties to the Rome Statute. They were also expected to submit their strategy to an extraordinary session of the executive council mandated to make decisions on the next steps.[120]

Once the committee was established, they considered proposals by the AU's Office of Legal Counsel as to what the withdrawal strategy might look like. The committee proposed multiple approaches, including the option of a collective withdrawal from the Rome Statute if particular reforms did not take place. In proposing the various approaches, the Open-Ended Committee outlined: (1) the need for continental and country-level ownership of international criminal justice through strengthening national judicial systems and working toward the ratification of the African Court; (2) the importance of engaging with the UNSC and clearly communicating that no referrals of particular situations on the African continent should be made without deference to AU Assembly; (3) the need for a robust strategy to enhance the ratification of the Malabo Protocol expanding the jurisdiction of the African Court of Justice and Human and Peoples' Rights to include international crimes; and (4) because of the slow pace of possible ICC reforms, the need for timelines for withdrawals. The ministerial committee insisted that the AUC should develop the comprehensive strategy as soon as possible. They emphasized the importance of soliciting input from various delegations and that a draft copy should be submitted to the ambassadors for consideration at the June 2016 meeting. In the end, two successive meetings were scheduled with the UNSC, and both of the formal meetings were canceled. Instead, representatives met informally and discussed the possibility of articulating new strategies through which to produce more equitable results for African states.

Key to the AU strategy laid out by the Open-Ended Committee meetings was the delivery of justice in a fair and equitable manner that allows for the regionalization of international criminal law on the continent. Without that, state withdrawals were understood as being the only viable mode of rectifying the way that law was encapsulating the terms for justice. They spoke of the need to create viable political solutions to structural inequalities and work toward building African judicial institutions within Africa. Protests in the form of prioritizing the peace and security of the countries that these leaders guard, resisting extraditions, and presenting new legal and political alternatives are also critical to the concept of reattribution at the core of this book.

In the domain of international lawmaking negotiations, a treaty is an agreement entered into by actors (such as international organizations and sovereign states) who give consent to assume obligations among themselves. Because the creation of a treaty involves painstaking negotiation and reflects a compromise among states regarding mutual obligations, the assumption is that the ratification of such treaties by states represents their acceptance of being bound by not just conditions of the treaties but their restrictions on termination or withdrawal. Thus, state consent is seen as an overarching principle governing the design and operation of all treaty exit clauses.[121] In guiding these rules, the Vienna Convention on the Law of Treaties sets out the conditions under which state parties can unilaterally withdraw from treaties and under which treaty obligations can be suspended and terminated.

The Rome Treaty for the ICC provides for withdrawal. The withdrawal question raised by African member states falls on Article 127, which is open ended in its execution: "A State Party may, by written notification addressed to the Secretary General of the United Nations, withdraw from this Statute. The withdrawal shall take effect one year after the date of receipt of the notification, unless the notification specifies a later date"—as seen with the Burundi withdrawal.[122] Central to the discussion of treaty withdrawal from the ICC by African states is the creation of a new notion of collective withdrawal as a way to demarcate their dissatisfaction with perceived inequality through selectivity.

Withdrawal from a treaty, according to Helfer, "can give a denouncing state additional voice, either by increasing its leverage to reshape the treaty to more accurately reflect its interests or those of its domestic constituencies, or by establishing a rival legal norm or institution together with other like-minded states."[123] We saw such developments over the course of the twentieth century when the League of Nations began to collapse, precisely when a large number of states—from Costa Rica and Brazil (in 1925 and 1926, respectively) to Japan and Germany (both in 1933) and then a host of other states in the late 1930s—withdrew from the organization. Such withdrawals were not necessarily coordinated, but they were also not coincidental or mutually indifferent. However, as a formal category of action, the notion of collective withdrawal has no formalized precedent. Rather, notions of "denunciation and withdrawal are . . . fundamentally unilateral acts."[124] They are not understood as collective acts, though when done within a region by successive states, in political terms they are actually seen as indicators of regional dissatisfaction. In this regard, while states have banded together to propose different legal alternatives to the dominant regimes, they have done so unilaterally by invoking the notice procedures established in the various treaties they were denouncing.

Collective withdrawal "by a smaller number of treaty parties may indicate an attempt to shift from an old equilibrium that benefits some states and disadvantages others to a new equilibrium with different distributional consequences."[125] States can sometimes band together to challenge international legal rules they perceive as unfair and objurgate international institutions that enforce those rules. The collectiveness of the action has the potential to "radically reconfigure existing forms of international cooperation."[126] This development raises questions about the norms that should shape international law and remains one of the most difficult of our time, thus the profound potential of such issues to create fissures and produce new alignments. While there are guidelines that establish treaty rules, customary rules are not static and provide an opening for social change. In this regard, once a general rule of CIL is established, continued *opinio juris* and state practice are necessary to preserve it.[127] Existing jurisprudence raises the uneasy question of whether state conduct that runs contrary to an existing rule, or reliance by states on a new principle, signifies the emergence of a new international norm, or whether it constitutes a breach of an existing rule—a strategy that describes one of the AU's legal directions.[128]

Members of the International Law Association, which is seen as being authoritative in international legal determinations, acknowledges that contrary state practice to which other states acquiesce can lead to changes in CIL.[129] As a result, it is possible that withdrawals of AU states and attempts to end ICC treaty obligations that do not follow conventional procedures set out in the Rome Statute, the Vienna Convention, and the broader customary law framework for ending treaty obligations could actually lead to a shift in those rules. This highlights the potential that such affective responses can have in changing norms. However, the prevailing thought in international law circles is that until conduct such as collective withdrawals and their associated acquiescence become sufficiently widespread to form a new rule, it will likely continue to be seen as a violation of existing international law or will need to be procured through individual state withdrawals.[130] And that is what has happened. State withdrawals from the Rome Statute for the ICC were part of a three-step strategy advanced by the African Union's ministerial group, established to report back to AU constituencies on Africa-ICC relations. The steps involved (1) reform of the Rome Statute, (2) reform of the UNSC referral system, and (3) ratification of both the Protocol on the Statute of the ACJHR and the Protocol on the Amendments on the Statute of the ACJHR by AU member states (the Malabo Protocol). They reflect AU attempts to promote equality in the international system and create new regional customs. Alongside these formations, concurrent withdrawals are also embodiments of political protest.

Such formations emerged from the AU's interest in being a shaper of international law rather than being shaped by it. In continuing this work, an important AU ministerial meeting in 2016 was concerned with African state party ICC withdrawals that resulted in a lack of consensus on the collective withdrawal of African states. Instead, individual states agreed to pursue withdrawal within a condensed time period, and one by one they began to submit their declarations of withdrawal to the UN secretary-general. First it was Burundi, then South Africa, then Gambia. In response, states such as Botswana and Senegal began to speak out against the withdrawal efforts. These acts of dissent were meant to ensure explicit recognition of the absence of consensus among African states. For it is well known among international law actors that "a small group of nations within a given region can threaten to object vocally to, and thereby derail, [its] attempts . . . to deviate from existing CIL rules."[131] What remains unclear is what fraction of states "need to explicitly object in order to prevent a new rule of CIL from forming," but ongoing legal commentaries about this matter suggest that "the fraction of nations that needs to object to bar the formation of a new CIL rule is significantly less than a majority, but greater than a handful."[132] These ambiguities have shaped the backdrop by which some AU states have sought to articulate their withdrawal strategy in relation to the possible and eventual formation of a new regional custom.

This chapter has considered the African Court's extension of its criminal jurisdiction and related forms of judicial action and protest in relation to the emotional and cultural sensibilities that sustain networks, shape practices, and transform attitudes around Africa's future. As we saw, AU representatives have responded to legal encapsulation through strategies that support African visions for a fair international system and new regional customs that, while contradictory and messy, shape alliances in critical ways. What we see is that bringing international law into African landscapes is about codifying various practices shaped in Europe and making them relevant to African lifeworlds. This importation of codified jurisprudence promoted through legal technocratic practices is not simply about the unimpassioned mimicry of European governance projects. It is also about intentional attempts to participate in biopolitical governance in the management of African lifeworlds while also refusing those forms of legality deemed not useful or irrelevant. Instead, it involves adapting and vernacularizing the law to put in place forms of legality that can be instrumentalized for African contexts in relation to very different histories and conditions of state formation. But with this comes emotionally-propelled innovations that respond in extreme ways to what is seen as structural injustice—such as Article 46A *bis*.

The introduction of Article 46A *bis* is an extraordinary act that reflects affective reattributive practices that are propelled through particular Pan-Africanist tropes and highlight African self-determination. Though they reflect core tenets of Europe's logics and traditions, these instrumentalizations of international law should also be seen through their relative forms of technocratic protest and the affective spaces that are opened up by some of the African elite, as no cultural practices are without tenets from other places. Justice making emerges out of rhizomatic formations, and through that messiness it reinscribes structural and emotional complexity.

With attention to the complex processes by which such projects are propelled, we have seen how issues that lie at the core problematic of the ICC and the formation of the African Court—struggles over inequality and selectivity—shape the emotional embodiments of affective justice that have propelled the formation of new institutions. To dismiss affective actions like reattributions, amendments, and withdrawals as irrelevant because they contravene international legality is to ignore the critical role of affective justice in the making and unmaking of international law.

Epilogue

Toward an Anthropology of International Justice

Something that transformed the way that I understood justice in my life? . . .
In that book there's a part where this young boy was running after this young
girl for some money [that] somebody had given them for helping to carry
some luggage. And the girl had escaped with this money and the guy was
chasing [her] when this old woman stepped in to stop this fight.

The old woman said, "Why do you do this?" So the boy went through this
explanation and at some point the old woman asked the young boy, "Where
is your dad?"

And the young man said, "My dad is dead." And the old woman asked,
"How did he die?" The young man explained that he was working in this
industry and his hand was chopped off and they could not provide medical
treatment for him.

And then the woman said something to the young man, and this is what
really influenced my life, having gone through the conflict [in Sierra Leone]
when I lost my dad.

So the woman said to the young man, "The day you ask yourself why your
dad died, you need to ask yourself: Why was it possible for him to die? And
then ask yourself: What should I do that another will not die under such circumstances? That day you will become a man."

I do what I do now to make sure that others do not go through what I went
through.

—Interview with activist and survivor of violence, Sierra Leone

This story, told to me with emotive bodily expressions and accentuated vocal fluctuations by a prominent African civil society activist, represents one person's take on what justice means, apart from its judicialization. It emphasizes the perspective that the circumstances of structural injustice related to the death of the boy's father are not insignificant when it comes to understanding notions of culpability and justice. What it also highlights is that these symbols and manifestations of justice are not communicated without particular bodily affects. What I have shown is that meanings of justice circulate through various biopolitical instruments but are also embodied, felt, and communicated in particular ways. People take those circumstances into account when considering not only how inequality should be addressed, but how justice should be realigned, and what social action to take—aesthetically, performatively, discursively. This message, then, highlights the issues at the heart of this book.

Throughout the chapters I have demonstrated how justice is constructed through affective formulations that are tied to various component parts that interact, converge, and diverge. The various component parts highlighted throughout the book constitute an international criminal law assemblage that comes together within that which is loosely called international justice. In these enmeshed spaces are the production, uses, and rethinking of justice as well as the emotions and regimes that propel its meanings. And though various tools to instrumentalize justice (such as laws, policies, rules), it has also become clear that international criminal law is not just about what the law says—it's not just about its black-letter manifestation. Law is not a tool that creates justice in and of itself. Law operates within unequal fields of power and governance. It reproduces the power that shapes it and also embodies spaces where global inequality can play out. It embodies social relations, and, at times, can be deployed strategically within those very unequal fields of power. For while the law is meant to protect the social contract as well as to address breaches in it, it can also enable their reproduction—for positive and negative.[1] As this book has shown, this dynamic is not new in the Global South—especially in Africa—where international law is being imaginatively inserted and engaged in daily life.

After decolonization in African states, new institutions of governance and regulation determined the way that postcolonial laws in Africa were structured. This was one of the ways that global inequality was reproduced. Law was deployed not just as an instrument of rules and norms, but also as a formulation of what law would be in new postcolonial domains. As we see in this book, law is a cultural artifact that embodies inequalities. As such, the story of justice in the African postcolony is a story about colonial and imperial law and the contemporary order of things. It is a story about political and economic restructuring made to align earlier forms of effective colonial control to the contemporary management of an international domain within which Africa's violence can trigger ICC action. As I have shown, this happens not because the court and its actors are targeting Africa. This happens because of the conditions of inequality in contemporary modernity. These forms of inequality are not just structural. They are biopolitical and operate through particular regimes of practice. Various instrumentalities and embodied modes of expression play a role in structuring what Michel Foucault called the conditions of possibility.[2] The rest is embedded in the afterlives of modernity, which is where affects, bodies, technologies, and governance effects come into sharp relief. For example, the racial imaginaries that have emerged at this junction of international justice and that are prominently displayed in relation to who the ICC indicts and who the victims of violence are, not unrelated to the modes of seeing, engaging, feeling, and speaking that are part of international rule of law assemblages. These affective modes of being shape the way that emotions produce particular institutional materialities and, as such, they invigorate the technocratic tools that circulate in the making of international criminal law.

Understanding these processes allows us to make sense of how affective states can be used to redraw lines of alliance and disjuncture. They highlight the way that figures and imaginaries, narrativized in particular ways, can contribute to the intensification of responses or the undermining of feelings. Here law is not just shaped by instrumental tools to be used by those who are formally trained in its logic. Law is also shaped by those engaged in its refusals, as well as those formal and expressive acts, such as renouncements, treaty withdrawals, and Twitter objections. These engagements with law highlight the way that protest speech can be deployed to subvert particular legal relationships and can reconfigure the terms by which it takes shape. Ultimately, we see how these affectivities that extend to technocratic knowledge and doctrine are ultimately tied to materialities that have real-world impact. One such afterlife is concerned with the residual life of the law and the pronounced or latent feelings that it instigates.

I have shown that to make sense of these dynamics we need to understand the life of the law through studying what various international and regional courts and their actors do. By studying their technocratic afterlives we can go beyond the black-letter language of the law to explore the technologies, governance, discourses, edicts, and emotional regimes that play key roles in establishing and legitimating meanings of justice. These justice formations produce alignments with particular symbolic regimes of power, which determine how and under what conditions such affective justice takes shape.

What we see is that affective justice shapes how justice feels, how justice is manifest in the everyday, and how it is decoupled from place and relocated in new feeling spaces. Through this process, the components that connect with such productions and circulations are fundamentally intertwined with the affective and sociocultural universes that shape it. So just as law is also what people make of it, how they see it, and how its force or pronouncements feel, justice is also about the production of meaning in the context of bodily and emotional responses to the social condition. But the processes of the production of law and justice are where the conflict lies, for not only are legal differences socially constituted, they are also constituted by and within particular structures of inequality. These logics contribute to the materialities of feeling and the domains within which they circulate and are rendered legible. For example, the ICC was created to respond to situations in postviolence states with decimated legal systems that cannot indict their own leadership or in places where violence is so widespread that a sense of collective responsibility pervades. But it is the conditions under which African stakeholders are in this predicament that raises fundamental questions about the place of inequality in our world. And further, those victimized by mass atrocity violence at the heart of ICC actions are often those who live in poverty and whose governmental officials have failed to protect them—whether in Africa or elsewhere. These structures of inequality exist alongside micropolitics of possibility and biopolitical domains that shape the resultant feelings that emerge.

Emotional invocations of and responses to injustice become the space for the materialization of justice, but their articulations are embedded in particular histories and power relations, providing the grammar through which social norms are instantiated and imaginaries brought to life. It is through the reinforcement of emotional regimes, which operate within particular frameworks of expectations and are propelled through various political and economic campaigns, that international justice is articulated. These articulations—often taking the form of protest campaigns, treaty withdrawals, photo imagery, or affirmations of values—reconstitute international publics through social movement campaigns and are supported by new technocratic tools such as international legal provisions and advocacy strategies. These modalities work through emotional expressions that become the basis for narrativizing justice imperatives and creating new social imaginaries of feeling that are expressed and regulated in particular ways.

While these imaginaries travel and often become decontextualized from their local cultural domains, they are then recontextualized in particular components of assemblages. The power to articulate narratives of justice or spheres of judicial or nonjudicial action is not benign. Rather, it operates in keeping with particular time and space horizons that are produced as relevant to the political mission of justice—and it is here that locating the effectiveness of the structures of emotion that shape social geographies of justice is critical. As such, looking at justice in relation to judicial and nonjudicial spaces reveals the relevance of history and politics in shaping the emotional meaning of social location. Judicial spaces operate within particular affective realms rooted in histories, memories, and experiences. Regardless of whether various stakeholders or audiences experienced those histories, the conditions of judicial possibility can be rationalized alongside shadows of the past—memories of colonialism, realities of economic disparity, complexities of violence and racial exclusion. For some, the vestiges of colonial inequalities, the workings of racialization, and the modernity of contemporary power operate and structure the postcolonial conditions within which individuals make seemingly free decisions. These decisions are shaped by psychic worlds and beliefs as much as they are by judicial constraints, political and economic considerations, and new digitized possibilities.

Justice making has also become increasingly accessible and therefore immediately sharable. Biomediated campaigns enable new forms of meaning making that transform the workings of the social imaginary. This reality calls on us to rethink the way that we privilege national state decisions to comply or not comply with international treaty provisions. Instead, through a range of competing ideations beyond the state or modern ontologies, it is important to render relevant the rhizomatic interrelations between state institutions, leaders, and everyday people.

Beyond the complexities of actors, spatiality and temporality are also critical. *Affective Justice* has made a case for understanding the relationships between space, time, modernity, and justice. In relation to various African encounters with the ICC, it makes a difference that the geographical spaces and persons under scrutiny by the court are African or from the continent of Africa. In the case of the AU, the Pan-Africanist pushback is about the politics of determining which crimes, committed when and why, by whom, and under what conditions are deemed relevant to the African continent, to African geography. It is also about the power to submit to the jurisdiction of one's own courts as well as to create new spaces in which the psychic life of possibility and change are forged. By focusing on these affectivities, especially in relation to the complex politics of protest in response to law's hegemony, nowhere is this more accentuated than in various parts of postcolonial Africa, in which both the law and its constituting political order are at play.

What we are seeing today through the ICC-AU pushback, then, is actually the playing out of a politics of recognition in which the legitimacy of various African stakeholders managing Africa's violence is negotiated in contemporary terms using the tools of global governance like the UN and the ICC. The key analytic challenge in making sense of the ICC, the AU, or the logic of an African Court in the twenty-first century is to understand the ways in which various multiply inspired commitments to justice imaginaries relate not to age-old senses of identity but to emotional performances and their regimentation. This involves making sense of the ways that relationships and emotional responses structure and are structured by feelings that have the power to command particular social relations and engage with the reality of the internationalization of daily life.

It behooves us to understand the way that Pan-Africanist forms of re-attributive initiatives are being crafted spatially. The recognition of these realities requires that we take seriously the complexities of the politics of the social and the affective life that informs those decisions. That is to say, we must take seriously which economies, moralities, social imaginaries, and psychic meanings shape decision making and how those decisions are legitimized with the moral force of the past. For they are part of the play of power that structures future possibilities in particular ways, all while exacerbating preexisting inequalities and psychic differences in responsibility, obligation, and histories. They are closely related to what Siba Grovogui has argued are age-old concerns about the future of Africa and Africans in relation to global governance and international morality.[3] And as such, they are tied to a more expansive domain by which to understand contemporary Pan-Africanism: through the social histories of European imperial power in Africa and broadening political economic and moral reparative aspirations. But it also means understanding the affective life of twentieth-century violence in Europe and the recognition that the anti-impunity fervor that has characterized the contemporary period refers to the desperate desire to make perpetrators of violence accountable to humanity. This reality however is not unrelated to the conditions of structural inequality that shape the conditions of possibility for violence in the first place. Recall the opening vignette where the old woman asked how the boy's dad died. The conclusion was that the boy's dad's death was a result of larger conditions of structural inequality—he was working in an "industry and his hand was chopped off and they could not provide medical treatment for him."

The story concludes with the woman asking the young man the key question: Why was it possible for him to die? The woman's answer was that the day you realize that justice is not just about addressing theft and violence through the law but that justice is about addressing the larger conditions within which theft and violence happen, is the day that your understanding of justice represents the issues at the core of the human condition.

Thus, my goal here has been to keep in tension these complexities of justice as a way to rethink the anthropology of international justice through the recognition of injustice. I have been interested in examining the multiplicities of contestations at the heart of the intertwined spaces between legal power and social displacement, and the challenges brought to bear on the conditions of modernity that make social reality legible, that is, the way that certain things are encapsulated by the law as legal, and made legible, while other things are seen as unrelated and dismissed as illegitimate. The reality is that in postcolonial Africa, as in other parts of the world, the judicial is one of many domains for ordering and performing power. But of particular interest here is the way that the judicialization of African politics increasingly occupies a space in the imagination as a site of international control. Interestingly, the production of the image of the African "victim" and the male "perpetrator" of violence, as well as a notion of an "international community" are part of the forging of international justice imaginaries whose work is being propelled through the social life of the law, which itself is dynamic. Its greatest power is in its commanding of order and objectivity. But this production is also part of the discursive power of its encapsulation through which certainty, fairness, procedural regularity, and an overriding sense of objectivity are produced. Its greatest effects are in its ability to produce a totalizing ideological order through which other logics are displaced—rendered marginal or irrelevant to the juridical order.

My concluding thoughts dwell in the middle space of the international rule of law assemblage, between the concerned recognition by African leaders, various African voting publics, Pan-Africanist activists, and intellectuals of the many harsh and contradictory realities on the African continent, the spaces of violence and social movements to rectify it, and the realities of international demands to create a world in which we can hold perpetrators of violence accountable. This middle space is where the affective life of law dwells—where alignments are made and others unraveled. Law's meanings and forms emerge from and constitute these emotional spaces, which are regimented according to the practices and aspirations of law's liberatory project.

Law's possibilities are found in emotional aspirations for social change, not in its core instrumentality. And this is where the key issues are about how we feel and what we do about what we feel. And these feelings are not absent from the historical and contemporary deployment of power. They are about determining the conditions under which the law is deployed, with what institutions, under whose jurisdiction, and in which geographical spaces—that is, the power to submit to the jurisdiction of one's own courts as well as to create spaces in which the psychic life of possibilities is forged. Indeed, one of the popular conceptions of the crisis of the African postcolony today is that it stems from a problem with the incorporation of things African. This involves disjunctures between imposed or legislated understandings and familiar cultural values and practices that are not always central to the development of new norms. And just as the understanding of rights in the West unfolded according to its own contested and unforeseeable logic so that, for instance, rights that once pertained to property-owning white men were made to include others, so it is the case on African terrain. Any number of African institutions continue to be reworked and reshaped.

There is no reason to think that notions of Pan-Africanism or other principles deemed sufficiently African cannot be mobilized to play increasingly critical roles in addressing the harsh realities of human rights violations. The key analytic challenge, however, in defining the work of agents engaged in the African Union or the ICC for the twenty-first century is to understand the ways in which multiply inspired commitments produce social imaginaries and relate to other institutions, treaties, or international justice institutions. This involves making sense of the ways that relationships and emotional responses structure affects that are deployed to build social institutions and erect policies that set social values and expectations.

For once we take on the core problem of affective justice—*the reality that justice is not necessarily about the absence of injustice but its complex mobilizing assemblages*—we see that as long as various stakeholders continue to encapsulate political histories and social problems and replace them with the rule of law, then a central part of justice processes will involve reattribution, a counterresponse that reinscribes justice in different terms. By expanding the juridical domain beyond the legal, we can see how surrender requests and their refusal or desires for compliance have political histories, the effects of which can be seen in a number of key attachments and social pacts mobilized through expressions of compliance or refusals to comply. But at the center is the power to decide to submit to the jurisdiction of one's own courts and to assert the tenets of its content in ways particular to one's life worlds. By focusing on technocratic legal knowledge, affects, and the emotional regimes through which they travel, we see how those engaged in African political decision making and social change mobilizations live in a space where feelings, reactions, and histories all come together to explain practice. It is where contemporary history is being forged, where cultural institutions and interior motives shape outward practices that are as dynamic and transforming in Africa as they are elsewhere. Making sense of this in relation to practices and power and the embodied responses it conjures—in Africa and beyond—is a challenge for twenty-first century social thought.

Notes

Acknowledgments

1 "Republicans Wage Anti–'Secret Science' Campaign against the EPA," Politics, HuffPost, June 25, 2014, https://www.huffingtonpost.com/2014/06/25/secret -science-epa_n_5529521.html.

Preface

1 Commentary, The African Court and Its Geographies of Justice, public forum in Addis Ababa, fall 2014.
2 Commentary, The African Court and Its Geographies of Justice.
3 Hannah Appel, lecture commentary to author, UCLA, October 2016.
4 Appel, lecture commentary.
5 Cantero, "Specters of the Market."
6 Mazzarella, "Affect," 299.
7 Asad, Formations of the Secular, 185.

Introduction. Formations, Dislocations, and Unravelings

1 ICC, Warrant of Arrest for Ali Kushayb (ICC-02/05-01/07-3).
2 ICC, Warrant of Arrest for Omar Hassan Ahmad Al Bashir (Al Bashir 9, ICC-02 /05-01/09-1).
3 ICC, Assembly of States Parties, Resolution 5, "Activation of the Jurisdiction of the Court over the Crime of Aggression," ICC-ASP/16/Res.5, December 14, 2017, https://asp.icc-cpi.int/iccdocs/asp_docs/Resolutions/ASP16/ICC-ASP-16-Res5 -ENG.pdf. After receiving the milestone ratification from Palestine in June 2016, the Assembly of States Parties, in their sixteenth session, decided to activate the court's jurisdiction over the crime of aggression as of July 17, 2018. It enters into force for those state parties that have accepted the amendments one year after the deposit of their instruments of ratification or acceptance. This is a his- toric activation that will enable the ICC to hold leaders individually criminally

responsible for the crime of aggression. Despite the calls for broader cooperation in ratifying the 2010 Kampala amendments on the crime of aggression, as of
March 31, 2019, none of the five permanent members and only three (Belgium,
Germany, and Poland) of the ten nonpermanent members of the UN Security
Council has ratified the Kampala agreement; Global Campaign for Ratification
and Implementation of the Kampala Amendments on the Crime of Aggression, "Status of Ratification and Implementation," Update No. 30, October 5,
2018, https://crimeofaggression.info/the-role-of-states/status-of-ratification-and
-implementation. United Nations, Rome Statute of the International Criminal
Court, UN Doc. A/CONF.183/9, July 17, 1998 (hereinafter Rome Statute), Art. 5,
http://legal.un.org/icc/statute/99_corr/cstatute.htm.

4 Rome Statute, Preamble, para. 6.

5 Rome Statute, Arts. 28, 25(3)(d), and 33.

6 International Criminal Court, "States Parties—Chronological List," Rome Statute,
https://asp.icc-cpi.int/en_menus/asp/states%20parties/Pages/states%20parties
%20_%20chronological%20list.aspx.

7 Arrest warrants were issued for the following individuals: Joseph Kony, Raska
Lukiya, Okot Ohiambo, Dominic Ongwen, Vincent Otti, Thomas Lubanga Dyilo,
Bosco Ntaganda, Ahmed Haroun, Ali Kushayb, Germain Katanga, Mathieu
Ngudjolo Chui, Jean-Pierre Bemba Gombo, Omar al-Bashir, Callixate Mbarushi-
mana, Muammar Gaddafi, Saif al-Islam Gaddafi, Abdullan al-Senussi, Laurent
Gbagbo, Charles Blé Goudé, Simone Gbagbo, Abdel Rahim Hussein, Sylves-
tre Mudacumura, Walter Barasa, Narcisse Arido, Jean-Jacques Kagongo, Aimé
Kilolo Musamba, and Fidèle Wandu. Summonses to appear were issued for Bahr
Idriss Abu Garda, Abdallah Banda, Saleh Jerbo, Mohammed Ali, Uhuru Kenyatta, Henry Kosgey, Francis Muthaura, William Samoei Ruto, and Joshua Sang.
As of March 2019, the following were on trial: Abdallah Banda, Bosco Ntaganda, and Dominic Ongwen. Thomas Luganga Dyilo and Germain Katanga
were convicted and serving sentences of fourteen and twelve years, respectively. Mathieu Ngudjolo Chui, Jean-Pierre Bemba Gombo, Laurent Gbagbo,
and Blé Goudé were acquitted. Charges were dismissed against Bahr Abu Garda,
Callixte Mbarushimana, Mohammed Ali, Henry Kosgey, William Samoei Ruto,
and Joshua Sang. Charges were withdrawn against Uhuru Kenyatta and Francis Muthaura. The case against Abdullah al-Senussi was declared inadmissible.
Finally, proceedings against Raska Lukiya, Saleh Jerbo, and Muammar Gaddafi
were terminated due to the death of the individuals.

8 Regarding countries outside of Africa, as of 2016, the ICC's Office of the Prosecutor was conducting eight preliminary examinations, including an assessment of
information about alleged war crimes by UK nationals during the conflict in Iraq
from 2003 to 2008; the violence committed in Ukraine since February 20, 2014;
an investigation in Afghanistan, in which they have indicated there is reasonable basis to believe that war crimes and crimes against humanity were and continue to be committed there; an examination of violence and alleged crimes in
the occupied Palestinian territory since June 13, 2014; and monitoring of national

prosecutions of crimes in Colombia. However, for the first thirteen years of its existence, all of the ICC cases involved Africans. This has shaped the charges that the ICC is engaged in the selective targeting of Africans. For updates on the investigations, see International Criminal Court (https://www.icc-cpi.int/).

9　On April 12, 2019, the ICC judges' refusal to permit the prosecutor of the ICC to open an investigation into US crimes in Afghanistan underscore the feeling that there are double standards in international law. See International Criminal Court (https://www.icc-cpi.int/).

10　Kimani, "Pursuit of Justice or Western Plot?"

11　"Sudanese President Bashir Charged with Darfur War Crimes: International Criminal Court Issues Warrant Alleging War Crimes and Crimes against Humanity," *The Guardian*, March 4, 2009, https://www.theguardian.com/world/2009/mar/04/omar-bashir-sudan-president-arrest. ICC, Decision on the Prosecution Application under Article 58(7) of the Statute, Harun (ICC-02/05-01/07-1).

12　ICC, Harun (ICC-02/05-01/07-1).

13　Jalloh, Akande, and Du Plessis, "Assessing the African Union Concerns about Article 16," 7.

14　Akhavan, "Are International Criminal Tribunals a Disincentive to Peace?," 648.

15　Murungi, "10 Years of the International Criminal Court."

16　Kimani, "Pursuit of Justice or Western Plot?"

17　Jalloh, Akande, and Du Plessis, "Assessing the African Union Concerns about Article 16," 8.

18　Note that a Kenyan court held that Kenya is under international obligation to arrest al-Bashir whenever he visits Kenya. Some scholars argue that he has immunity and that Act 98(1) of the Rome Statute protects him. This is a counterargument by Dapo Akande that the Security Council referral suspends his immunity. See Akande, "The Legal Nature of Security Council Referrals to the ICC"; Akande, "The Bashir Indictment"; Akande, "The Jurisdiction of the International Criminal Court over Nationals of Non-Parties." See also Jalloh, Akande, and Du Plessis, "Assessing the African Union Concerns about Article 16," 8.

19　Kimani, "Pursuit of Justice or Western Plot?"

20　Kimani, "Pursuit of Justice or Western Plot?"

21　As stated by Colonel General Omar Zein Abedeen of Sudan's Transitional Council. See public speech, Associated Press, April 12, 2019.

22　Derrida, *Specters of Marx*; Rawls, *Theory of Justice*; Rawls, *Political Liberalism*; Rawls, *The Law of Peoples*; Derrida, "Force of Law."

23　Locke, *Two Treatises of Civil Government*; Locke, *The Works of John Locke*; Russell, *Marriage and Morals*; Russell, *An Inquiry into Meaning and Truth*; Russell, *The Problems of Philosophy*; Wittgenstein, *Philosophical Investigations*; Malcolm, *Ludwig Wittgenstein*; Frege, Black, and Geach, *Translations from the Philosophical Writings of Gottlob Frege*; Frege, *Logical Investigations*.

24　Nosek, Hawkins, and Frazier, "Implicit Social Cognition"; O'Connor and Aardema, "The Imagination"; Bargh et al., "Automaticity in Social-Cognitive Processes"; Nanda et al., "Lessons from Neuroscience."

25 The AU decided to merge the currently functional African Court of Human and Peoples' Rights, which was established in 2004, and the African Court of Justice, which was envisioned in the Constitutive Act of the African Union but not established, in 2008. This was mostly due to concern over the cost required to maintain two continental judicial bodies. Before the Merger Protocol came into force, African states agreed to revise the composition of the court once again with the aim of expanding the subject matter jurisdiction of the proposed court. In 2014, the AU adopted the Protocol on Amendments to the Protocol on the Statute of the African Court of Justice and Human Rights (ACJHR). In addition to human rights (jurisdiction currently being exercised by the African Court on Human and Peoples' Rights) and general affairs (jurisdiction essentially to be exercised by the African Court of Justice), the newly proposed court would also have jurisdiction over international crimes. The amended protocol has yet to be ratified by any African state. See Werle and Vormbaum, *The African Criminal Court*.

26 Deleuze and Guattari, "The Geology of Morals," in *A Thousand Plateaus*.

27 De Landa, *A New Philosophy of Society*.

28 De Landa, *A New Philosophy of Society*.

29 Deleuze and Guattari, *A Thousand Plateaus*.

30 Bourdieu, *Outline of a Theory of Practice*.

31 Eltringham, "When We Walk Out."

32 Kersten, *Justice in Conflict*.

33 Fraser, *Scales of Justice*; Valverde, *Chronotopes of Law*. See also Jonas Bens, "Gerechtigkeitsgefühle und die Legitimität des Internationalen Strafgerichtshofs in Norduganda," *Gerechtigkeitsgefühle: Zur affektiven und emotionalen Legitimität von Normen*, January 2017, transcript; Latour, *Reassembling the Social*.

34 Deleuze and Guattari, *A Thousand Plateaus*, 8.

35 Shaw, *Colonial Inscriptions*; Mamdani, *When Victims Become Killers*; Ciaran Cross, "'Whoever Owns the Land, the Natives Do Not': In Re Southern Rhodesia," Critical Legal Thinking, July 26, 2018, http://criticallegalthinking.com/2018/07/26/whoever-owns-the-land-the-natives-do-not-in-re-southern-rhodesia/; Burgis, *The Looting Machine*; Privy Council, In re Southern Rhodesia.

36 See Shaw, *Colonial Inscriptions*.

37 Li, "Practices of Assemblage and Community Forest Management"; Li, "What Is Land?"; Ong and Collier, *Global Assemblages*; Puar, *Terrorist Assemblages*; De Landa, *A New Philosophy of Society*; Marcus and Saka, "Assemblage"; Ong and Roy, *Worlding Cities*.

38 UN General Assembly, Convention on the Prevention and Punishment of the Crime of Genocide, December 9, 1948, 78 UNTS 277.

39 ICRC, *Geneva Convention I for the Amelioration of the Condition of the Wounded and Sick in Armed Forces in the Field*, August 12, 1949, Art. 49. See also ICRC, *Geneva Convention II for the Amelioration of Wounded, Sick and Shipwrecked Members of the Armed Forces at Sea*, August 12, 1949, Art. 50; ICRC, *Geneva Convention III Relative to the Treatment of Prisoners of War*, August 12, 1949, Art. 129;

ICRC, *Geneva Convention IV Relative to the Protection of Civilian Persons in Time of War*, August 12, 1949.

40 ICRC, "Rule 158, Prosecution of War Crimes," in IHL Database: Customary IHL, https://ihl-databases.icrc.org/customary-ihl/eng/docs/v1_rul_rule158.

41 Ross, *Mixed Emotions*.

42 On sociocultural anthropology, see Williams, "A Philosophy of Emotion"; Sahlins, *Culture and Practical Reason*; Stewart, *Ordinary Affects*; Stewart, "In the World That Affect Proposed"; Rosaldo, "Introduction"; Lutz and White, "The Anthropology of Emotions"; Obeyesekere, "Depression, Buddhism, and the Work of Culture," 135; Scheper-Hughes, *Death without Weeping*; Abu-Lughod, *Veiled Sentiments*; Schieffelin, *The Sorrow of the Lonely and the Burning of the Dancers*; Geertz, *The Interpretation of Cultures*. On emotion research, see Critical Legal Conference Utrecht, "'Great Expectations': Multiple Modernities of Law," Utrech University, September 2010, http://uu.academia.edu/CriticalLegalConference2010: Barreto, Jose-Manuel, "The Turn to Emotions"; Bertolino, "Body, Emotions, and Human Rights Justice"; Davies, "The Rational Primacy of Emotion in Law and Governance"; Ridler, "Justice as Sentiment." See also Clough and Halley, *The Affective Turn*; Gregg and Seigworth, *The Affect Theory Reader*.

43 Throop, *Suffering and Sentiment*; Hollan, "Emerging Issues in the Cross-Cultural Study of Empathy"; Hollan, "Vicissitudes of 'Empathy' in a Rural Toraja Village"; Hollan and Throop, "Whatever Happened to Empathy?"

44 Shaw, "Memory Frictions"; Nordstrom, *A Different Kind of War Story*.

45 Richard Wilson's unpublished essay titled, "The Anthropology of Justice after Atrocity."

46 See Richard Wilson, "The Anthropology of Justice after Atrocity," in *Oxford Handbook of Law and Anthropology*, edited by Marie-Claire Foblets, Mark Goodale, Olaf Zenker, and Maria Sapignoli (forthcoming).

47 Exemplary studies include Ulla Berg and Ana Ramos-Zayas, "Racializing Affect," on the interrelationship between emotion and the sociocultural production of sensual moods; Segal, "The Burden of Being Exemplary," an analysis of the expected performance of wifely strength through the suppression of emotions by Palestinian women married to Palestinian men jailed in Israel; and Alessandra Gribaldo, "The Paradoxical Victim," a look at violence and victimhood in Italy, in which she examines the expectation of particular forms of performative speech. See also Friedner, "Deaf Bodies and Corporate Bodies"; Magee, "Of Love and Fur"; Englund, "Multivocal Morality"; and Kravel-Tovi, "Corrective Conversion."

48 Ahmed, *The Promise of Happiness*; Ahmed, *The Cultural Politics of Emotion*; Ahmed, "Affective Economies."

49 Foucault, *The History of Sexuality*, 140.

50 Foucault, *Discipline and Punish*, 252–253.

51 Foucault, *The History of Sexuality*.

52 Schuller, *The Biopolitics of Feeling*.

53 Harding, *The Book of Jerry Falwell*.

54 Clarke, "Refiguring the Perpetrator."

55 Spinoza, *A Theologico-Political Treatise*; Spinoza and Parkinson, *Ethics*; Spinoza, *The Collected Works of Spinoza*; Deleuze and Guattari, *A Thousand Plateaus*.

56 Hirschkind, *Ethical Soundscape*, 85; also see Massumi, *The Politics of Affect*; and Massumi, "The Autonomy of Affect."

57 Leys, *The Turn to Affect*.

58 Massumi, *Parables for the Virtual*, 29.

59 Reddy, *The Navigation of Feeling*, 129.

60 The Silencing the Guns campaign represents the AU's efforts to address violence in Africa before 2020.

61 Nussbaum, *Political Emotions*; Wilson and Brown, *Humanitarianism and Suffering*; Laqueur, "Mourning, Pity, and the Work of Narrative"; Valverde, *Chronotopes of Law*.

62 Foucault, *Archaeology of Knowledge*; Foucault, *Discipline and Punish*.

63 See also Berg Ulla and Ramos-Zayas, "Racializing Affect"; and Berlant, *Compassion*.

64 Assembly of the African Union, "Decisions and Declarations," Thirteenth Ordinary Session, Sirte, Great Socialist People's Libyan Arab Jamahiriya, July 1–3, 2009, 8, https://au.int/sites/default/files/decisions/9560-assembly_en_1_3_july_2009_auc_thirteenth_ordinary_session_decisions_declarations_message_congratulations_motion_0.pdf.

65 The ICC had already passed a decision of noncooperation against Malawi six months earlier because the country failed to arrest and surrender al-Bashir when he was attending a summit of the Common Market for Eastern and Southern Africa in the capital city, Lilongwe. See International Criminal Court, "Situation in Darfur, Sudan," Corrigendum to the Decision Pursuant to Article 87(7) of the Rome Statute on the Failure by the Republic of Malawi to Comply with the Cooperation Requests Issued by the Court with Respect to the Arrest and Surrender of Omar Hassan Ahmad Al Bashir, ICC-02/05-01/09-139-Corr.

66 Joyce Banda, public statement at a press conference in Malawi in May 2012. See also "African Union Pulls Summit from Malawi in Row over Sudan's President," *The Guardian*, June 8, 2012, https://www.theguardian.com/world/2012/jun/08/african-union-malawi-summit-sudan.

67 The acronym BRICS stands for particular newly industrialized countries: Brazil, Russia, India, China, and South Africa. See M. Taddele Maru, "Why South Africa Let Bashir Get Away," *Al Jazeera*, June 15, 2015, http://www.aljazeera.com/indepth/opinion/2015/06/south-africa-bashir-150615102211840.html.

68 United Nations Human Rights Council, "United Nations Independent Investigation on Burundi (UNIIB) Established Pursuant to Human Rights Council Resolution S-24/1," A/HRC/33/37, Thirty-Third Session, accessed January 25, 2018, http://www.ohchr.org/EN/HRBodies/HRC/UNIIB/Pages/UNIIB.aspx.

69 "Communique de Presse de la Réunion du Conseil des Ministres du Jeudi 06 Octobre, 2016," Gouvernement du Burundi, Bujumbura, October 7, 2016, http://www.burundi.gov.bi/spip.php?article1534. See also ICC, "Situation in the Repub-

lic of Burundi," ICC-01/17, 2017, https://www.icc-cpi.int/burundi; James Butty, "Burundi Officially Informs UN of Intent to Leave ICC," Voice of America, October 27, 2016, https://www.voanews.com/a/burundi-icc-withdrawal/3568311.html; "Burundi Is Officially Not a Member of the International Criminal Court," *Africa News*, October 27, 2017, http://www.africanews.com/2017/10/27/burundi-is-officially-not-a-member-of-the-international-criminal-court-icc/.

70 United Nations, "Declaratory Statement by the Republic of South Africa on the Decision to Withdraw from the Rome Statute." In law, a declaratory statement is known as a letter of notification.

71 United Nations, "Declaratory Statement by the Republic of South Africa on the Decision to Withdraw from the Rome Statute."

72 "Gambia to Withdraw from International Criminal Court," *Daily Monitor*, October 26, 2016, http://www.monitor.co.ug/News/World/Gambia-withdraw-International-Criminal-Court/688340-3430480-oljwloz/index.html. "Gambia Announces Withdrawal from International Criminal Court," Reuters, October 25, 2016, https://www.reuters.com/article/us-gambia-icc/gambia-announces-withdrawal-from-international-criminal-court-idUSKCN12P335.

73 Yang, "On the Principle of Complementarity in the Rome Statute of the International Criminal Court," 122. On sovereignty, see Shaw, "International Law," 902.

74 Hamilton, "Case Admissibility at the International Criminal Court," 306–308.

75 Triffterer and Ambos, "The Rome Statute of the International Criminal Court: A Commentary," 803–804.

76 International Criminal Court, "States Parties—Chronological List," n.d., https://asp.icc-cpi.int/en_menus/asp/states%20parties/Pages/states%20parties%20_%20chronological%20list.aspx.

77 Fatou Bensouda, speech, Albany Law School, Albany, New York, 2015.

78 See Simpson, "The Sentimental Life of International Law"; also see Ross, *Mixed Emotions*.

79 Observational notes on file with the author. See also "US President Trump Rejects Globalism in Speech to UN General Assembly's Annual Debate," *UN News*, September 25, 2018, https://news.un.org/en/story/2018/09/1020472; "Full Text of John Bolton's Speech to the Federalist Society," *Al Jazeera*, September 10, 2018, https://www.aljazeera.com/news/2018/09/full-text-john-bolton-speech-federalist-society-180910172828633.html.

80 Mbembe and Dubois, *Critique of Black Reason*, at 32.

81 Mbembe and Dubois, *Critique of Black Reason*, at 32.

82 Mbembe and Dubois, *Critique of Black Reason*.

83 For earlier work on discourse and its operationalization, see also Goffman, *Frame Analysis*; or Luhmann, *Social Systems*.

84 Cooper, *Africa in the World*.

85 Thanks to Erin Baines, private communication, June 2017, for her further clarification of the key point here.

86 Brants, "Guilty Landscapes."

87 See Chris McGreal, "Is Kagame Africa's Lincoln or a Tyrant Exploiting Rwanda's Tragic History?," *The Guardian*, May 19, 2013, https://www.theguardian.com /world/2013/may/19/kagame-africa-rwanda. See also Robert Mbaraga, "International Law Biased against Africa," *East African*, August 6, 2016.

88 See also scholarly discussions about the judicialization of politics in Comaroff and Comaroff, *Law and Disorder in the Postcolony*; Randeria, "De-politicization of Democracy and Judicialization of Politics"; Blichner and Molander, "Mapping Juridification"; Eckert et al., *Law against the State*.

89 African Union meeting notes on file with author.

90 Yoweri Museveni, interview with author.

91 See also Clair MacDougall, "Uganda's President Holds On in the Face of Growing Public Unrest," *Time*, March 4, 2016, http://time.com/4246766/uganda -president-yoweri-museveni/.

92 Mamdani, *When Victims Become Killers*.

93 Hannah Appel, lecture commentary, UCLA, October 2016.

94 Massumi, *The Autonomy of Affect*, 90.

95 Mazzarella, "Affect," 299.

96 See Verges, *De la stratégie judiciaire*.

97 Sikkink, *The Justice Cascade*.

98 An emerging body of literature on the sociology of emotions has unpacked how the microcreation of sense making through emotion becomes shared and ultimately institutionalized; see Colombetti, *The Feeling Body*; Bandes, *The Passions of Law*; Bandes and Blumenthal, "Emotion and Law"; Maroney, "Law and Emotion"; and Popovski, "Emotions and International Law."

99 Li, "What Is Land?"

100 Political crimes are compared with crimes that are considered the root causes of violence. They are seen as enabling violence, but do not directly address the crimes that are central to Africa's economic resource wars and illegal economies; instead, they manifest as the political actions that produce violence.

101 Legum, *Pan-Africanism*, 14–15.

102 Legum, *Pan-Africanism*, 14–15.

103 Legum, *Pan-Africanism*.

104 Constable, *Our Word Is Our Bond*, 11; Richland, "Jurisdiction."

105 Mbembe and Dubois, *Critique of Black Reason*.

106 Hochschild, "Emotion Work, Feeling Rules, and Social Structure."

107 Fischer, *Emergent Forms of Life and the Anthropological Voice*; Haraway, *Modest_Witness@Second_Millennium.FemaleMan©_ Meets_OncoMouse*; Masco, *The Nuclear Borderlands*; Cazdyn, *The Already Dead*; Rajan, *Lively Capital*.

108 Dominic Ongwen's case provides an excellent example of how one can be both a victim (he was abducted as a child) and a perpetrator (he allegedly climbed the ranks of the LRA to be Joseph Kony's second in command) and the role of understandings and temporality in the construction of the perpetrator.

Chapter 1. Genealogies of Anti-Impunity

1 Bärbel Bohley was known to have said, "We wanted justice and got the rule of law." She was strongly criticized for saying that, as the governing sentiment about the (West German) rule of law was that while it was oriented toward justice, the rules of the law had to be respected because achieving legality was more import-ant than bending the law in order to secure justice. As quoted in "Bärbel Bohley," *The Economist*, September 23, 2010, http://www.economist.com/node/17090837; and in German, original quote, "Wir wollten Gerechtigkeit und bekamen den Rechtsstaat"; Claus Christian Malzahn, "Sie wollte Gerechtigkeit und bekam den Rechtsstaat," *Welt*, September 11, 2010, https://www.welt.de/politik/deutschland /article9566915/Sie-wollte-Gerechtigkeit-und-bekam-den-Rechtsstaat.html.

2 William Ruto, ICC Status Conference in Ruto/Sang case, P 46/47, May 14, 2013.

3 William Pace, Assembly of States Parties Address, November 2013.

4 David Smith, "New Chief Prosecutor Defends International Criminal Court," *The Guardian*, May 23, 2012.

5 Kendall and Nouwen, "Representational Practices at the International Criminal Court."

6 Uhuru Kenyatta, ICC Status Conference, February 5, 2014, The Hague, Nether-lands. Note also that the name Mungiki (mūngĩkĩ) referred to in the Kikuyu lan-guage means "a united people." In the 1980s, it emerged as a secretive religious cult group and eventually took on characteristics closer to a gang-like secretive society. It is now banned.

7 Waddell and Clark, *Courting Conflict?*, 11.

8 Baxi, "What May the 'Third World' Expect from International Law?"

9 Franceschet, "The Rule of Law, Inequality, and the International Criminal Court."

10 Meister, *After Evil*.

11 Clarke, *Fictions of Justice*.

12 Clarke, *Fictions of Justice*.

13 Sikkink, *The Justice Cascade*, 11.

14 Engle, Miller, and Davis, *Anti-Impunity and the Human Rights Agenda*.

15 Thabo Mbeki and Mahmood Mamdani, "Courts Can't End Civil Wars," Opinion, *New York Times*, February 5, 2014.

16 Teitel, "Transitional Justice Genealogy."

17 International Criminal Tribunals and Special Courts, Global Policy Forum, accessed August 30, 2017, https://www.globalpolicy.org/international-justice /international-criminal-tribunals-and-special-courts.html.

18 Teitel, "Humanity's Law," 355; and Malamud-Goti, "Transitional Governments in the Breach."

19 Luckham et al., "Conflict and Poverty in Sub-Saharan Africa," 17.

20 N'Diaye, "Not a Miracle after All."

21 Savo Heleta, "Roots of Sudanese Conflict Are in the British Colonial Policies," *Sudan Tribune*, January 12, 2008, http://www.sudantribune.com/spip.php?article 25558.

22 From independence to the present, France has intervened in African countries using military force in over thirty situations. It has military bases in Djibouti, Senegal, Gabon, Mayotte, and Réunion, and army deployments in Somalia, the Ivory Coast, Chad, the Central African Republic, and Malia.

23 See International Bank for Reconstruction and Development, "The Berg Report and the Model of Accumulation."

24 Rodrik, "Goodbye Washington Consensus, Hello Washington Confusion?"

25 Mueller, "The IMF, Neoliberalism and Hegemony."

26 Krever, "The Legal Turn in Late Development Theory."

27 Chalfin, *Neoliberal Frontiers*; Ferguson, *Global Shadows*; Comaroff and Comaroff, *Millennial Capitalism and the Culture of Neoliberalism*.

28 Krever, "The Legal Turn in Late Development Theory"; Santos, "The World Bank's Uses of the 'Rule of Law' Promise"; Shihata, *The World Bank in a Changing World*.

29 Santos, "The World Bank's Uses of the 'Rule of Law' Promise."

30 Krever, "The Legal Turn in Late Development Theory."

31 Kaufmann, Kraay, and Mastruzzi, "The Worldwide Governance Indicators."

32 World Justice Project, "Rule of Law Index, 2014–2015," accessed January 30, 2019, https://worldjusticeproject.org/sites/default/files/documents/civ_com_law.pdf.

33 Safarty, "Regulating through Numbers"; also see Kendall, "Donors' Justice."

34 Davis, Kingsbury, and Engle Merry, "Introduction."

35 Serban, "Rule of Law Indicators as a Political Technology of Power in Romania."

36 Such as the MacArthur Foundation, the Open Society Foundations, Bill and Melinda Gates Foundation, and Ford Foundation. See also Oomen, "Donor-Driven Justice and Its Discontents"; and Parsons et al., *Developing Indicators to Measure the Rule of Law*.

37 Teitel, "Transitional Justice Genealogy."

38 Rowen, "Searching for Truth in the Transitional Justice Movement," 5. See also Teitel, "Transitional Justice Genealogy"; Gready, *The Era of Transitional Justice*.

39 "Background: The Road to Reconciliation," in "Tutu and His Role in the Truth and Reconciliation Commission," South African History Online, October 6, 2016, https://www.sahistory.org.za/article/tutu-and-his-role-truth-reconciliation -commission.

40 Dullah Omar, "Justice in Transition Booklet Explaining the Role of the TRC," Truth and Reconciliation Commission, accessed January 30, 2019, http://www .justice.gov.za/trc/legal/justice.htm.

41 "Background: The Road to Reconciliation."

42 David Smith, Giles Tremlett, Kate Hodal, Jonathan Franklin, Julian Borger, and Sibylla Brodzinsky, "Special Report: Truth, Justice and Reconciliation," *The Guardian*, June 24, 2014, https://www.theguardian.com/world/2014/jun/24 /truth-justice-reconciliation-civil-war-conflict.

43 "Background: The Road to Reconciliation.

44 Smith et al., "Special Report"; "Background: The Road to Reconciliation."

45 "What Place for Forgiveness after Genocide?," Forgiveness Project, July 18, 2016.

46 "What Place for Forgiveness after Genocide?"

47 "What Place for Forgiveness after Genocide?"

48 "After the Rupture: Understanding Transitional Justice and Reconciliation," ICTJ, https://www.ictj.org/news/rupture-relationships-transitional-justice-reconciliation, paras. 7–8.

49 "Background: The Road to Reconciliation.

50 "After the Rupture," para. 9; Ensalako, "Truth Commission for Chile and El Salvador."

51 González and Varney, *Truth Seeking*.

52 González and Varney, *Truth Seeking*.

53 Clarke, *Fictions of Justice*.

54 Kofi Annan, "The Secretary-General Address to the United Nations General Assembly," United Nations Meeting Coverage and Press Releases, September 20, 1999.

55 Koulen, "The Responsibility to Protect."

56 ICISS, *The Responsibility to Protect*, 18.

57 ICISS, *The Responsibility to Protect*, 10.

58 Kioko, "The Right of Intervention under the African Union's Constitutive Act."

59 African Union, Constitutive Act of the African Union, Article 4, para. (h), 7, https://au.int/sites/default/files/pages/32020-file-constitutiveact_en.pdf.

60 United Nations, "A More Secure World," 56–57, paras. 201–203; Stahn, "Notes and Comments."

61 Stahn, "Notes and Comments"; Focarelli, "The Responsibility to Protect Doctrine and Humanitarian Intervention"; Schimmel, "The Moral Case for Restorative Justice."

62 See Feldman and Ticktin, *In the Name of Humanity*; Fassin and Pandolfi, *Contemporary States of Emergency*; Fassin, *Humanitarian Reason*; Redfield, *Life in Crisis*.

63 Etymology: *impunity*, mid-sixteenth century, from Latin *impunitas*, from *impunis* "unpunished," from *in-* "not" + *poena* "penalty" or *punire* "punish."

64 The relevant part of the recommendation stated, "In these circumstances, the Commission desire to state expressly that in the hierarchy of persons in authority, there is no reason why rank, however exalted, should in any circumstances protect the holder of it from responsibility when that responsibility has been established before a properly constituted tribunal. *This extends even to the case of heads of States* . . . even if, in some countries, a sovereign is exempt from being prosecuted in a national court of his own country the position from an international point of view is quite different." Commission on the Responsibility of the Authors of the War and on Enforcement of Penalties, "Report Presented to the Preliminary Peace Conference, 29 March 1919," reprinted in *American Journal of International Law* 14 (1920), https://www.legal-tools.org/en/browse/record/63159c/.

65 1945 Charter of the International Military Tribunal, Nuremberg, Article 7, http://www.un.org/en/genocideprevention/documents/atrocity-crimes/Doc.2_Charter%20of%20IMT%201945.pdf.

66 "International Military Tribunal (Nuremberg), Judgment of 1 October 1946,"
    55–56, https://crimeofaggression.info/documents/6/1946_Nuremberg_Judgement
    .pdf.

67 Jackson, "Second Day, Wednesday,"

68 Jackson, "Second Day, Wednesday," 98–102.

69 Jackson, "The Besieged Strongholds of the Mind."

70 Loretta E. Lynch, "Commemoration of the 70th Anniversary of the Nuremberg
    Trials," Nuremberg, Germany, September 29, 2016, https://www.justice.gov/opa
    /speech/attorney-general-loretta-e-lynch-delivers-remarks-10th-international
    -humanitarian-law.

71 United Nations, "Updated Statute of the International Criminal Tribunal for the
    Former Yugoslavia."

72 The ICTY declared, "Individuals are personally responsible, whatever their offi-
    cial position, even if they are heads of State or government ministers: Article
    7(2) of the Statute and article 6(2) of the Statute of the International Criminal
    Tribunal for Rwanda . . . *are indisputably declaratory of customary international
    law.*"

73 John Hocking, "Judicial Transparency: Lessons Learned and Ways Forward,"
    BIRN Regional Conference, "Transparency of Courts and Responsibility of the
    Media," Sarajevo, September 1–3, 2009.

74 Crawford, *The International Law Commission's Articles on State Responsibility.*

75 Preparatory Committee on the Establishment of an International Criminal
    Court, A/AC.249/1997/WG.2/CRP.2/Add.1), February 14, 1997, http://iccnow.org
    /documents/WrkGrp2IrrelevanceFeb97.pdf.

76 The only suggestion came from Garcia Labajo of Spain, who said that he had res-
    ervations about Article 24. He stated that for Para. 2 of Article 24, it might be bet-
    ter to say, for example, "jurisdiction in relation to acts for which that person is
    responsible." This was not considered, and the articles were passed.

77 Schabas, *The International Criminal Court,* 446; Rome Statute, Article 27, Irrele-
    vance of Official Capacity: "1. This Statute shall apply equally to all persons with-
    out any distinction based on official capacity. In particular, official capacity as
    a Head of State or Government, a member of a Government or parliament, an
    elected representative or a government official shall in no case exempt a per-
    son from criminal responsibility under this Statute, nor shall it, in and of itself,
    constitute a ground for reduction of sentence. 2. Immunities or special proce-
    dural rules which may attach to the official capacity of a person, whether under
    national or international law, shall not bar the Court from exercising its jurisdic-
    tion over such a person."

78 Rome Statute of the International Criminal Court, text of the Rome Statute cir-
    culated as document A/CONF.183/9 of July 17, 1998, and corrected by process-
    verbaux of November 10, 1998, July 12, 1999, November 30, 1999, May 8, 2000,
    January 17, 2001, and January 16, 2002. The statute entered into force on July 1,
    2002.

79 Teitel, *Transitional Justice.*

80 See CICC promotion campaign, "Global Justice for Atrocities," accessed November 15, 2016, http://www.coalitionfortheicc.org/fight/global-justice-atrocities.

81 Emma Green, "The Last Man at Nuremberg," *The Atlantic*, May 9, 2014, http://www.theatlantic.com/international/archive/2014/05/the-last-man-at-nuremberg/361968/.

82 Green, "The Last Man at Nuremberg."

83 Ben Ferencz, interview with author, 2014.

84 Rome Statute, Preamble, 1.

85 See also Constable, *Just Silences.*

86 Teitel, *Transitional Justice.*

87 See Okello et al., *Where Law Meets Reality*; also see Editorial Note, *International Journal of Transitional Justice* 7, no. 1 (March 2013): 1–7.

88 See AU Commission of Inquiry on South Sudan, Executive Summary; Mamdani, "A Separate Opinion"; and Mahmood Mamdani, "Who's to Blame in South Sudan?," *Boston Review*, June 28, 2016, http://bostonreview.net/world/mahmood-mamdani-south-sudan-failed-transition.

89 Warrant of Arrest for Omar Hassan Ahmad Al Bashir; Baldo, "Sudan."

90 Murungi, "10 Years of the International Criminal Court."

91 See AU Assembly, "Decision of the Meeting of African States Parties to the Rome Statute of the International Criminal Court," 8; PSC, "Communiqué of the 207th Meeting of the Peace and Security Council at the Level of the Heads of State and Government," 5.

92 Baldo, "Sudan."

93 Ero, "Understanding Africa's Position on the International Criminal Court," 11–14.

94 See United Nations–African Union Hybrid Operation in Darfur, http://unamid.unmissions.org/.

95 See United Nations–African Union Hybrid Operation in Darfur.

96 See "Security Council Extends UN–African Union Operation in Darfur for Another Year," UN News, June 29, 2015, https://www.un.org/apps/news/story.asp?NewsID=51285#.VcKwCJNViko.

97 See commentary, "South Sudan: Stop Delays on Hybrid Court; Four Years in Conflict, Rampant Abuse," Human Rights Watch, December 14, 2017, https://www.hrw.org/news/2017/12/14/south-sudan-stop-delays-hybrid-court.

98 See African Union, "Communique of 547th Meeting of the Peace and Security Council," para. 22(ii)(a); also "Agreement on the Resolution for the Conflict in the Republic of South Sudan."

99 Interview data and author's field notes, 2015, 2016, 2017.

100 Till Papenfuss, "Interview with Luis Moreno-Ocampo, Chief Prosecutor of the International Criminal Court," Global Observatory, January 25, 2012, https://theglobalobservatory.org/2012/01/interview-with-luis-moreno-ocampo-chief-prosecutor-of-the-international-criminal-court/.

101 Papenfuss, "Interview with Luis Moreno-Ocampo."

102 Papenfuss, "Interview with Luis Moreno-Ocampo."

103 Jennings, "Cosmopolitan Subjects," 3.

104 Jennings, "Cosmopolitan Subjects."

105 Jennings, "Cosmopolitan Subjects," 6–7. See also the Tadic Decision "Judgment," *Tadić* (IT-94-1-A), Appeals Chamber, July 15, 1995, §186.

106 Focarelli, "The Responsibility to Protect Doctrine and Humanitarian Intervention."

107 International Criminal Court, "Rules of Procedure and Evidence," Rule 85(b), 31, https://www.icc-cpi.int/iccdocs/PIDS/legal-texts/RulesProcedureEvidenceEng .pdf.

108 Schabas, *An Introduction to the International Criminal Court.*

109 The Rome Statute of the International Criminal Court, Articles 75 and 79. Article 75 establishes that the court "may order reparations against a convicted person specifying appropriate reparations to, or in respect of, victims, including restitution, compensation and rehabilitation." Article 79 establishes the TFV "for the benefit of victims of crimes within the jurisdiction of the Court, and the families of such victims."

110 War Crimes Research Office and Judge Sang-Hyun Song, *Victim Participation before the International Criminal Court.*

111 "Kenyans Set Benchmarks for Implementation of Jubilee Manifesto," Ipsos Synovate, July 13, 2013.

112 Trust Fund for Victims, "Mobilising Resources and Supporting the Most Vulnerable Victims through Ear-Marked Funding," Programme Progress Report, winter 2012, http://www.nuhanovicfoundation.org/user/file/tfv_programme _progress_report_winter_2012finalcompressed.pdf.

113 Van den Wyngaert, "Victims before International Criminal Courts," 482.

114 Van den Wyngaert, "Victims before International Criminal Courts," 483.

115 ICC Trial Chamber V, Decision on Victims' Participation and Representation, October 3, 2012.

Chapter 2. Founding Moments?

1 Ahmed, *The Cultural Politics of Emotion*, 117.

2 The Kapenguria Six, a group of political activists in Kenya, were all members of the Mau Mau society. In 1953 they were arrested and convicted of conspiracy against the colonial government and of pressuring locals into pledging alliance to the Mau Mau. They were later released, as elections for an independent government took place, in which Kenyatta won the majority vote. Both the colonial government and the Mau Mau activists competed to gain people's support through relentless propaganda. See "The Case That Immortalised Kenya's 'Kapenguria Six,'" *East African*, July 1, 2017, https://www.theeastafrican.co.ke/magazine/Case -that-immortalised-Kenya-Kapenguria-Six-/434746-3995106-s8sxn5z/index.html; for more on the propaganda war, see Osborne, "The Rooting Out of Mau Mau."

3   Previously known as Kenyatta Day, celebrated to commemorate the detention
    of the Kapenguria Six. However, following the establishment of the new Kenyan
    Constitution in August 2010, Kenyatta Day was renamed Mashujaa Day.
4   See "Mashujaa Day Speech by Uhuru Kenyatta," *Capital FM*, December 20, 2013.
5   See "Mashujaa Day Speech by Uhuru Kenyatta."
6   See "Mashujaa Day Speech by Uhuru Kenyatta."
7   Bakhtin, *The Dialogic Imagination*, especially "Forms of Time and the Chrono-
    tope in the Novel: Notes toward a Historical Poetics."
8   De Rivera and Páez, "Emotional Climate, Human Security, and Cultures of
    Peace"; Valsiner, "Process Structure of Semiotic Mediation"; also see Tallgren,
    "The Durkheimian Spell of International Criminal Law?"
9   Interestingly, despite Kenyatta's attempt to highlight the wealth and power of the
    West, Kenyatta's own family's wealth and power is ironic as it is seen by the Office
    of the Prosecutor as an impediment to its investigations, as Kenyatta was seen as
    using his financial and political resources to influence witnesses and the political
    and legal process.
10 See Freud, *The Ego and the Id*.
11 Clarke, Knottnerus, and de Volder, *Africa and the ICC*.
12 Anghie, *Imperialism, Sovereignty, and the Making of International Law*. See also
    Gevers and Du Plessis, "Another Stormy Year for the International Criminal
    Court"; Baxi, "What May the 'Third World' Expect from International Law?";
    Mutua, "The International Criminal Court in Africa"; Okafor, "Critical Third
    World Approaches to International Law"; Anand, *International Law and the
    Developing Countries*; Rajagopal, *International Law from Below*; Gathii, "The Past
    and Future of African International Law Scholarship"; Nesiah, "Local Ownership
    of Global Governance."
13 Van Schaack and Slye, "A Concise History of International Criminal Law," 21.
14 Van Schaack and Slye, "A Concise History of International Criminal Law."
15 Van Schaack and Slye, "A Concise History of International Criminal Law."
16 Van Schaack and Slye, "A Concise History of International Criminal Law."
17 Van Schaack and Slye, "A Concise History of International Criminal Law," 23.
18 Schabas, *An Introduction to the International Criminal Court*, 3.
19 Treaty of Peace between the Allied and Associated Powers and Germany (Treaty
    of Versailles) (1919), TS 4, Art. 227.
20 Schabas, *An Introduction to the International Criminal Court*.
21 Van Schaack and Slye, "A Concise History of International Criminal Law," 24.
22 Schabas, *An Introduction to the International Criminal Court*, 4.
23 Cassese, "From Nuremberg to Rome," 4–5.
24 Cassese, "From Nuremberg to Rome."
25 Schabas, *An Introduction to the International Criminal Court*, 5–6.
26 Van Schaack and Slye, "A Concise History of International Criminal Law," 30–31.
27 Cassese, "From Nuremberg to Rome," 7.
28 Van Schaack and Slye, "A Concise History of International Criminal Law," 30–32.

29 Van Schaack and Slye, "A Concise History of International Criminal Law," 32; Schabas, *An Introduction to the International Criminal Court*, 7.
30 Van Schaack and Slye, "A Concise History of International Criminal Law," 34.
31 Van Schaack and Slye, "A Concise History of International Criminal Law," 37.
32 Van Schaack and Slye, "A Concise History of International Criminal Law"; Cassese, "From Nuremberg to Rome," 8.
33 Jones, *Genocide, War Crimes, and the West*; Kiernan and Gellately, *The Specter of Genocide*; Taithe, *The Killer Trail*; Fernandes, "Accomplice to Mass Atrocities"; Martínez Salazar, *Global Coloniality of Power in Guatemala*; Woolford, Hinton, and Benvenuto, *Colonial Genocide in Indigenous North America*; Lawson, "Memorializing Colonial Genocide in Britain"; Brett, "'The Miserable Remnant of this Ill-Used People'"; Mandel, *How America Gets Away with Murder*.
34 Van Schaack and Slye, "A Concise History of International Criminal Law," 38.
35 Schabas, *An Introduction to the International Criminal Court*, 8–9; Cassese, "From Nuremberg to Rome," 9–10.
36 Schabas, *An Introduction to the International Criminal Court*, 9.
37 See Anthony S. Franklin, "Prevention and Suppression of Transnational Organized Crime," Discussion Panel on Maritime Security and Safety, UN Headquarters, New York, June 24, 2008, http://www.un.org/depts/los/consultative_process /documents/9_franklin_presentation.pdf.
38 Franklin, "Prevention and Suppression of Transnational Organized Crime."
39 UN Doc. SC Res. 780, October 6, 1992.
40 UN Doc. SC Res. 827, May 25, 1993.
41 Schabas, *An Introduction to the International Criminal Court*, 12; Cassese, "From Nuremberg to Rome," 14.
42 See Report of the Ad Hoc Committee on the Establishment of an International Criminal Court, G.A., 50th Sess., Supp. No. 22, A/50/22, 1995; *Report of the Preparatory Committee on the Establishment of an International Criminal Court, Volume 1 (Proceedings of the Preparatory Committee during March, April and August 1996)*, G.A., 51st Sess., Supp. No. 22, A/51/22, 1996, p. 193; *Report of the Preparatory Committee on the Establishment of an International Criminal Court, Volume 2*, G.A., 51st Sess., Supp. No. 22, A/51/22, 1996.
43 The clearest location of Mahmood Mamdani's argument that it was necessary to produce Nuremberg and the model it created for transitional justice is in his "The Logic of Nuremberg." The point about the Nuremberg model is clarified more substantively in Mamdani, "Beyond Nuremberg."
44 See Abass, "Prosecuting International Crimes in Africa," 937, citing UN Doc. GA Res. 2202 A (XXI), December 16, 1966; International Convention on the Suppression and Punishment of the Crime of Apartheid, New York, November 30, 1973, in force July 18, 1976, 1015 UNTS 243, Art. V.
45 See Abass, "Prosecuting International Crimes in Africa," 937, citing J. Dugard, "International Convention on the Suppression and Punishment of the Crime of Apartheid" (Audiovisual Library of International Law, 2008). See also Art. V of the Apartheid Convention.

46 Grovogui, *Beyond Eurocentrism and Anarchy.*
47 Interview notes on file with author. See also Ernest Ochonma, "IMF, World Bank and African Economies," Global Policy Forum, February 1, 2001, https://www .globalpolicy.org/component/content/article/209-bwi-wto/43291.html; and Chris Huggins, "A Historical Perspective on the 'Global Land Rush,'" Academia, January 2011, https://www.academia.edu/835652/A_historical_perspective_on_the_ Global_Land_Rush.
48 See Article 5 of the Rome Statute of the ICC, 3.
49 The states that have so far ratified this jurisdiction are overwhelmingly countries in the developing world, with a striking absence of all five UNSC permanent-member states: China, France, the Russian Federation, the United Kingdom, and the United States. See "Status of Ratification and Implementation of the Kampala Amendments on the Crime of Aggression," Update No. 28, as of December 8, 2017, https://crimeofaggression.info/the-role-of-states/status-of -ratification-and-implementation/.
50 "Report on the Facilitation on the Activation of the Jurisdiction of the International Criminal Court over the Crime of Aggression," ICC-ASP/16/24.
51 "Activation of the Jurisdiction of the Court over the Crime of Aggression," Resolution ICC-ASP/16/Res.5, para. 2.
52 See Annex 2 of the report, ICC-ASP/16/24, 15.
53 The states that have ratified this are Liechtenstein, Samoa, Trinidad and Tobago, Luxembourg, Estonia, Germany, Botswana, Cyprus, Slovenia, Andorra, Uruguay, Belgium, Croatia, Slovakia, Austria, Latvia, Spain, San Marino, Georgia, Malta, Costa Rica, Czech Republic, Switzerland, Lithuania, Finland, the former Yugoslav Republic of Macedonia, El Salvador, Iceland, the State of Palestine, the Netherlands, Chile, Portugal, Argentina, and Panama. On December 6, 2017, Panama deposited its instrument of ratification of the Kampala amendments, becoming the thirty-fifth state to ratify the amendments.
54 Odinkalu, "International Criminal Justice, Peace and Reconciliation in Africa."
55 "Report on the Facilitation on the Activation of the Jurisdiction of the International Criminal Court."
56 On file with author: prevalent narrative collected in fieldwork interviews.
57 Wetherall, *Affect and Emotion*, 142.
58 Durkheim, *Elementary Forms of the Religious Life.*
59 Laqueur, "Bodies, Details, and the Humanitarian Narrative."
60 For more on the politics of resentment, see also Hogget, Wilkinson, and Beedell, "Fairness and the Politics of Resentment"; and Engels, "The Politics of Resentment and the Tyranny of the Minority."
61 Clarke and Goodale, *Mirrors of Justice.*
62 Durkheim, *Elementary Forms of the Religious Life*; Wetherall, *Affect and Emotion.*
63 Wetherall, *Affect and Emotion.*
64 Van Schaack and Slye, "A Concise History of International Criminal Law," 7; Sikkink, *The Justice Cascade.*

Chapter 3. Biomediation and the #BringBackOurGirls Campaign

1 See Matfess, *Women and the War on Boko Haram*; see also Walker, *"Eat the Heart of the Infidel"*; and "The Popular Discourses of Salafi Radicalism and Salafi Counter-Radicalism in Nigeria."

2 "Boko Haram Threaten to Sell Abducted Nigerian Schoolgirls 'as Slaves,'" *South China Morning Post*, May 6, 2014, http://www.scmp.com/news/world/article /1505194/boko-haram-threatens-sell-hundreds-abducted-nigerian-schoolgirls -slaves.

3 Quoted in Kathryn Urban-Oberberg, "Actress Jolie Takes Plight of Kidnapped Nigerian Girls to Red Carpet," Reuters, May 9, 2014, https://www.reuters.com /article/us-nigeria-girls-jolie/actress-jolie-takes-plight-of-kidnapped-nigerian -girls-to-red-carpet-idUSKBN0DP14720140509.

4 John Kerry, "Commitment to Africa," U.S. Department of State, May 3, 2014, https://2009-2017.state.gov/secretary/remarks/2014/05/225571.htm.

5 President Goodluck Jonathan was a Christian southerner and was president in 2014 when the Chibok girls were kidnapped. The popular discourse is that he was interested in resolving this crisis because the disorder in the northeast bolstered his political prospects in the next presidential election to be seen as a political success.

6 Michelle Faul, "How Did 21 Chibok Schoolgirls Get Released?," *Global News*, October 14, 2016, https://globalnews.ca/news/3002479/how-did-21-chibok -schoolgirls-get-released/.

7 ICC-OTP Report on Preliminary Examinations, December 13, 2011, 12–13.

8 Joe Parkinson and Drew Hinshaw, "Two Bags of Cash for Boko Haram: Freedom for the World's Most Famous Hostages Came at a Heavy Price," *Wall Street Journal*, December 24, 2017, https://www.wsj.com/articles/two-bags-of-cash-for-boko -haram-the-untold-story-of-how-nigeria-freed-its-kidnapped-girls-1513957354. As of December 30, 2017, one hundred girls remained captive since their abduction in May 2014. The way Nigeria's leadership under President Goodluck handled the Chibok girls' kidnapping should be compared with the more recent (February 19, 2018) kidnapping by Boko Haram of schoolgirls in Dapchi, Yobe State, which was addressed almost immediately by the next Nigerian president, Muhammadu Buhari. The release of the girls in these regions was negotiated and they were freed a month later.

9 Ross, *Mixed Emotions*. See also publications on victimhood, human rights, and humanitarianism, such as Allen, "Martyr Bodies in the Media"; McLagan, "Principles, Publicity, and Politics"; see also Khoja-Moolji, "Becoming an 'Intimate Publics,'" on hashtag feminism as it relates to #BringBackOurGirls, exploring the politics of saving Muslim women. See also Abu-Lughod, *Do Muslim Women Need Saving?*; Hirschkind and Mahmood, "Feminism, the Taliban, and Politics of Counter-Insurgency"; and Chouliaraki, *The Spectatorship of Suffering* and the literature on posthumanitarianism concerning how social media changes the affective landscape of humanitarian mobilization and erases the need for suffering.

10 Barad, *Meeting the Universe Halfway*; Haraway, *When Species Meet*.

11 For a discussion on the link between technology and charity, see Glenn, "Activism or 'Slacktivism'?"; Brachotte and Frame, *Citizen Participation and Political Communication in a Digital World*; Dahlberg-Grundberg, "Technology as Movement"; McLean and Fuller, "Action with(out) Activism." See also Clyde Haberman, "Philanthropy That Comes from a Click," *New York Times*, November 13, 2016, https://www.nytimes.com/2016/11/14/us/philanthropy-that-comes-from -a-click.html. For more on the term *slacktivism*, see Anna Rudenko, "Slacktivism: An Illusion of a Good Behaviour or the First Step towards Real Help?," *Popsop*, July 19, 2013, http://popsop.com/2013/07/slacktivism-an-illusion-of-good -behaviour-or-a-first-step-towards-a-real-help/. On the link between NGOs and supporting causes through social media, see Katrina VanHuss and Otis Fulton, "Constituents Do More Than Wear Your Wristbands," *NonProfit Pro*, November 22, 2017, http://www.nonprofitpro.com/post/constituents-wear-wristbands/.

12 Wilson and Brown, *Humanitarianism and Suffering*, 19–20.

13 They point to political theorist Richard Rorty, "Human Rights, Rationality and Sentimentality," and anthropologists Veena Das in "The Act of Witnessing," and Arthur Kleinman in "The Violences of Everyday Life," as well as Thomas Laqueur, "Mourning, Pity, and the Work of Narrative in the Making of 'Humanity,'" to explore the role of narrative in conjuring emotion. See also Das and Kleinman, "Introduction," in *Violence and Subjectivity*; and Das and Kleinman, *Remaking a World*.

14 These campaigns are not only funded by multimillion-dollar donor organizations, such as the Bill and Melinda Gates Foundation, the MacArthur Foundation, Open Society, and the Ford Foundation, they also reveal how particular forms of activism have carried over to the business of advocacy.

15 Shaw, "Memory Frictions"; Wilson, *The Politics of Truth and Reconciliation in South Africa*.

16 Kony 2012: Invisible Children (website), accessed January 2, 2018, https:// invisiblechildren.com/kony-2012/.

17 Kony 2012: Invisible Children. The image can be found on the main page of their website.

18 Kony 2012: Invisible Children.

19 Kony 2012: Invisible Children.

20 Obiageli Ezekwesili is a chartered accountant and was the federal minister of solid materials and, later, federal minister of education under Olusegun Obasanjo, the president of Nigeria from 1999 to 2007.

21 Barthes, "Shock-Photos."

22 Rancière, *The Future of the Image*; also see Rancière, *The Politics of Aesthetics*.

23 Ramaa Mosley, "Bring Back Our Girls," Facebook, accessed January 2, 2018, https://www.facebook.com/bringbackourgirls.

24 This was the US branding for disadvantaged students that was advanced by President George W. Bush's educational platform. The message prioritized literacy for all children through ensuring that all children's educational needs would be

addressed through the new plan. It was legislated through the US Congress's No Child Left Behind Act of 2001 (NCLB).

25 Tracy McVeigh, "Michelle Obama Raises Pressure over Kidnapped Schoolgirls," *The Guardian,* May 11, 2014, https://www.theguardian.com/world/2014/may/10 /michelle-obama-nigeria-presidential-address.

26 Michelle Obama, "Weekly Address: The First Lady Marks Mother's Day and Speaks Out on the Tragic Kidnapping in Nigeria," Obama White House Archives, May 10, 2014, https://obamawhitehouse.archives.gov/the-press-office/2014/05/10 /weekly-address-first-lady-marks-mother-s-day-and-speaks-out-tragic-kidna.

27 Whoopi Goldberg (@WhoopiGoldberg), Twitter, May 6, 2014, 5:09 A.M., https:// twitter.com/WhoopiGoldberg/status/463651861187534848.

28 Ian Somerhalder (@iansomerhalder), Twitter, May 7, 2014, 8:36 A.M., https:// twitter.com/iansomerhalder/status/464066303561854977.

29 Mia Farrow (@MiaFarrow), Twitter, May 5, 2014, 12:37 P.M., https://twitter.com /MiaFarrow/status/463402048340238336.

30 Iman Abdulmajid (@The_Real_IMAN), Twitter, May 7, 2014, 10:05 A.M., https:// twitter.com/The_Real_IMAN/status/464088568206356480.

31 Reese Witherspoon (@RWitherspoon), Twitter, May 7, 2014, 9:04 P.M., https:// twitter.com/RWitherspoon/status/464254571662295041.

32 Gina Carano (@ginacarano), Twitter, May 7, 2014, 8:29 P.M., https://twitter.com /ginacarano/status/464245790806794240.

33 Rashida Jones (@iamrashidajones), Twitter, May 7, 2014, 11:37 P.M., https://twitter .com/iamrashidajones/status/464293083476017152.

34 Kim Kardashian (@KimKardashian), Twitter, May 8, 2014, 10:26 A.M., https:// twitter.com/KimKardashian/status/464456438837157888.

35 Cara Delevingne (@Caradelevingne), Twitter, May 8, 2014, 7:50 A.M., https:// twitter.com/Caradelevingne/status/464416968481599488.

36 Kendall (@KendallJenner), Twitter, May 8, 2014, 8:26 A.M., https://twitter.com /KendallJenner/status/464426229831958528.

37 Kerry Washington (@kerrywashington), replying to @ABCWorldNews, Twitter, May 7, 2014, 4:23 P.M., https://twitter.com/kerrywashington/status /464183846989078528.

38 Naomi Campbell (@NaomiCampbell), Twitter, May 7, 2014, 10:25 A.M., https:// twitter.com/NaomiCampbell/status/464093657268621312.

39 Paula Abdul (@PaulaAbdul), Twitter, May 7, 2014, 10:08 A.M., https://twitter.com /PaulaAbdul/status/464089323894091776.

40 Queen Latifah (@IAMQUEENLATIFAH), Twitter, May 7, 2014, 1:37 P.M., https:// twitter.com/IAMQUEENLATIFAH/status/464141873007693824.

41 Mary J. Blige (@maryjblige), Twitter, May 7, 2014, 10:46 A.M., https://twitter.com /maryjblige/status/464098955093999618.

42 Daisy Fuentes Marx (@DaisyFuentes), Twitter, May 8, 2014, 8:15 A.M., https:// twitter.com/DaisyFuentes/status/464423379101949952.

43 Stacey Dash (@REALStaceyDash), Twitter, May 6, 2014, 12:47 P.M., https://twitter .com/REALStaceyDash/status/463767077036118016.

44 Chelsea Clinton (@ChelseaClinton), Twitter, May 6, 2014, 8:38 A.M., https://twitter.com/ChelseaClinton/status/463704298556493824.

45 Ellen DeGeneres (@TheEllenShow), Twitter, May 8, 2014, 2:22 P.M., https://twitter.com/TheEllenShow/status/46451572018160026.

46 Jessica Biel (@JessicaBiel), Twitter, May 6, 2014, 12:30 P.M., https://twitter.com/JessicaBiel/status/463762747449413632.

47 Teresa Palmer (@teresapalmer), Twitter, May 7, 2014, 6:14 P.M., https://twitter.com/teresapalmer/status/464211773680152578.

48 Poppy Delevingne (@DelevingnePoppy), Twitter, May 8, 2014, 12:37 A.M., https://twitter.com/DelevingnePoppy/status/464308120299507713.

49 See Ariana Hernandez Reguant's argument about racism and American anthropology, unpublished paper.

50 Williams, *Stains on My Name, War in My Veins*.

51 Mamdani, *When Victims Become Killers*; Cooper, *Africa in the World*.

52 For a historical view on inequality in Nigeria, see Diejomaoh and Bienen, *Inequality and Development in Nigeria*. Also, for a discussion of contemporary structural inequality, see Ariyo and Olaniyan, "Structural Transformation and Inequality."

53 A Brookings Institute report indicated that Nigeria overtook India in May 2018 "to become the country with the world's highest number of people—87 million—living in extreme poverty." Many of these 87 million persons live in northern Nigeria. See Peter Beaumont and Isaac Abrak, "Oil-Rich Nigeria Outstrips India as Country with Most People in Poverty," *The Guardian*, July 16, 2018, https://www.theguardian.com/global-development/2018/jul/16/oil-rich-nigeria-outstrips-india-most-people-in-poverty.

54 Nicolson, *The Administration of Nigeria*.

55 Mbembe, *On the Postcolony*; see also Mbembe, "Provisional Notes on the Postcolony."

56 In relation to the question of legitimate victims, see also Ticktin, "The Gendered Human of Humanitarianism"; Ticktin, "How Biology Travels"; and Fassin, "Humanitarianism as a Politics of Life."

57 Augé, *Non-Places*.

Chapter 4. From "Perpetrator" to Hero

1 De Rivera and Páez, "Emotional Climate, Human Security, and Cultures of Peace."

2 This message was formally articulated in Uhuru Kenyatta's official announcement that introduced the Jubilee Coalition in February 2013, where he set the tone for the message that our fate is in our hands, promoted by the Jubilee campaign. See also Agathangelou and Killian, *Time, Temporality and Violence in International Relations*.

3 See also Vladimir Petrović's book on juridical and historical time, *The Emergence of Historical Forensic Expertise*; Bevernage, "Time, Presence, and Historical

Injustice"; Beverage, *History, Memory, and State-Sponsored Violence*; and Stauffer, "Speaking Truth to Reconciliation."

4 See BTP Advisers (website), http://btpadvisers.com.

5 See "A Million Vote Victory," Kenya Elections 2013, BTP Advisers, accessed February 6, 2019, http://btpadvisers.com/work/kenya-elections-2013.

6 See Dikembe Disembe, "Sovereignity [*sic*] Hoax? Uhuru's British Consultants Who 'Delivered' Presidency," *Kenya Today*, April 7, 2013, https://www.kenya -today.com/opinion/jubilee-alliance-pr-consultants; also see "Kenya: The Team That Made Uhuru," All Africa, March 11, 2013, http://allafrica.com/stories/2013 03111894.html.

7 Sikkink, *The Justice Cascade.*

8 Hart, "The Aims of the Criminal Law."

9 Similarly, the law literature describing the choice to reject the collectivization of guilt often suggests that holding a few accountable allows the rest to be cleansed, rid of guilt, and free to move beyond the period of violence. Scholars such as Madoka Futamura, for instance, wrote that avoiding the collectivization of guilt has "the effect of endorsing the transformation of the nation by freeing it from the burden of collective guilt while detaching those responsible for war crimes from the society concerned and eliminating their political influence." See Futamura, "Individual and Collective Guilt." Writing on the Tokyo Tribunal, the Nuremberg IMT's less famous counterpart, she reflects, "Consciously or unconsciously, the Japanese displaced the burden of their war guilt and responsibility onto the shoulders of the defendants at the Tribunal." This position was further explored by Mark Drumbl, who argued, "Absolving the many might be more conducive to the grand project of social healing. Such absolution may have currency . . . in the process of peace. . . . Implicating too many individuals might threaten peace and, as such, the fiction of collective innocence could serve important political purposes." See Drumbl, *Atrocity, Punishment, and International Law*, 41.

10 On emotions, see Ahmed, *The Promise of Happiness.*

11 See Futamura, "Individual and Collective Guilt"; and Drumbl, *Atrocity, Punishment, and International Law.*

12 Simpson, *Law, War and Crime.*

13 Cassese, *International Criminal Law*, 136.

14 "Judgment," *Tadić* (IT-94-1-A), Appeals Chamber, July 15, 1995, §186.

15 "The Prosecutor versus Jean-Paul Akayesu," ICTR Case No. ICTR-96-4-T, Judgement (ICTR Trial Chamber I, September 2, 1998).

16 In the midst of Liberia and Sierra Leone's war, the president of Nigeria, Olusegun Obasanjo, gave Charles Taylor asylum in the southern state of Calabar, Nigeria, in exchange for brokering a peace deal in Liberia and an agreement to put an end to the raging war. However, while in exile Taylor was accused of breaking the agreement by continuing to engage in Liberian politics. In January 2006, when President Ellen Johnson Sirleaf took office in Liberia, she made the extradition request for Taylor. President Obasanjo agreed to release Taylor into Liberia's

custody. Taylor fled and was recaptured and repatriated to Liberia. He was then taken to Sierra Leone and turned over to the Special Court for Sierra Leone. In the end, his trial was administered in the first ICC building in The Hague, where in April 2012 he was convicted of eleven charges of aiding and abetting war crimes.

17 ICC Pre-trial Chamber II, "Situation in the Republic of Kenya, Request for Authorization of an Investigation Pursuant to Article 15," 3.

18 ICC Pre-trial Chamber II, "Situation in the Republic of Kenya, Decision on the Prosecutor's Appeal against the Decision on the Request to Amend the Updated Document Containing the Charges Pursuant to Article 61(9) of the Statute."

19 Juma, "African Mediation of the Kenyan Post-2007 Election Crisis."

20 Kagwanja and Southall, "Introduction."

21 See Waki, *Report of the Commission of Inquiry into Post-Election Violence*. In the Kikuyu language, Mungiki (mūngīkī) means "a united people." It was first a secretive religious cult group and is now a banned gang-like secret organization.

22 The first defeat was in 2009 when the government failed to obtain enough support in Parliament to pass the relevant laws to set up the tribunal.

23 See also Brown, "International Criminal Justice and Electoral Violence"; Sriram and Brown, "Kenya in the Shadow of the ICC"; Kendall, "'UhuRuto' and Other Leviathans"; and Höhn, "New Start or False Start?"

24 Kenyan National Dialogue and Reconciliation Monitoring Project, "Progress in Implementation of the Constitution and Other Reforms," 45.

25 Mueller, "Kenya and the International Criminal Court (ICC)."

26 See International Criminal Court, "Decision on the Prosecutor's Application for Summonses to Appear for Francis Kirimi Muthaura, Uhuru Muigai Kenyatta and Mohammed Hussein Ali"; and International Criminal Court, "Decision on the Prosecutor's Application for Summons to Appear for William Samoei Ruto, Henry Kiprono Kosgey and Joshua Arap Sang."

27 Charged pursuant to articles 7(l)(a), 7(l)(d), 7(l)(h), and 25(3)(a) of the Rome Statute.

28 Charged pursuant to articles 7(l)(a), 7(l)(d), 7(l)(g), 7(l)(k), 7(l)(h), and 25(3)(a) of the Rome Statute.

29 Cheeseman, "The Kenyan Elections of 2007."

30 Human Rights Watch, "High Stakes: Political Violence and the 2013 Elections in Kenya," February 2013, https://www.hrw.org/report/2013/02/07/high-stakes /political-violence-and-2013-elections-kenya.

31 Human Rights Watch, "High Stakes"; see also Kagwanja and Southall, "Introduction."

32 Interview 0037, by Kamari Clarke, July 18, 2013.

33 On January 23, 2012, the Pre-trial Chamber II decided to move cases against Ruto, Sang, Muthaura, and Kenyatta to trial (see *The Prosecutor v. William Samoei Ruto and Joshua Arap Sang*, ICC-01/09-01/11-859, 16-08-2013; *The Prosecutor v. Uhuru Muigai Kenyatta*, ICC-PIDS-KEN-02-010/14-2014). Judges declined to confirm charges against Henry Kiprono Kosgey and Mohammed Hussein

Ali. The charges against Francis Muthaura were dropped before being brought to trial. The decision to move the majority of the Kenyan cases to trial is bound to provide a window into another set of international juridical processes on the world stage and assessments on the extent to which the ICC has the potential to produce justice.

34 Dworkin, *Law's Empire*.

35 Decision Pursuant to Article 15 of the Rome Statute on the Authorization of an Investigation into the Situation in the Republic of Kenya, March 31, 2010, ICC-01/09, para. 173–174.

36 Rome Statute of the International Criminal Court, Article 11.

37 ICC, "Decision Pursuant to Article 15 of the Rome Statute on the Authorization of an Investigation into the Situation in the Republic of Kenya," ICC-01/09, March 31, 2010, https://www.legal-tools.org/doc/focaaf/pdf/. The court reaffirmed this analysis twice in the Ruto case. First, in the March 8, 2011, Decision on Summons to Appear, ICC-01/09/01/11, para. 10–11 (reaffirming the analysis of temporal jurisdiction from the March 31, 2010, decision, finding "no need to reiterate its finding"), and second, in the January 23, 2012, Decision on the Confirmation of Charges Pursuant to Article 61(7)(a) and (b) of the Rome Statute, ICC-01/09-01/11, para. 26–27 (finding that the court's territorial and temporal parameters are still satisfied, and accordingly, there is no reason to repeat its previous finding on these two aspects of jurisdiction). The court reaffirmed this analysis twice more in the Kenyatta case. See Decision on the Prosecutor's Application for Summonses to Appear, March 8, 2011, ICC-01/09-02/11, para. 10–11; Decision on the Confirmation of Charges Pursuant to Article 61(7)(a) and (b) of the Rome Statute, January 23, 2012, ICC-01/09-02/11, para. 24–25.

38 Decision on the Confirmation of Charges Pursuant to Article 61(7)(a) and (b) of the Rome Statute, para. 107.

39 *The Prosecutor v. William Samoei Ruto and Joshua Arap Sang*, ICC-01/09-01/11-859. The prosecutor did seek permission to amend the charges against Ruto and Sang to include events on December 30 and 31, 2007, but the judges deemed this request inadmissible at the time it was made, as it was after the confirmation of charges hearing and no postponement was requested in order to amend the charges. For the ICC's narrowing of the relevant time period for Ruto, see Decision on the Confirmation of Charges Pursuant to Article 61(7)(a) and (b) of the Rome Statute, para. 349.

40 *The Prosecutor v. Uhuru Muigai Kenyatta*, ICC-PIDS-KEN-02-010/14, 2014.

41 See Rome Statute, Article 61(7). The ICC sua sponte undertook the decision to narrow the charges by time period.

42 Request for Authorization of an Investigation Pursuant to Article 15, ICC-01/09, para. 55–56.

43 Rome Statute of the International Criminal Court, Article 7(2)(h).

44 Rome Statute of the International Criminal Court, Article 7(1)(a).

45 See also Nissel, "Continuing Crimes in the Rome Statute."

46 See Case Concerning the Difference between New Zealand and France Concern-

ing the Interpretation or Application of Two Agreements, Concluded on 9 July 1986 between the Two States and Which Related to the Problems Arising from the Rainbow Warrior Affair (N.Z./Fr.), 20 R.I.A.A. 217 (1990).

47 Citing *Prosecutor v. Musema*, ICTR Case No. ICTR-96-13-A, P164 (ICTR Trial Chamber, January 27, 2000), Judgment and Sentence.

48 ICTR Case No. ICTR-99-52-T, P103 (ICTR Trial Chamber, December 3, 2003).

49 ICTR Case No. ICTR-97-19-AR72 (ICTR Appeals Chamber, September 12, 2000).

50 Eltringham, *Accounting for Horror*; and Wilson, *Incitement on Trial*.

51 See Mamdani, *When Victims Become Killers*.

52 Engel, "Law, Time, and Community."

53 Uhuru Kenyatta, speech, February 2013, announcing the launch of the Jubilee Coalition.

54 Uhuru Kenyatta, speech, February 2013.

55 Uhuru Kenyatta, speech, February 2013.

56 Uhuru Kenyatta, speech, February 2013.

57 Ogot, *Zamani*, 249.

58 Oathing rituals among the Mau Mau involved a campaign in which members of the Gikuyu masses took oaths to show their support of particular social decisions or conditions. The oaths involved the alignment of particular beliefs understood as ideological and expressed through solemn commitments in songs and at rallies—all for the expression of those alliances.

59 Kinyatti, *History of Resistance in Kenya*, 144–150. The question of ethnicity in the Mau Mau struggle is one of the most controversial in the historiography. The debate revolves around whether the struggle was of a nationalist nature or was only a Kikuyu affair. For details of this debate, see Kinyatti, "Mau Mau"; and Atieno-Odhiambo, "The Production of History in Kenya."

60 It is worth noting here that Kenyatta denied involvement with the Mau Mau during the Kapenguria trial.

61 Home Guards were African village policemen who were working for the British colonial government in Kenya to quash the Mau Mau struggle. They had a reputation for being extremely vicious in their anti–Mau Mau campaigns.

62 Interview data collected in Nairobi, on file with author.

63 Nicoll and Delaney, "Kenya's Election," vii–ix.

64 Robins, "'To Live as Other Kenyans Do.'"

65 Field notes/data collection on file with author.

66 See Nissel, "Continuing Crimes in the Rome Statute."

67 Ngugi, interview with author in Nairobi. Note that following the violence over Kenya's disputed 2007 general elections, the Kenyan Dialogue and Reconciliation Forum was created to facilitated mediation among the various parties. As part of this process, four agendas were identified as areas of focus for national dialogue and reconciliation. Agenda 4 focused on long-term issues and solutions such as land reform, legal and institutional reform, unemployment, and several more. See the National Accord and Reconciliation Act 2008 signed in Nairobi, Kenya, on February 1, 2008.

68 Ngugi, interview with author.

69 Ngugi, interview with author.

70 The Truth, Justice and Reconciliation Commission of Kenya report tried to address these very questions, but the process was significantly delayed and marked with internal wrangling, which served to discredit the process significantly.

Chapter 5. Reattribution through the Making of an African Criminal Court

1 "50th Anniversary Solemn Declaration," African Union, May 30, 2013, http://www.un.org/en/africa/osaa/pdf/au/50anniv_declaration_2013.pdf.

2 "50th Anniversary Solemn Declaration."

3 "50th Anniversary Solemn Declaration."

4 Nkosazana Dlamini Zuma, "Silencing Guns in Africa: Building a Roadmap to a Conflict-Free Continent" [press release], African Union, April 29, 2014, https://au.int/en/newsevents/20140429.

5 "African Union Agenda 2063: A Shared Strategic Framework for Inclusive Growth and Sustainable Development," African Union, August 2013, https://www.au.int/web/sites/default/files/newsevents/workingdocuments/29732-wd-27_08_agenda_2063_background_note_en_0.pdf; "From the Organisation of African Unity (OAU) to the African Union (AU): The 50-Year Path towards African Unity," Africa-EU Partnership Organization, May 28, 2013, https://www.africa-eu-partnership.org/en/stay-informed/news/organisation-african-unity-oau-african-union-au-50-year-path-towards-african.

6 United Nations Economic Commission for Africa, "Youth and Children's Forum: Theme: African Renaissance/Africa We Want to See 2063," Addis Ababa, Ethiopia, April 2013, https://au.int/sites/default/files/newsevents/conceptnotes/29076-cn-concept_note_auc-eca_20may_0.pdf.

7 African Union Commission, "Agenda 2063: The Africa We Want," June 2014, Issuu, 68–69, https://issuu.com/assogbavi/docs/au_agenda_2063_-_draft_june_2014.

8 Gordon, *Ghostly Matters*.

9 For more on this, see Pahuja, *Decolonising International Law*; Ferguson, *Global Shadows*; Grovogui, *Beyond Eurocentricism and Anarchy*.

10 See Hobsbawm and Ranger, *The Invention of Tradition*; and Anderson, *Imagined Communities*.

11 Eisikovits, "Peace versus Justice in Transitional Settings," 715.

12 Thabo Mbeki and Mahmood Mamdani, "Courts Can't End Civil Wars," Opinion, *New York Times*, February 5, 2014, https://www.nytimes.com/2014/02/06/opinion/courts-cant-end-civil-wars.html.

13 See Murithi, "The African Union and the International Criminal Court"; Akhavan, "Are International Criminal Tribunals a Disincentive to Peace?"; Branch, "Uganda's Civil War and the Politics of ICC Intervention"; Eisikovits, "Peace versus Justice in Transitional Settings," 717.

14   See, for example, Mallinder, "Beyond the Courts?"; Mnookin, "Rethinking the Tension between Peace and Justice," 145; Olsen, Payne, and Reiter, "The Justice Balance."

15   Eisikovits, "Peace versus Justice in Transitional Settings," 715.

16   Eisikovits, "Peace versus Justice in Transitional Settings," 715.

17   Connal Parsley, "Global Spectatorship: The Power of Appearance and the Construction of Authority," Contemporary Trends Speaker Series (Carleton University, Ottawa, Canada, March 17, 2016).

18   See also Kai, Pouvoir et Poursuite.

19   See the "I am African, I am the African Union" branding campaign highlighted at African Union Newsletter, May 25, 2012: https://au.int/ar/newsevents/26526 /launch-au-branding-campaign-%E2%80%9Ci-am-african-i-am-african-union% E2%80%9D.

20   Nkosazana Dlamini Zuma, "Welcome Remarks by HE Dr. Nkosazana Dlamini Zuma, Chairperson of the African Union Commission, at the Opening Session of the 24th Ordinary Session of the Permanent Representatives Committee (PRC)," African Union, Addis Ababa, Ethiopia, January 21, 2013, https://au.int/en /speeches/20130121.

21   Legum, Pan-Africanism.

22   Blyden, "The Aims and Methods of a Liberal Education for Africans," 11.

23   African Union, "OAU Charter," Addis Ababa, Ethiopia, May 25, 1963, https://au.int /en/treaties/oau-charter-addis-ababa-25-may-1963.

24   Kwame Nkrumah, "The People of Africa Are Crying for Unity," May 24, 1963, Pan African News Wire, posted September 4, 2012, http://panafricannews .blogspot.ca/2012/09/kwame-nkrumah-speech-at-founding.html; also see collection of speech transcripts by President Nyerere at Nyerere Centre for Peace Research, http://www.juliusnyerere.org/resources/category/speeches_and _statements.

25   Mwanasali, "From the Organization of African Unity to the African Union," 205.

26   African Union, "OAU Charter."

27   Article 17 and the protocol to the treaty establishing the African Economic Community relating to the Pan-African Parliament. On the Pan-African Parliament generally, see Musila, "United States of Africa." Constitutive Act of the African Union, Articles 14, 15, and 16, Lome, Togo, July 11, 2000, https://au.int /en/constitutive-act. The African Commission on Human and Peoples Rights, though established by a separate instrument, is regarded as an organ of the AU, while the African Court on Human and Peoples' Rights is to be subsumed in the proposed African Court of Justice and Human Rights established by the Malabo Protocol. The Peace and Security Council, another organ of the union, was established by a separate instrument, the Protocol Relating to the Establishment of the Peace and Security Council of the African Union.

28   Constitutive Act, Article 9.

29   "From the Organisation of African Unity (OAU) to the African Union (AU)."

30   Ferguson, Global Shadows.

31 Dlamini, "Towards a Regional Protection of Human Rights in Africa."

32 Dlamini, citing Weinstein, "Africa's Approach to Human Rights at the United Nations," unpublished manuscript.

33 These include the following: "Seminar on Measures to Be Taken on the National Level for the Implementation of the United Nations Instrument Aimed at Combating and Eliminating Racial Discrimination and for the Promotion of Harmonious Racial Relations," held in Yaounde, Cameroon, June 16–21, 1971; "Seminar on the Participation of Women in Economic Life," Libreville, Gabon, July 27–29, 1971; "Seminar on the Study of New Ways and Means for Promoting Human Rights with Special Attention on the Problems and Needs of Africa," Dar es Salaam, Tanzania, October 23–November 5, 1973. See Dlamini, "Towards a Regional Protection of Human Rights in Africa," citing Omozurike, "The African Charter on Human and Peoples' Rights," 190. Beyond the 1961 conference, the UN and the International Commission of Jurists organized several other conferences and seminars on the rule of law in Dakar (1976 and 1978) and Dar es Salaam (1976).

34 Dlamini, citing a report prepared for the International League for Human Rights by Kannyo, "Human Rights in Africa: Problems and Prospects," 198, 24 et seq.

35 In January 1981, an OAU Council of Ministers adopted a preliminary draft of an African charter in Banjul, the Gambia, that had been written in 1979 by a committee of experts headed by Keba Mbaye. The charter was adopted at the OAU Assembly Summit held in June in Nairobi, Kenya (see Dlamini, "Towards a Regional Protection of Human Rights in Africa," 193, citing Kannyo, "Human Rights in Africa," 20) and came into force in 1986. The African Commission, the institution established under the charter to interpret, protect, and promote human rights in Africa, was established in November 1987 (African Charter, Article 45). In 1998, a protocol to the charter was adopted that created the African Court of Human and Peoples' Rights (ACHPR). That protocol entered into force on January 25, 2005, and currently twenty-seven of fifty-four possible states are party to it (see Dlamini, "Towards a Regional Protection of Human Rights in Africa," 7–8). The ACHPR sits in Arusha, Tanzania, and may hear applications relating to human rights violations brought before it by the AUC as well as African intergovernmental organizations and member states, but the path to adjudicating international crimes has taken much longer (see Dlamini, "Towards a Regional Protection of Human Rights in Africa," 8).

36 Dlamini, "Towards a Regional Protection of Human Rights in Africa," 191. Dlamini records that a meeting of experts subsequently convened by the UN in Morovia in September to discuss the creation of the African Commission would make proposals to the OAU on a model of the commission.

37 See Abass, "The Proposed International Criminal Jurisdiction for the African Court," citing UN GA Res 2202 A (XXI), December 16, 1966; Article 5 of the Apartheid Convention, see note 14 above.

38 See Abass, "Prosecuting International Crimes in Africa," citing J. Dugard, International Convention on the Suppression and Punishment of the Crime of Apartheid (2008). See also Article 5 of the Apartheid Convention.

39 Pan-African Citizens Network, formerly the Center for Citizen Participation on the African Union, accessed January 3, 2018, http://ccpau.org/.

40 AUC, "Strategic Plan, 2009–2012," para. 97, https://europafrica.files.wordpress.com/2009/07/au-strategic-plan-2009-2012.pdf.

41 Constitutive Act, Articles 10–13.

42 The AGA was mandated by the AU Assembly in July 2010 at its Fourteenth Ordinary Session. See AU, "Decisions, Declarations and Resolutions," Fourteenth Ordinary Session of the AU Assembly, January 31–February 2, 2010, Addis Ababa, Ethiopia, https://au.int/sites/default/files/decisions/9561-assembly_en_31 _january_2_feburuary_2010_bcp_assembly_of_the_african_union_fourteenth _ordinary_session.pdf; see also "Decision on the Theme, Date and Venue of the Sixteenth Ordinary Session of the Assembly of the African Union" adopted during its Fifteenth Ordinary Session, July 25–27, Kampala, Uganda, Assembly /AU/Dec.304(XV). The AGA arose out of a series of deliberations within the AU (between the Department of Political Affairs and AUC) driven by the desire to "facilitate policy and programme convergence on Governance amongst AU Member States as a means to accelerate deeper integration," as stated in African Union, "Framework of the African Governance Architecture," n.d., http://www .iag-agi.org/IMG/pdf/aga-framewor9183.pdf.

43 See AU, "Decisions," Fourteenth Ordinary Session of the AU Assembly; see also "Decision on the Theme, Date and Venue of the Sixteenth Ordinary Session of the Assembly of the African Union."

44 See AU, "Decisions," Fourteenth Ordinary Session of the AU Assembly; see also "Decision on the Theme, Date and Venue of the Sixteenth Ordinary Session of the Assembly of the African Union."

45 On the structure and status of AGA, see Mukundi, "Consolidating the African Governance Architecture."

46 Mukundi, "Consolidating the African Governance Architecture."

47 Mukundi, "Consolidating the African Governance Architecture."

48 "The AGA's policy approach rests on three principal pillars: the existence of necessary norms, the institutions that house them and the processes through which they are implemented" (Mukundi, "Consolidating the African Governance Architecture," para. 7–19). With links between peace, security, and democracy, AGA is envisioned as complementary to the PSC and the associated institutions that support its work, together with the REC, jointly constituting the African Union's Peace and Security Architecture (APSA). On APSA, see generally Powell, "The African Union's Emerging Peace and Security Regime." Through APSA, the assembly works closely with the PSC, a fifteen-member body elected on a regional basis, which serves as the AU's standing decision-making organ responsible for the maintenance of continental peace and security (AU, "PSC," http://www .peaceau.org). According to the outlined structure, the AU's PSC is supported by a number of associated units: the commission, a Panel of the Wise, a Continental Early Warning System, an African Standby Force, and a Special Fund (Protocol Relating to the Establishment of the Peace and Security Council). Since starting

work in 2004, the PSC has addressed a variety of issues on the African continent, such as armed conflicts (e.g., Somalia and Sudan), unconstitutional changes of government (though the PSC position on these—and the role of popular uprisings in particular—has yet to be solidified), peace building, and issues such as terrorism and the illicit trade in small arms and light weapons (Williams, "The Peace and Security Council of the African Union").

49 African Union Panel of the Wise, "Peace, Justice, and Reconciliation in Africa 1. African Union Panel of the Wise.

50 For a case for humanitarian intervention in Darfur, noting that legal (judicial) responses have limits and their role should be contextualized, see Smith, "Moral Hazard and Humanitarian Law"; on responses to the Darfur conflict and the role of the AU, see Musila, "New Posture and Old Rhetoric?," 15–17. See also Grono, "Briefing," 621–631; on humanitarian intervention, see Udombana, "Still Playing Dice with Lives"; and Kuwali, "The End of Humanitarian Intervention."

51 On the AU's earliest peace missions, see generally Aboagye, "The African Mission in Burundi"; and Murithi, "The African Union's Evolving Role in Peace Operations."

52 On the support mission in Mali, the multidimensional integrated mission, and UN-AU cooperation in peacekeeping in general, see Williams and Dersso, "Saving Strangers and Neighbors." On features of AU peacekeeping missions, see Norwegian Institute of International Relations, "Strategic Options for the Future of African Peace Operations 2015–2025."

53 PSC, "Communiqué of the PSC at Its 411th Meeting Held at the Level of Heads of State and Government in Banjul the Gambia." See also Human Rights Council, "Report of the Commission on Human Rights in South Sudan"; and Mamdani, "A Separate Opinion."

54 See African Union, "Communique of 547th Meeting of the Peace and Security Council"; see also "Agreement on the Resolution for the Conflict in the Republic of South Sudan."

55 PSC, "Communiqué of the PSC 207th Meeting of the Peace and Security Council at the Level of Heads of State and Government."

56 UN Security Council, "Report of the International Commission of Inquiry Mandated to Establish the Facts and Circumstances of the Events of 28 September 2009 in Guinea," 3.

57 For a related report, see ICC-OTP, "Preliminary Examination: Guinea," http://www.icc-cpi.int/en_menus/icc/structure%20of%20the%20court/office%20of%20the%20prosecutor/comm%20and%20ref/pe-ongoing/guinea/Pages/guinea.aspx.

58 Kuperman, "A Model Humanitarian Intervention?"

59 I. H. Daalder and J. G. Stavridis, "NATO's Victory in Libya," *Foreign Affairs*, March/April 2012, https://www.foreignaffairs.com/articles/libya/2012-02-02/natos-victory-libya.

60 Kuperman, "A Model Humanitarian Intervention?," 105.

61 See Kuperman, "A Model Humanitarian Intervention?," 110. Kuperman argues

that evidence that Qaddafi avoided targeting civilians comes from HRW's report on the city of Misurata, which showed that of the 949 people wounded there in the rebellion's initial seven weeks, only thirty were women or children, meaning that Qaddafi's forces focused narrowly on combatants. During that same period, only 257 people were killed among the city's population of 400,000—a fraction less than 0.0006—providing additional proof that the government avoided using force indiscriminately. Moreover, Qaddafi did not perpetrate a "bloodbath" in any of the cities that his forces recaptured from rebels prior to NATO intervention—including Ajdabiya, Bani Walid, Brega, Ras Lanuf, Zawiya, and much of Misurata—so there was virtually no risk of such an outcome if he had been permitted to recapture the last rebel stronghold of Benghazi.

62 Kuperman, "A Model Humanitarian Intervention?," 113–114.

63 Kuperman argues that NATO attacked Libyan forces indiscriminately, including some in retreat and others in Qaddafi's hometown of Sirte, where they posed no threat to civilians. Moreover, NATO continued to aid the rebels even when they repeatedly rejected government cease-fire offers that could have ended the violence and spared civilians. Such military assistance included weapons, training, and covert deployment of hundreds of troops from Qatar, eventually enabling the rebels to capture and summarily execute Qaddafi and seize power in October 2011.

64 Kuperman, "A Model Humanitarian Intervention?"

65 See International Criminal Court, "Situation in Libya."

66 Mnookin, "Rethinking the Tension between Peace and Justice."

67 Mnookin, "Rethinking the Tension between Peace and Justice."

68 Kuperman, "A Model Humanitarian Intervention?"

69 Akuffo, "The Politics of Interregional Cooperation," 109.

70 Akuffo, "The Politics of Interregional Cooperation."

71 Akuffo, "The Politics of Interregional Cooperation."

72 African Union, Constitutive Act of the African Union.

73 Article 4 of the Protocol Relating to the Establishment of the Peace and Security Council of the African Union, July 9, 2002.

74 "AU Demands End to Libya Strikes," South African, May 26, 2011, https://www.thesouthafrican.com/au-demands-end-to-libya-strikes/.

75 Akuffo, "The Politics of Interregional Cooperation," 120.

76 IRRI, Proposed AU Amendments to Rome Statute for Kampala Review Conference, 2010.

77 See Nouwen, Complementarity in the Line of Fire; also see Abbas, "The Proposed International Criminal Jurisdiction for the African Court"; Udombana, "'Can These Dry Bones Live?,'" 1.

78 See Smith, "Moral Hazard and Humanitarian Law," making a case for humanitarian intervention in Darfur, noting that legal (judicial) responses have limits, and their role should be contextualized; Musila, "New Posture and Old Rhetoric?," 15–17 (on responses to the Darfur conflict and the role of the AU); see also Grono, "Briefing." On humanitarian intervention, see Udombana, "Still Playing Dice with Lives"; Kuwali, "The End of Humanitarian Intervention."

79 African Union, *Report of the African Union High-Level Panel on Darfur* (AUPD).

80 See also Shaw, Waldorf, and Hazan, *Localizing Transitional Justice*; Anders and Zenker, "Transition and Justice"; Branch, *Displacing Human Rights*; and also see Lucey and Kumalo, "How the AU Can Promote Transitional Justice in South Sudan." See also Rotberg and Thompson, *Truth v. Justice*; Sriram and Pillay, *Peace versus Justice?*; Roht-Arriaza and Mariezcurrena, *Transitional Justice in the Twenty-First Century*; Collins, *Post-Transitional Justice*.

81 See African Union, The African Governance Architecture (AGA) and Platform, http://aga-platform.org; "The African Governance Architecture," Europafrica .net, March 2011, https://europafrica.net/2011/03/10/the-african-governance -architecture/. See also Muhuthi, "The Advent of a Differentiated Accountability System."

82 Musila, "New Posture and Old Rhetoric?," 18–20.

83 Musila, "New Posture and Old Rhetoric?"

84 African Union, "Report on the Preparations for the Commemoration of the 50th Anniversary of the Organization of the African Unity/African Union (OAU/AU)."

85 AU Assembly, "Decision on the Implementation of the Assembly Decision on the Abuse of the Principle of Universal Jurisdiction" para. 9.

86 Protocol of the ACJ, note 7 above, Article 60 (requiring fifteen ratifications to enter into force). A list of countries that have signed or ratified/acceded to the Protocol of the Court of Justice of the African Union, as of June 15, 2017, is at https://au.int/sites/default/files/treaties/7784-sl-protocol_of_the_court_of_ justice_of_the_african_union_1.pdf.

87 Protocol to the African Charter on Human and Peoples' Rights on the Establishment of an African Court on Human and Peoples' Rights, see note 1 above, Article 3(1).

88 African Union, "42nd Activity Report of the African Commission on Human and Peoples' Rights."

89 AU Assembly, Decision on the Single Legal Instrument on the Merger of the African Court on Human and Peoples' Rights and the African Court of Justice.

90 AU Assembly, Decision on the Meeting of African States Parties to the Rome Statute of the International Criminal Court, para. 5.

91 AU Assembly, Decision on the Meeting of African States Parties to the Rome Statute of the International Criminal Court, annex Article 6 (replacing Article 16). Note that as of May 2018, only eleven countries have signed the protocol and none have ratified it.

92 See also Deya, "Worth the Wait."

93 Jalloh, Clarke, and Nmehielle, "Introduction."

94 *Situation in Darfur, Sudan Prosecutor v. Omar Hassan Al Bashir*, https://www .icc-cpi.int/CaseInformationSheets/AlBashirEng.pdf.

95 AU Assembly, "Decision on the Application by the International Criminal Court Prosecutor for the Indictment for the President of the Republic of Sudan."

96 AU Assembly, "Decision on the Meeting of African States Parties to the Rome Statute of the International Criminal Court," para. 2.

97   AU Assembly, Decision on the Meeting of African States Parties to the Rome
     Statute of the International Criminal Court, Thirteenth Ordinary Session, held
     in Sirte Libya on July 1–3, 2009, para. 3.
98   "Senegal Court Rejects Habre Extradition to Belgium," ICTJ, January 11, 2012,
     https://www.ictj.org/news/senegal-court-rejects-habre-extradition-belgium.
99   Habre Trial; see also Amnesty International Report, "Open Letter from Amnesty
     International to the Chairperson of the African Union on the Options for Trial
     of Hissène Habré," AI Index: IOR 63/001/2006, March 23, 2006, https://www
     .amnesty.org/download/Documents/68000/afr200022006en.pdf.
100 "Bringing a Dictator to Justice," Human Rights Watch, September 29, 2005,
     http://www.hrw.org/legacy/english/docs/2005/09/30/chad11797.htm; see also
     "Historical Background: The War against Libya and Internal Conflicts in Chad,"
     Human Rights Watch, https://www.hrw.org/reports/2005/chad0705/3.htm.
101 Michael Bronner, "Our Man in Africa," *Foreign Policy*, July 20, 2015, http://
     foreignpolicy.com/2014/01/24/our-man-in-africa/.
102 Ruth Maclean, "Chad's Hissène Habré Found Guilty of Crimes against Human-
     ity," *The Guardian*, May 30, 2016, https://www.theguardian.com/world/2016/may
     /30/chad-hissene-habre-guilty-crimes-against-humanity-senegal.
103 The PALU draft of the amended criminal jurisdiction was considered at validation
     workshops attended by legal counsel attached to AU organs and institutions, as
     well as representatives from some RECs (see Marc, Verjee, and Mogaka, *The Chal-
     lenge of Stability and Security in West Africa*). In July 2010, the second draft of the
     protocol was prepared following that meeting with AU Office of the Legal Coun-
     sel. The AU OLC organized internal review meetings in Midrand, South Africa, in
     November 2010, where piracy and aggression were reinstated and the subject mat-
     ter jurisdiction of the proposed court expanded to include transnational crimes
     (November 2010 [Midrand Draft] Protocol, document on file with author).
104 On January 19–20, the AU OLC organized a review meeting of African experts
     and Chief Security Officer actors of the Midrand Draft Protocol, held in Nai-
     robi, Kenya. This meeting was organized by PALU in collaboration with Open
     University of Tanzania and Open Society Initiative of East Africa. In Octo-
     ber and November 2011, AU OLC then organized two meetings of government
     legal experts in Addis Ababa to assess the Midrand Draft of the protocol. This
     was followed by a May 2012 AU summit meeting of the justice ministers and
     attorneys general, in Addis Ababa (see "Report of the Meeting of Govern-
     ment Experts and Ministers of Justice/Attorneys General on Legal Matters on
     the Draft Protocol on Amendments to the Protocol on the Statute of the Afri-
     can Court of Justice and Human Rights"). Following this, the executive coun-
     cil reviewed and endorsed the report of the Meeting of Ministers of Justice
     /Attorneys General ("Decision of the Executive Council Adopted during Its
     Twenty-First Ordinary Session").
105 Abraham, "Africa's Evolving Continental Court Structures," 7.
106 See Article 16 of African Union, Protocol on Amendments to the Protocol on
     the Statute of the African Court of Justice and Human Rights.

107 See Clarke, *Fictions of Justice*.

108 Donald Deya, interview with author, 2012.

109 See Article 16 of the Protocol on the Statute of the African Court of Justice and Human Rights.

110 Countries that have signed the protocol: Kenya, Benin, Chad, Congo, Ghana, Guinea-Bissau, Guinea, Sierra Leone, São Tomé and Principe, and Mauritania.

111 These are the African Commission on Human and People's Rights (Banjul Commission), the African Committee of Experts on the Rights and Welfare of the Child, the African Union Advisory Board on Corruption, the African Union Commission on International Law, the Peace and Security Council, the Courts of the Regional Economic Communities, the African Standby Force, and the African Capacity for the Immediate Response to Crises.

112 Powell, "The African Union's Emerging Peace and Security Regime."

113 As cited in Powell, "The African Union's Emerging Peace and Security Regime."

114 In relation to affects argued as both internalities and externalities, see Navaro, *The Make-Believe Space*.

115 Appel, *The Licit Life of Capitalism*.

Chapter 6. Reattributing the Irrelevance of the Official Capacity Movement

1 "Communique de Presse de la Réunion du Conseil des Ministres du Jeudi 06 Octobre 2016," Gouvernement du Burundi, Bujumbura, October 7, 2016, http://www.burundi.gov.bi/spip.php?article1534.

2 Tshililo Michael Masuthao, "Opening Statement," General Debate, Sixteenth Session of the Assembly of States Parties of the International Criminal Court, New York, December 4, 2017, https://asp.icc-cpi.int/iccdocs/asp_docs/ASP16/ASP -16-ZA.pdf.

3 Burundi's withdrawal will not affect the country's existing obligations in relation to ongoing proceedings or investigations, and it will not come into effect until after a one-year waiting period has elapsed and the subsequent notification of withdrawal is registered with UN treaty office.

4 Citing Lambert Nigarura in "Burundi on Regressive Path Following ICC Withdrawal Vote" (press release), Coalition for the International Criminal Court, October 12, 2016, http://www.iccnow.org/documents/CICCPR_BurundiICC withdrawal_Oct2016_(1).pdf.

5 Just one week after that, on October 25, 2016, Gambia announced its intent to withdraw as well. This was reversed in February 2017 when the country, under new leadership, decided to cancel its withdrawal from the ICC.

6 "Gambia Withdraws from International Criminal Court," *Al Jazeera*, October 25, 2016, https://www.aljazeera.com/news/2016/10/gambia-withdraws-international -criminal-court-161026041436188.html.

7 Camila Domonoske, "South Africa Announces Withdrawal from International Criminal Court," *National Public Radio*, October 21, 2016, https://www .npr.org/sections/thetwo-way/2016/10/21/498817513/south-africa-announces

-withdrawal-from-international-criminal-court; Eamon Aloyo, Geoff Dancy, Tessa Alleblas, and Yvonne Dutton, "Is the International Criminal Court Biased against Africans? Kenyan Victims Don't Think So," *Washington Post*, March 6, 2017, https://www.washingtonpost.com/news/monkey-cage/wp/2017/03/06/is-the -international-criminal-court-biased-against-africans-kenyan-victims-dont -think-so/?utm_term=.74a2833ac246.

8 "Mandela Legacy on the Line as South Africa Moves to Leave ICC" (press release), Coalition for the International Criminal Court, October 21, 2016, http:// www.iccnow.org/documents/CICCPR_SouthAfrica_Oct2016.pdf.

9 "Mandela Legacy on the Line as South Africa Moves to Leave ICC."

10 "Mandela Legacy on the Line as South Africa Moves to Leave ICC."

11 "Gambia Urges U.N. Inquiry into 'Deliberate' Migrant Shipwrecks," Reuters, World News, September 25, 2014, https://www.reuters.com/article/us-un-assembly -gambia/gambia-urges-u-n-inquiry-into-deliberate-migrant-shipwrecks-id USKCN0HK2TB20140925.

12 "Gambia urges U.N. Inquiry into 'Deliberate' Migrant Shipwrecks."

13 Pap Saine, "Gambia's Jammeh Wants ICC to Investigate Migrant Deaths," *Daily Mail*, June 8, 2015, http://www.dailymail.co.uk/wires/reuters/article-3115847 /Gambias-Jammeh-wants-ICC-investigate-migrant-deaths.html#ixzz53DhcSKlZ.

14 Elise Keppler, "Gambia Rejoins ICC: South Africa, Burundi Now Outliers on Exit," Human Rights Watch, February 17, 2017, https://www.hrw.org/news/2017 /02/17/gambia-rejoins-icc.

15 "South Africa: Revocation of Withdrawal from the ICC a Chance to Rethink Thwarting Pursuit of Justice," Amnesty International, March 8, 2017, https://www .amnesty.org/en/latest/news/2017/03/south-africa-revocation-of-withdrawal -from-the-icc-a-chance-to-rethink-thwarting-pursuit-of-justice/.

16 Arrest Warrant of 11 April 2000 (Democratic Republic of the Congo v. Bel- gium), International Court of Justice. See *Case Concerning the Arrest Warrant of 11 April 2000 (Democratic Republic of the Congo v. Belgium)*, ICJ, February 14, 2012, https://www.refworld.org/cases,ICJ,3c6cd39b4.html; Tladi, "The Immunity Provision in the AU Amendment Protocol," 12.

17 Tladi, "The Immunity Provision in the AU Amendment Protocol," 12.

18 Tladi, "The Immunity Provision in the AU Amendment Protocol," 12.

19 Tladi, "The Immunity Provision in the AU Amendment Protocol," 12–13.

20 Vienna Convention on the Law of Treaties, Article 34; see also International Criminal Court, "Situation in Darfur, Sudan: In the Case of *The Prosecutor v. Omar Hassan Ahmad Al-Bashir*," Decision on the Cooperation of the Democratic Republic of the Congo Regarding Omar Al Bashir's Arrest and Surrender to the Court, April 9, 2014, para. 26; AU Press Release No. 002/2012, 2.

21 ICC, "Situation in Darfur, Sudan: In the Case of *The Prosecutor v. Omar Has- san Ahmad Al-Bashir*," Decision on the Cooperation of the Democratic Repub- lic of the Congo Regarding Omar Al-Bashir's Arrest and Surrender to the Court, April 9, 2014, at para. 26; ICC, "Situation in Darfur, Sudan: In the Case of *The Pros- ecutor v. Omar Hassan Al-Bashir*," Case No. ICC-02/05-01/09, decision under Arti-

cle 87(7) of the Rome Statute on noncompliance by South Africa with the request by the court for the arrest and surrender of Omar Al-Bashir, July 6, 2017, para. 82; Akande, "The Legal Nature of Security Council Referrals to the ICC," 339.

22 ICC, "Situation in Darfur, Sudan: In the Case of *The Prosecutor v. Omar Hassan Al-Bashir*," Case No. ICC-02/05-01/09, decision under article 87(7) of the Rome Statute on the noncompliance by Jordan with the request by the court for the arrest and surrender of Omar Al-Bashir, December 11, 2017, para. 37–38; ICC, "Situation in Darfur, Sudan: In the Case of *The Prosecutor v. Omar Hassan Ahmad Al-Bashir*," decision under Article 87(7) of the Rome Statue on the noncompliance by South Africa with the request by the Court for the arrest and surrender of Omar Al-Bashir, para. 85–86; see also Akande, "The Legal Nature of Security Council Referrals to the ICC," 340.

23 ICC, "Situation in Darfur, Sudan: In the Case of *The Prosecutor v. Omar Hassan Al-Bashir*," Case No. ICC-02/05-01/09, decision under Article 87(7) of the Rome Statute on the noncompliance by Jordan with the request by the court for the arrest and surrender of Omar Al-Bashir, at para. 15 (describing Jordan's argument); ICC, "Situation in Darfur, Sudan: In the Case of *The Prosecutor v. Omar Hassan Al-Bashir*," Case No. ICC-02/05-01/09, submission from the government of the Republic of South Africa for the purposes of proceedings under Article 87(7) of the Rome Statute, March 17, 2017, para. 52.2; AU Press Release No. 002 /2012, 2; see also Arrest Warrant of 11 April 2000 (*Democratic Republic of the Congo v. Belgium*), International Court of Justice; see *Case Concerning the Arrest Warrant of 11 April 2000 (Democratic Republic of the Congo v. Belgium)*, ICJ, February 14, 2012, https://www.refworld.org/cases,ICJ,3c6cd39b4.html; Mwangi and Mphepo, "Developments in International Criminal Justice in Africa during 2011."

24 Rome Statute of the ICC, Article 98(1). South Africa's submission in the Al Bashir case, at para. 52.2, 52.6, 61, 65; see also Dapo Akande, "ICC Issues Detailed Decision on Bashir's Immunity (. . . at long Last . . .) but Gets the Law Wrong," *EJIL: Talk!*, December 15, 2011, https://www.ejiltalk.org/icc-issues-detailed-decision -on-bashir%E2%80%99s-immunity-at-long-last-but-gets-the-law-wrong/; Tladi, "Interpretation and International Law in South African Courts," 331; Gaeta, "Official Capacity and Immunities," 329.

25 Akande, Du Plessis, and Jalloh, "Position Paper," 5. See also AU report, "Decision of the Meeting of African States Parties to the Rome Statute of the International Criminal Court," Thirteenth Ordinary Session, July 1–3, 2009, 8, https:// reliefweb.int/report/sudan/decision-meeting-african-states-parties-rome-statute -international-criminal-court-icc; PSC, "Communiqué of the 207th Meeting of the Peace and Security Council at the Level of the Heads of State and Government."

26 Akhavan, "Are International Criminal Tribunals a Disincentive to Peace?," 648; Akande, Du Plessis, and Jalloh, "Position Paper," 6.

27 Akande, Du Plessis, and Jalloh, "Position Paper," 6.

28 ICC Decision on Jordan's Noncompliance, at para. 33; ICC Decision on South Africa's Noncompliance, at para. 74–76, 91, 93–94; see also Akande, "The Legal Nature of Security Council Referrals to the ICC," 338.

29 ICC Decision on Jordan's Noncompliance, at para. 33, 39.

30 ICC Decision on the DRC's Cooperation, at para. 29; ICC Decision on South Africa's Noncompliance, at para. 87–89.

31 ICC, Warrant of Arrest for Omar Hassan Ahmad Al Bashir.

32 UN General Assembly, "Request for an advisory opinion of the International Court of Justice on the consequences of legal obligations of State under different sources of international law with respect to immunities of Heads of State and Government and other senior officials." From the permanent representative of Kenya to the United Nations, Seventy-Third Session, July 18, 2018, https://digitallibrary.un.org/record/1636896/files/A_73_144-EN.pdf.

33 "Warrant 'Subverts Peace and Solidarity' in Africa," *Business Day*, July 26, 2010, cited in Du Plessis, *The International Criminal Court That Africa Wants*, 89.

34 Abraham, "Africa's Evolving Continental Court Structures," 10.

35 Abraham, "Africa's Evolving Continental Court Structures," 10.

36 Abraham, "Africa's Evolving Continental Court Structures," 10.

37 Abraham, "Africa's Evolving Continental Court Structures," 10.

38 African Union, "Decisions and Declarations, Extraordinary Session of the Assembly of the African Union," para. 52.

39 The word *bis* comes from old Latin and means "repeat" and "twice" in Old High German. It is applied to various modern protocol standards to indicate the second version of the protocol.

40 Tladi, "The Immunity Provision in the AU Amendment Protocol," 11.

41 Hobbs, in notes on file with author.

42 While Article 38 of the Statute of the International Court of Justice (and before it Article 38 of the Statute of the Permanent Court of International Justice) lists international treaties and CIL as the two most significant "sources of international law," it also goes on to list two other sources, "general principles of law recognized by civilized nations" and "judicial decisions and the teachings of the most highly qualified publicists of the various nations." Many international lawyers have since sought to add UN resolutions, both Security Council and General Assembly resolutions, to that list of "soft law," *jus cogens* norms, obligations *erga omnes*, and a litany of other modes of international legality, each with varying claims to formal validity and substantive coherence.

43 S. R. Adjovi, "Immunities in International Criminal Law: The Challenges from Africa," International Commission of Jurists, May 2015, http://www.icj-kenya.org/dmdocuments/papers/discussion%20paper%20on%20immunities.pdf, 1.

44 Du Plessis, *The International Criminal Court That Africa Wants*, 77.

45 Tladi, "The Immunity Provision in the AU Amendment Protocol," 10. Tladi cites the following: AU Commission Press Release 02/2012 on the Decision of Pre-trial Chamber of the ICC Pursuant to Art. 87(7) of the Rome Statute on the Alleged Failure by the Republic of Chad and the Republic of Malawi to Comply with the Cooperation Requests Issued by the Court with Respect to the Arrest and Surrender of President Omar Hassan Al Bashir of the Republic of the Sudan, January 9, 2012. See also Dapo Akande, "The African Union's Response to the ICC's

Decisions on Bashir's Immunity: Will the ICJ Get Another Immunity Case?,"
EJIL Talk!, February 8, 2012, https://www.ejiltalk.org/2012/02/page/2/, who states
that "what the AU wants is an opinion [from the ICJ] that would clarify the
immunity (or otherwise) of State officials from prosecution by the ICC and from
enforcement action taken by States acting at the request of the ICC."

46 ICC, "Situation in Darfur, Sudan: In the Case of *The Prosecutor v. Omar Hassan
Ahmad Al-Bashir.*

47 Akande and Shah, "Immunities of State Officials, International Crimes, and Foreign Domestic Courts," 819.

48 ICC-02/05-01/09-139, "Corrigendum to the Decision Pursuant to Article 87(7) of
the Rome Statute on the Failure by the Republic of Malawi to Comply with the
Cooperation Requests," para. 36.

49 ICC-02/05-01/09-195, "Decision on the Cooperation of the Democratic Republic
of the Congo," para. 27.

50 ICC-02/05-01/09-195, para. 29.

51 ICC-02/05-01/09-302, "Decision under Article 87(7) of the Rome Statute on the
Noncompliance by South Africa with the Request by the Court," para. 91–93.

52 ICC-02/05-01/09-302, para. 74.

53 ICC-02/05-01/09-302, para. 93.

54 Coalition for the International Criminal Court, "Report on the 12th Session of
the Assembly of States Parties to the Rome State."

55 Djenaba Diarra, comment at Assembly of States Parties, November 2013, The
Hague.

56 Djenaba Diarra in discussion with the author at Assembly of States Parties,
November 2013, The Hague.

57 Comment at Assembly of States Parties, November 2013, The Hague.

58 Comment at Assembly of States Parties, November 2013, The Hague.

59 Comment at Assembly of States Parties, November 2013, The Hague.

60 Comment at Assembly of States Parties, November 2013, The Hague.

61 Comment at Assembly of States Parties, November 2013, The Hague.

62 Charles Jalloh speaking at the Twelfth Session of the Assembly of States Parties
(ICC_ASP/12/61), The Hague, November 20–28, 2013. See also Gaeta, "Official
Capacity and Immunities," 978.

63 See International Court of Justice, Reports of Judgement, Advisory Opinions
and Orders: Case Concerning the "Arrest Warrant of 11 April 2000 (*Democratic
Republic of the Congo v. Belgium*)," Judgement of 14 February 2002, para. 61,
p. 25, https://www.icj-cij.org/files/case-related/121/121-20020214-JUD-01-00-EN
.pdf.

64 Du Plessis, *The International Criminal Court That Africa Wants*, 77.

65 Akande, "International Law Immunities and the International Criminal Court,"
409.

66 See also Foucault, *Discipline and Punish*; Agamben, *Homo Sacer*; Agamben, *State
of Exception*; and Foucault, *The History of Sexuality*.

67 Rao, "The Concept of International Community in International Law," 102;

"Brief Profile: P. S. Rao," National Law University, http://www.nlujodhpur.ac.in
/downloads/profile-rao.

68 United Nations Security Council, Frequently Asked Questions (FAQ), accessed
March 31, 2019, https://www.un.org/securitycouncil/content/faq.

69 United Nations Security Council, Frequently Asked Questions.

70 United Nations Security Council, Frequently Asked Questions.

71 United Nations Security Council, "Voting System," UN News Center, accessed
March 31, 2019, https://www.un.org/securitycouncil/content/voting-system.

72 General Assembly of the United Nations, "Functions and Powers of the General Assembly," accessed March 31, 2019, https://www.un.org/en/ga/about
/background.shtml.

73 General Assembly of the United Nations, "Functions and Powers of the General
Assembly."

74 General Assembly of the United Nations, "Functions and Powers of the General
Assembly."

75 The International Criminal Court can assume jurisdiction if a case is referred to
it by the UNSC, per Article 13 of the Rome Statute.

76 Schabas, *The International Criminal Court*, 446.

77 Gaeta, "Official Capacity and Immunities," 978.

78 Gaeta, "Official Capacity and Immunities."

79 Akande, "International Law Immunities and the International Criminal Court,"
413.

80 Akande, "International Law Immunities and the International Criminal Court,"
413.

81 Jakobsen, "Immunity versus Impunity?"; see also Cassese, "When May Senior
State Officials Be Tried for International Crimes?," 13.

82 *Eichmann v. Attorney-General of Israel*, Supreme Court of Israel (1962) 136 ILR, at
277; Jakobsen, "Immunity versus Impunity?," 20.

83 *R v. Bow Street Metropolitan Stipendiary Magistrate, Ex Parte Pinochet
Ugarte* (H.L. 1998), 3 WLR 1, 456.

84 See *R v. Bow Street Metropolitan Stipendiary Magistrate*; see also Wirth, "Immunities, Related Problems, and Article 98 of the Rome Statute," 434.

85 Wirth, "Immunities, Related Problems, and Article 98 of the Rome Statute,"
434–437.

86 Akande, "International Law Immunities and the International Criminal Court,"
409. Diplomatic agents also enjoy a type of personal immunity referred to as
diplomatic immunity, governed by United Nations, Vienna Convention on
Diplomatic Relations, 1961, http://legal.un.org/ilc/texts/instruments/english
/conventions/9_1_1961.pdf.

87 Akande, "International Law Immunities and the International Criminal Court,"
409–410.

88 Akande, "International Law Immunities and the International Criminal Court,"
410; confirmed by the ICJ in Arrest Warrant of 11 April 2000 (Democratic
Republic of the Congo v. Belgium), para. 54.

89   Akande, "International Law Immunities and the International Criminal Court,"
     410.
90   See Article 27, para. 2, p. 8 of the Vienna Convention on Diplomatic Relations.
91   "Report of the Working Group on Amendment of the Assembly of States Parties
     of the International Criminal Court," ICC-ASP/13/31, 16.
92   Secretariat of the Assembly of States Parties, Compilation of proposals to amend
     the Rome Statute, January 23, 2015, 15:30. Document on file with author.
93   "Report of the Working Group," ICC-ASP/13/31, para. 12.
94   "Report of the Working Group," ICC-ASP/13/31, para. 12.
95   See Preamble of African Union Protocol on Amendments to the Protocol on the
     Statute of the African Court of Justice and Human Rights, June 27, 2014.
96   Amended ACJHR Statute, Article 46(H).
97   Rome Statute, Article 86.
98   Conclusions of the Meeting of the Open Ended Committee of Ministers of For-
     eign Affairs on the International Criminal Court at the Level of Permanent Rep-
     resentatives, fieldwork notes on file with author.
99   International Court of Justice, Asylum Case (Colombia/Peru), 266.
100 Tladi, "Interpretation and International Law in South African Courts."
101 For further discussion, see Adjovi, "Immunities in International Criminal
     Law"; Imoedemhe, "Unpacking the Tension between the African Union and the
     International Criminal Court"; Du Plessis, *Shambolic, Shameful and Symbolic*;
     Abraham, "Africa's Evolving Continental Court Structures"; Igwe, "The ICC's
     Favourite Customer."
102 See Cassese, *International Criminal Law*, 320; Gaeta, "Official Capacities and
     Immunities," 975, 983–989. See also the Ghaddafi case, Arrêt no. 1414 (2001),
     125 ILR, 456 (France: Cour de Cassation); Castro case (Spain: Audiencia Nacio-
     nal, 1999), cited in Cassese, *International Criminal Law*, 320n24; Re Sharon and
     Yaron, 42 ILM (2003) 596 (Belgium: Cour de Cassation); *R v. Bow Street Sti-
     pendiary Magistrate and Others, Ex Parte Pinochet* (No. 3), [1999] 2 All E.R. 97,
     126–127, 149, 179, 189 (UK House of Lords, per Lords Goff, Hope, Millett, and
     Phillips).
103 Special Court for Sierra Leone, "Decision on Immunity from jurisdiction,"
     (SCSL-2003-01-I), Freetown, Sierra Leone, May 31, 2004, note 53, http://www
     .worldcourts.com/scsl/eng/decisions/2004.05.31_Prosecutor_v_Taylor.pdf.
104 Arrest Warrant, April 11, 2000, *Democratic Republic of the Congo v. Belgium*.
105 Nouwen, "The Special Court for Sierra Leone and the Immunity of Taylor," 668.
106 Nouwen, "The Special Court for Sierra Leone and the Immunity of Taylor," 668.
107 Nouwen, "The Special Court for Sierra Leone and the Immunity of Taylor," 668.
108 See Kujenga Amani, "Article 46A bis: Implications for Peace, Justice, and Rec-
     onciliation in Africa," Social Science Research Council, October 21, 2014, http://
     forums.ssrc.org/kujenga-amani/2014/10/21/article-46a-bis-implications-for
     -peace-justice-and-reconciliation-in-africa/#.VkptHd-rSRt.
109 For example, the international crime of unconstitutional change of government.
110 In January 2012, during the Nineteenth African Union Summit, over thirty civil

society organizations from close to twenty African countries wrote to the African member states of the ICC and urged them to renew their support for the ICC's efforts to combat grave international crimes.

111 See Du Plessis, *Shambolic, Shameful and Symbolic*, 11; Amnesty International, "Africa: Malabo Protocol," 27, 35; also Dey, "Protecting the Powerful."

112 Vuki Ezrom Sibia and Michelle Nel, "Withdrawal from the International Criminal Court: Does Africa Have an Alternative?," African Centre for the Constructive Resolution of Disputes, September 12, 2017, http://www.accord.org.za/ajcr-issues/withdrawal-international-criminal-court/.

113 See "Joint Letter to the Justice Ministers and Attorneys General of the African States Parties to the International Criminal Court," Human Rights Watch, May 3, 2012, https://www.hrw.org/news/2012/05/03/joint-letter-justice-ministers-and-attorneys-general-african-states-parties; and "Statement Regarding Immunity for Sitting Officials," Human Rights Watch, November 13, 2014, https://www.hrw.org/news/2014/11/13/statement-regarding-immunity-sitting-officials-expanded-african-court-justice-and; and Karim Lahidji et al., "Immunity of Heads of State and Government for International Crimes?," International Federation for Human Rights, June 20, 2014, https://www.fidh.org/International-Federation-for-Human-Rights/15601-immunity-of-heads-of-state-and-government-for-international-crimes-the; and "AU Summit Decision a Backward Step for International Justice," Amnesty International, July 1, 2014, https://www.amnesty.org/en/latest/news/2014/07/au-summit-decision-backward-step-international-justice/; "IBA and SALC Express Alarm at AU's Endorsement of Immunity for Heads of State," International Bar Association, July 9, 2014, http://www.ibanet.org/Article/Detail.aspx?ArticleUid=f0c41e45-693d-4712-98c8-3da28c2b949d.

114 African Union, Constitutive Act of the African Union, Article 4(h).

115 On Article 46A *bis*, see sections by Idayat Hassan and Anne Kubai; African Union, Constitutive Act of the African Union, Article 4(o), http://www.au.int/en/sites/default/files/ConstitutiveAct_EN.pdf.

116 Amani, "Article 46A bis."

117 Abass, "Prosecuting International Crimes in Africa."

118 Odinkalu, "International Criminal Justice, Peace and Reconciliation in Africa."

119 Assembly of the Union, Twenty-Sixth Ordinary Session, Assembly/AU/Dec.590 (XXVI), 3.

120 Clarke and Kassaye, "African State Withdrawals from the Rome Statute for the International Criminal Court."

121 Helfer, "Terminating Treaties," 636.

122 Rome Statute (last amended January 2002), July 17, 1998, 2187 UNTS 90 art. 127.

123 Helfer, "Exiting Treaties," 1588.

124 Helfer, "Exiting Treaties," 1582.

125 Helfer, "Exiting Treaties," 1646.

126 Helfer, "Terminating Treaties," 645.

127 *Opinio juris* is the second element (along with state practice) in international law that is necessary to establish a legally binding custom.

128 See International Court of Justice, *Reports of Judgements, Advisory Opinions and Orders.*

129 International Law Association, *Statement of Principles Applicable to the Formation of General Customary International Law.*

130 Bradley and Gulati, "Withdrawing from International Custom," 212.

131 Bradley and Gulati, "Withdrawing from International Custom," 250.

132 Bradley and Gulati, "Withdrawing from International Custom," 249 n. 202.

Epilogue. Toward an Anthropology of International Justice

1 Thomas Spijkerboer, "The International Refugee Regime" (lecture, Carleton University, Ottawa, December 2017).

2 Foucault, *The Order of Things.*

3 Grovogui, "To the Orphaned, Dispossessed, and Illegitimate Children."

Bibliography

Abass, Ademola. "The Proposed International Criminal Jurisdiction for the African Court: Some Problematical Aspects." *Netherlands International Law Review* 60 (2013): 27–50.

Abass, Ademola. "Prosecuting International Crimes in Africa: Rationale, Prospects and Challenges." *European Journal of International Law* 24, no. 3 (2013): 933–946.

Aboagye, Festus. "The African Mission in Burundi: Lessons Learned from the First African Union Peacekeeping Operation." *Conflict Trends* 2 (2004): 9–15.

Abraham, Garth. "Africa's Evolving Continental Court Structures: At the Crossroads?" Occasional Paper 209. South African Institute of International Affairs, January 2015.

Abu-Lughod, Lila. *Do Muslim Women Need Saving?* Cambridge, MA: Harvard University Press, 2013.

Abu-Lughod, Lila. *Veiled Sentiments: Honor and Poetry in a Bedouin Society.* Berkeley: University of California Press, 1986.

Agamben, Giorgio. *Homo Sacer: Sovereign Power and Bare Life.* Stanford, CA: Stanford University Press, 1998.

Agamben, Giorgio. *State of Exception.* Chicago: University of Chicago Press, 2005.

Agathangelou, Anna M., and Kyle D. Killian. *Time, Temporality and Violence in International Relations: (De)Fatalizing the Present, Forging Radical Alternatives.* Abingdon, UK: Routledge, 2017.

Ahmed, Sara. "Affective Economies." *Social Text* 79, no. 2 (2004): 117–139.

Ahmed, Sara. *The Cultural Politics of Emotion.* Edinburgh: Edinburgh University Press, 2004.

Ahmed, Sara. *The Promise of Happiness.* Durham, NC: Duke University Press, 2010.

Akande, Dapo. "The Bashir Indictment: Are Serving Heads of State Immune from ICC Prosecution?" *Oxford Transitional Justice Research Working Paper Series,* July 30, 2008.

Akande, Dapo. "International Law Immunities and the International Criminal Court." *American Journal of International Law* 98, no. 3 (2004): 407–433.

Akande, Dapo. "The Jurisdiction of the International Criminal Court over Nationals of Non-Parties: Legal Basis and Limits." *Journal of International Criminal Justice* 1, no. 3 (2003): 618–650.

Akande, Dapo. "The Legal Nature of Security Council Referrals to the ICC and Its Impact on Al Bashir's Immunities." *International Journal of Criminal Justice* 7, no. 2 (2009): 333–352.

Akande, Dapo, M. Du Plessis, and C. C. Jalloh. "Position Paper: An African Expert Study on the African Union Concerns about Article 16 of the Rome Statute of the ICC." Institute for Security Studies, October 28, 2010, 1–30. https://papers.ssrn.com/sol3/papers.cfm?abstract_id=1969124.

Akande, Dapo, and S. Shah. "Immunities of State Officials, International Crimes, and Foreign Domestic Courts." *European Journal of International Law* 21 (2011): 815–852.

Akhavan, Payam. "Are International Criminal Tribunals a Disincentive to Peace? Reconciling Judicial Romanticism with Political Realism." *Human Rights Quarterly* 31, no. 3 (2009): 624–654.

Akuffo, E. A. "The Politics of Interregional Cooperation: The Impact of NATO's Intervention in Libya on Its Relations with the African Union." *African Conflict and Peacebuilding Review* 4 (2014): 108–128.

Allen, Lori A. "Martyr Bodies in the Media: Human Rights, Aesthetics, and the Politics of Immediation in the Palestinian Intifada." *American Ethnologist* 36, no. 1 (2009): 161–180.

Anand, R. P. *International Law and the Developing Countries: Confrontation or Cooperation?* New Delhi: Banyan, 1987.

Anders, Gerhart, and O. Zenker. "Transition and Justice: Negotiating the Terms of New Beginnings in Africa." *Development and Change* 45, no. 3 (2014): 395–414.

Anderson, Benedict R. O. *Imagined Communities: Reflections on the Origin and Spread of Nationalism.* Rev. ed. New York: Verso, 2006.

Anghie, Antony. *Imperialism, Sovereignty, and the Making of International Law.* Cambridge: Cambridge University Press, 2004.

Appel, Hannah. *The Licit Life of Capitalism: U.S. Oil in Equatorial Guinea.* Durham, NC: Duke University Press, 2019.

Arendt, Hannah. *Responsibility and Judgment.* New York: Schocken, 2003.

Ariyo, Ademola, and Olanrewaju Olaniyan. "Structural Transformation and Inequality: Evidence from Nigeria." *Development* 57, nos. 3–4 (2014): 531–539.

Asad, Talal. *Formations of the Secular: Christianity, Islam, Modernity.* Stanford, CA: Stanford University Press, 2003.

Atieno-Odhiambo, E. S. "The Production of History in Kenya: The Mau Mau Debate." *Canadian Journal of African Studies* 25, no. 2 (1991): 300–307.

Augé, Marc. *Non-Places: Introduction to an Anthropology of Supermodernity.* London: Verso, 2009.

Bakhtin, M. M. *The Dialogic Imagination: Four Essays.* Edited by Michael Holquist, translated by Caryl Emerson and Michael Holquist. Austin: University of Texas Press, 1981.

Baldo, Suliman. "Sudan: Impact of the Rome Statute and the International Criminal Court." International Center for Transitional Justice, May 1, 2010. https://www .ictj.org/publication/sudan-impact-rome-statute-and-international-criminal -court.

Bandes, Susan A. *The Passions of Law*. New York: New York University Press, 1999.

Bandes, Susan A., and J. A. Blumenthal. "Emotion and Law." *Annual Review of Law and Social Science* 8, no. 1 (2012): 161–181.

Barad, Karen Michelle. *Meeting the Universe Halfway: Quantum Physics and the Entanglement of Matter and Meaning*. Durham, NC: Duke University Press. 2007.

Barreto, Jose-Manuel. "The Turn to Emotions: Law, Geopolitics, Aesthetics." Paper presented at the Critical Legal Conference Utrecht, "'Great Expectations': Multiple Modernities of Law." Utrech University, Netherlands, September 10–12, 2010.

Bargh, John A., Kay L. Schwader, Sarah E. Hailey, Rebecca L. Dyer, and Erica J. Boothby. "Automaticity in Social-Cognitive Processes." *Trends in Cognitive Sciences* 16, no. 12 (2012): 593–605.

Barthes, Roland. "Shock-Photos." In *The Eiffel Tower and Other Mythologies*. New York: Hill and Wang, 1979.

Baxi, Upendra. "What May the 'Third World' Expect from International Law?" *Third World Quarterly* 27 (2006): 713–725.

Berg, Ulla, and Ana Ramos-Zayas. "Racializing Affect: A Theoretical Proposition." *Current Anthropology* 56, no. 5 (2015): 654–677.

Berlant, Lauren. *Compassion: The Culture and Politics of an Emotion*. New York: Routledge, 2004.

Bertolino, Elisabetta. "Body, Emotions, and Human Rights Justice." Paper presented at the Critical Legal Conference Utrecht, "'Great Expectations': Multiple Modernities of Law." Utrech University, Netherlands, September 10–12, 2010.

Bevernage, Berber. *History, Memory, and State-Sponsored Violence*. New York: Routledge, 2012.

Bevernage, Berber. "Time, Presence, and Historical Injustice." *History and Theory* 47, no. 2 (2008): 149–167.

Blichner, L. C., and A. Molander. "Mapping Juridification." *European Law Journal* 14, no. 1 (2008): 36–54.

Blyden, Edward W. "The Aims and Methods of a Liberal Education for Africans." Inaugural address, January 5, 1881. Cambridge: Cambridge University Press, 1882.

Bonilla, Yarimar, and Jonathan Rosa. "#Ferguson: Digital Protest, Hashtag Ethnography, and the Racial Politics of Social Media in the United States." *American Ethnologist* 42, no. 1 (2015): 4–17.

Bourdieu, Pierre. *Outline of a Theory of Practice*. Cambridge Studies in Social and Cultural Anthropology 16. Cambridge: Cambridge University Press, 1977.

Brachotte, Gilles, and Alex Frame, eds. *Citizen Participation and Political Communi-*

cation in a Digital World. Routledge Studies in New Media and Cyberculture 32. New York: Routledge, 2015.

Bradley, Curtis A., and Mitu Gulati. "Withdrawing from International Custom." Yale Law Journal 120 (2010): 202–275.

Branch, Adam. Displacing Human Rights: War and Intervention in Northern Uganda. Oxford: Oxford University Press, 2011.

Branch, Adam. "Uganda's Civil War and the Politics of ICC Intervention." Ethics and International Affairs 21, no. 2 (2007): 179–198.

Brants, Chrisje. "Guilty Landscapes." In Cosmopolitan Justice and Its Discontents, edited by Cecilia Baillet and Katja Frank Aas. New York: Routledge, 2011.

Brett, André. "'The Miserable Remnant of This Ill-Used People': Colonial Genocide and the Moriori of New Zealand's Chatham Islands." Journal of Genocide Research 17, no. 2 (2015): 133–152.

Brown, Stephen. "International Criminal Justice and Electoral Violence: The Stakes of the ICC 's Involvement in Kenya." Revue Tiers Monde, no. 205 (2011): 85–100.

Burgis, Tom. The Looting Machine: Warlords, Oligarchs, Corporations, Smugglers, and the Theft of Africa's Wealth. New York: Public Affairs, 2015.

Cantero, Lucia E. "Specters of the Market: Consumer-Citizenship and the Visual Politics of Race and Inequality in Brazil." PhD diss., Yale University, 2015. ProQuest Dissertations (AAT 1701284804).

Cassese, Antonio. "From Nuremberg to Rome." In The Rome Statute of the International Criminal Court: A Commentary, edited by Antonio Cassese, P. Gaeta, and J. Jones. Oxford: Oxford University Press, 2002.

Cassese, Antonio. International Criminal Law. 3rd ed. Oxford: Oxford University Press, 2008.

Cassese, Antonio. "When May Senior State Officials Be Tried for International Crimes? Some Comments of the Congo v. Belgium Case." European Journal of International Law 13, no. 4 (2002): 853–875.

Cazdyn, Eric. The Already Dead: The New Time of Politics, Culture, and Illness. Durham, NC: Duke University Press, 2012.

Chalfin, Brenda. Neoliberal Frontiers: An Ethnography of Sovereignty in West Africa. Chicago: University of Chicago Press, 2010.

Cheeseman, Nic. "The Kenyan Elections of 2007: An Introduction." Journal of Eastern African Studies 2, no. 2 (2008): 166–184.

Chouliaraki, Lilie. The Spectatorship of Suffering. Thousand Oaks, CA: Sage, 2006.

Clarke, Kamari Maxine. Fictions of Justice: The International Criminal Court and the Challenge of Legal Pluralism in Sub-Saharan Africa. New York: Cambridge University Press, 2009.

Clarke, Kamari Maxine. "Refiguring the Perpetrator: Culpability, History and International Criminal Law's Impunity Gap." International Journal of Human Rights 19, no. 5 (2015): 592–614.

Clarke, Kamari Maxine, and Mark Goodale, eds. Mirrors of Justice: Law and Power in the Post–Cold War Era. New York: Cambridge University Press, 2009.

Clarke, Kamari Maxine, and Ermias Kassaye. "African State Withdrawals from the

Rome Statute for the International Criminal Court." African Court Research Initiative, November 1, 2016.

Clarke, Kamari M., Abel S. Knottnerus, and Eefje de Volder, eds. *Africa and the ICC: Perceptions of Justice*. New York: Cambridge University Press, 2016.

Clough, Patricia Ticineto, and Jean Halley, eds. *The Affective Turn: Theorizing the Social*. Durham, NC: Duke University Press, 2007.

Collins, C. *Post-Transitional Justice: Human Rights Trials in Chile and El Salvador*. University Park: Pennsylvania State University Press, 2010.

Colombetti, G. 2014. *The Feeling Body: Affective Science Meets the Enactive Mind*. Cambridge, MA: MIT Press, 2014.

Comaroff, Jean, and John L. Comaroff. "Law and Disorder in the Postcolony: An Introduction." In *Law and Disorder in the Postcolony*. Chicago: University of Chicago Press, 2006.

Comaroff, Jean, and John L. Comaroff. *Millennial Capitalism and the Culture of Neoliberalism*. Durham, NC: Duke University Press, 2001.

Constable, Marianne. *Just Silences: The Limits and Possibilities of Modern Law*. Princeton, NJ: Princeton University Press, 2005.

Constable, Marianne. *Our Word Is Our Bond: How Legal Speech Acts*. Stanford, CA: Stanford University Press, 2014.

Cooper, Frederick. *Africa in the World: Capitalism, Empire, Nation-State*. Cambridge, MA: Harvard University Press, 2014.

Crawford, James. *The International Law Commission's Articles on State Responsibility: Introduction, Text and Commentaries*. Cambridge: Cambridge University Press, 2002.

Dahlberg-Grundberg, Michael. "Technology as Movement: On Hybrid Organizational Types and the Mutual Constitution of Movement Identity and Technological Infrastructure in Digital Activism." *Convergence* 22, no. 5 (2016): 524–542.

Das, Veena. "The Act of Witnessing: Violence, Poisonous Knoweldge, and Subjectivity." In *Violence and Subjectivity*, edited by Veena Das, Arthur Kleinman, and Mamphela Ramphele, 205–225. Berkeley: University of California Press, 2000.

Das, Veena, and Arthur Kleinman. "Introduction." In *Violence and Subjectivity*, edited by Veena Das, Arthur Kleinman, and Mamphela Ramphele, 1–18. Berkeley: University of California Press, 2000.

Das, Veena, and Arthur Kleinman, eds. *Remaking a World: Violence, Social Suffering, and Recovery*. Berkeley: University of California Press, 2001.

Davies, Gareth. "The Rational Primacy of Emotion in Law and Governance." Paper presented at the Critical Legal Conference Utrecht, "'Great Expectations': Multiple Modernities of Law." Utrech University, Netherlands, September 10–12, 2010.

Davis, Kevin, B. Kingsbury, and S. Engle Merry. "Introduction: Global Governance by Indicators." In *Governance by Indicators: Global Power through Classification and Rankings*, edited by K. Davis, A. Fisher, and S. Engle Merry, 3–28. Oxford: Oxford University Press, 2010.

De Landa, Manuel. *A New Philosophy of Society: Assemblage Theory and Social Complexity*. London: Continuum, 2006.

Deleuze, Gilles, and Félix Guattari. *A Thousand Plateaus: Capitalism and Schizophrenia*. Minneapolis: University of Minnesota Press, 1987.

De Rivera, Joseph, and D. Páez. "Emotional Climate, Human Security, and Cultures of Peace." *Journal of Social Issues* 63, no. 2 (2007): 233–253.

Derrida, Jacques. "Force of Law: The 'Mystical Foundation of Authority.'" Translated by Mary Quaintance. *Cardozo Law Review* 11 (1990): 919–1045.

Derrida, Jacques. *Specters of Marx: The State of the Debt, the Work of Mourning, and the New International*. Translated by Peggy Kamuf. New York: Routledge, 1994.

Dey, Shantanu. "Protecting the Powerful: The African Union's Response to Allegations of Human Rights Violations." *Cambridge International Law Journal*, February 2, 2015. http://cilj.co.uk/2015/02/02/protecting-powerful-african-unions-response-allegations-human-rights-violations/.

Deya, Don. "Worth the Wait: Pushing for the African Court to Exercise Jurisdiction for International Crimes." Open Society Initiative for Southern Africa, March 6, 2012.

Diejomaoh, Victor P., and Henry Bienen. *Inequality and Development in Nigeria*. New York: Holmes and Meier, 1981.

Dlamini, C. R. M. "Towards a Regional Protection of Human Rights in Africa: The African Charter on Human and Peoples' Rights." *Comparative and International Law Journal of Southern Africa* 24, no. 2 (1991): 189–203.

Drumbl, Mark. *Atrocity, Punishment, and International Law*. New York: Cambridge University Press, 2007.

Du Plessis, Max. *The International Criminal Court that Africa Wants*. Institute for Security Studies Monographs 172. Pretoria: Institute for Security Studies, 2010.

Du Plessis, Max. *Shambolic, Shameful and Symbolic: Implications of the African Union's Immunity for African Leaders*. Pretoria: Institute for Security Studies, 2014.

Durkheim, Emile. *Elementary Forms of the Religious Life*. London: Hollen Street Press, 1915.

Dworkin, Ronald M. *Law's Empire*. Cambridge, MA: Belknap, 1986.

Eckert, J., B. Donahoe, C. Strümpel, and Z. O. Biner, eds. *Law against the State: Ethnographic Forays into Law's Transformations*. Cambridge: Cambridge University Press, 2012.

Editorial Note. *International Journal of Transitional Justice* 7, no. 1 (March 2013): 1–7. https://doi.org/10.1093/ijtj/ijs039.

Eisikovits, Nir. "Peace versus Justice in Transitional Settings." *Quinnipiac Law Review* 32, no. 3 (2014): 707.

Eltringham, Nigel. *Accounting for Horror: Post-Genocide Debates in Rwanda*. London: Pluto Press, 2004.

Eltringham, Nigel. "'When We Walk Out, What Was It All About?' Views on New Beginnings from within the International Criminal Tribunal for Rwanda." *Development and Change* 45, no. 3 (2014): 543–564.

Engel, David M. "Law, Time, and Community." *Law and Society Review* 21, no. 4 (1987): 605–638.

Engels, Jeremy. "The Politics of Resentment and the Tyranny of the Minority: Rethinking Victimage for Resentful Times." *Rhetoric Society Quarterly* 40, no. 4 (2010): 303–325.

Engle, Karen, Zinaida Miller, and D. M. Davis. *Anti-Impunity and the Human Rights Agenda.* New York: Cambridge University Press, 2017.

Englund, Harri. "Multivocal Morality: Narrative, Sentiment, and Zambia's Radio Grandfathers." *HAU: Journal of Ethnographic Theory* 5, no. 2 (2015): 251–273.

Ensalako, Mark. "Truth Commission for Chile and El Salvador: A Report and Assessment." *Human Rights Quarterly* 6 (1994): 663–664.

Ero, Comfort. "Understanding Africa's Position on the International Criminal Court." Oxford Transitional Justice Research Working Paper Series, March 10, 2010. http://otjr.crim.ox.ac.uk/materials/papers/122/Justice_in_Africa.pdf.

Fassin, Didier. "Humanitarianism as a Politics of Life." *Public Culture* 19, no. 3 (2007): 499–520.

Fassin, Didier. *Humanitarian Reason: A Moral History of the Present Times.* Berkeley: University of California Press, 2011.

Fassin, Didier. "On Resentment and Ressentiment: The Politics and Ethics of Moral Emotions." *Current Anthropology* 54, no. 3 (June 2013): 249–267.

Fassin, Didier, and M. Pandolfi. *Contemporary States of Emergency: The Politics of Military and Humanitarian Interventions.* New York: Zone, 2010.

Feldman, Ilana, and Miriam Ticktin. *In the Name of Humanity: The Government of Threat and Care.* Durham, NC: Duke Univeristy Press, 2010.

Ferguson, James. *Global Shadows: Africa in the Neoliberal World Order.* Durham, NC: Duke University Press, 2006.

Fernandes, Clinton. "Accomplice to Mass Atrocities: The International Community and Indonesia's Invasion of East Timor." *Politics and Governance* 3, no. 4 (2015): 1–11.

Fischer, Michael. *Emergent Forms of Life and the Anthropological Voice.* Durham, NC: Duke University Press, 2003.

Focarelli, Carlo. "The Responsibility to Protect Doctrine and Humanitarian Intervention: Too Many Ambiguities for a Working Doctrine." *Journal of Conflict and Security Law* 13 (2008): 191–213.

Foucault, Michel. *Archaeology of Knowledge.* New York: Psychology Press, 2002.

Foucault, Michel. *Discipline and Punish: The Birth of the Prison.* New York: Vintage, 1977.

Foucault, Michel. *The History of Sexuality.* Harmondsworth: Penguin, 1981.

Foucault, Michel. *The Order of Things: An Archaeology of the Human Sciences.* London: Routledge, 2002.

Foucault, Michel. *Security, Territory, Population.* London: Palgrave Macmillan, 2009.

Foucault, Michel. *The Will to Knowledge: The History of Sexuality, Volume 1.* London: Penguin, 1998.

Foucault, Michel, and Colin Gordon. *Power/Knowledge: Selected Interviews and Other Writings, 1972–1977.* New York: Pantheon, 1980.

Franceschet, Antonio. "The Rule of Law, Inequality, and the International Criminal Court." *Alternatives: Global, Local, Political* 29 (2004): 23–42.

Fraser, Nancy. *Scales of Justice: Reimagining Political Space in a Globalizing World.* New York: Columbia University Press, 2009.

Frege, Gottlob. *Logical Investigations.* Oxford: Blackwell, 1977.

Frege, Gottlob, Max Black, and P. T. Geach. *Translations from the Philosophical Writings of Gottlob Frege.* Oxford: Blackwell, 1952.

Freud, Sigmund. *The Ego and the Id.* Edited by J. Strachey. Translated by J. Riviere. New York: Norton, 1960.

Friedner, Michele. "Deaf Bodies and Corporate Bodies: New Regimes of Value in Bangalore's Business Process Outsourcing Sector." *Journal of the Royal Anthropological Institute* 21, no. 2 (2015): 313–329.

Futamura, Madoka. "Individual and Collective Guilt: Post-War Japan and the Tokyo War Crimes Tribunal." *European Review* 14, no. 4 (2006): 471–483.

Gaeta, Paola. "Official Capacity and Immunities." In *The Rome Statute of the International Criminal Court: A Commentary*, edited by Antonio Cassese, Paola Gaeta, and J. Jones. Oxford: Oxford University Press, 2002.

Gathii, James Thuo. "The Past and Future of African International Law Scholarship." *Proceedings of the Annual Meeting, American Society of International Law* 107 (2013): 187.

Geertz, Clifford. *The Interpretation of Cultures: Selected Essays.* New York: Basic Books, 1973.

Gevers, Christopher, and Max Du Plessis. "Another Stormy Year for the International Criminal Court and Its Work in Africa: Notes and Comments." *South African Yearbook of International Law* 35 (2010): 163–180.

Glenn, Cerise L. "Activism or 'Slacktivism'? Digital Media and Organizing for Social Change." *Communication Teacher* 29, no. 2 (2015): 81.

Goffman, Erving. *Frame Analysis: An Essay on the Organization of Experience.* Cambridge, MA: Harvard University Press, 1974.

González, Eduardo, and Howard Varney. *Truth Seeking: Elements of Creating an Effective Truth Commission.* Brasilia: Amnesty Commission of the Ministry of Justice of Brazil, 2013.

Gordon, Avery. *Ghostly Matters: Haunting and the Sociological Imagination.* Minneapolis: University of Minnesota Press, 2008.

Gready, Paul. *The Era of Transitional Justice: The Aftermath of the Truth and Reconciliation Commission in South Africa and Beyond.* Milton Park, UK: Routledge, 2010.

Gregg, Melissa, and Gregory J. Seigworth. *The Affect Theory Reader.* Durham, NC: Duke University Press, 2010.

Gribaldo, Alessandra. "The Paradoxical Victim: Intimate Violence Narratives on Trial in Italy." *American Ethnologist* 41, no. 4 (November 2014): 743–756.

Grono, Nick. "Briefing: The International Community's Failure to Protect." *African Affairs* 105, no. 421 (2006): 621–631.

Grovogui, Siba. *Beyond Eurocentrism and Anarchy: Memories of International Order and Institutions.* London: Palgrave Macmillan, 2006.

Grovogui, Siba. "To the Orphaned, Dispossessed, and Illegitimate Children: Human Rights beyond Republican and Liberal Traditions." *Indiana Journal of Global Legal Studies* 18, no. 1 (2011): 41–63.

Hamilton, Tomas. "Case Admissibility at the International Criminal Court." *Law and Practice of International Courts and Tribunals* 14 (2015): 305–317.

Haraway, Donna. *Modest_Witness@Second_Millennium.FemaleMan©_Meets_ OncoMouse™: Feminism and Technoscience.* New York: Routledge, 1997.

Haraway, Donna Jeanne. *When Species Meet.* Minneapolis: University of Minnesota Press, 2008.

Harding, Susan Friend. *The Book of Jerry Falwell: Fundamentalist Language and Politics.* Princeton, NJ: Princeton University Press, 2000.

Hart, Henry M. "The Aims of the Criminal Law." *Law and Contemporary Problems* 23, no. 3 (1958): 401–441.

Helfer, Laurence R. "Exiting Treaties." *Virginia Law Review* 91, no. 7 (2005): 1579–1648.

Helfer, Laurence R. "Terminating Treaties." In *The Oxford Guide to Treaties*, edited by Duncan Hollis. Oxford: Oxford University Press, 2012.

Heller, Kevin Jon. "Power, Subjectification and Resistance in Foucault." *SubStance* 25, no. 1 (1996): 78–110.

Hirschkind, Charles. *Ethical Soundscape: Cassette Sermons and Islamic Counterpublics.* New York: Columbia University Press, 2006.

Hirschkind, Charles, and Saba Mahmood. "Feminism, the Taliban, and Politics of Counter-Insurgency." *Anthropological Quarterly* 75, no. 2 (2002): 339–354.

Hobsbawm, Eric, and Terence Ranger, eds. *The Invention of Tradition.* Cambridge: Cambridge University Press, 1983.

Hochschild, Rusell Arlie. "Emotion Work, Feeling Rules, and Social Structure." *American Journal of Sociology* 85, no. 3 (1979): 551–575.

Hogget, Paul, Hen Wilkinson, and Pheobe Beedell. "Fairness and the Politics of Resentment." *Journal of Social Policy* 42, no. 3 (2013): 567.

Höhn, Sabine. "New Start or False Start? The ICC and Electoral Violence in Kenya." *Development and Change* 45, no. 3 (2014): 565–588.

Hollan, Douglas. "Emerging Issues in the Cross-Cultural Study of Empathy." *Emotion Review* 4, no. 1 (2012): 70–78.

Hollan, Douglas. "Vicissitudes of 'Empathy' in a Rural Toraja Village." In *The Anthropology of Empathy: Experiencing the Lives of Others in Pacific Societies*, edited by D. W. Hollan and C. J. Throop, 195–214. New York: Berghahn, 2011.

Hollan, Douglas, and C. Jason Throop. "Whatever Happened to Empathy? Introduction." *Ethos* 36, no. 4 (2008): 385–401.

Hordern, Joshua. *Political Affections: Civic Participation and Moral Theology.* Oxford: Oxford University Press, 2012.

Igwe, C. S. "The ICC's Favourite Customer: Africa and International Criminal Law."

Comparative and International Law Journal of Southern Africa 41, no. 2 (2008): 294–323.

Imoedemhe, Ovo. "Unpacking the Tension between the African Union and the International Criminal Court: The Way Forward." *African Journal of International and Comparative Law* 23, no. 1 (2015): 74–105.

Jakobsen, Meghan. "Immunity versus Impunity? Reconciling Articles 27(2) and 98(1) of the Rome Statute." Riga Graduate School of Law, RGSL Working Papers No. 23, 2005.

Jalloh, Charles, Dapo Akande, and Max Du Plessis. "Assessing the African Union Concerns about Article 16 of the Rome Statute of the International Criminal Court." *African Journal of Legal Studies* 4, no. 1 (2011): 5–50. doi:10. 1163/170873811 IX563947.

Jalloh, Charles C., Kamari M. Clarke, and Vincent O. Nmehielle. "Introduction." In *The African Court of Justice and Human and Peoples' Rights in Context: Development and Challenges.* New York: Cambridge University Press, 2019.

Jennings, Ronald C. "Cosmopolitan Subjects: Critical Reflections on Dualism, International Criminal Law and Sovereignty." *African Journal of Legal Studies* 7, no. 3 (2014): 321–350.

Jones, Adam. *Genocide, War Crimes, and the West: History and Complicity.* New York: Zed, 2013.

Juma, Monica Kathina. "African Mediation of the Kenyan Post-2007 Election Crisis." *Journal of Contemporary African Studies* 27, no. 3 (2009): 407–430.

Kagwanja, Peter, and Roger Southall. "Introduction: Kenya—A Democracy in Retreat?" *Journal of Contemporary African Studies* 27, no. 3 (2009): 259–277.

Kai, Ambos. *Pouvoir et Poursuite: Défis et Opportunites pour la Justice Penale Internationale en Afrique SubSaharienne.* Göttingen: Universitätsverlag Göttingen Press, 2012.

Kaufmann, Daniel, A. Kraay, and Massimo Mastruzzi. "The Worldwide Governance Indicators: Methodology and Analytical Issues." World Bank, Policy Research Working Paper No. 5430, 2011, 220–246.

Kendall, Sara. "Donors' Justice: Recasting International Criminal Accountability." *Leiden Journal of International Law* 24, no. 3 (2011): 585–606.

Kendall, Sara. "'UhuRuto' and Other Leviathans: The International Criminal Court and the Kenyan Political Order." *African Journal of Legal Studies* 7, no. 3 (2014): 399–427.

Kendall, Sara, and Sarah Nouwen. "Representational Practices at the International Criminal Court: The Gap between Juridified and Abstract Victimhood." *Law and Contemporary Problems* 76, nos. 3–4 (2013): 1–211.

"Kenyans Set Benchmarks for Implementation of Jubilee Manifesto." Ipsos Synovate, July 13, 2013.

Kersten, Mark. *Justice in Conflict: The Effects of the International Criminal Court's Interventions on Ending Wars and Building Peace.* Oxford: Oxford University Press, 2016.

Khoja-Moolji, Shenila. "Becoming an 'Intimate Publics': Exploring the Affective Intensities of Hashtag Feminism." *Feminist Media Studies* 15, no. 2 (2015): 347–350.

Kiernan, Ben, and Robert Gellately. *The Specter of Genocide: Mass Murder in Historical Perspective.* New York: Cambridge University Press, 2003.

Kimani, Mary. "Pursuit of Justice or Western Plot?" *African Renewal* 23, no. 3 (2009): 12–15.

Kinyatti, Maina Wa. *History of Resistance in Kenya: 1884–2002.* North Charleston, SC: Createspace, 2010.

Kinyatti, Maina Wa. "Mau Mau: The Peak of African Political Organization in Colonial Kenya." *Kenya Historical Review* 5, no. 2 (1977): 287–311.

Kioko, Ben. "The Right of Intervention under the African Union's Constitutive Act: From Non-interference to Non-intervention." *IRRC* 85 (2003): 807–825.

Kleinman, Arthur. *The Illness Narratives: Suffering, Healing, and the Human Condition.* New York: Basic Books, 1988.

Kleinman, Arthur. "The Violences of Everyday Life: The Multiple Forms and Dynamics of Social Violence." In *Violence and Subjectivity*, edited by Veena Das, Arthur Kleinman, and Mamphela Ramphele, 226–241. Berkeley: University of California Press, 2000.

Koulen, Sarah-Jane. "The Responsibility to Protect: A Critique of Motherhood and Apple Pie." Unpublished manuscript, 2009.

Kravel-Tovi, Michal. "Corrective Conversion: Unsettling Citizens and the Politics of Inclusion in Israel." *Journal of the Royal Anthropological Institute* 21, no. 1 (2015): 127–146.

Krever, Tor. "The Legal Turn in Late Development Theory: The Rule of Law and the World Bank's Development Model." *Harvard International Law Journal* 52, no. 1 (2011): 287–319.

Kuperman, Alan. "A Model Humanitarian Intervention? Reassessing NATO's Libya Campaign." *International Security* 38, no. 1 (2013): 105–136.

Kuwali, Dan. "The End of Humanitarian Intervention: An Evaluation of the African Union's Right of Intervention." *African Journal on Conflict Resolution* 9, no. 1 (2009): 41–61.

Laqueur, Thomas. "Bodies, Details, and the Humanitarian Narrative." In *The New Cultural History*, edited by Lynn Hunt. Berkeley: University of California Press, 1989.

Laqueur, Thomas. "Mourning, Pity, and the Work of Narrative in the Making of 'Humanity.'" In *Humanitarianism and Suffering: The Mobilization of Empathy*, edited by Richard Wilson and Richard Brown. New York: Cambridge University Press, 2009.

Latour, Bruno. *Reassembling the Social: An Introduction to Actor-Network-Theory.* New York: Oxford University Press, 2005.

Lawson, Tom. "Memorializing Colonial Genocide in Britain: The Case of Tasmania." *Journal of Genocide Research* 16, no. 4 (2014): 441–461.

Legum, Colin. *Pan-Africanism: A Short Political Guide.* New York: Frederick A. Praeger, 1964.

Leys, Ruth. "The Turn to Affect: A Critique." *Critical Inquiry* 37, no. 3 (spring 2011): 437–443.

Li, Tania Murray. "Practices of Assemblage and Community Forest Management." *Economy and Society* 36, no. 2 (2007): 263–293.

Li, Tania Murray. "What Is Land? Assembling a Resource for Global Investment." *Transactions of the Institute of British Geographers* 39, no. 4 (2014): 589–602.

Locke, John. *Two Treatises of Civil Government*. London: Dent, 1966.

Locke, John. *The Works of John Locke*. Rev. ed. Aalen, Germany: Scientia Verlag, 1963.

Lucey, Amanda, and Liezelle Kumalo. "How the AU Can Promote Transitional Justice in South Sudan." *East Africa Report* 14 (September 2017). https://issafrica.s3 .amazonaws.com/site/uploads/ear14-1.pdf.

Luckham, R., I. Ahmed, R. Muggah, and S. White. "Conflict and Poverty in Sub-Saharan Africa: An Assessment of the Issues and Evidence." IDS Working Paper 128. Institute of Development Studies, University of Sussex, Brighton, UK, 2001.

Luhmann, Niklas. *Social Systems*. Stanford, CA: Stanford University Press, 1995.

Lutz, Catherine A., and Geoffrey M. White. "The Anthropology of Emotions." *Annual Review of Anthropology* 15 (1986): 405–436.

Magee, Siobhan. "Of Love and Fur: Grandmothers, Class, and Pre-mortem Inheritance in a Southern Polish City." *Journal of the Royal Anthropological Institute* 21, no. 1 (2015): 66–85.

Malamud-Goti, Jaime. "Transitional Governments in the Breach: Why Punish State Criminals?" *Human Rights Quarterly* 12, no. 1 (1990): 1–16.

Malcolm, Norman. *Ludwig Wittgenstein: A Memoir*. Oxford: Clarendon, 1984.

Mallinder, L. "Beyond the Courts? The Complex Relationship of Trials and Amnesties." *SSRN Electronic Journal*, May 2011. doi:10.2139/ssrn.1630418.

Mamdani, Mahmood. "The Logic of Nuremberg." *London Review of Books* 35, no. 21 (2013): 33–34.

Mamdani, Mahmood. "Beyond Nuremberg: The Historical Significance of the Post-Apartheid Transition in South Africa." *Politics and Society* 43, no. 1 (2015): 61–88.

Mamdani, Mahmood. "A Separate Opinion." Addis Ababa: African Union Commission of Inquiry on South Sudan, October 20, 2014. http://www.peaceau.org /uploads/auciss.separate.opinion.pdf.

Mamdani, Mahmood. *When Victims Become Killers: Colonialism, Nativism, and the Genocide in Rwanda*. Princeton, NJ: Princeton University Press, 2001.

Mandel, Michael. *How America Gets Away with Murder: Illegal Wars, Collateral Damage and Crimes against Humanity*. London: Pluto, 2004.

Marc, Alexandre, Neelam Verjee, and Stephen Mogaka. *The Challenge of Stability and Security in West Africa*. Africa Development Forum Series. Washington, DC: World Bank, 2015. doi:10.1596/978-1-4648-0464-9.

Marcus, George E., and Erkan Saka. "Assemblage." *Theory, Culture and Society* 23, nos. 2–3 (2006): 101–106.

Maroney, T. A. "Law and Emotion: A Proposed Taxonomy of an Emerging Field." *Law and Human Behavior* 30, no. 2 (2006): 119–142.

Martínez Salazar, Egla. *Global Coloniality of Power in Guatemala: Racism, Genocide, Citizenship*. Lanham, MD: Lexington, 2012.

Masco, Joseph. *The Nuclear Borderlands: The Manhattan Project in Post–Cold War New Mexico*. Princeton, NJ: Princeton University Press, 2006.

Massumi, Brian. "The Autonomy of Affect." *Cultural Critique* 31 (1995): 83–109.

Massumi, Brian. *The Politics of Affect*. Malden, MA: Polity, 2015.

Massumi, Brian. *Parables for the Virtual: Movement, Affect, Sensation*. Durham, NC: Duke University Press, 2002.

Matfess, Hilary. *Women and the War on Boko Haram: Wives, Weapons, Witnesses*. London: Zed, 2017.

Mazzarella, William. "Affect: What Is It Good For?" In *Enchantments of Modernity: Empire, Nation, Globalization*, edited by Saurabh Dube, 291–309. London: Routledge, 2009.

Mbembe, Achille. *On the Postcolony*. Berkeley: University of California Press, 2001.

Mbembe, Achille. "Provisional Notes on the Postcolony." *Africa: Journal of the International African Institute* 62, no. 1 (1992): 3–37.

Mbembe, Achille, and Laurent Dubois. *Critique of Black Reason*. Durham, NC: Duke University Press, 2017.

McLagan, Meg. "Principles, Publicity, and Politics: Notes on Human Rights Media." *American Anthropologist* 105, no. 3 (2003): 605–612.

McLean, Jessica Emma, and Sara Fuller. "Action with(out) Activism: Understanding Digital Climate Change Action." *International Journal of Sociology and Social Policy* 36, no. 9–10 (2016): 578–595.

Meister, Robert. *After Evil: A Politics of Human Rights*. New York: Columbia University Press, 2010.

Mnookin, R. H. "Rethinking the Tension between Peace and Justice: The International Criminal Prosecutor as Diplomat." *Harvard Negotiation Law Review* 18 (2013): 145–174.

Mueller, Julie L. "The IMF, Neoliberalism and Hegemony." *Global Society* 25 (2011): 377–402.

Mueller, Sussane. "Kenya and the International Criminal Court (ICC): Politics, Election and the Law." *Journal of Eastern African Studies* 8, no. 1 (2014): 25–42.

Muhuthi, Timothy. "The Advent of a Differentiated Accountability System: The African Court of Justice and Human Rights and the AU Transitional Justice Architecture." In *The African Court of Justice and Human and Peoples' Rights in Context: Development and Challenges*, edited by Charles C. Jalloh, M. Kamari Clarke, and Vincent O. Nmehielle. New York: Cambridge University Press, 2019.

Mukundi, W. George. "Consolidating the African Governance Architecture." SAIIA Policy Brief 96, Governance and APRM Programme, 2014. https://saiia.org.za/wp-content/uploads/2014/07/saia_spb_96_wachira_20140704.pdf.

Murithi, Tim. "The African Union and the International Criminal Court: An Embattled Relationship?" Policy Brief, Institute for Justice and Reconciliation, 2013. http://www.ijr.org.za/home/wp-content/uploads/2017/05/IJR-Policy-Brief-No-8-Tim-Miruthi.pdf.

Murithi, Tim. "The African Union's Evolving Role in Peace Operations: The African Union Mission in Burundi, the African Union Mission in Sudan and the African Union Mission in Somalia." *African Security Review* 17, no. 1 (2008): 69–82.

Murungi, Phoebe. "10 Years of the International Criminal Court: The Court, Africa, the United Nations Security Council (UNSC) and Article 16 of the Rome Statute." *SSRN*, September 10, 2012, 1–16. https://ssrn.com/abstract=2169819.

Musila, Godfrey. "New Posture and Old Rhetoric? The Role of the African Regional and Sub-regional Organisations in International Criminal Justice." *SSRN*, February 21, 2016. https://papers.ssrn.com/sol3/papers.cfm?abstract_id=2782871.

Musila, Godfrey. "United States of Africa: Positioning the Pan-African Parliament and Court in the Political Union Debate." *SSRN* June 1, 2007. http://dx.doi .org/10.2139/ssrn.2593597.

Mutua, Makau W. "The International Criminal Court in Africa: Challenges and Opportunities." Norwegian Peacebuilding Centre Working Paper, September 2010; Buffalo Legal Studies Research Paper No. 2011-003.

Mwanasali, Musifiky. "From the Organization of African Unity to the African Union." In *From Cape to Congo: Southern Africa's Evolving Security Challenges*, edited by Mwesiga Laurent Baregu and Christopher Landsberg. New York: International Peace Academy, 2003.

Mwangi, Wambui, and Tiyanjana Mphepo. "Developments in International Criminal Justice in Africa during 2011: Recent Developments." *African Human Rights Law Journal* 12, no. 1 (2012): 254–291.

Nanda, Upali, Debajyoti Pati, Hessam Ghamari, and Robyn Bajema. "Lessons from Neuroscience: Form Follows Function, Emotions Follow Form." *Intelligent Buildings International* 5, no. 1 (2013): 61–78.

Navaro, Yael. *The Make-Believe Space: Affective Geography in a Postwar Polity*. Durham, NC: Duke University Press, 2012.

N'Diaye, Boubacar. "Not a Miracle after All . . . Côte d'Ivoire's Downfall: Flawed Civil-Military Relations and Missed Opportunities." *Scientia Militaria—South African Journal of Military Studies* 33, no. 1 (2011): 89–118.

Nesiah, Vasuki. "Local Ownership of Global Governance." *Journal of International Criminal Justice* 14, no. 4 (2016): 985–1009.

Nicoll, Alexander, and Jessica Delaney. "Kenya's Election: Risk of Renewed Violence." *International Institute for Strategic Studies* 3, no. 1 (2013). https://doi.org/10.1080 /13567888.2013.779523.

Nicolson, I. F. *The Administration of Nigeria, 1900–1960: Men, Methods, and Myths*. Oxford: Clarendon, 1969.

Nissel, Alan. "Continuing Crimes in the Rome Statute." *Michigan Journal of International Law* 25, no. 3 (2004): 653–665.

Nordstrom, Carolyn. *A Different Kind of War Story*. Philadelphia: University of Pennsylvania Press, 1997.

Nosek, Brian A., Carlee Beth Hawkins, and Rebecca S. Frazier. "Implicit Social Cognition: From Measures to Mechanisms." *Trends in Cognitive Sciences* 15, no. 4 (2011): 152–159.

Nouwen, Sarah. *Complementarity in the Line of Fire: The Catalysing Effect of the International Criminal Court in Uganda and Sudan.* Cambridge: Cambridge University Press, 2013.

Nouwen, Sarah. "The Special Court for Sierra Leone and the Immunity of Taylor: The Arrest Warrant Case Continued." *Leiden Journal of International Law* 18 (2005): 645–669.

Nussbaum, Martha Craven. *Political Emotions: Why Love Matters for Justice.* Cambridge, MA: Belknap, 2013.

Obeyesekere, Gananath. "Depression, Buddhism, and the Work of Culture." In *Culture and Depression: Studies in the Anthropology and Cross-Cultural Psychiatry of Affect and Disorder,* edited by Arthur Kleinman and Byron Good, 134–152. Berkeley: University of California Press, 1985.

O'Connor, Kieron P., and Frederick Aardema. "The Imagination: Cognitive, Precognitive, and Meta-cognitive Aspects." *Consciousness and Cognition* 14, no. 2 (2005): 233–256.

Odinkalu, Chidi Anselm. "International Criminal Justice, Peace and Reconciliation in Africa: Re-imagining an Agenda beyond the ICC." *Africa Development* 40, no. 2 (2015): 257–290.

Ogot, Bethwell. *Zamani: A Survey of East African History.* Nairobi: East African Publishing and Longman, 1974.

Okafor, Obiora Chinedu. "Critical Third World Approaches to International Law (TWAIL): Theory, Methodology, Or Both?" *International Community Law Review* 10, no. 4 (2008): 371–378.

Okello, C. Moses, Chris Dolan, Undine Whande, Nokukhanya Mncwabe, Levis Onegi, and Stephen Oola, eds. *Where Law Meets Reality: Forging African Transitional Justice.* Cape Town: Pambazuka, 2012.

Olsen, T. O., L. A. Payne, and A. G. Reiter. "The Justice Balance: When Transitional Justice Improves Human Rights and Democracy." *Human Rights Quarterly* 32, no. 4 (2010): 980–1007.

Ong, Ahiwa, and Stephen J. Collier, eds. *Global Assemblages: Technology, Politics, and Ethics as Anthropological Problems.* Malden, MA: Blackwell, 2005.

Ong, Aihwa, and Ananya Roy. *Worlding Cities: Asian Experiments and the Art of Being Global.* Malden, MA: Wiley-Blackwell, 2011.

Oomen, Barbara. "Donor-Driven Justice and Its Discontents: The Case of Rwanda." *Development and Change* 36 (2005): 887–910.

Osborne, Myles. "The Rooting Out of Mau Mau from the Minds of the Kikuyu Is a Formidable Task: Propaganda and the Mau Mau War." *Journal of African History* 56, no. 1 (2015): 77–97.

Pahuja, Sundhya. *Decolonising International Law: Development, Economic Growth, and the Politics of Universality.* Cambridge: Cambridge University Press, 2011.

Parsons, Jim, Monica Thornton, Hyo Eun (April) Bang, Ben Estep, Kaya Williams, and Neil Weiner. *Developing Indicators to Measure the Rule of Law: A Global Approach. A Report to the World Justice Project.* New York: Vera Institute of Justice, July 2008.

Petrović, Vladimir. *The Emergence of Historical Forensic Expertise*. Florence: Routledge, 2016. doi:10.4324/9781315536828.

Popovski, Vesselin. "Emotions and International Law." In *Emotions in International Politics: Beyond Mainstream International Relations*, edited by Vesselin Popovski, Yohan Ariffin, and Jean-Marc Coicaud. Cambridge: Cambridge University Press, 2016.

"The Popular Discourses of Salafi Radicalism and Salafi Counter-Radicalism in Nigeria: A Case Study of Boko Haram." *Journal of Religion in Africa* 42, no. 2 (2012): 118–144.

Powell, Kristiana. "The African Union's Emerging Peace and Security Regime: Opportunities and Challenges for Delivering on the Responsibility to Protect." Pretoria: Institute for Security Studies, 2005.

Puar, Jasbir K. *Terrorist Assemblages: Homonationalism in Queer Times*. Durham, NC: Duke University Press, 2007.

Rajagopal, Balakrishnan. *International Law from Below: Development, Social Movements, and Third World Resistance*. New York: Cambridge University Press, 2003.

Rajan, Sunder Kaushik, ed. *Lively Capital: Biotechnologies, Ethics, and Governance in Global Markets*. Durham, NC: Duke University Press, 2012.

Rancière, Jacques. *The Future of the Image*. New York: Verso, 2007.

Rancière, Jacques. *The Politics of Aesthetics*. New York: Continuum, 2004.

Randeria, Shalini. "De-politicization of Democracy and Judicialization of Politics." *Theory, Culture and Society* 24, no. 4 (2007): 38–44.

Rao, Pemmaraju Sreenivasa. "The Concept of International Community in International Law: Theory and Reality." In *International Law between Universalism and Fragmentation: Festschrift in Honour of Gerhard Hafner*, edited by Isabelle Buffard, James Crawford, Alain Pellet, and Stephan Wittich, 85–105. Boston: Martinus Nijhoff, 2008. doi:10.1163/ej.9789004167278.v-1086.

Rawls, John. *The Law of Peoples: With the Idea of Public Reason Revisited*. Cambridge, MA: Harvard University Press, 1999.

Rawls, John. *Political Liberalism*. Vol. 4. New York: Columbia University Press, 1993.

Rawls, John. *Theory of Justice*. Cambridge, MA: Harvard University Press, 1971.

Reddy, William M. *The Navigation of Feeling: A Framework for the History of Emotions*. New York: Cambridge University Press, 2001.

Redfield, Peter. *Life in Crisis: The Ethical Journey of Doctors without Borders*. Berkeley: University of California Press, 2013.

Richland, Justin. "Jurisdiction: Grounding Law in Language." *Annual Review of Anthropology* 42 (2013): 209–226.

Ridler, Victoria. "Justice as Sentiment and the Argument for an Asymmetric Legality." Paper presented at the Critical Legal Conference Utrecht, "'Great Expectations': Multiple Modernities of Law." Utrech University, Netherlands, September 10–12, 2010.

Robins, Simon. "'To Live as Other Kenyans Do': A Study of the Reparative Demands of Kenyan Victims of Human Rights Violations." *International Center for Transitional Justice* 52 (2011): 1–75.

Rodrik, Dani. "Goodbye Washington Consensus, Hello Washington Confusion?" *Journal of Economic Literature* 44 (2006): 973–987.

Roht-Arriaza, N., and J. Mariezcurrena, eds. *Transitional Justice in the Twenty-First Century: Beyond Truth versus Justice*. Cambridge: Cambridge University Press, 2006.

Rorty, R. "Human Rights, Rationality, and Sentimentality." In *On Human Rights: The Oxford Amnesty Lectures 1993*, edited by S. Shute and S. Hurley, 112–134. New York: Basic Books, 1993.

Rosaldo, Renato. "Introduction: Grief and a Headhunter's Rage." In *Culture and Truth: The Remaking of Social Analysis*, 1–24. Boston: Beacon, 1989.

Ross, Andrew. *Mixed Emotions: Beyond Fear and Hatred in International Conflict*. Chicago: University of Chicago Press, 2012.

Rotberg, R. I., and D. F. Thompson. 2000. *Truth v. Justice: The Morality of Truth Commissions*. Princeton, NJ: Princeton University Press.

Rowen, Jamie. *Searching for Truth in the Transitional Justice Movement*. Cambridge: Cambridge University Press, 2017.

Russell, Bertrand. *An Inquiry into Meaning and Truth*. Nottingham, UK: Spokesman, 2007.

Russell, Bertrand. *Marriage and Morals*. London: Routledge, 2009. doi:10.4324 /9780203875346.

Russell, Bertrand. *The Problems of Philosophy*. New York: Prometheus, 1988.

Safarty, Galit. "Regulating through Numbers: A Case Study of Corporate Sustainability Reporting." *Virginia Journal of International Law* 54 (2013): 575–622.

Sahlins, Marshall. *Culture and Practical Reason*. Chicago: University of Chicago Press, 1976.

Santos, Alvaro. "The World Bank's Uses of the 'Rule of Law' Promise in Economic Development." In *The New Law and Economic Development: A Critical Appraisal*, edited by David Trubek and Alvaro Santos, 253–300. New York: Cambridge University Press, 2006.

Schabas, William. *The International Criminal Court: A Commentary on the Rome Statute*. Oxford: Oxford University Press, 2010.

Schabas, William. *An Introduction to the International Criminal Court*. 4th ed. Cambridge: Cambridge University Press, 2011.

Scheper-Hughes, Nancy. *Death without Weeping: The Violence of Everyday Life in Brazil*. Berkeley: University of California Press, 1993.

Schieffelin, Edward L. *The Sorrow of the Lonely and the Burning of the Dancers*. New York: St. Martin's, 1976.

Schimmel, Noam. "The Moral Case for Restorative Justice as a Corollary of the Responsibility to Protect: A Rwandan Case Study of the Insufficiency of Impact of Retributive Justice on the Rights and Well-Being of Genocide Survivors." *Journal of Human Rights* 11, no. 2 (2012): 161–188.

Schuller, Kyla. *The Biopolitics of Feeling: Race, Sex, and Science in the Nineteenth Century*. Durham, NC: Duke University Press, 2017.

Segal, Lotte Buch. "The Burden of Being Exemplary: National Sentiments, Awkward Witnessing, and Womanhood in Occupied Palestine." *Journal of the Royal Anthropological Institute* 21, no. S1 (May 2015): 30–46.

Serban, Mihaela. "Rule of Law Indicators as a Political Technology of Power in Romania." In *The Quiet Power of Indicators: Measuring Governance, Corruption, and Rule of Law*, edited by Sally Engle Merry, Kevin E. Davis, and Benedict Kingsbury. Cambridge: Cambridge University Press, 2015.

Shaw, Carolyn Martin. *Colonial Inscriptions: Race, Sex, and Class in Kenya*. Minneapolis: University of Minnesota Press, 1995.

Shaw, Malcolm N. *International Law*. 8th ed. Cambridge: Cambridge University Press, 2017.

Shaw, Rosalind. "Memory Frictions: Localizing the Truth and Reconciliation Commission in Sierra Leone." *International Journal of Transitional Justice* 1, no. 2 (2007): 183–207.

Shaw, Rosalind, Lars Waldorf, and Pierre Hazan. *Localizing Transitional Justice: Interventions and Priorities after Mass Violence*. Palo Alto, CA: Stanford University Press, 2010.

Shihata, Ibrahim. *The World Bank in a Changing World: Selected Essays*. Leiden: Brill, 1991.

Sikkink, Kathryn. *The Justice Cascade: How Human Rights Prosecutions Are Changing World Politics*. New York: Norton, 2011.

Simpson, Gerry. *Law, War and Crime: War Crime Trials and the Reinvention of International Law*. Cambridge: Polity, 2007.

Simpson, Gerry. "The Sentimental Life of International Law." *London Review of International Law* 3, no. 1 (2015): 3–29.

Smith, Thomas. "Moral Hazard and Humanitarian Law: The International Criminal Court and the Limits of Legality." *International Politics* 39, no. 2 (2002): 175–192.

Spinoza, Benedictus de. *A Theologico-Political Treatise*. Boulder, CO: Project Gutenberg, 1990.

Spinoza, Benedictus de. *The Collected Works of Spinoza*. Edited and translated by E. M. Curley. Princeton, NJ: Princeton University Press, 1985.

Spinoza, Benedictus de. *Ethics*. Edited and translated by G. H. R. Parkinson. New York: Oxford University Press, 2000.

Sriram, Chandra Lekha, and Stephen Brown. "Kenya in the Shadow of the ICC: Complementarity, Gravity and Impact." *International Criminal Law Review* 12 (2012): 219–244.

Sriram, Chandra Lekha, and Suren Pillay, eds. *Peace versus Justice? The Dilemma of Transitional Justice in Africa*. Oxford: James Currey, 2010.

Stahn, Carsten. "Notes and Comments. Responsibility to Protect: Political Rhetoric or Emerging Legal Norm?" *American Journal of International Law* 101 (2007): 99–120.

Stauffer, Jill. "Speaking Truth to Reconciliation: Political Transition, Recovery, and the Work of Time." *Humanity* 4 (2013): 27–48.

Stewart, Kathleen. "In the World That Affect Proposed." *Cultural Anthropology* 32, no. 2 (2017): 192–198.

Stewart, Kathleen. *Ordinary Affects*. Durham, NC: Duke University Press, 2007.

Taithe, B. *The Killer Trail: A Colonial Scandal in the Heart of Africa*. Oxford: Oxford University Press, 2009.

Tallgren, Immi. "The Durkheimian Spell of International Criminal Law?" *Revue Interdisciplinaire d'Études Juridiques* 71, no. 2 (2013): 137–169.

Teitel, Ruti G. "Humanity's Law: Rule of Law for the New Global Politics." *Cornell International Law Journal* 35, no. 2 (2002): 355.

Teitel, Ruti G. *Transitional Justice*. Oxford: Oxford University Press, 2002.

Teitel, Ruti G. "Transitional Justice Genealogy." *Harvard Human Rights Journal* 16 (2003): 69–94.

Throop, C. Jason. *Suffering and Sentiment: Exploring the Vicissitudes of Experience and Pain in the Yap*. Berkeley: University of California Press, 2010.

Ticktin, Miriam. "The Gendered Human of Humanitarianism: Medicalizing and Politicizing Sexual Violence." *Gender and History*, 23, no. 2 (2011): 250–265.

Ticktin, Miriam. "How Biology Travels: A Humanitarian Trip." *Body and Society* 17, no. 2–3 (2011): 139–158.

Tladi, Dire. "The Immunity Provision in the AU Amendment Protocol: Separating the (Doctrinal) Wheat from the (Normative) Chaff." *Journal of International Criminal Justice* 13, no. 1 (2015): 3–17.

Tladi, Dire. "Interpretation and International Law in South African Courts: The Supreme Court of Appeal and the Al Bashir Saga." *African Human Rights Law Journal* 16 (2016): 310: 1–338.

Triffterer, Otto, and Kai Ambos. "The Rome Statute of the International Criminal Court: A Commentary." *Journal of International Criminal Justice* 13, no. 3 (2018): 663–668.

Udombana, Nsongurua. "'Can These Dry Bones Live?' In Search of a Lasting Therapy for AU and ICC Toxic Relationship." *African Journal of International Criminal Justice* 1 (2014): 57–76.

Udombana, Nsongurua. "Still Playing Dice with Lives: Darfur and Security Council Resolution 1706." *Third World Quarterly* 28, no. 1 (2007): 97–116.

Valsiner, Jaan. "Process Structure of Semiotic Mediation in Human Development." *Human Development* 44, no. 2–3 (2001): 84–97.

Valverde, Mariana. *Chronotopes of Law: Jurisdiction, Scale and Governance*. New York: Routledge, 2015.

Van den Wyngaert, Christine. "Victims before International Criminal Courts: Some Views of an ICC Trial Judge." *Case Western Reserve Journal of International Law* 44 (2011): 475–496.

Van Schaack, Beth, and Ronald Slye. "A Concise History of International Criminal Law: Chapter 1 of Understanding International Criminal Law." *Legal Studies Research Paper Series*, 2007, 7–42.

Velasquez, Eduardo, ed. *Love and Friendship: Rethinking Politics and Affection in Modern Times*. Portland: Ringgold, 2003.

Verges, Jacques. *De la stratégie judiciaire*. Paris: Les Editions de Minuit, 1981.

Waddell, Nicholas, and Phil Clark, eds. *Courting Conflict? Justice, Peace and the ICC in Africa*. London: Royal African Society, 2008.

Walker, Andrew. *"Eat the Heart of the Infidel": The Harrowing of Nigeria and the Rise of Boko Haram*. London: Hurst, 2016.

Werle, Gerhard, and Moritz Vormbaum, eds. *The African Criminal Court: A Commentary on the Malabo Protocol*. The Hague: T.M.C. Asser, 2017.

Wetherall, Margaret. *Affect and Emotion: A New Social Science Understanding*. London: Sage, 2012.

Williams, Brackette F. *Stains on My Name, War in My Veins: Guyana and the Politics of Cultural Struggle*. Durham, NC: Duke University Press, 1991.

Williams, Paul. "The Peace and Security Council of the African Union." In *The African Union Peace and Security Council*, edited by Tim Murithi and Halleluja Lulie. Pretoria: Institute for Security Studies, 2012.

Williams, Paul, and Solomon Dersso. "Saving Strangers and Neighbors: Advancing UN-AU Cooperation on Peace Operations." New York: International Peace Institute, 2015.

Williams, Raymond. "A Philosophy of Emotion." *The Guardian*, December 28, 1962.

Wilson, Richard. *The Politics of Truth and Reconciliation in South Africa: Legitimizing the Post-Apartheid State*. Cambridge: Cambridge University Press, 2001.

Wilson, Richard, and Richard D. Brown. *Humanitarianism and Suffering: The Mobilization of Empathy*. Cambridge: Cambridge University Press, 2009.

Wilson, Richard Ashby. *Incitement on Trial: Prosecuting International Speech Crimes*. Cambridge: Cambridge University Press, 2017.

Wirth, S. "Immunities, Related Problems, and Article 98 of the Rome Statute." *Criminal Law Forum* 12, no. 4 (2001).

Wittgenstein, Ludwig. *Philosophical Investigations*. Oxford: Basil Blackwell, 1953.

Woolford, Andrew John, Alexander Laban Hinton, and Jeff Benvenuto. *Colonial Genocide in Indigenous North America*. Durham, NC: Duke University Press, 2014.

Yang, Lijun. "On the Principle of Complementarity in the Rome Statute of the International Criminal Court." *Chinese Journal of International Law* 4, no. 1 (June 2005): 121–132.

Legal and Other Documents

African Union. "Communique of 547th Meeting of the Peace and Security Council." September 29, 2015. http://www.peaceau.org/en/article/communique-of-547th -meeting-of-the-psc-at-the-level-of-heads-of-state-and-government-on-the -situation-in-south-sudan.

African Union. Constitutive Act of the African Union. Lome, Togo, July 11, 2000. https://au.int/sites/default/files/pages/32020-file-constitutiveact_en.pdf.

African Union. "Decisions and Declarations, Extraordinary Session of the Assembly of the African Union." October 12, 2013. Ext/Assembly/AU/Dec.1–2 (October 2013) EX.CL/952 (XXVIII).

African Union. "42nd Activity Report of the African Commission on Human and Peoples' Rights." African Commission on Human and Peoples' Rights, 2017. http://www.achpr.org/activity-reports/42/.

African Union. "Framework of the African Governance Architecture." n.d. http://www.iag-agi.org/IMG/pdf/aga-framewor9183.pdf.

African Union. On the Decisions of Pre-trial Chamber I of the International Criminal Court (ICC) Pursuant to Article 87(7) of the Rome Statute on the Alleged Failure by the Republic of Chad and the Republic of Malawi to Comply with the Cooperation Requests Issued by the Court with Respect to the Arrest and Surrender of President Omar Hassan Al Bashir of the Republic of the Sudan. Press Release No. 002/2012, January 9, 2012. http://www.iccnow.org/documents/PR-_002-_ICC_English_2012.pdf.

African Union. Protocol on Amendments to the Protocol on the Statute of the African Court of Justice and Human Rights. June 27, 2014.

African Union. Protocol Relating to the Establishment of the Peace and Security Council of the African Union. July 9, 2002.

African Union. *Report of the African Union High-Level Panel on Darfur (AUPD).* Addis Ababa, October 29, 2009, PSC/AHG/2 (CCVII). http://www.africalegalaid.com/download/human_rights_instruments_and_treaties_in_africa/Report_of_the_African_Union_High_Level_Panel_on_Darfur_The_Quest_for_Peace_Justice_and_Reconcilation_October_2009.pdf.

African Union. "Report on the Preparations for the Commemoration of the 50th Anniversary of the Organization of the African Unity/African Union (OAU/AU)." December 19, 2012. https://portal.africa-union.org/DVD/Documents/DOC-AU-WD/EX%20CL%20771%20%28XXII%29%20_E.pdf.

African Union Commission. "Strategic Plan, 2009–2012." EX.CL/501 (XV) Rev. 2, May 19, 2009. https://europafrica.files.wordpress.com/2009/07/au-strategic-plan-2009-2012.pdf.

African Union Panel of the Wise. "Peace, Justice, and Reconciliation in Africa: Opportunities and Challenges in the Fight against Impunity," The African Union Series. New York: International Peace Institute, 2013.

"Agreement on the Resolution for the Conflict in the Republic of South Sudan." Intergovernmental Authority on Development, Addis Ababa, August 17, 2015. https://www.igad.int.

Amnesty International. "Africa: Malabo Protocol: Legal and Institutional Implications of the Merged and Expanded African Court." January 22, 2016. Index number AFR 01/3063/2016.

Amnesty International. "AU Summit Decision a Backward Step for International Justice." July 1, 2014.

"Arrest Warrant of 11 April 2000 (Democratic Republic of the Congo v. Belgium)." International Court of Justice, February 14, 2002. General List No. 121.

Arrêt no. 1414 (2001), 125 ILR 456. Muammar Gaddafi. France: Cour de Cassation.

Assembly of the Union. "Decision on the Implementation of the Assembly Decision on the Abuse of the Principle of Universal Jurisdiction." Twelfth Ordinary Session. Addis Ababa, Ethiopia, February 1–3, 2009. Assembly/AU/3 (XII).

Assembly of the Union, Fourteenth Ordinary Session. Addis Ababa, Ethiopia, January 30–31, 2011. Assembly/AU/Dec.332–361 (XVI).

Assembly of the Union, Fourteenth Ordinary Session. Addis Ababa, Ethiopia, January 31–February 2, 2010. Assembly/AU/Dec.268–288 (XIV).

Assembly of the Union. Twenty-Sixth Ordinary Session. Addis Ababa, Ethiopia, January 30–31, 2016. Assembly/AU/Dec.590 (XXVI).

AU Assembly. "Decision on the Application by the International Criminal Court Prosecutor for the Indictment for the President of the Republic of Sudan." Twelfth Ordinary Session. Addis Ababa, Ethiopia, February 3, 2009. Assembly/AU/Dec.221 (XII).

AU Assembly. Decision on the Meeting of African States Parties to the Rome Statute of the International Criminal Court. Addis Ababa, Ethiopia, July 1–3, 2009. Assembly/AU/13 (XIII).

AU Assembly. Decision on the Meeting of African States Parties to the Rome Statute of the International Criminal Court (ICC). Sirte, Libya, July 3, 2009. Doc. Assembly/AU/13 (XIII).

AU Assembly. Decision on the Meeting of African States Parties to the Rome Statute of the International Criminal Court. Addis Ababa, Ethiopia, July 25, 2010. Assembly/AU/Dec.289–331 (XV).

AU Assembly. Decision on the Single Legal Instrument on the Merger of the African Court on Human and Peoples' Rights and the African Court of Justice. June 30–July 1, 2008. Assembly/AU/Dec.196 (XI); Assembly/AU/13 (XI).

AU Commission of Inquiry on South Sudan. Executive Summary. Addis-Ababa, October 15, 2014. https://reliefweb.int/sites/reliefweb.int/files/resources/auciss .executive.summary.pdf.

Case Concerning the Difference between New Zealand and France Concerning the Interpretation or Application of Two Agreements, Concluded on July 9, 1986 between the Two States and Which Related to the Problems Arising from the Rainbow Warrior Affair (N.Z./Fr.). 20 R.I.A.A. 217 (1990).

Coalition for the International Criminal Court. "Report on the 12th Session of the Assembly of States Parties to the Rome Statute." The Hague, November 20–28, 2013. http://www.iccnow.org/documents/asp12_report.pdf.

"Decision of the Executive Council Adopted during Its Twenty-First Ordinary Session Held on 9–13 July 2012 in Addis Ababa, Ethiopia on the Protocol on Amendments to the Protocol on the Statute of the African Court of Justice and Human Rights." EX.CL/Dec.706 (XXI) Doc. EX.CL/731 (XXI)a.

"Decision on the Confirmation of Charges Pursuant to Article 61(7)(a) and (b) of the Rome Statute." ICC-01/09-02/11.

Eichmann v. Attorney-General of Israel. Supreme Court of Israel (1962) 136 ILR.

Human Rights Council. "Report of the Commission on Human Rights in South Sudan." Thirty-fourth session, February 27–March 24, 2017. Agenda Item 4: Human Rights Situation That Requires the Attention of the Council. A/HRC/34/63. https://www.refworld.org/pdfid/58bd7d6f4.pdf.

ICC. Decision on the Prosecution Application under Article 58(7) of the Statute, Harun (ICC-02/05-01/07-1). Pre-trial Chamber I, April 27, 2007.

ICC. Report on the Situation in the Republic of Burundi. ICC-01/17. October 2017. https://www.icc-cpi.int/burundi.

ICC. Status Conference in Ruto/Sang case. William Ruto. May 14, 2013.

ICC. Status Conference. Uhuru Kenyatta. February 5, 2014. The Hague, Netherlands.

ICC. Warrant of Arrest for Ali Kushayb (ICC-02/05-01/07-3). Pre-trial Chamber I, April 27, 2007.

ICC. Warrant of Arrest for Omar Hassan Ahmad Al Bashir (Al Bashir 9, ICC-02 /05-01/09-1). Pre-trial Chamber I, March 4, 2009.

ICC-01/09-01/11-859, 16-08-2013 (*The Prosecutor v. William Samoei Ruto and Joshua Arap Sang*).

ICC-OTP. Preliminary Examination: Guinea. Focus: Alleged crimes against humanity committed in the context of the 28 September 2009 events in Conakry, Guinea. http://www.icc-cpi.int/en_menus/icc/structure%20of%20the%20court/office%20 of%20the%20prosecutor/comm%20and%20ref/pe-ongoing/guinea/Pages/guinea .aspx.

ICC-PIDS-KEN-02-010/14-2014 (*The Prosecutor v. Uhuru Muigai Kenyatta*).

ICC Pre-trial Chamber II. "Situation in the Republic of Kenya, Decision on the Prosecutor's Appeal against the Decision on the Request to Amend the Updated Document Containing the Charges Pursuant to Article 61(9) of the Statute." December 13, 2013. http://www.icc-cpi.int/iccdocs/doc/doc1699466.pdf.

ICC Pre-trial Chamber II. "Situation in the Republic of Kenya, Request for Authorization of an Investigation Pursuant to Article 15." November 26, 2009. http://www .icc-cpi.int/iccdocs/doc/doc785972.pdf.

ICC Trial Chamber V. Decision on Victims' Participation and Representation. October 3, 2012.

ICISS. *The Responsibility to Protect: Report of the International Commission on Intervention and State Sovereignty*. Ottawa: International Commission on Intervention and State Sovereignty, 2001.

ICRC. *The Geneva Conventions of 12 August 1949*. Geneva: International Committee of the Red Cross, n.d. https://www.icrc.org/en/doc/assets/files/publications/icrc -002-0173.pdf.

ICTR. Case No. ICTR-96-4-T, Judgement (ICTR Trial Chamber I, September 2, 1998).

ICTR. Case No. ICTR-97-19-AR72 (ICTR Appeals Chamber, September 12, 2000).

ICTR. Case No. ICTR-99-52-T, P103 (ICTR Trial Chamber, December 3, 2003).

International Bank for Reconstruction and Development. "The Berg Report and the Model of Accumulation in Sub-Saharan Africa: An Agenda for Action." New York: World Bank, 1981.

International Convention on the Suppression and Punishment of the Crime of Apartheid, New York, November 30, 1973, in force July 18, 1976. 1015 UNTS 243.

International Court of Justice. Asylum Case (Colombia/Peru). Judgment of November 20th 1950: ICJ Reports 1950. https://www.icj-cij.org/files/case-related/7/007 -19501120-JUD-01-00-EN.pdf.

International Court of Justice. Reports of Judgements, Advisory Opinions and

Orders. In *Case Concerning Military and Paramilitary Activities in and against Nicaragua* (Nicaragua v. United States of America). Jurisdiction of the Court and Admissibility of the Application. Judgment of November 26, 1984.

International Criminal Court. "Activation of the Jurisdiction of the Court over the Crime of Aggression." Resolution ICC-ASP/16/Res.5, December 14, 2017. https:// asp.icc-cpi.int/iccdocs/asp_docs/Resolutions/ASP16/ICC-ASP-16-Res5-ENG .pdf.

International Criminal Court. "Decision on the Prosecutor's Application for Summonses to Appear for Francis Kirimi Muthaura, Uhuru Muigai Kenyatta and Mohammed Hussein Ali." ICC-01/09-02/11-1. March 8, 2011. https://www.icc-cpi .int/Pages/record.aspx?docNo=ICC-01/09-02/11-1.

International Criminal Court. "Decision on the Prosecutor's Application for Summons to Appear for William Samoei Ruto, Henry Kiprono Kosgey and Joshua Arap Sang." ICC-01/09-01/11-1. March 8, 2011. https://www.icc-cpi.int/Pages /record.aspx?docNo=ICC-01/09-01/11-1.

International Criminal Court. "Situation in Darfur, Sudan: In the Case of *The Prosecutor v. Omar Hassan Ahmad Al-Bashir*." Corrigendum to the Decision Pursuant to Article 87(7) of the Rome Statute on the Failure by the Republic of Malawi to Comply with the Cooperation Requests Issued by the Court with Respect to the Arrest and Surrender of Omar Hassan Ahmad Al Bashir. ICC-02/05-01/09-139, December 13, 2011. https://www.icc-cpi.int/CourtRecords /CR2011_21750.PDF.

International Criminal Court. "Situation in Darfur, Sudan: In the Case of *The Prosecutor v. Omar Hassan Ahmad Al-Bashir*." Decision under Article 87(7) of the Rome Statute on the noncompliance by South Africa with the request by the Court for the arrest and surrender of Omar Al-Bashir. ICC-02/05-01/09, July 6, 2017. https://www.icc-cpi.int/CourtRecords/CR2017_04402.PDF.

International Criminal Court. "Situation in Darfur, Sudan: in the Case of *The Prosecutor v. Omar Hassan Ahmad Al-Bashir*." Submission from the government of the Republic of South Africa for the purposes of proceedings under Article 87(7) of the Rome Statute, ICC-02/05-01/09, March 17, 2017. https://www.icc-cpi.int /CourtRecords/CR2017_01350.PDF.

International Criminal Court. "Situation in Darfur, Sudan: In the Case of *The Prosecutor v. Omar Hassan Ahmad Al-Bashir*." Decision under article 87(7) of the Rome Statute on the noncompliance by Jordan with the request by the Court for the arrest and surrender of Omar Al-Bashir. ICC-02/05-01/09, December 11, 2017. https://www.icc-cpi.int/CourtRecords/CR2017_07156.PDF.

International Criminal Court. "Situation in Darfur, Sudan: In the Case of *The Prosecutor v. Omar Hassan Ahmad Al-Bashir*." Decision on the Cooperation of the Democratic Republic of the Congo Regarding Omar Al Bashir's Arrest and Surrender to the Court. ICC-02/05-01/09, April 9, 2014. https://www.icc-cpi.int /CourtRecords/CR2014_03452.PDF.

International Criminal Court. "Situation in Libya: *The Prosecutor v. Saif Al-Islam Gaddafi*." ICC-PIDS-CIS-LIB-01-011/15_Eng, Case Information Sheet, June 13,

2016. https://thenewlibyareport.files.wordpress.com/2016/07/saif-gaddafi-case
-information-sheet.pdf.

International Law Association. *Statement of Principles Applicable to the Formation of General Customary International Law*. London Conference, 2000.

International Military Tribunal (Nuremberg). "Judgment of 1 October 1946." https:// crimeofaggression.info/documents/6/1946_Nuremberg_Judgement.pdf.

IRRI. Proposed AU Amendments to Rome Statute for Kampala Review Conference, 2010.

Jackson, Robert. "The Besieged Strongholds of the Mind: Address to the Assembly of the International Student Service." RHJP box 42, September 2, 1942, Washington, DC. https://www.roberthjackson.org/wp-content/uploads/2015/01/The _Besieged_Strongholds_of_the_Mind.pdf.

Jackson, Robert. "Second Day, Wednesday, 11/21/1945, Part 04." In *Trial of the Major War Criminals before the International Military Tribunal*. Vol. 2, *Proceedings: 11/14/1945–11/30/1945*. Nuremberg, IMT, 1947, 98–102. https://www.famous-trials .com/nuremberg/1897-jacksonopen.

"Judgment." *Prosecutor v. Tadić* (IT-94-1-A). Appeals Chamber, July 15, 1999, §186. http://www.icty.org/x/cases/tadic/acjug/en/tad-aj990715e.pdf.

Kalla, Kristin, Judicael Elidje, Katharina Peschke, Aude Le Goff, Scott Bartell, and Marita Nadalutti. "Mobilising Resources and Supporting the Most Vulnerable Victims through Ear-Marked Funding." Trust Fund for Victims, Programme Progress Report, Winter 2012. http://www.nuhanovicfoundation.org/user/file/ tfv_programme_progress_report_winter_2012finalcompressed.pdf.

Kenyan National Dialogue and Reconciliation (KNDR) Monitoring Project. "Progress in Implementation of the Constitution and Other Reforms." Review Report (funded by Open Society Institute), October 2011.

1945 Charter of the International Military Tribunal, Nuremberg. http://www.un.org/ en/genocideprevention/documents/atrocity-crimes/Doc.2_Charter%20of%20 IMT%201945.pdf.

Norwegian Institute of International Relations. "Strategic Options for the Future of African Peace Operations 2015–2025." NUPI Seminar Report, 2015, 11–13.

Office of the Prosecutor. "Report on Preliminary Examination Activities." ICC. December 13, 2011. https://www.icc-cpi.int/nr/rdonlyres/63682f4e-49C8-445d -8C13-f310a4f3aeC2/284116/otpreportonpreliminaryexaminations13december 2011.pdf.

Organization of African Unity. OAU Charter. Addis Ababa, Ethiopia, May 25, 1963. https://au.int/sites/default/files/treaties/7759-file-oau_charter_1963.pdf.

Pace, William. "Assembly of States Parties Address." Coalition for the International Criminal Court, Twelfth Session of the Assembly of States Parties to the Rome Statute, The Hague, November 2013.

Privy Council. In re Southern Rhodesia. Matter Specially Referred to the Judicial Committee. July 26, 1918. http://www.uniset.ca/other/cs2/1919AC211.html.

Prosecutor v. Musema. ICTR Case No. ICTR-96-13-A, P164. ICTR Trial Chamber January 27, 2000. Judgment and Sentence.

PSC. "Communiqué of the 207th Meeting of the Peace and Security Council at the Level of the Heads of State and Government." October 29, 2009. Doc. PSC/AHG/COMM.1 (CCVII).

PSC. "Communique of the 411th PSC Meeting Held at the Level of Heads of State and Government in Banjul the Gambia." December 30, 2013. PSC/AHG/COMM.1 (CDXI) Rev. 1.

Report of the Ad Hoc Committee on the Establishment of an International Criminal Court, G.A., 50th Sess., 1995, Supp. No. 22, A/50/22.

Report of the Preparatory Committee on the Establishment of an International Criminal Court, Vol. 1 (Proceedings of the Preparatory Committee during March, April and August 1996), G.A., 51st Sess., Supp. No. 22, A/51/22, 1996.

Report of the Preparatory Committee on the Establishment of an International Criminal Court, Vol. 2, G.A., 51st Sess., Supp. No. 22, A/51/22, 1996.

"Report of the United Nations Independent Investigation on Burundi (UNIIB) Established Pursuant to Human Rights Council Resolution S-24/1." Office of the High Commissioner and the Secretary-General, Technical Assistance and Capacity-Building. Thirty-third session, September 20, 2016. https://reliefweb.int/sites/reliefweb.int/files/resources/A_HRC_33_37_E_AUV_.pdf.

"Report of the Working Group on Amendment of the Assembly of States Parties of the International Criminal Court." December 7, 2014. ICC-ASP/13/31.

"Report on the Facilitation on the Activation of the Jurisdiction of the International Criminal Court over the Crime of Aggression." ICC-ASP/16/24.

"Report on the Meeting of Government Experts and Ministers of Justice/Attorneys General on Legal Matters on the Draft Protocol on Amendments to the Protocol on the Statute of the African Court of Justice and Human Rights: Revisions up to 15 May 2012." Addis Ababa, Ethiopia, May 7–11 and 14–15, 2012. Exp/Min/IV/Rev.7.

R v. Bow Street Metropolitan Stipendiary Magistrate. Ex Parte Pinochet Ugarte (H.L. 1998) 3 WLR 1,456.

Treaty of Peace between the Allied and Associated Powers and Germany ("Treaty of Versailles") (1919). TS 4, Art. 227.

UN Doc. SC Res. 780, October 6, 1992.

UN Doc. SC Res. 827, May 25, 1993.

UN General Assembly. Convention on the Prevention and Punishment of the Crime of Genocide. 78 UNTS 277, December 9, 1948.

United Nations. "Declaratory Statement by the Republic of South Africa on the Decision to Withdraw from the Rome Statute of the International Criminal Court." C.N.786.2016.TREATIES-XVIII.10 (Depositary Notification). July 17, 1998. https://treaties.un.org/doc/Publication/CN/2016/CN.786.2016-Eng.pdf.

United Nations. "Final Report of the Mission of Independent Experts to Burundi." UN Human Rights Council Session 33. Geneva, September 13–30, 2016. A/HRC/33/37. http://wunrn.com/2016/09/un-human-rights-council-session-33-reports-gender/.

United Nations. "A More Secure World: Our Shared Responsibility." Report of the High-Level Panel on Threats, Challenges and Change, 2004.

United Nations. Rome Statute of the International Criminal Court. July 17, 1998. UN Doc. A/CONF.183/9.

United Nations. "Updated Statute of the International Criminal Tribunal for the Former Yugoslavia." International Tribunal for the Prosecution of Persons Responsible for Serious Violations of International Humanitarian Law Committed in the Territory of the Former Yugoslavia since 1991, September 2009. http://www.icty .org/x/file/Legal%20Library/Statute/statute_sept09_en.pdf.

United Nations. *Vienna Convention on the Law of Treaties*, May 23, 1969.

UN Security Council. "Report of the International Commission of Inquiry Mandated to Establish the Facts and Circumstances of the Events of 28 September 2009 in Guinea." December 18, 2009. S/2009/693.

Waki, Philip N. *Report of the Commission of Inquiry into Post-Election Violence*. Nairobi: Government Printer, 2008. http://www.kenyalaw.org/s/Reports /Commission_of_Inquiry_into_Post_Election_Violence.pdf.

War Crimes Research Office and Judge Sang-Hyun Song. *Victim Participation before the International Criminal Court*. 7th Consultative Assembly of Parliamentarians for the International Criminal Court and the Rule of Law and World Parliamentary Conference of Human Rights, International Human Rights Day, December 10, 2012.

Index

Abass, Ademola, 251

Abdullahi, Ibrahim, 123

accountability, 56; AU and, 13, 31; forgiveness transition to, 64–67; legal, 13; for mass atrocity crimes, 14–15, 33; of perpetrator, 66. *See also* criminal accountability

ACHPR (African Court on Human and Peoples' Rights), 203–4, 294n35

ACJ. *See* African Court of Justice

ACJHR (African Court of Justice and Human Rights), 183, 255, 270n25

"Activation of the Jurisdiction of the Court over the Crime of Aggression," 267n3

activism, 285n14; biomediated, 119, 261; do-good, 120; hashtag, 118, 120; justice, contemporary, 119

actor-network theory, 9

ad hoc tribunals, 74, 101. *See also* International Criminal Tribunal for Rwanda; International Criminal Tribunal for Yugoslavia

affect: emotional, 14–21, notion of, 18

affective justice, 173, 260; amending, 237–43; biomediation and, 119; debating, 229–37; digital media justice campaigns and, 119; emotional affect and, study of, 14–21; forms of, 224; ICC and, 5; international criminal law and, con-

temporary, 6; justice assemblages and, 39; mechanisms, 44–45; online justice campaigns and, 41–42; in practice, 28–29; reattribution and, 43; as of rule of law assemblages theorization, 4–13; structural inequality and, 90; term, 5

affective regimes, Pan-Africanist, 35–38

affective retribution, in practice, 28–29

affective transference, 108–14; reattribution and, 41

Afghanistan, 268n8; United States crimes in, 269n9

Africa: civil wars, 60; colonialism in, 31; dictatorships in, 60; economic development in, 61, 215; economic reforms in, 61–62; First Conference of Independent African States, 36–37; France and, 276n22; future of, 186, 262; governance challenges in, 60; human rights in, 190; ICC and, 2–3, 32, 82, 104–5, 255; independence negotiations, 102–3; independence struggles, 186–87; international criminal law institutions, 79–80, 103; international criminal tribunals in, 80; international justice in, failures of, 189–90; international law and, 182, 203; justice in, 27–29, 36, 183, 207–14, 216; national security, 188; politics, judicialization of, 263; postcolonialism in, 33, 58, 209, 244;

Africa (*continued*)
Rome Statute ratification in, 28; rule of law in, 80; self-determination, 187; state establishment in, 59; UN Economic Commission for, 179; UN failures in, 213–14; UNSC and, 238, 255; Western powers in, 60. *See also specific countries*

African bias, 50

African Charter on Human and Peoples' Rights, 203, 211

African Commission, 294n35

African Court for Justice and Human and Peoples' Rights, 4, 35–38, 193; criminal jurisdiction of, 209, 211–12, 214, 243; establishment of, 204–5; jurisdiction of, 201, 203, 209, 211–12, 214, 243; Malabo Protocol for, 183–84, 202–7; self-determination and, 37–38; as sentimentally Pan-African project, 214–16

African Court of Justice (ACJ), 203, 270n25; Protocol of, 43, 298n86

African Court of Justice, Human Rights, and Criminal Justice, 204–5

African Court of Justice and Human Rights (ACJHR), 183, 255; Protocol on Statute of, 270n25

African Court on Human and Peoples' Rights (ACHPR), 203–4, 294n35

African Development Bank, 179

African diaspora, 187

African Economic Community, 293n27

African Governance Architecture (AGA), 192, 295n48; preventive diplomacy and, 193

African leaders, 210–11; abuse of power perception of, 146; extradition of, 170; ICC and unfair targeting of, 222–23; ICC indictments of, 170, 222–23; immunity for, 226, 245, 251. *See also specific leaders*

African perpetrator, 140, 143–44

"African solutions for African problems," 185, 201, 210, 225, 250

African state sovereignty, 222

African Union (AU): accountability and, 13, 31; Agenda 2063, 179–81; Article 4,
68; Article 6, 188–89; Assembly, 188–89, 192–93, 197; al-Bashir arrest and, 3–4, 22; al-Bashir extradition and non-cooperation of, 246, 272n65, 303n45; CIL and, 246; Commission of Inquiry on South Sudan, 81, 196–97; conflict resolution missions, 195–96; Constitutive Act, 188–89, 199, 203, 250–51, 270n25; on Darfur, 82; establishment of, 187–88; Executive Council, 192–93; fiftieth anniversary, 202; "50th Anniversary Solemn Declaration," 177–78; Golden Jubilee, 177; Habré trial and, 208; High-Level Panel on Darfur, 200; ICC and, 192, 212, 229–30; ICC and oppositional stance of, 3, 13, 221, 262; on immunity, 245–46; immunity provision in, disputes over, 247–51; institutions, 183; legal accountability in, pushback against, 13; Libya and, 199; Merger Protocol, 270n25; NATO and, 199; Pan-Africanism and, 181, 185–92, 215; Panel of the Wise, 80–81, 194–95; peace and justice strategy, 196; popularization movement, 192; Protocol Relating to the Establishment of the Peace and Security Council of, 293n27; Rome Statute and, 236; Rome Statute, withdrawal of states from, 23–24, 223, 252–56; Silencing the Guns campaign, 19; summits, 22; Transitional Justice Policy Framework, 80, 81, 194–95; transition to, 203; Twenty-Second Summit of, 185–86

African Union Commission (AUC), 69, 178–79; Silencing Guns in Africa: Building a Roadmap to a Conflict-Free Continent, 179; Strategic Plan of 2009–2012, 192

African Union Peace and Security Architecture (APSA), 193, 295n48

African violence: apartheid, 31; colonial injustice and, 11; contemporary, 11, 58; ICC and, 80–81; mass atrocity, 33; political nature of, 204; postcolonial, 54–55. *See also* Kenyan 2007–8 post-electoral violence

Cassese, Antonio, 101, 114; individualized liability and, 147; *International Criminal Law*, 84

Cavell, Stanley, 39

Chad, 209, 221; al-Bashir extradition and noncooperation of, 303n45

Charter of the International Military Tribunal, 70–71; Article 7 of, 70

Chibok kidnapping, 116–18, 135–36, 284n5, 284n8. *See also* #BringBackOurGirls campaign

CICC (Coalition for the International Criminal Court), 76

CIL. *See* customary international law

clicktivism, 132

Coalition for the International Criminal Court (CICC), 76

collective consciousness, 39

"collective effervescence," 106–7

collective responsibility, 89; Kenyan 2007–8 post-electoral violence and, 159–60; temporality of, 164

collective sentiment, 95

collective violence, 144–45

collective withdrawals, 254–55

collectivization of guilt, 288n9

colonial inequality, 135

colonial injustice, in Africa, 26, 29, 94; contemporary violence and, 11

colonial institutions, 38

colonialism, 27; Home Guards and, 158, 163; ICC and, 31, 34; in Kenya, 93–94, 109; neocolonialism, 31; in Nigeria, 133–34; Pan-Africanism and, 37. *See also* British colonialism; postcolonialism

colonial oppression, 111

Columbia, 245

command responsibility, 147

Commission of Inquiry into Post-election Violence (Waki Commission), 149–51, 164–65

Commission of Inquiry on South Sudan, 81, 196–97

Constable, Marianne, 39

Constitutive Act, AU, 188–89, 199, 203; Article 4(h), 250; Article 4(o), 250–51

contemporary state form, 58–59

continuing or composite crime, 153–54

Convention on the Prevention and Punishment of the Crime of Genocide (Genocide Convention), 12, 74, 98, 240

Cover the Night campaign, 122

criminal accountability, 14; African perpetrator and, 144; hierarchies of, 136; for mass atrocity violence, 144; post-World War II and, 100

criminal responsibility, individualization of, 52, 64, 88, 89. *See also* individual criminal responsibility

criminal tribunals, 57; in Africa, 80; international, 29, 80, 98–99

culpability, 35, 37, 42; attributing, 169; for collective violence, 145; definitions of, 169; determining, 169; in international law, 53; Jubilee Coalition campaign and, 143; justice and, 172; for Kenyan 2007–8 post-electoral violence, 143, 161–68; legal time and, 154–55; re-attribution and, 140–74; rethinking of, 144–45; structural inequalities and, 258; structural violence and, 155–61; temporality of, 169

culpable negligence (*culpa gravis*), 84

customary international law (CIL), 218, 224, 303n42; AU and, 246; immunity in, 247; rules of, shifting, 254–55

Darfur region, Sudan, 3, 82, 199, 207; High-Level Panel on, 200

DDPD (Doha Document for Peace in Darfur), 82

DDS (Directorate of Documentation and Security), 208–9

Declaration of Basic Principles of Justice for Victims of Crime and Abuse of Power (Victims' Declaration), 85

DeGeneres, Ellen, 126–27, 129

Deleuze, Gilles, 7, 9, 18

Democratic Republic of Congo, 227

Derrida, Jacques, 4

Desalegn, Hailemariam, 31, 33

Deya, Don, 205, 210, 212–13

Diarra, Djenaba, 229

diaspora, 36; African, 187
dictatorships, African, 60
Directorate of Documentation and Security (DDS), 208–9
displacement, legal encapsulation and, 52
Dlamini Zuma, Nkosazana, 186
do-good activism, 120
Doha Document for Peace in Darfur (DDPD), 82
Drumbl, Mark, 288n9
Du Plessis, Max, 250
Durkheim, Émile, 106
duty to prosecute, 12–13; Nuremberg Trials and, 77

Economic Commission for Africa, UN, 179
Economic Community of West African States (ECOWAS), 197
economic crimes, 36; corporate actors and, 205
economic development: in Africa, 61, 215; neoliberalism and, 62; *Washington Consensus*, 61
economic inequality, 62; in Kenya, 157–58
economics, postcolonialism and, 59
ECOWAS (Economic Community of West African States), 197
Eichmann v. Attorney-General of Israel, 240
electoral violence, postcolonialism and, 62
embodied affects, 21, 41; international criminal justice assemblages and, 18; social transference and institutionalization of, 114–15
emotion, 39–40, 57; international criminal justice assemblages and, 16; sociology of, 274n98
emotional affect, affective justice and study of, 14–21
emotional regimes, 19–21, 94–95, 243, 260; attribution and, politics of, 168–72; international criminal justice assemblages and, 19–20; justice interpretations and, 13; Pan-African, 29–30, 169, 182; postcolonial, 79–83. *See also* feeling regimes

empathy mobilization, humanitarian narratives and, 120–21
Ethiopia, 185, 191
ethnography: global, 40; transnational, 9
evidence, 51
exceptionalism, of leaders, 70
Ezekwesili, Obiageli, 123, 285n20
Ezulwini Consensus, 68

Facebook, 119, 125
feeling regimes, 13, 91; history and, 112–13
female body, 88
Ferencz, Ben, 77–79
Ferguson, Jim, 189
Fife, Rolf, 233–34
First Conference of Independent African States, 36–37
forgiveness, 28; accountability and transition from, 64–67; of perpetrator, 66; reconciliation and, 65
France, 154, 205; Africa and, 276n22
freedom fighter, 34, 160; Mau Mau, 92, 95, 156–58, 280n2, 291n58; in Pan-African emotional regimes, 29–30
Futamura, Madoka, 288n9
The Future of Human Rights (Sikkink), 57

gachacha (traditional justice), 29
Gambia, 24; Rome Statute withdrawal of, 218–19, 300n5
Gaynor, Fergal, 51–52
gender-based violence, 166
General Assembly, UN, 101, 238; "Principles and Guidelines on the Right to a Remedy and Reparation for Victims of Gross Violations of International Human Rights Law and Serious Violations of International Humanitarian Law," 68; Principles of International Law Recognized in the Charter of the Nuremberg Tribunal, 71; Universal Declaration of Human Rights, 58; Victims' Declaration adopted by, 85
Geneva Convention, 12
genocide, 12; Rwandan, 65–66

on Peace and Stability and Reconciliation, 229
individual (subjective) consciousness, 39
individual criminal responsibility, 278n72; attribution and, 147; for collective violence, 145; command responsibility and, 147; immunity and, 249; Uhuru Kenyatta and, 146–51; in Malabo Protocol, 225; root causes versus, 184; Ruto and, 146–51; Taylor and, 147–48
individualism, language of, 54
individualization of criminal responsibility, 52, 64, 89; anti-impunity movement and, 88
individualized liability, 147
inequality: biopolitics and, 259; colonial, 135; economic, 62, 157–58; ICC and, 217, 231–32, 238; Islamic, 132–37; postcolonial, 132, 258–59. *See also* structural inequalities
Instagram, 125
International Center for Transitional Justice (ICTJ), 67, 161
International Committee of the Red Cross (ICRC), 12–13, 98, 118; racism, accusations of, 27
international community, 137; notion of, 67; responsibility of, 68–70; as victim proxy, 130–31
international court, mass atrocity crimes and, 78. *See also specific international courts*
International Court of Justice (ICJ), 191; *Arrest Warrant* case, 220, 247–48; *Asylum Case*, 245–46
International Criminal Court (ICC): affective justice and, 5; Africa and, 2–3, 32, 82, 104–5, 255; African leaders indicted by, 170; African leaders unfairly targeted by, 222–23; African violence and, 80–81; anti-impunity sentiments, 12; Assembly of States Parties, 229, 267n3; AU and, 192, 212, 229–30; AU oppositional stance to, 3, 13, 221, 262; al-Bashir and, 81, 207, 221–22, 227; al-Bashir extradition noncooperation and, 246, 272n65; colonialism

and, 31, 34; Commission of Inquiry into Post-election Violence, 149–51; as court of last resort, 230–31; Democratic Republic of Congo and, 227; on immunity, 221–22; Indictment of Sitting Heads of State and Government and Its Consequences on Peace and Stability and Reconciliation, 229; inequality and, 217, 231–32, 238; injustice and, 2; jurisdiction of, 1–2, 104–5, 151; justice provided by, 33; Kenya and, 230–31, 235–36; Kenyan postelectoral violence and, 152–53; Uhuru Kenyatta and, 32, 110, 222; as lawfare, 31; legal processes, 7; legal time and, 151, 171; legitimacy of, 34; Malabo Protocol and, 242–43; mass atrocity violence and, 1–2; Mbizvo on, 113; Open-Ended Committee of African Ministers on, 252–53; opposition to, 219; OTP, 96; Pan-Africanism and, 182; in peace processes, 83; *propio mutu* referral power in, 2; purpose of, 96; referral power under Rome Statute, 3; restorative mandate, 87–88; Ruto and, 222; sentimental narrative of, 96–97; South Africa and, 218–19, 227; state engagement in, 104; structural inequalities and, 228; victim reparations and, 86; Victims Participation and Reparations Section, 86–87
international criminal justice: differentiated formations of, 70–79; emergence of, 70–79; victims and, 87
international criminal justice assemblages, 7–8; embodied affects and, 18; emotional regimes and, 19–20; emotion and, 16; legal technocratic practices and, 16–18
international criminal law, 258–59; affective justice and contemporary, 6; modern, development of, 99; narratives, 114; post–World War II, 99–100
International Criminal Law (Cassese), 84
international criminal law institutions: Africa and, 79–80, 103; Uhuru Kenyatta on, 109–10

Kampala agreement, 268n3; ratification of, 283n53
Kampala Review Conference, 104–5
Kapenguria Six, 92, 280n2
Kaunda, Kenneth, 186
Kay, Stephen, 143
Kegoro, George, 235
Kenya, 30; al-Bashir arrest and, 269n18; British colonialism in, 156–57; colonialism in, 93–94, 109; Commission of Inquiry into Post-election Violence, 149–51; economic inequality in, 157–58; ethnic divisions in, 167, 172; Home Guards and, 158, 163; ICC and, 230–31, 235–36; independence, 92–95, 157; Kapenguria Six and, 280n2; #kenya decides, 110, 141; Kenyatta Day, 281n3; land ownership in, 155–57; National Accord and Reconciliation Act of 2008, 291n67; postcolonialism in, 158, 172; Rift Valley, 158–59, 167; Rome Statute and, 239, 241; UhuRuto 2013 campaign, 140–43; "willing buyer, willing seller" land policy, 157–58
#kenyadecides, 110, 141
Kenyan Human Rights Commission, 235
Kenyans for Peace with Truth and Justice, 235
Kenyan 2007–8 post-electoral violence, 49–50, 140, 148; agendas proposed after, 167; British colonialism and, 162; collective responsibility and, 159–60; Commission of Inquiry into Post-election Violence, 149–51, 164–65; culpability for, 143, 161–68; ethnic groups and, 153, 160, 163–64; legal time and, limits of, 151–55; perpetrators of, 161–62; responsibility for, 159–61, 166–67; scale of, 153; state involvement in, 167; victims of, 162
Kenyatta, Jomo, 30, 91–92, 111
Kenyatta, Uhuru, 42, 51, 88, 275n6, 280n2, 281n9; collective responsibility and, 160; Commission of Inquiry into Post-election Violence and, 149–51; as freedom fighter, 160; Heroes' Day speech, 92–95, 97, 106, 108–13; ICC

and, 32, 110, 222; individual criminal responsibility and, 146–51; on international criminal institutions, 109–10; Jubilee Coalition and, 155, 287n2; Kenyan postelectoral violence and, 148–49, 152–53, 159–61, 163, 166; on land ownership, 155–56; *The Prosecutor v. Uhuru Muigai Kenyatta*, 289n33, 290n40; public support of, 111–12; UhuRuto 2013 campaign, 140–43, 172; "willing buyer, willing seller" land policy, 157–58
Kenyatta Day, 281n3
Kerry, John, 117
Kiamu, 53, 162, 164
Kibaki, Mwai, 143, 150, 160–61, 168
Kikuyu ethnic group, 162–65, 167, 172
Kony, Joseph, 121–22, 274n108; campaign, 42
Kony 2012 (film), 121–22
#Kony2012 campaign, 121–23
Kosgey, Henry Kiprono, 149, 151, 289n33
Kuperman, Alan, 198, 296nn61–63

Labajo, Garcia, 278n76
Lagos Conference on Primacy of Law, 189
land ownership, in Kenya, 155–57
land redistribution, 60–61
Laqueur, Thomas, 107
Latin America, 61–62
Latour, Bruno, 25
leaders: anti-impunity movement and, 75; exceptionalism of, 70. *See also* African leaders; heads of state
League of Nations, 100, 254
legal encapsulation, 17, 29, 38, 42, 108; displacement and, 52; of perpetrator, 58; of victim, 58
legal temporality, 38, 42; continuing or composite crime and, 153–54; culpability and, 169; hegemonic production of, 17–18; strict, 153
legal time, 168–69; apartheid and, 153; culpability and, 154–55; guilt and, 171; ICC and, 151, 171; limits of, 151–55; notion of, 171; *Rainbow Warrior* case, 153–54; substructure of, 151

practice-oriented justice, 4

Principles of International Law Recognized in the Charter of the Nuremberg Tribunal, 71

proprio motu, 2, 105

prosecution: of apartheid, 190–91; duty to prosecute, 12–13, 77; of mass atrocity crimes, 57–58

prosecutorial justice, 59, 102; cascade, 144; international law and, 203

Prosecutor v. Jean-Bosco Barayagwiza, 154

Prosecutor v. Musema, 154

The Prosecutor v. Omar Hassan Ahmad Al-Bashir, 302nn22–23

The Prosecutor v. Uhuru Muigai Kenyatta, 289n33, 290n40

The Prosecutor v. William Samoei Ruto and Joshua Arap Sang, 289n33

Protocol of the Merged Court, 204

PSC (Peace and Security Council), 197, 293n27, 295n48

al-Qaddafi, Muammar, 197–99, 221, 247, 296n61

race, 26–27; Pan-Africanism and, 37

racial imagery, 180

racism, 26–27

Rainbow Warrior case, 153–54

Rao, Pemmaraju Sreenivasa, 237

rationae materiae immunity, 226, 240

rationae personae immunity, 74–75, 240

Rawls, John, 4

reattribution, 10, 35–36, 108; affective justice and, 43; affective transference and, 41; African Criminal Court and, 177–216; concept of, 20; culpability and, 140–74; justice and, 30–35; of official capacity movement, 217–56; practices, 20; workings of, 42

reconciliation, 51; forgiveness and, 65; South Africa strategy for, 28

RECS (Regional Economic Communities), 192

Reddy, William, 19

redistribution: justice and, 173; land, 60–61

Regional Economic Communities (RECS), 192

responsibility: to act, international justice and, 138; collective, 89, 147, 159–60, 164; command, 147; of international community, 68–70; moral, to victims, 78–79; to protect, 96, 197. *See also* criminal responsibility, individualization of

retribution: affective, 28–29; judicial proceedings driven by, 88

retributive justice, 69, 123

revenge speech, 14

rhetorical strategies, 41

Richland, Justin, 39

right to protect, discourse of, 69

de Rivera, Joseph, 141

Rome Statute, 1, 96, 98–102; African states and ratification of, 28; African states and withdrawal from, 23–24, 223, 252–56; Article 5, 104; Article 11, 152; Article 13, 2–3; Article 16, 221, 223, 237–39; Article 17, 25; Article 24, 73–74, 278n76; Article 27, 73–75, 220–21, 223, 225–27, 232–33, 239–41, 278n77; Article 28, 146; Article 54, 200; Article 61, 290n37, 290n39; Article 63, 223; Article 75, 280n109; Article 79, 280n109; Article 87, 302nn22–23; Article 98, 221, 226–27, 245, 302n24; Article 127, 253; AU and, 236; Burundi withdrawal from, 217, 300n3; Draft, 74; drafting of, 233–34; Gambia withdrawal from, 218–19, 300n5; ICC referral power under, 3; immunity provisions of, 220–21, 225–27, 232, 240–41; *Jurisdiction ratione temporis*, 152; jurisdiction under, 104–5, 151–52; Kenya and, 239, 241; South Africa and, 238–39; subject matter jurisdiction under, 211; temporal jurisdiction under, 151–52; victim reparations under, 85–86

Ross, Andrew, 118

rule of law, 20, 58–64; actors, actants, and, 25; in Africa, 80; application of, unreliability in, 237; discourse, 2; indicators,

www.ingramcontent.com/pod-product-compliance
Lightning Source LLC
Chambersburg PA
CBHW030906270326
41929CB00008B/594

* 9 7 8 1 4 7 8 0 0 6 7 0 1 *